From *The Halcyon Era* by Lord Ernest Hamilton
(by courtesy of John Murray Ltd.)

THE MARLBOROUGH
HOUSE SET

Also by *Anita Leslie*

RODIN—IMMORTAL PEASANT

TRAIN TO NOWHERE

LOVE IN A NUTSHELL

THE FABULOUS LEONARD JEROME

MRS FITZHERBERT

MR FREWEN OF ENGLAND

JENNIE:

The Life of Lady Randolph Churchill

Anita Leslie

THE
MARLBOROUGH
HOUSE SET

Doubleday & Company, Inc., Garden City
New York   1973

PHOTO CREDITS:

Radio Times Hulton Picture Library—1, 2, 3, 4, 6, 7, 12, 13, 25, 26, 28, 31, 32
From the collection of the Earl of Rosse—5
Courtesy of the Marquess of Londonderry—8
Courtesy of Hugh R. Tennant—9
Courtesy of the Leslie family—11, 16
Courtesy of Desmond Leslie—15
Courtesy of the Tate Gallery, London—17
From the collection of Major Anthony Brett, courtesy of the Hon. Mrs. Maurice Brett—18
From the collection of Prince Hansel of Pless—22
Courtesy of Mary, Duchess of Roxburghe—23
Courtesy of Henry P. McIlhenny—29
Courtesy of the Earl of Fingall—30

ISBN: 0-385-01448-1
Library of Congress Catalog Card Number 72–89949

For

Acknowledgements

THE AUTHOR WISHES to express thanks to the following who have provided copyright permission for unpublished letters: Mr. Mark Bonham-Carter (Margot, Countess of Oxford and Asquith); Mr. Seymour Leslie (Leonie, Lady Leslie); the late Mrs. Cicely Mure and the Earl of Warwick (Daisy, Countess of Warwick).

For reminiscences the author is especially grateful to Princess Marthe Bibesco, the late Mrs. Denton Carlisle, Lady Betty Cartwright, Francesca, Countess of Gosford, Mr. Seymour Leslie, the Prince of Pless and Count Edmond de Pourtalés. Above all I wish to acknowledge thanks to my father, Sir Shane Leslie, who was aiding me with notes for this book up to the week he died.

Sincere thanks are also due to the following who have provided illustrations: Major Anthony Brett, the Hon. Mrs. Maurice Brett, the Earl of Fingall, Lady Laycock, the Marquess of Londonderry, Mr. Henry P. McIlhenny, the Prince of Pless, the Earl and Countess of Rosse, Mary, Duchess of Roxburghe and Mr. hugh R. Tennant.

The author also wishes to acknowledge indebtedness to the following publishers and owners of copyright for permission to quote from the works indicated: H.R.H. Princess Alice and Evans Brothers Ltd. (*For My Grandchildren* by H.R.H. Princess Alice); Mr. Mark Bonham-Carter (*Autobiography of Margot Asquith*); Harcourt, Brace, Jovanovich (*Winston Churchill: An Intimate Portrait* by Lady Violet Bonham-Carter); the Hon. Mrs. S. C. Cubitt (*Edwardian Daughter* by Sonia Cubitt); Curtis Brown Ltd. (*Recollections of Three Reigns* by Sir Frederick Ponsonby); the Earl of Fingall and Pamela Hinkson (*Seventy Years Young* by Daisy, Countess of Fingall); the Fitzwilliam Museum (*My Diaries* by Wilfrid Scawen Blunt); David Higham Associates Ltd. (*Great Morning* by Sir Osbert Sitwell); Hutchinson & Co. (Publishers) Ltd. (*Things Past* by the Duchess of Sermoneta, *Memoirs* by Sir Almeric Fitzroy and *The Last Grand Duchess* by Ian Vorres); *Diaries: 1915–1918,* by Lady Cynthia Asquith. Copyright © 1968 by Michael and Simon Asquith. Reprinted by permission of Alfred A. Knopf, Inc.; Lord Knutsford (*In Black and White* by Lord Knutsford); John Murray Ltd. (*The Halcyon Era* by Lord Ernest Hamilton and *From My Diaries* by Daisy, Princess of Pless); Macmillan & Co. Ltd. (*Letters from Disraeli to Frances Anne, Marchioness of Londonderry* and *Vacant Thrones* by Sir Ian Malcolm); Eileen Quelch (*Edwardian Heyday* by George Cornwallis-West); A. D. Peters, Ltd. (*From Peace to War* by Lord Chandos); Weybright and Talley (*Superior Person: A Portrait of Curzon and His Circle* by Kenneth Rose).

Contents

"If our passion has been great, so also
has been our uplifting."

—*Letter from Lady Warwick to
Joe Laycock, spring 1902*

THE MARLBOROUGH
HOUSE SET

Who Were the Edwardians?

WHAT WOULD THE small group of people known as the Edwardians have thought if they could have read today's attempts to reconstruct the complicated game of their love life! They might be indignant at revelations and yet unable to resist contradicting errors. I must be among the few to whom a delicious grandmother—American and therefore slightly an outsider—recounted the intricate rules of the Prince of Wales's set before 1900.

The First World War swept away need for decorum and the Second ended strict chaperonage of girls and the stigma of divorce. Now the Pill has completely destroyed audaciousness in illegal lovemaking. The mystery and the danger are gone, pent-up emotions freed. Hemlines may rise and fall but moral restraint has been thrown to the four winds.

How difficult it is for this classless generation to visualise a world where so many automatic restrictions were in force; where a well-brought-up girl was never allowed to be alone with a man even for half an hour in the drawing room; and where all women expected all men to make up to them the instant they found themselves alone. That was the convention of the time. All males were in search of prey. All females must be protected from what was called then, but not now, deflowering.

The amorous adventures described in this book occurred over a period of about fifty years—from 1860 when Albert Edward, Prince of Wales, stepped into the social scene as a handsome young rip until his death in 1910 as the portly Edward VII. The term 'Edwardian' covers, therefore, his forty lusty years as heir to the throne as well as ten years of kingship. The code of conduct which we term Edwardian originated in Queen Victoria's reign when, to the applause of all Europe, the Prince, who was in his mid-twenties, started to be unfaithful to his beautiful delicate wife.

As soon as Albert Edward began to have 'affairs' with noble ladies as well as with actresses, guide lines were laid out, not only for H.R.H. but for the gentlemen of his entourage. These firm rules were intended to ensure that the even tenor of family life, the graciousness and dignity which all enjoyed, should not be spoiled by sexual embroilments.

If religious banns did not count, what did? Unmarried girls were never considered fair game. All Victorian mamas took care to prevent loss of their daughters' reputations as well as loss of the real thing. Men were odd creatures and if rumour spread that a girl had disappeared for an hour or so it meant that *something could have happened*. Potential suitors then evaporated.

An old French lady once told me that when an ignorant governess walked in the Bois de Boulogne wearing brown boots instead of black her mother's friends wrote horrified notes saying that her marriage prospects had been jeopardised—brown boots were worn by *cocottes!* Eventually she married an English officer coming from a sporting caste which cared less about outward errors if the actual goods remained undamaged.

In order to avoid malicious rumour it was imperative that young women should be constantly on view. An unmarried American friend of my grandmother's happened to disappear in her own continent for six months on a business trip. On returning to London she was 'cut' by dowagers, who calculated that she could have 'got into a scrape.' They chose, however, to disregard the months spent out of view when she became Countess of Essex.

An eminent historian of medieval life recently wrote asking me if my grandmother and her sister 'slept around with a lot of chaps.' I was genuinely surprised at the question. The clothes of the time alone made casual affairs impossible, and all 'ladies' lived under the constant surveillance of servants. They were wakened by maids and dressed by maids. Their meals were served to them. There were no midnight snacks in the kitchen; no journeys in the backs of cars. They played their social roles in public—riding in Rotten Row each morning, attending political dinners, dancing in their jewelled tiaras at balls, driven home by their own liveried coachmen and then once more undressed by sleepy ladies' maids. Their amours had to be carefully disciplined, for the rules were rigid and woe betide the offender—she would be cast out from the great houses, and never invited to a good party again.

The Prince of Wales rejoiced in rich food and lovely women. The former killed him, the latter enlivened the tedium of long years during which the Queen allowed him no responsibility. All men in Victorian England were able to find and enjoy sex in the poorer classes, but only the special set around the Prince devised a code which permitted liaisons with gentlewomen as long as no scandal undermined the family unit.

Girls must remain virginal and ignorant. Once married, a young woman could be eyed thoughtfully, but it would not be *de rigueur* to attempt to waylay her before she produced a few sons to carry on her husband's name and inherit his estates. If this rule was broken, as in the Aylesford case, there was the devil to pay—and nobody wanted *that*. When the nursery had been sufficiently stocked up, a kindly husband might discreetly look the other way—in the direction of other wives, in fact! It did not matter terribly if one or two rather different-looking children arrived at the *tail end* of the family, but there was no time in a lady's life when a love affair did not carry an element of danger. Jealousy and the pain of desperate love existed then, as now, and unexpected dramas flared up because these creatures parading in top hats and silken gowns were human beings often consumed by passions too strong to control.

The Edwardians, overfed and with too much leisure and no reliable contraceptives, had sex on the brain, but months of glances, sighs, blushes, protestations and trembling assignations preceded the organisation necessary for a physical culmination. During the three-month London season there was a sporting chance for romance at teatime. This must have been pretty dicey, but husbands were *expected* to go out to tea (with other men's wives if not to the club) and it was quite proper to invite a few gentlemen to the drawing room. Etiquette demanded that they should never leave their tall hats, gloves and sticks in the hall, but lay them on the drawing-room floor as if just ready to go, as if merely 'looking in.' This tea invitation could be carefully reduced to one caller—and servants did *not* enter rooms unless rung for. Of course, there was always the possibility of a half-trained footman barging in with more cucumber sandwiches, but on the whole it was safe to flirt, if not to attempt carnal exercises. There were always big sofas around, but the strategy needed must have taxed ingenuity. To have any peace with a loved one a lady must arrange a double invitation to some big country house party where the hostess approved of the liaison, so that rooms could be discreetly allotted along those interminable, icy, creaking corridors. Then the husband had to be sent off to some other country house where the sport was more to his taste—thank heaven for those grouse moors and all that fishing and stalking up north! Then the anxious swain had to bide his time until the last lady's maid had departed, and keep his wits about the right door to open.

Even the craftiest did not always succeed in his stratagems. Lord Charles Beresford (who was in love with Lady Warwick at the same time as the Prince of Wales) told my grandfather that on one occasion he tiptoed into a dark room and jumped into the vast bed shouting, 'Cock-a-doodle-doo,' to find himself, when trembling hands had lit a paraffin lamp, between the Bishop of Chester and his wife. The situation seemed very difficult to explain and he left the house before breakfast next morning. A man might get away with this sort of error but a woman could not. The double standard remained.

To sleep discreetly with Albert Edward, Prince of Wales, was, of course, an impossibility. Everyone would know the hours his carriage waited outside a front door. The heir to the throne was given opportunities for dalliance in a manner which I have heard was not common for other men. His Royal Highness did not have to adhere to the tea hour only; for him, and I think for him alone, it was permissible to lunch with a great lady or to entertain her to a midnight supper in seclusion. There could be no secrecy about the Prince's amours and he himself wrote the name of every person he met each day in his engagement diary. He was neither ashamed nor boastful of his lady loves. He took it for granted that they and those around him considered he was conferring an honour.

All this was done with pomp and decorum. All was extremely grand. And a great deal of staff work went into it. The privilege of sleeping with the Prince of Wales was not accompanied by gifts or display. He chose mature women according to the rules of the game. Most of them carried ancient names and were hung with their own family jewels. They did not expect to be the recipients of obvious favours. The Prince and Princess together gave expensive presents to their friends at Christmas, but a love affair with the Prince was considered its own reward. No very young women came into this orbit. Young women can be a bother. They are prone to be acquisitive and indiscreet. And not even a King of England wants *many* bastards.

The Prince got into plenty of hot water in his life but not actually over his own mistresses. The most unfortunate affair was probably that with Lady Warwick. She was the most tempestuous and most fascinating of his great ladies, and on the young side. Emotion played too great a part. She squandered her own fortune entertaining him and the Prince suffered his disastrous quarrel with Admiral Lord Charles Beresford on her account. And the most fortunate affairs were undoubtedly the later ones with the wise, intelligent Mrs. Keppel and the worthy Miss Keyser.

A great deal of trouble went into the arrangement of such liaisons, to prevent anything slapdash or out of control. Never was more decorum demanded for such indecorous proceedings. In the end His Royal Highness grew satiated. Enough is as good as a feast and ambitious political hostesses intent on a horizontal rendezvous can be wearying. After 1900, while his courtiers continued to devise amorous excursions, King Edward VII grew a little tired of sex, a little moody. During the last ten years what the King craved had a more ordinary name: friendship.

They are fading into the shadows of history, those rich, rustling characters who once belonged to the Prince of Wales's set. A hand-ful of people, picked almost entirely from the six hundred families who formed London society, they presented for forty years a spe-cial segment in the nation's life. How Europe envied the men and women who were drawn into the orbit of Albert Edward during the long frustrating wait for the throne, and who shared his con-fidences during the ten years he reigned.

Now those teen-age girls who watched their mothers being dressed for Edwardian parties are themselves eighty-year-olds. The stories about this curious moral vacuum which the heir to the throne created in Victorian England must be recorded before it is too late to get firsthand accounts.

The environment and the code of conduct appear so strange to us, who have been purged by two world wars, that it is difficult to realise that these people were human beings like ourselves. But top hats and flounced skirts do not alter the fundamental urges, for-mality and grandeur do not preclude lust, true love, self-sacrifice, bitter anguish or sense of comedy.

Can we see the Edwardians as they really were seventy or eighty years ago, playing that game of specially permitted amours devised by the Prince, as goldfish might play in a bowl cut off from the rest of the ocean? The game never became casual. The rules were as strict and complicated as those of chess, and a mistake meant banishment. If the consort Alexandra is regarded as Queen, her role was never to move at all, to remain standing upright in the centre of the board. The King could move in all directions, as far as he wished and even out of turn. Rules for other pieces differed. Unmarried girls were kept off the board and bishops could not compete with knights, though they attended the same house parties. As for the pawns—those self-important ladies on whom the whole game depended—one must realise that *their* moves were very restricted indeed. They must hop, slide, and capture in secret.

Were they contented? Presumably yes. No one remained in the Prince's expensive set who did not want to be there. It was perfectly easy to fall out, to slip back into the dull routine of Queen Victoria's court, or to save money by staying in the country, or to take up politics seriously, or even to go abroad. There was a certain coming and going in Albert Edward's circle, but on the whole his friends remained friends, for the Prince of Wales was an affable man anxious to hold on to affection, and this was genuinely given to him by the people who knew him intimately and whom he called by their Christian names.

Apart from the German-Jewish Sir Ernest Cassel and Baron Hirsch and the Rothschilds and Sassoons and the Portuguese Marquis de Soveral, the men and women who were intimates of the Prince of Wales came from old English families which, whether carrying titles or not, were deeply rooted in the land. The English love of soil can in no way compare with the feeling of European nobility towards their estates. Englishmen do not merely own their land, they belong to it. A family home in the country, surrounded by its park and farm, was the most important factor in English life. The English upper classes were pastoral. Bejewelled, they attended the London three-month summer season as if it was a long-drawn-out village fair. The gentlemen who were Members of Parliament opened their town houses for the winter season, that 'little season' poisoned by pea-soup fog, before Christmas. But apart from the summer frolic, most English upper-class entertaining took place in the country. If the new rich, emerging from the industrial Midlands, had social ambitions, they bought a country house and organised good shooting and rode about their estates. If they had the nerve, they rode to hounds. It took years for them to merge into the rural scene sufficiently to be called gentlemen, but a sure entry lay in sporting prowess. New titles did not impress the ancient strata known as 'the county.' It was family history that mattered and the old home (not necessarily large) in which generations had been reared to special standards in England's service. They entered Parliament, the Army, Navy, the Church or worked on local affairs. England had never known a Versailles. Her lords were earthy. The manor houses and castles bred sportsmen and courtiers.

Almost without exception the children born into aristocratic English families were brought up in the country. Outdoor life was considered basically more important than education. Our first glimpse of almost any personage of the Edwardian set will almost surely reveal a small figure galloping on a pony, and the passionate love letters which have survived often contain sporting entries. Both men and women care so much about their horses that an ardent lover cannot resist describing a good gallop in detail while the beloved is quite likely to intersperse her vows of constancy with veterinary advice.

Amidst the roar of modern motorways, in the fumes of our petrol-scented cities, can we imagine the silences of that fresher England where it was possible for the upper class to enjoy riding over the countryside all winter, and around Rotten Row in the summer mornings? These were rulers who remained rustic amidst their magnificence and their power, and who did not mix with the professional classes depicted in Galsworthy's *Forsyte Saga*.

Nor really did they think it wise to mix with foreigners. In a letter of 1861 Lord Clarendon records the remarks he hears an old lady make concerning Lady Shaftesbury and the Italian envoy who were too often seen together: '. . . so natural that she should be tired of Lord Shaftesbury—such a tiresome man—but why must she go first to Germany and then to Italy for someone—why cannot she take some nice Englishman there are so many, and I hate these foreigners—they are never safe.'

2

The Framework

LADY BETTY CARTWRIGHT, who was a teen-ager during King Edward's reign, has described to me the peculiar strictnesses with which she and her elder sister Gwendoline (who married Jack Churchill) were brought up. Their parents, the Earl and Countess of Abingdon, lived in Oxfordshire, where a famous family named Brassey gave a 'children's party' each year in their great house, Heythrop. The occasion was unique. No one gave parties for children at that time. Sometimes a couple of children might go out to tea in another nursery, but the idea of entertaining for the young did not exist. The glamour of this Brassey event seeped into schoolroom talk, stirring up longing and ruining digestions. Small children were invited from 3 to 6 P.M., older children from 6 to 8 P.M., and teen-agers from 8 to 10 P.M. Carriages, pony traps and motorcars dropped and picked up for seven hours. Cakes, lemonade and balloons were lavishly distributed.

'I was never once allowed to go and I have really never got over it,' Lady Betty sighed. 'Mother said all that excitement would be bad for us!'

She was a first-class horsewoman and the breeding of hunters and show hacks loomed importantly in her parents' lives. The daughter of the house was allowed to train horses but never to show them; to lead a young horse around the ring would have been considered competitive and vulgar.

After she had 'come out' her parents took a hunting box for the winter season at Brackley, in the Grafton country, but Lady Betty also liked to hunt with distant packs. Accompanied as far as the station by a groom, the girl was allowed to book a box for her hunter and travel off with him by train early in the morning, returning mud-splattered and weary quite late at night. The one stipulation was that she did not enter a railway carriage. It was considered perfectly proper for a young lady to travel in the straw with her horse, who was presumably relied on to kick to death any man who entered, but she must not sit in an ordinary carriage unchaperoned. Lady Betty reflects quizzically: 'I was allowed out alone in the dark with my horse, but if I wanted a morning walk across Hyde Park to see a girl friend, a maid had to accompany me.'

In all these great English mansions, manors and castles the same pattern of existence lasted up until 1914. There were plenty of rooms, hordes of servants, masses of food and a cosy nursery wing.

In this setting arose that unique race, the English nanny, which all extolled. Humorous and unselfish, Nanny had the power of creating an 'atmosphere' which their charges never forgot. The fear of doing something which Nanny would have thought shoddy has restrained English men and women all their lives. And foreign princes too! The English nanny exported to the Continent had more 'influence' than the United Nations today. I have never heard of a nanny who was not loved. The parents of Victorian times seem to have been unamused by their offspring. Mothers might see their little ones once a day, the fathers about once a year. It is curious, really, that they did not want small children tumbling around when there were so many servants to clear the debris away.

On reaching the age of five or six, a new and wondrous world would open, for the children could now venture farther afield to make friends with the outside men, the grooms and stableboys and the gamekeepers. How often do the memoirs of men born into that vanished English world start by recounting what they learned from gamekeepers and foresters, for these characters, close to nature, full of the love of wild animals, fascinated children. Early on the boys were given their first gun and sternly trained not to shoot each other before they popped at a first rabbit. Maybe our Irish gamekeepers were lax about the importance of unloading, for my father's gun went off sometime in the early nineties while he was climbing a fence beside Professor Mahaffy, the greatest scholar of Dublin, who turned slowly to him and said, 'Six inches lower and you'd have blown half the Greek out of Ireland.' He remembered this reprimand all his life.

There are many stories of first ponies, for often they made an impression as deep as that of first love. Peering back into those childhoods of the 1850s, we see Lord Randolph Churchill, aged ten, following hounds on his black pony, The Mouse, which he had begged to buy from the post boy and had himself trained to be a 'hunter that jumped.' With flushed cheeks the little boy revels in his victory on the day he keeps ahead of the big horses over the fences of Oxfordshire. And Daisy Warwick, who was to rock the Prince's affections—how does *she* spend her girlhood? In the stables, learning to jump her wonderful white pony, the first of many famous mounts who would carry her over the ditches and hedges of England. And Lord Charles Beresford, who quarrelled with the Prince over darling Daisy—what was *he* doing as a boy? Why, hunting in Ireland where he even had the fun of seeing his uncle Lord Waterford break his neck.

This idyllic equestrian non-intellectual routine continued for the girls until they came out at the age of eighteen, but for the boys there would be a horrible break.

During Victoria's reign it had become necessary to turn out an increasing number of young men capable of serving her vast empire. To create the suitable type, a number of new public schools had arisen, for Eton, Harrow and Winchester could not produce sufficient administrators of the required calibre. Prior to going to these schools at the age of thirteen it was, of course, imperative to learn *something*—not *much*—for character formation was the essential part of an English boy's education; but reading, writing, elementary mathematics and Latin had to begin. The old eighteenth-century habit of letting the parson educate the squire's sons along with the brighter village boys had ceased, and upper-class Victorians could not concoct any better idea than that of sending their sons off to boarding school at the age of eight. It seems unbelievable that parents, who were not necessarily brutal or callous, could have been so stupid, so unimaginative, as to risk sending such little boys to those unsupervised institutions. Any slightly educated man who wanted to make money could open his house and call it a 'prep' school. The masters were miserably paid and not necessarily qualified. The surest way of making money was to save on the boys' food. There were never any inspections, and when a man could retire on his profits he just closed the school or sold it to some type who could carry out a plausible interview with parents.

There were many stories concerning cruelty and perversion. My own grandfather told me that he never got over his absolute hatred for the headmaster of his preparatory school; in fact, he would shake with indignation when describing what had been done to him during the five years before Eton. He was the only son of Sir John Leslie, a dreamy Victorian artist, and Lady Constance Dawson-Damer, a beauty much painted by Watts, and a friend of Thackeray and Dickens. Yet both parents remained blind to the sufferings of their adored little boy. They were not stupid people—only unobservant. Old Sir John had not himself been sent to a prep school. In his days boys went to Harrow aged ten, and he used to travel all alone from Ireland, sitting from Liverpool to London on the outside of the coach without an overcoat. He told my father that in winter he would arrive half frozen, but boys were 'not expected to complain.'

Dozens of gentlemen of later generations have related horrific stories about their 'prep' schools. An exception was Lord Randolph Churchill, who was happy at his, and certainly never expected the school selected for seven-year-old Winston to be run by an arch-sadist. Had it not been for his American wife and that most splendid of all nannies, Mrs. Everest, who were outraged by the marks of beatings, Lord Randolph would never have known what was being perpetrated.

If these were schools for the élite, one wonders what the cheaper ones could have been like. The extroverts and the toughs survived, but the delicate and sensitive never quite recovered from these five years—or so many have told me.

At thirteen, all upper-class boys went to the 'public schools' selected by their family. Eton, Harrow, Winchester and Rugby topped the list. These were famous *institutions* where improvements could be made over the years. Often the masters came from the very school they served. They could remember and alter and they were proud of their profession. Many were delightful scholars, some were fitted to discipline youth, some were not, but the atmosphere and traditions at these famous schools could not be destroyed by a passing master. And the boys who went to them received a veneer and a basic attitude which no other educational establishments in the world could give.

Having somehow survived the nightmare of early schooldays, English youths emerged at eighteen curiously relaxed and mature, taking it for granted that they were leaders of men and that honour counted above all. The boys with brain usually went into law or politics, but the duds and the average fellows were equally sure of their importance to England. In a way they were not far wrong. A far-flung empire needs a caste trained to be trustworthy—and that was the supreme virtue of the English upper and middle classes, who merged into each other through these schools. Individuals might be conceived, dim-witted or weak, but in an emergency they could be counted on. Their reactions would be automatic.

And what of their sisters? When the eight-year-old boys went off to boarding school what happened to the girls? They learned to read and write with Nanny or a nursery governess. Then some poor scholarly woman would be interviewed and installed in a room which was a step up from the nursery. This place would contain a table and bookshelves, and presumably some books. Sometimes a professional look was given by a blackboard. Here for seven or eight years the future *grandes dames* of England would fidget and yawn for a few hours each day, casting their eyes longingly towards the window to see if the weather was good enough to go riding.

Just as nannies were always adored, so the unfortunate governesses were usually hated. That may have been due to the fact that nannies had chosen their fate, they were natural and jolly and under no strain, whereas no woman ever *chose* to be a governess. This role was forced upon them by circumstances. Coming from a wide lower-middle-class range, these unfortunate individuals had been schooled in the homes of fathers who might have been impecunious clergymen or professors, or they might simply have been penniless girls who could not find a husband. This situation was wretched and the task of enforcing learning on resentful children is exhausting at the best of times. None of these governesses had any training. They just had to produce textbooks and try to ram the contents into reluctant pupils.

Apart from insisting on languages, parents took very little interest in female education. It was considered sufficient virtue to be able to play a piece on the piano, paint a water colour and know an outline of history. Girls with a literary bent could pull dust-covered volumes out of their fathers' libraries, but how bitterly lonely the governesses were, and how heartless their charges! Children never hesitate to show their preferences, and the grooms and servants and country retainers with their uninhibited wit and cheerful ways made much more amusing companions.

My Leslie great-aunts, who were all brought up until the age of eighteen in a particularly isolated family home in the middle of Ireland, shared one German governess throughout all these years. They grew rather fond of her, for, not a natural disciplinarian, she appears to have relinquished the losing battle and allowed her charges to spend most of the day with the delightful old forester Gilroy, whose lodge still bears his name, or with Bob Weir the coachman and his small army of grooms. Each girl had a dogcart and her own pony—they could drive out alone for miles and miles across the bog roads, to visit friends in distant cottages. Or they could ride through the forest. This absolute freedom in the countryside contrasted completely with the rigorous chaperonage deemed necessary when a girl came to London. My great-aunt Olive told me how she once got off to open a difficult gate and her pony kicked her on the knee. Sick with pain, she lay in the grass until she could drag herself up into the sidesaddle and ride home, trying not to faint until she had handed her mount to a groom and reached the schoolroom. There she collapsed by the bookshelf, where she could pretend she had been trying to reach a lesson book.

The girls and the governess came down to the big dining room for lunch only and they sat at a separate table. Afternoon tea was carried up to the schoolroom and it is interesting to note that after this snack at five o'clock the children got nothing more. My great-aunts said they were allowed *either* butter or jam on their bread, never both, and only one slice of cake. This was washed down by plenty of fresh milk. When they were big girls of fifteen and sixteen they invariably went to bed hungry. While the governess had a tray carried up to her in the schoolroom, on which lay portions of the large delicious dinner being served downstairs, her charges would tiptoe out barefoot to the servants' stone staircase to see what pickings were to be had, and they described the pathos of that solitary tray being carried to the 'Gov' alone in her schoolroom while shrieks of laughter came from the grownups' dining room and louder, coarser shrieks from the servants' hall.

Sometimes the unnaturalness of this life twisted a woman. Lord Curzon suffered psychological torture from his governess even before he went off to the floggings of his preparatory school. His ill luck in slipping from female sadist to male sadist may have been unusual. On the whole these governesses were merely unfortunate beings, neither fish, flesh nor fowl, just too well bred and ladylike to find a mate.

In families which did not 'do the season' in London, governesses got no break at all, but most families closed down their country houses in mid-April and opened the town ones. In the case of my own family the entire staff travelled over from Ireland. The carriages and the second coachman went first, the horses and the first coachman next (horses were more precious than vehicles); there also came two grooms, several footmen, the butler, and the head housekeeper with the minions of her choice. The great houses of Mayfair and Belgravia would be painted afresh, and window boxes of bright flowers appeared on the lower floors. For nearly three months, while parents 'did the season,' the girl children would live on the top floor doing the same old lessons with the same old governess.

Some of them briefly attended classes, and when they reached the teens French and German had to be added to the curriculum. It was considered imperative that girls should speak two languages, so numerous mademoiselles and fräuleins were imported. What a sense of isolation must have been added to the already lonely routine as these poor foreigners climbed to the schoolroom floor! And, with the cruelty innate in children, how horrid their charges could be. The servants scorned foreigners, they also scorned failures— and no woman who had to endure the status of a governess could be deemed a success. There were, of course, a few happy exceptions—some governesses found husbands, but precious few; some were adored and remained on as old family friends; some were naturally erudite women to whom books and the imparting of knowledge atoned for their austere life.

This educational picture was only true in England. French girls were far more polished, and Russian and German girls worked intensively and always learned three or four languages perfectly. Yet these half-educated English girls became politically the most powerful women in the world. At the age of eighteen an astonishing change would occur. Without any 'finishing' or preliminary instruction, girls had to be 'brought out.' This meant putting their hair up and accompanying parents to dinner parties and balls. They would, of course, be presented to Queen Victoria at a 'drawing room'— a function which necessitated full evening dress and long trains at three in the afternoon. Apart from table manners, no particular training was considered necessary for this entry into the blazing world of Disraeli's novels. The girls stepped straight from the schoolroom into the ballroom, and were expected to behave as the grownups did. Princess Marie Louise has described coming down to dinner at Balmoral when a very young girl and finding herself sitting next to the Lord Chancellor. She felt inarticulate until her grandmother whispered in her ear: 'The Queen wishes the young Princesses to remember that their duty is to entertain their neighbours at table.'

My Irish great-aunts always hated being dragged away from their Irish home in the spring. The exile only lasted three months, but they lamented with the cottagers each year and longed to get back to their lake at the end of July. Yet the dogs and horses accompanied them to London and they rode before breakfast just as they had done in Ireland. It is difficult to imagine the empty Mayfair streets in those days. One of my Leslie aunts was riding down

Oxford Street towards Hyde Park when an unexpected gust of wind blew her riding skirt up, revealing boots and breeches. Embarrassed, she glanced the length of Oxford Street and was relieved to see not a soul in sight. This incident occurred where Selfridge's now stands.

One would have thought it terrifying for girls reared in isolated castles to be suddenly launched into society, but most of them had caught the gift of the gab from the country folk.

At the required age, each of my great-aunts ceased lessons and travelled to London in April with a few simple white dresses. Having never actually dined at a grown-up table before, they had to accompany their parents and chatter as best they could with statesmen and eligible gentlemen. Girls were not expected to *know*, they were expected to *amuse*. The fact that the better-bred girls had spent so much time in the stableyard probably helped to overcome shyness, for stableboys have a quick turn of wit, and the important gentlemen who were looking for wives wanted them innocent but also able to make them laugh.

My great-aunt Olive, who married at the end of her first season in the 1890s, tried to tell me what it was like to leave her Irish schoolroom in April and find herself married and the chatelaine of a great Scottish castle by October. She had been awe-struck at coming down to dinner with her parents for the first time, but gentlemen were kind and took pains with a little redheaded Irish girl who easily lapsed into the brogue of County Monaghan. At balls the formal politeness helped because girls stood with their families, watching the great ladies in their jewels and the ambassadors and generals in their decorations. When a young man was introduced and asked for a dance his name would be inscribed on the little card handed out for the purpose. There were no scrimmages, no drunkenness, no bad manners, no wallflowers.

At the last ball of the season Olive's parents went home, leaving her in charge of a married sister. Although only just out of the schoolroom, she let herself be led to the conservatory where proposals of marriage were supposed to be made. When he popped the question—the tall, dark stranger whom she had sat next to at dinner a few times—she accepted for the best of reasons: 'He was so good-looking!'

Olive was too happy to realise that this was the end of childhood, that the little room overlooking that misty lake would no longer be hers. From now on she would sit at the head of her own long dining table, laden with the huge emeralds which were heirlooms of her husband's family—a young girl with ministers of the Crown sitting on her right and big households to attend to. She was very much in love and yet there was something sad about it.

Other girls married when they were not in love at all, simply because they wished to attain the status of married women. One, who knew much unhappiness, told me that she accepted wedlock to escape a mother who kept telling her not to sit with her ankles crossed! Many girls, however, married men they hardly knew, and were extremely happy. The fact that choice is limited and that swains are carefully vetted does not necessarily blight romance.

The seventh Lord Londonderry told me that when he contemplated wedlock he had met only six or seven possible girls. Each of these young ladies had been purposely placed next to him at dinner because they were by birth and upbringing qualified to entertain as a great political hostess should.

A late Edwardian description of a debut into London society comes from the pen of Lady Violet Bonham-Carter, daughter of the Liberal Prime Minister, Lord Asquith:

'Coming out in those days was an event which happened suddenly. Overnight, in the twinkling of an eye, one was magically transformed from a child into a grown-up person. The process by which this transformation was, as a rule, accomplished, was a large dinner party followed by a ball. Eager as I was to be grown-up I found the rite bewildering and painful. For the first time in my life the hair that dangled down my back was put up in a disfiguring pile. I was *laced* into a white satin dress by Worth, and feeling rather breathless and a little cold I went downstairs to face the forty strangers who had come to dinner. I had never seen one of them before, and the twenty young men all dressed like waiters (only a little better) looked as anonymous as supers.'

There were no 'young people's parties.' Dinners and balls were given by the older generation to entertain royalty, statesmen and politicians—the governing class. Young people were merely *allowed to attend* these magnificent functions.

The men wore white tie and identical tail suits enlivened by decorations if royalty was present. Young girls were expected to dress simply in white. Not until they married would jewels and bright colours be *de rigueur*. Innocence was highly valued. No man wanted to marry a girl with a 'bold eye.' The double standard prevailed. It was considered natural for young gentlemen to keep mistresses but their sisters must not even suspect the facts of life—those were to be learned on the wedding night. It was the men who liked it this way—presumably it amused them to cause consternation.

This was the atmosphere in which the English upper classes brought up their young, casual in the country, splendidly formal in London. From the rough, tough schools came the statesmen and from muddly schoolrooms stepped the great hostesses of tomorrow. Half-educated, horse-loving girls turned quickly into the most politically minded women of Europe. They did not always spell very well, but they listened to the conversation of their elders and soon they had their own views and were not shy to air them. English women were extremely sure of themselves. Issuing out of England's green parklands, brought up amidst her ancient oaks and beeches, they understood their role in life—a role that could not be learnt out of books.

3

The Young Prince

How CRUELLY DIFFERENT was the upbringing of Albert Edward to that of his subjects. Young Queen Victoria and her well-meaning conscientious consort were awed by the 'sacred duty' of training a future King of England. They allowed their German adviser, Baron von Stockmar, to work out the proper upbringing for a 'perfect being.'

The pressure on the boy's nervous system must have been terrible. During those early years, when the children of England's aristocracy were hobnobbing with nanny, cook and the stableboys, this little Prince had to face day after day of study under a team of experts. Pitilessly they strove to cram his mind until he verged on a nervous breakdown. Indeed his mother did worry when he had fits of uncontrollable, baffled fury, stamping his feet and hysterically shrieking at his tormentors, but this was merely considered 'naughty.'

The fashionable boarding schools to which his contemporaries went may have been brutal, but at least the atmosphere was alive and the boys learned to fend for themselves and to make friends. Also they had wonderful holidays in country homes in which to recover from term-time horrors.

It is strange that Queen Victoria, who had been raised without companions of her own age, and who recorded that she had been 'extremely crushed and kept under, and hardly dared say a word,' should have allowed her son to be brought up without seeing any children except his brothers and sisters; yet she did so.

The narrow-minded old Bishop of Oxford laid down this dreadful dictum: 'The great object in view is to make him the most perfect man.'

Poor little boy! He started lessons at the age of five with three governesses who taught him to speak English, French and German fluently (but they could not teach him the racy natural idiom of the English country gentleman and he never lost the German way of pronouncing 'r'). The fact that his elder sister Victoria was exceptionally precocious started an inferiority complex, but at the age of seven Bertie was transferred from the governesses and put in the charge of a team of tutors headed by one paragon of virtue, a Mr. Henry Birch, who had been captain of the school at Eton and taught there as a master. From now on the young Prince had to study five subjects every day, including Saturdays, each period lasting an hour or half an hour. Birch taught him mathematics, geography and English, the other tutors taught religion, German, French, handwriting, drawing and music. Those hateful boarding schools at least allowed their pupils three to four months' holiday a year, but for the royal children lessons were continuous except for a few days at Christmas and Easter and to celebrate family birthdays. They were intensively trained from morning to night and kept completely away from the 'frivolous atmosphere' of other English children.

Prince Albert Edward would be taught fencing and riding by experts, but there was no casual adventure, no fun, no pretending, no galloping off alone on a pony to explore the hidden corners of Windsor Great Park, no magic hours fishing for minnows with bent pins. Every minute of the day must be organised and every step of progress reported to his parents.

When Albert Edward was eleven years old Mr. Birch departed, after frankly reporting to Prince Albert that he thought many of his pupil's peculiarities resulted from 'want of contact with boys of his own age. . . . He has no standard by which to measure his own powers. . . . I have always found that boys' characters at Eton were formed as much by contact with others as by the precepts of their tutors.' Royal princes were not allowed this contact, however.

Prince Albert considered it a sufficient treat to take his son to hear the sixth-form boys recite in Latin and Greek on speech days. 'I can see his poor bored little face now. It was pitiful,' wrote Lord Redesdale.

The eleven-year-old Prince now faced lessons of six or seven hourly periods six days a week. Several of his tutors vainly appealed to Prince Albert not to overtax the young mind, but that 'dearest Papa' could not see that his son was being hard pressed. He never spared himself—why should the children slack off? It was Queen Victoria who worried because at times the little Prince hung his head and looked at his feet prior to one of those 'fits of nervous unmanageable temper.'

When Bertie and his younger brother Alfred visited Eton for a few hours with carefully selected companions they did not know how to behave. Being shy and overanxious, they appeared to be aggressive and rude. What they craved, of course, was to frolic with the other boys and to be liked. Merely to read the curriculum worked out by Prince Albert for his sons makes one dizzy. There seemed to be no subject in the world that the Princes must not study—and no sport, no pastime, which could not be turned into an onerous duty under 'expert tuition.'

Yet the Prince's natural *joie de vivre* survived. He immensely enjoyed his first visit to Paris when in 1856 he accompanied his parents on a state visit to Napoleon III's court, and the French nation was enchanted by the slim, good-looking boy in a kilt. On departure he begged to be allowed to stay behind.

At sixteen the Prince departed with three tutors and four Eton boys of his own age on a trip to Germany where a surprising incident on the first night had to be discreetly handled by Colonel Henry Ponsonby, the equerry in charge. The Prince of Wales kissed a girl! He had dined slightly too well, and that naturally affectionate nature, which would so soon become obsessively amorous, caused him to try his luck with the first pretty creature he met.

One of the 'selected companions' described the incident in a letter home to his father, the great Gladstone, who seemed deeply shocked: 'Evidently the Prince of Wales has not been educated up to his position.' But educating did not come into it. The sixteen-year-old Albert Edward had discovered without the help of any tutors that the touch of a girl's cheek was very pleasant.

Back in England the naughty Prince was sent to the White Lodge in Windsor Park for several months of intensive preparation for military examinations. It was not easy to find suitable paragons for company, but three exemplary young men were finally selected, and Prince Albert wrote a confidential memorandum outlining the ideas they were to try to instil into his son:

APPEARANCE, DEPORTMENT AND DRESS
. . . A gentleman does not indulge in careless self-indulgent lounging ways, such as lolling in armchairs or on sofas, slouch-

ing in his gait, or placing himself in unbecoming attitudes with his hands in his pockets. . . . He will borrow nothing from the fashions of the groom or the gamekeeper, and whilst avoiding the frivolity and foolish vanity of dandyism, will take care that his clothes are of the best quality. . . .

The Prince of Wales had, of course, been carefully coached by a dancing master, but his first ball—that given to celebrate his elder sister's engagement to the Crown Prince of Prussia—does not sound very amusing as Disraeli describes it:

Jan 23, 1858

On Wednesday we were at the Bridal Ball at Court. It was more brilliant than numerous, being, as I thought, unbecomingly limited, for the new Ball Room was only half full, and all the other rooms were open and empty.

However, I liked it as I got a seat. There were as many princes as at the Congress of Vienna. The Royal Party did nothing but dance with each other and, I thought, perhaps in consequence, looked bored. I saw the Princess of Prussia cram her handkerchief into her mouth to stifle a yawn. The Princess Royal, however, looked bright and gay, tho' I understand she is continually crying about leaving home, but then, they say, she is very childish and always cries.

Poor tearful Vicky was to become Empress of Germany and mother of England's enemy, the Kaiser Wilhelm II.

At the end of 1858 Disraeli formed his first opinion of the heir to the throne: 'I sat next to the Prince of Wales at dinner the other day, and was very much pleased with him—intelligent, informed and with a singularly sweet manner. He was going off next day to Berlin and seemed full of delight at the prospect.'

It was always refreshing to get out of England, even to Berlin. Paris, where morals were so lightly regarded, could not be considered suitable. According to Disraeli, Princess Metternich, wife of the Austrian Ambassador there, was behaving in a way she could not possibly have adopted in London: 'The Princess adores Paris and the French call her irresistibly fascinating. She seems to be what in *argot* would be called "rather fast," sees and does everything, and tho' of course respectably escorted, is found talking in the *coulisses* to fashionable actresses.'

When the Prince visited Italy he was invited by King Victor Emmanuel II to stay with him at Turin, but although Queen Victoria said that of all the Knights of the Garter he was the only one who looked likely to best the Dragon, she feared his rough habit of speech would not be a good example for her son. But there was more to worry about in King Victor Emmanuel's court than speech. On December 1, 1958, Count Cavour wrote to the Sardinian Minister in London: 'It appears that the Queen hesitates to consent to let him come to Turin, fearing that he might run some danger of losing his innocence. . . . If they speak to you about it, you may reassure the Court on the score of this precious quality of the Heir to the Throne. If it arrives with him as far as Turin, it is not here that he will lose it.'

Daniele Varè who translated this private letter adds that the words he uses are not as graphic and precise as in the original.

It was perhaps with relief that the Prince learned he was to attend Oxford and Cambridge universities successively. His mother, who was non-intellectual by nature, showed a touch of understanding when she wrote to her naturally studious eldest daughter 'Bertie is my caricature. That is the misfortune, and in a man, this is so much more. You are quite your dear beloved Papa's child.'

The Prince was not allowed to reside in college like other Oxford undergraduates. He had to rent an independent establishment and live under the eye of his equerry. Special professors delivered courses of instruction to him and his six selected companions.

It was about this time that Albert Edward first showed symptoms of that nervous habit we call compulsive eating. His parents added his increasing stoutness to their other anxieties. They approved of exercise, but when he wanted to go fox hunting they were afraid he would break his neck.

Studies ceased during the long vacation when he visited Canada to open bridges and lay foundation stones. Accepting an invitation from the President of the United States, the Prince of Wales enjoyed a triumphal tour through the major American cities, culminating with a ball at the Academy of Music in New York, to which five thousand people, who considered themselves socially eligible, found their way. The floor collapsed but no one was hurt; trumpets blew, the Americans grew wild with excitement and only the young Prince felt vexed—for he was expected to partner illustrious matrons when he was longing to dance with girls of his own age.

After a year at Oxford Albert Edward moved to Trinity College, Cambridge. Once again he had to live in a special establishment four miles from the town, but this was pleasant, for he could ride in on horseback each morning or drive his phaeton.

In the summer vacation of 1861 the Prince was sent for a ten-week course of infantry training at the Curragh Camp near Dublin where he was to be under the 'strictest discipline.' The Prince Consort directed that his son should wear a staff colonel's uniform and be attached to the Grenadier Guards. The camp was to be treated as 'a school of social as well as military instruction,' and the Prince of Wales's relationship with fellow officers was to be placed on a 'becoming and satisfactory footing.' Twice weekly he must give dinners to senior officers and twice weekly he was to dine in the regimental mess, while once a week he would be guest of honour to other regiments. The remaining evenings were to be spent quietly writing or reading edifying books.

It was not long before his fellow officers took pity on H.R.H. They all had mistresses and it seemed a shame that their Prince should not enjoy the delights which he so obviously, almost innocently, craved. Albert Edward's living quarters had purposely been situated in the very centre of the camp, but they managed to smuggle Nellie Clark, a pretty actress, into his hut nightly. The G.O.C. never knew of these happenings, but every soldier in Ireland soon heard the news and soon after the Prince returned to Cambridge Miss Clark was boasting around London of her adventures.

The 'scandal' which broke out in the following November, just after dear Bertie's twentieth birthday, was particularly embarrassing in that the Prince had recently met the beautiful Princess Alexandra of Schleswig-Holstein, and wished to ask her hand in marriage.

On November 16, 1861, the Prince Consort wrote to his eldest son of the 'greatest pain I have ever felt in my life.' Reluctantly he had made enquiries and discovered that the 'story current in the Clubs' was true—the Prince had had an affair with an actress—the whole country knew, Queen Victoria knew and dearest beloved Papa was on his way to exhort a wicked son to mend his ways: 'You *must* not, you *dare* not be lost.'

Prince Albert travelled to Cambridge by special train on November 25 to have the matter out with his son, who proved penitent and obtained forgiveness. A few days later Prince Albert fell ill and wrote to his eldest daughter: 'I am at a very low ebb. Much worry and great sorrow (about which I beg you not to ask questions) have robbed me of sleep during the past fortnight.' Within a week he had collapsed with typhoid fever and on the night of December 14 he died.

Queen Victoria was stunned with grief, and during her first unbalanced weeks of widowhood she cruelly blamed Bertie for causing the sudden death of his father. In vain the contrite son tried to offer comfort. She could hardly bear to see him. Fortunately Bertie's nature proved resilient. He could not bring himself to believe that his father's typhoid death had been *entirely* his fault. A letter of Disraeli's gives the atmosphere of that December week: 'It is a great calamity for this country. The Prince of Wales, as you probably know, has been perpetrating some scrapes, and was about to be sent abroad. They say he has brought about all this—others say that it was the King of Portugal's death, who was a sort of pupil of the Prince Consort and by whom he managed to govern Portugal, as well as England.'

Later Disraeli wrote: 'The Prince of Wales seems anxious to take his place: and I hear behaves with great tact and feeling. The funeral strictly private. . . . They wish to move the Queen to Osborne but she puts it off every day, dreading the sight of the glaring daylight, it being impossible for the yacht to bring up under Osborne after dark. As matters now stand she will go today, the Prince of Wales escorting her and returning. . . . He wrote yesterday to Palmerston, by desire of his mother, to say that Lord P. would always find her mindful of duty and of her people, but that her worldly career was at an end.'

This was Victoria, widowed at forty-two, a censorious yet loving mother who would stand by her son when he got into trouble but never seek to mitigate the feeling of guilt. The blow had slightly unhinged her. When discussing Prince Albert's death with her old friend Lord Hertford she mentioned that he had been killed by 'that dreadful business at the Curragh. . . .'

'Oh, no, madam,' interposed Lord Hertford firmly.

Vainly her ministers tried to reason with the distraught Queen, vainly they tried to explain that it was quite natural for a young man to have affairs with actresses. She could not bear to look at her son, so it was sensibly decided to send him off on a tour of the Near East and then tie him up safely with beautiful Princess Alexandra. 'The marriage is the thing, and beloved Papa was most anxious for it.' So Queen Victoria comforted herself.

How lucky that a lot of jolly places remained open to an English Prince after disasters of this magnitude. Having been entertained in Vienna, H.R.H. sailed down the Dalmatian coast in the royal yacht *Osborne*. He explored Corfu, shot wild boar in Albania and wrote cheerfully to his friend Lord Carrington that the trip would be 'especially well adapted to a gay fellow like you.' It is evident that the Prince of Wales had no intention of being the only nobleman in Europe denied mistresses.

After Cairo sightseeing, the royal party started up the Nile in a luxuriously equipped steamer provided by the spendthrift Viceroy Said Pasha. Albert Edward shocked Canon Stanley, his guide and chaplain, by 'levity and frivolity.' The twenty-year-old Prince preferred taking pot shots at crocodiles to inspecting tumble-down temples.

In the Holy Land the Prince found himself constantly attended by vast cavalcades. After a dutiful glance at historical places his greatest interest seemed to be shooting. He was never parted from his gun and would bang off at lizards, owls, larks, vultures, when the more edible partridges and quail were not in view. On the Palestinian hills he collected and dried wild flowers for sister Vicky, Crown Princess of Prussia.

During the return journey he received a kindly letter from his mother, who seemed to be recovering from her shock, and an observer wrote of the Prince's touching desire for approbation: 'I wish you could have seen the Prince of Wales's face when he read the Queen's letter to him. It was actually beaming with pleasure.'

The heir to the throne craved affection, he loved his mother and he wanted to be loved by all around him, and the knowledge he now had of his own physical attraction made the idea of a romantic marriage to Europe's loveliest Princess very alluring indeed.

After disembarking at Marseilles, Albert Edward spent several days at the British Embassy in Paris and paid a fortuitous visit to Louis Napoleon at Fontainebleau, where the Empress Eugénie, quickly realising that the young Prince longed to meet people of his own age, decided to summon the most attractive young women of her court for an informal soirée. 'You are going to enjoy yourself for once,' she said, 'and don't worry about your keeper. I know he has orders to get you off to bed at 11 P.M. but I'll corner him and keep him talking.'

So the Prince was introduced to the Duchesse de Morny, the Comtesse Greffuhle, the Comtesse Edmond de Pourtalés, the wondrously beautiful Duchesse de Mouchy, the Princesse de Sagan and other young women who charmed and amused him and became his friends for life. None of them was over twenty-five, but, of course, there were no unmarried girls, for they would be compromised if they danced twice with a Prince and, besides, they were too shy to tease and sparkle.

While Albert Edward enjoyed this animated company, the Empress chatted to Sir Charles Phipps, Keeper of Queen Victoria's Privy Purse and temporary keeper of her son, whose eye kept anxiously rolling towards the sound of happy laughter. 'Do not worry, I will write explaining it all to Queen Victoria,' the Empress remonstrated. 'Let him have one evening that is all pleasure and no duty.'

So the Prince danced and flirted, but only one of the lovely throng would become his mistress. This was the handsome heiress, the Princesse de Sagan, whose witty, unfaithful husband, most elegant of dandies, known in Paris as the '*fleur des pois*,' was even then causing her indignation.

When a few days later the Prince returned to England the Queen noted: 'His time away has done him so much good, he is improved in every respect, so kind and nice to the younger children, more serious in his ways and views, and most anxious for his marriage.'

As the Curragh story had reached Denmark, Queen Victoria thought it wise, and indeed only fair to the parties concerned, to ask her daughter Vicky to communicate frankly with Princess Alexandra's parents, telling them 'that *wicked wretches* had led our poor innocent boy into a scrape which had caused his beloved father and myself the deepest pain . . . but that both of us had forgiven him the *one sad mistake* . . . and that I was very confident he would make a steady Husband. . . .'

After suitable manœuvring the Prince travelled to Denmark, asked Princess Alexandra to marry him and was accepted on September 9, 1863. The wedding was arranged for the following March. London went wild with excitement and curiosity when the eighteen-year-old Princess arrived and drove through the city wearing a violet fur-trimmed jacket and a white bonnet adorned with red rosebuds.

At Windsor Castle Queen Victoria felt too desolate to join the dinner party, but she was touched by Alexandra's 'sweet loving expression.'

Next day there came a visit to the mausoleum where the Prince Consort had been buried, and if Alexandra shed a few tears on her wedding morning she was able to say frankly to the Prince's elder sister, 'You may think I like marrying Bertie for his position, but if he were a cowboy I would love him just the same and would marry no one else.' Vicky must have repeated these words to the bridegroom and he would not have been human had he not burned with pride.

The marriage service took place in St. George's Chapel in medieval splendour. The Prince wore his velvet Garter robes, the fairy-tale Princess shimmered in silver. All the men present were in uniform, the ladies glittering in court dresses heavy with jewels. Queen Victoria sat alone in Catherine of Aragon's balcony, a tiny dramatic figure dressed in black relieved only by the blue ribbon and star of the Order of the Garter. The pathos of the unsmiling widow made a deep impression; so did her little grandson, Prince

Wilhelm of Prussia, who threw his aunt's muff out of the carriage window, picked the cairngorms out of his dirk and bit the bare knees of his kilted uncle, Prince Arthur.

But Queen Victoria rejoiced for Bertie—that boy she had feared for, that 'caricature' of herself. With such a wife he would find virtue easy. 'She is one of those sweet creatures who seem to come from the skies to help and bless poor mortals and lighten for a time their path.'

On returning from a week's honeymoon in gloomy Osborne, the young couple moved into Marlborough House, the great cut-stone and brick edifice which was to be their home for nearly forty years. Balls and festivities started immediately and within weeks the grimmer members of the old aristocracy were referring with long faces and raised eyebrows to what they called that fast Marlborough House set. By June Queen Victoria was scolding them for looking tired, but the country delighted in its lively Prince and Princess. Never had there been such a London season. After all the years of restraint, this glamorous young pair proved perfect social leaders. They would set the tone not only for England but for Europe. Queen Victoria could not predict the patterns of behaviour which her amiable, lusty son would devise, but she may have had shrewd suspicions. She might comment, she might deplore, but she could not restrain. Albert Edward, Prince of Wales, would personally dictate the code of social behaviour for the next fifty years, and it would be unique in history.

4

Albert Edward Emerges

WHAT WAS IT LIKE—the society of which the twenty-one-year-old
Prince of Wales and his eighteen-year-old bride found themselves
the applauded leaders?

For two decades the court had been ruled by dutiful Prince Albert while his busy, virtuous Queen attended to state affairs. There
had been precious little fun in the royal entourage, but, as always
happens, there were individuals in the very rich, very powerful
aristocracy who could be as eccentric as they pleased.

Between the sexes a double standard existed in a way that is
difficult for today's youth to visualise. Even cultivated men often
stipulated that they did not wish their daughters to learn more
than French and to dance lightly in case they became *bores*. Flirtatious girls had to pretend to know nothing and physical innocence was a necessity. Males could seduce at random as long as
they carried on these activities out of view of their families. It
must have been difficult for respectable mamas to explain away
the high-class cocottes who took their carriage outings in Hyde
Park. Maybe daughters were just ordered to 'look the other way.'

It was considered perfectly natural for a man to keep mistresses,
but they must remain in a separate world. A mistress had to be
paid, therefore she would invariably be of a lower class than her
keeper. The hungry workers did not take a particularly dismal
view of daughters who went astray with a 'nob,' but the girls had
a rough time if 'cads' abandoned them with illegitimate babies.

The composite misery based on the frequency of this occurrence must have been terrible. For a penniless girl there was so much temptation and such unfair retribution. For every merry little shopgirl who skipped around as a 'kept woman' there were hundreds whose lives were broken. A man could lie, or threaten, or bribe, or force a working-class girl to give in to him. She would have no redress. And the children suffered the stigma of being bastards even when financially supported. Beneath the gracious surface lay this ugly world. To the inevitable sorrows of human life, cruel scorn was deliberately added. The ordinary woman in Victorian England could find no halfway path. She had to be rigidly virtuous or branded immoral and this hypocrisy must have destroyed much natural joy, while the natural pervert had a field day. The ones who must have suffered most in this queer censorious atmosphere were the gay, naturally sexy women who were born into the respectable classes. After 'catching a husband' they were supposed to spend the rest of their lives just hating what he forced them to do. Extramarital affairs were almost impossible—although much thought of—always *thought of!*

But whatever the rules, human character emerges and there were many daring individuals in young Queen Victoria's land, and certain aristocratic ladies took lovers without incurring odium. Sex relationships with royalty were considered *different*. To give an idea of the atmosphere one could pick out Frances Anne Vane Tempest, that Marchioness of Londonderry who conducted a long correspondence with Disraeli, whom she met at a ball when he was thirty and she was thirty-five. An heiress in her own right, Frances Anne had deliberately chosen to be the second wife of a man twenty years older than herself, who established her as the great Tory hostess of her time. After bearing him a son and daughter she conducted a dramatic love affair with the good-looking Tsar Alexander I, whose superb gifts of jewelry were added to the Londonderry collection without anyone batting an eyelid. Here is an eyewitness account of this lady at one of her great political receptions: 'In her own house her manner was polite and high-bred but stately and frigid such as invariably inspired awe in those who were introduced to or had occasion to pass her.'

In middle age she used to seat herself on a gilded chair with a gold brocade baldachin over her head and there she presided between the statue gallery and the drawing rooms, receiving the departing salutes of her nervous guests.

But ambitious young Disraeli was not intimidated—or only slightly so. A letter to his sister describes his first meeting at a fancy-dress ball: 'Lady Londonderry as Cleopatra, was in a dress literally embroidered with emeralds and diamonds from top to toe. It looked like armour and she like a rhinoceros. Castlereagh introduced me most particularly to her by her desire, and I was with her a great deal.'

Disraeli, quickly realising the value of Lady Londonderry's patronage, requested permission to write to her. Their correspondence lasted twenty years and is written in the lightest of veins, full of malicious gossip concerning such unfortunates as Mrs. Caroline Norton, whose beastly husband had cited the Prime Minister, Lord Melbourne, in divorce proceedings. As this brute used his full husbandly rights to impound his wife's literary earnings as well as every penny of her personal fortune *and* took her young children away, this *cause célèbre* did result in some improvements concerning married women's property rights later in the century. But at the time poor Mrs. Norton aroused as much laughter as sympathy.

Disraeli alludes frequently to his Marchioness' 'bright eyes,' but there is no bedroom talk except concerning that famous Bedroom Plot when Lord Peel refused to take office unless Her Majesty's ladies of the bedchamber, belonging to Whig families, should retire in favour of Tory ladies of his own choosing.

Disraeli was often invited to the thatched cottage at Richmond where Lord and Lady Londonderry were wont to play at being rustics, and described it thus: ' 'Tis the prettiest baby house in the world—a pavilion rather than a villa, all green paint, white chintz and looking-glass. The grounds, however, are considerable, and very rich, bordering the Thames. The dinner was admirable but no silver plate; porcelain fresh as the room, with a bouquet by every guest, and five immense pyramids of roses down the table.'

This desire to escape to rural simplicity was more real than the urge which prompted Marie Antoinette. English women loved gardens and were knowledgeable about all that grew. Their architects built enormous glass conservatories in which tea would be served, but it was the flower garden and, indeed, the kitchen garden of which they were proud.

Less fortunate Victorian ladies suffered acute boredom, but the Marchioness of Londonderry was part of England, not merely part of London. Although she may have been unusually energetic and unusually well endowed, I have chosen Frances Anne as an example because she could not have been found in any other land. Society was run by such as she when the romantic young Prince stepped out of his mother's court to form a world of his own. He bowed to the great ladies and started to draw his own pattern from scratch,

and among the first of his friends would be the thirty-year-old
German-born Louisa, Duchess of Manchester, ten years older than
himself, who had already run foul of his mother and been forbidden the court. She entertained in great style, at Kimbolton Castle in
Huntingdonshire in the winter, where her lover, the famous Liberal Lord Hartington, enjoyed fox hunting, and during the summer
at Manchester House in London. What the Duke of Manchester did
is obscure. He rode to hounds, broke his bones frequently, gambled, dabbled in politics, gave Louisa five children and lived in
Hartington's shadow for thirty years. Perhaps he felt it was enough
to just be a duke and have the most beautiful wife in England.

The routine which the Prince of Wales devised as a young married
man remained the same throughout his life. January and February
would be spent at Sandringham, which he and the Princess regarded
as their home. It is interesting to note that when the 7000-acre estate had been bought no other big country place was available. During Victoria's reign a family place scarcely ever changed hands.
English gentry owned England and lived on the land they owned.
The Hon. C. S. Cowper of Sandringham had chosen to retire to the
Continent after marrying his former mistress, Lady Harriet d'Or-
say. Norfolk was no place in which to sit out a scandal—and so the
Prince benefited. He paid £220,000 for the only large property on
the market, and spent £80,000 rebuilding the house in Victorian-
Tudor style.

In mid-March Albert Edward always visited the French Riviera
en garçon for five weeks, spending a few days in Paris at either end
so that he could call on his friends and, as time went by, have their
children and eventually their grandchildren presented to him. After reference to private diaries it appears that no lady of the nobility became his mistress except the Princesse de Sagan, and this famous affair can slip into place later. One must realise that it was
impossible for the Prince of Wales to have an affair with *une grande
dame* without the circumstances being known to the whole of Paris.
When in his mid-twenties and early thirties the Prince enjoyed visiting the demi-mondaines—birds of paradise who vied for his favour: nor did their wealthy keepers object to lending bejewelled
mistresses to England's heir. These classy cocottes lived in fantastic
style and would arrive at the races sparkling with jewels in their
own carriages, yet they knew their role and never thought of trying to enter the enclosure where they might have brushed up
against 'a lady.' They did not *want* to mix. They had their own
world where they could show off and they were respected in it.

These were the fabled demi-mondaines of Paris—enticing and intriguing and collecting great fortunes. One of them, with the delicious name of Emilienne d'Alençon, always used heliotrope scent and had her carriage upholstered in mauve satin.

But let us get back to royal Aprils. At the end of this month the Prince, refreshed rather than otherwise by six solid weeks of dinners and festivities in the South of France, would return to Marlborough House. It is understandable that he should have delighted the French—he was so spontaneous and appreciative of all they had to give, but it does seem extraordinary that any man should have been able to stand up to weeks of intensive entertaining *just before* the rigorous London season. The Prince of Wales would now face three solid months of dinners, operas and balls, with a great deal of official work thrown in.

Not until the end of July, when he went to Cowes for a few weeks' sailing, could there be any break. And even there the round of parties continued. When he returned from the sailing races he so enjoyed there would always be dinners and dances and occasionally a summons to dine with his mother at Osborne.

After Cowes he generally proceeded to a health spa in Germany or Austria before returning to Abergeldie, near Balmoral, for grouse shooting and deerstalking. His own and the Princess' birthdays (November 9 and December 1) were always spent at Sandringham and so was Christmas. They loved this place more than any other, and always felt lighthearted and happy there.

From the day she had been widowed, Queen Victoria avoided going to London. She attended to her duties from Windsor Castle or Balmoral or Osborne—the vast, hideous structure designed by her consort at East Cowes. Although Victoria refused to discuss affairs of state with her son, she continually expressed regret that Bertie's incorrigible love of pleasure did not appear to be fading. During the very first London season she began scolding him for encouraging 'that sweet wife' to overdo things. 'For although Bertie says he is anxious to take care of her, he goes on going out every night until she will become a skeleton. . . . Oh how different poor foolish Bertie is to adored Papa. . . .'

The first baby appeared prematurely, but this was not really Bertie's fault. The Princess had wished to be whirled out on a sledge to watch her husband play ice hockey. Then she had to be rushed back to Frogmore and a little son was born before the Home Secretary could be summoned. A local doctor, arriving on horseback at full gallop, was knighted for his services. The Queen recorded in her diary that there were 'no clothes for the poor little boy who was just wrapped up in cottonwool.' This baby, named Albert Victor after his paragon grandparents, would prove a great trial in the future.

Alexandra bore six children within seven years, then she became extremely ill, and it seems likely that she did not wish to risk childbirth again. The Prince of Wales loved his children dearly but he was unable to relax in the family circle. That naturally enquiring mind which had been trained to ceaseless activity could not be still. Rushing from one social engagement to another, he never complained of overwork. On the contrary, a ceaseless stream of friends were bidden to enliven every spare moment. Albert Edward did not *want* to be alone. After so much bookish education he now preferred to get his information from people.

The marriage was really ideally happy for several years. Then, after visits to St. Petersburg and Paris, the Prince, realising that he could, if he wished, seduce almost any lady he chose, started to try his luck in England. Indeed, he found it almost too easy. When word went around that the heir to the throne was susceptible, a number of married ladies, who had already given their husbands male heirs and were therefore fair game, responded with alacrity. Their husbands may have been bored with them—anyway, none raised objections. A carefully organised loosening of morals was such a relief after the last twenty-five years under Victoria. The whisper that the handsome Prince of Wales, around whom society centred, would flirt and graciously pay court to every lady who gave him hope enchanted Europe. And the gentlemen of his entourage were anything but averse to this altered tempo in upper-class behaviour. After all, the Prince could not behave thus all on his own. Within bounds they also felt free to think about the wives of friends in a new context. Most of their marriages had been arranged years before. The ignorant brides were now eager, mature women —sauce for the goose must be sauce for the gander. Very discreetly, carefully and romantically, the Prince's set began to copy the domestic habits of His Royal Highness.

It was easy to love Albert Edward—he had such a warm nature that the ladies who acquiesced to his bantering overtures did not do so entirely because it had become the smart thing. There was a very real pleasure in giving affection to this Prince who genuinely craved it. Queen Victoria wrote admiringly of Alexandra: 'I often think her lot is no easy one, but she is very fond of Bertie, though not blind. . . .'

Yet again she wrote: 'Bertie is so full of good and amiable qualities that it makes one forget and overlook much that one would wish different.' But London society wished nothing different. They were delighted at the change. For the first time in years it had become possible for a gentleman to contemplate having an affair with a woman of his own class.

The hard-gambling Duke of Sutherland and the beautiful domineering Duchess of Manchester, who had with Lord Hartington anticipated the new moral code, were foundation members of the 'fast set' to which the Queen particularly objected. Their names occur frequently in the early pages of the Prince's engagement diary which he kept in his own hand and in which he noted the names of every person he met each day—whether approved of by the Queen or not. It certainly seems harsh that while bewailing her son's excursions into 'frivolous society' and the 'fast racing set' the Queen should deliberately debar her son from affairs of state which might have taken his mind off much nonsense. She would not even allow him to represent her in public: '. . . Her Majesty thinks it would be most undesirable to constitute the heir to the Crown a general representative of Herself, and particularly to bring him forward too frequently before the people. This would necessarily place the Prince of Wales in a position of competing, as it were, for popularity with the Queen.'

So the Prince of Wales, with that highly trained lively mind, had to content himself with being president of various societies, chairman or governor of colleges and colonel-in-chief of regiments. It was particularly bitter for him not to be allowed to serve in the Army or Navy when his Prussian brother-in-law saw active service and two of his younger brothers enjoyed serious military careers. In 1870 Gladstone would gloomily observe: 'To speak in rude and general terms, the Queen is invisible, and the Prince of Wales is not respected.' Laying foundation stones and making public speeches could not satisfy a man of the Prince's calibre. Yet he was permitted no more. His inner frustrations must have been terrible. It is a wonder that he did not get into trouble more often, and no one can follow up the detailed record of his life without becoming very sorry for Albert Edward. Of course he got bored, and when he did find stimulating friends the Queen wrote asking him to show disapproval by 'not asking them to dinner, nor down to Sandringham—and, above all, not going to their houses.'

To these admonitions he paid no attention whatever.

5

The World of
the Princesse de Sagan

As THE HABIT of compulsive eating grew upon him, the Prince worried about his increasing girth. Even before the age of thirty he had become much too fat. Cures became regular annual fixtures, but it never seemed to cross his doctors' minds that he might be cajoled into reducing the intake of huge quantities of rich food.

The Prince demolished an enormous breakfast as well as a vast lunch and dinner every day of his life. When in the country he tucked into a hearty tea of scones and cake as well, and during the season he could cheerfully consume a fifth meal—midnight supper.

An energetic course of amours might have been expected to diminish this unnatural appetite, but H.R.H. seems to have become hungrier and hungrier as more ladies came his way. In 1867 *The Times* and other newspapers gave such embarrassing publicity to his relationship with the actress Hortense Schneider that Queen Victoria pressed her son to forgo the London season. But he answered manfully from Marlborough House, 'We have certain duties to fulfil here and your absence from London makes it more necessary that we should do all we can for society, trade and public matters.'

Public matters were splendidly attended to—it was private matters which needed less zeal. For, while London hummed about Miss

Schneider, the gossips in Empress Eugénie's court had a glint in
their eyes. After several years of separation from her husband the
Princesse de Sagan had organised a brief reconciliation and given
birth to a second son—her first child after a nine-year interval. Parisian calendars were being consulted and wicked fingers ticked off
the months since the Prince's last visit. H.R.H. used Jeanne de
Sagan's houses as he did that of the Duc and Duchesse de Mouchy
—as his own.

Yet despite his roving eye the Prince remained devoted to his
lovely Princess Alexandra and in July 1868 she bore her fourth
child—Alexandra Victoria—only four months before setting out
with her husband on a six-month tour of Europe and the Far East.
It was sad for the young mother to leave so young a baby, but she
was allowed to take the three older children as far as Copenhagen
for one of those cosy visits to her parents' home.

The Prince and Princess travelled with a doctor and thirty-three
servants. Louis Napoleon and Eugénie gave a fabulous ball at Compiègne where Alexandra's beauty won all hearts—even that of the
Princesse de Sagan, who felt perhaps even more deeply the honour
that had been conferred on her!

Queen Victoria had deplored certain aspects of the French court,
saying: '. . . the proceedings at Compiègne and Fontainebleau
make it undesirable that the Prince and Princess should visit either
of these places,' but the ball passed off splendidly and decorously.

Now Her Majesty expressed displeasure at learning that the
Duke of Sutherland was waiting to join the royal party in Egypt: 'If
you ever become King you will find all these friends most inconvenient.' *Inconvenient*—with what exactitude Victoria could choose
words!

In Egypt the Khedive spared no expense when entertaining England's heir. The Ezbekiya Palace had been extravagantly redecor-
ated, and the Prince and Princess humorously stared at their bedroom, nearly fifty yards long, with massive silver twin beds, and
gold-plated chairs too heavy to move. They sailed a thousand miles
up the Nile in six blue and gold steamers, each towing a barge filled
with campaign comforts such as three thousand bottles of champagne, four thousand of claret, four French chefs and a milk-white
donkey for Alexandra's sightseeing. On returning to Cairo, the
Prince, understandably, sought exercise by climbing the Great Pyr-
amid.

After inspection of the Suez Canal came an amusing visit to the
Sultan of Turkey, where the Prince had to distribute large numbers
of jewelled snuffboxes and his wife glanced into the harem. Then

came a few happy days in Athens where they stayed with Alexandra's brother, King George of Greece. They were back in Paris by mid-May, where the Emperor Napoleon produced another ball for the Princess and a military review for the Prince.

Queen Victoria poured out advice: 'I hope dear Alix will not spend much on dress in Paris. There is besides, a *very* strong feeling against the luxuriousness, extravagance and frivolity of Society . . . added to the many scandalous stories current in Society.'

The Prince wrote back frankly: 'You need not be afraid, dear Mama, that Alix will commit any extravagances with regard to dresses, as I have given her two simple ones, as they make them better here than in London; but if there is anything I dislike, it is extravagant or outré dresses—at any rate on my wife.

'Sad stories have indeed reached our ears from London of scandals in high life, which is indeed much to be deplored, and still more so the way in which . . . "they wash their dirty linen in public."'

There indeed lay the unforgivable sin—PUBLIC LAUNDERING! The Prince took pains to conduct his love affairs with discretion and his entourage knew they would ruin their own pleasures if scandals broke loose.

The Prince was very unlucky in being drawn into one divorce case as a witness, but this isolated mischance was not his fault. Counsel for the twenty-one-year-old mentally deranged Lady Mordaunt, accused of adultery, insisted on calling on the Prince of Wales (who had known her since childhood and frequently visited her in London) as a witness in her defence. It was unfortunate that the name of H.R.H. should be connected with any divorce case, but the law of England stands firm and fair. Royal princes can be subpoenaed. The two co-respondents cited by Mordaunt happened to be friends of the Prince and some pleasant notes written by H.R.H. to the lady existed—her counsel intended these to enhance her reputation, not to hint that the Prince was infatuated; but the fact that he had known her and associated with immoral men friends sullied his reputation.

When the Lord Chancellor advised the Prince not to raise any question of privilege, Albert Edward attended the court and underwent a seven-minute cross-examination in the witness box with dignity and composure. The case was dismissed on the grounds of insanity and the Prince's wife and mother stood by him loyally, only expressing indignation that Lady Mordaunt's counsel had ever thought fit to subpoena the heir to the throne. Queen Victoria was showing her usual perspicacity when she wrote to the Lord Chancellor: 'Still, the fact of the Prince of Wales's intimate acquaintance with a young married woman being publicly proclaimed, will show an amount of imprudence which cannot but damage him in the eyes of the middle and lower classes, which is to be lamented in these days when the higher classes, in their frivolous, selfish and pleasure-seeking lives, do more to increase the spirit of democracy than anything else.'

It seems extremely unfair that for some weeks after the Mordaunt case both the Prince and Princess should have aroused hisses as they drove through London streets and at the theatre where they inadvisedly appeared with the Duchess of Manchester in their box.

Louisa Manchester was not a wise companion to choose at this juncture. As Queen Victoria wrote, when pressing Princess Alexandra to drop her, the Duchess had 'done more harm to Society from her *tone*, her love of Admiration and her "fast" style, than almost anyone.'

Despite the care with which the Prince and his entourage conducted their affairs, rumours were bound to escape. The man in the street enjoyed salacious gossip concerning 'the nobs,' but middle-class, nonconformist England looked down its long nose and Queen Victoria noted with pain a growing immodesty of behaviour. 'The animal side of our nature is to me too dreadful and now one of the new fashions of our very elegant society is to go in perfectly light-coloured dresses without a particle of Shawl or Scarf (as I was always accustomed to wear and to see others wear), and to dance within a fortnight of the confinement, even waltzing at 7 months!!!'

This must have been a fairly difficult feat even for ladies with first-class balance, but it shows how dance-mad society had become. The Prince of Wales indulged his tastes without self-consciousness. Watched by all Europe, he set the pace and created the Marlborough House set. Romantic liaisons were permissible, but the even tenor of life must not be disturbed. Love was made to enhance festivities, not to destroy homes. Young girls had to remain strictly guarded as before—they would not get husbands if not absolutely, idiotically innocent, but when a married woman who had done her duty by producing sufficient sons cared to glance around, she now might notice a certain thoughtful expression on the faces of gentlemen who hoped to emulate the Prince of Wales. At first came only the glance, then the careful game of modest recoil and soft innuendo. The chatelaines of the English countryside were no longer entirely intent on politics and on running their great mansions. They found time to consider and count conquests. Society now recognised a certain way of arranging rooms in country houses if the husband (who usually slept in an adjoining dressing room) did not object. Presumably husbands who were padding off to other ladies' rooms did not object at all, but it took a lot of discreet probing to be sure. These were no *casual* affairs, they needed strategy and tact. Scandal must never ensue; if it did the woman was out of society for life. A man with a bad reputation could creep in again, under that unfair double standard, but no divorced person, man or woman, could be invited to court, nor could non-divorced but separated couples. Marriage was the cement which held up the whole social edifice. To sin in secret was one story, to shake the home by getting into the newspapers or law courts another. Naturally intent on preserving itself and its good times, society turned pitilessly on those who tumbled openly into trouble. Behind the few hundreds constituting the Prince's set lay stern middle-class England, where Puritan tendencies had become solidified. The toiling hungry workers hardly came into the picture. They didn't care if the gentry carried on—all they wanted was enough to eat.

The discomforts of these splendid English country houses would appal ordinary folk today. Central heating did not exist, so that all large rooms were cold despite open fires. Most bathrooms were built on at the end of freezing corridors and there was never enough hot water. In fact, the earlier habit of having a hip bath in front of one's own bedroom fire was infinitely preferable. My grandmother, sitting in front of her own bedroom fire in Ireland, used to sigh for this 'forgotten luxury.' We still had a dozen hip baths at Castle Leslie which we played boats in as children. Our grandmother said it used to be delicious sitting in a hip bath by flickering firelight while the towel warmed on a nearby chair. The maids always carried up one brass water can of cold water and two of hot. She poured in the cold first, then a hot can, then the lady would get in, sit down, and keep warming up the water from the third can. After she had dried in the warm towel my grandmother's maid would reappear to dress her, do her hair up with diamond pins (the mean Leslie family never produced a tiara to punish her for being American), pull in her waist and hook up the gorgeous evening gown with its fluffy sleeves and pneumonia-inviting décolleté. The Prince scolded women who did not wear jewels in their hair at dinner. 'I take the trouble to dress. Why can't you?' 'Oh, sir, I'm so sorry . . .'—downcast eyes, blushes and then would come the kindly unscolding which he never could resist, even when people had done something dreadful.

At Londesborough Lodge near Scarborough, where Lady Londesborough gave a royal house party in October 1871, not only were the bathrooms few but the drains seeped into the drinking water. Several guests, including the Prince and his groom and Lord Chesterfield, contracted typhoid fever. When Chesterfield and the groom died the doctors abandoned hope for the Prince. Queen Victoria, who had moved to Marlborough House during the crisis, wrote: 'I hardly knew how to pray aright, only asking God, if possible, to spare my Beloved Child.'

Suddenly on December 14, the anniversary of his father's death, the Prince's delirium ended and he fell into a healing sleep. At the news that Albert Edward might live the entire nation rejoiced. England suddenly realised how fond she had grown of 'Teddy,' her magnificent profligate. Henceforth he would seem more precious and his lusty ways more endearing. In the hour of danger Queen Victoria forgot that her eldest son had ever caused her to 'shudder,' and 'poor foolish Bertie' had become once more 'my Beloved Child.'

After a three-month convalescence the Prince realised that Gladstone was striving to arrange a sort of super-Viceroy job for him in Ireland. When the Prime Minister spent a constrained weekend at Sandringham to discuss possible employment, Queen Victoria wrote him bluntly that 'The P. of W. has *never* been fond of reading, and from his earlier years it was *impossible* to get him to do so. Newspapers and, *very rarely*, a novel, are all he ever reads.'

Bertie craved action, not books. He had had his fill of study in the past and the duties now assigned him were insufficient to satisfy an intelligent overeducated man. He was pathetically eager to play his part. He had charm and intelligence and energy and gradually he acquired experience of human beings. When his brother, the Duke of Edinburgh, married the attractive Grand Duchess Marie, daughter of Tsar Alexander II of Russia, her family made a fuss because she was not granted precedence *above* the Princess of Wales. Albert Edward soothed ruffled feelings by inviting the Tsarevitch and his wife Marie Feodorovna (who was Alexandra's sister) to stay for two months and be entertained at Cowes. Such preoccupation with relatives whose noses were out of joint over *precedence* was hardly worthy of the talents of a clever man of thirty-three, but Queen Victoria insisted on good nature and friendliness in the royal dovecots.

The one really important result of this summer honey-up could not have been foreseen by anyone. At the dance on the cruiser *Ariadne* which the Prince gave in honour of the Tsarevitch and his Grand Duchess, a certain young man met an American girl of nineteen. This chance meeting, due entirely to the fact that the Prince was sufficiently broad-minded to allow non-aristocratic foreigners to be presented and enter his circle, resulted in the marriage which produced Winston Churchill. If the Grand Duchess Marie had not protested at having to walk *behind* the Princess of Wales, this dance would not have been given and Lord Randolph Churchill might never have set eyes on Miss Jennie Jerome of New York.

Because his sister was Crown Princess of Prussia, Albert Edward's tact had to be severely tested when entertaining those French friends whose lives had been blighted by Sedan. But he always showered kindnesses on people who were *down*, and in spite of her own strongly pro-German feelings Queen Victoria took pains to show her sympathy to the exiled Empress Eugénie. When in the winter of 1874 Louis Napoleon died at Chiselhurst, Victoria gave her son permission to attend the funeral, but to the Prince's chagrin, Gladstone asked him not to go. The role of a Prince of Wales can be very painful when political duty interferes with generous impulses.

Criticism began to arise in certain English circles when Bonapartists visited Sandringham. The Prince trod on delicate ground, but with his sensitivity and inbred courtesy he managed to receive impoverished French friends and to let them entertain him in Paris in reduced circumstances without hurting their feelings. Overthrown aristocrats are naturally edgy, but he handled them with just the right mixture of sympathy and respect, and carefully avoided mentioning to them those occasions when he had to meet ministers of the Third Republic.

When the Comtesse Edmond de Pourtalés came to England to visit the Empress Eugénie, the Prince asked her to attend a reception at Marlborough House, but she wrote excusing herself on the grounds that France was in mourning, and she in yet deeper mourning than many others, for the Pourtalés home in northern Alsace had been annexed by Germany. In fact, she was building up a small court of her own there, cutting Germans who crossed her path and inviting only French intellectuals and writers. Far from being offended when the Comtesse declined his invitation to Marlborough House, the Prince took trouble to show that he understood her feelings. A week later the Comtesse received a wide gold bracelet studded with a few pearls and engraved on the inside were the words, '*Les larmes d'Alsace.*' It was this sensitivity to other people that aroused absolute devotion. The Pourtalés family, who have since seen Alsace captured and recaptured, still possess this bracelet. They remain very pro-Edouard! This trait of kindness in the Prince's character overweighs what appears to be a certain callousness when playing practical jokes, and the thoughtlessness of permitting silly courtiers to bankrupt themselves in their efforts to entertain him.

An extraordinary story concerning the Princesse de Sagan (her husband also carried the title Duc de Talleyrand-Périgord) has been told me by her family connections. It reveals the awe with which the French aristocracy regarded an affair with the Prince of Wales, and the utter disregard all parents had for psychological effects of aristocratic amours on their offspring in France. The Princess had long been regarded as *maîtresse en titre*. She was an industrial heiress who had made a grand match. Her father, a rich banker, had been delighted when his daughter married into the great family of Talleyrand-Périgord with the added estates of Sagan which had been procured by the famous Talleyrand for his nephews. Maybe the girl was also delighted at the time—it was a great step up for her. The Prince de Sagan and his caustic wit kept him popular in society. Only his wife detested him. She may have had good reason, for they say he was extremely unfaithful and irrepressibly funny about it. Madame la Princesse lived in splendour and sulks. She has been called beautiful but the only Frenchman I've met who, as a little boy, actually set eyes on her says she had too big a nose. Certainly she was not exquisite like the Duchesse de Mouchy or the Comtesse Greffuhle, but her extravagance and her voluptuous inclinations led many men to court her. Although she possessed a great mansion in the Rue St. Dominique, most of her time was spent at her properties at Cannes and Deauville and also at the Château de Mello, some hundred kilometres south of Paris, where she used her fortune to embellish the existing castle and to build vast stone arches into the stableyard through which the Prince could drive in a coach drawn by four horses. It was all very, very grand and Jeanne de Sagan's love affairs were as ostentatious as her stonework. While the Prince de Sagan strutted around the clubs dropping *bons mots* his wife developed a country pursuit of her own at Mello—building laboratories for the distillation of perfumes. The wits had it that she would end with a laboratory for husband-poison.

Be that as it may, she found consolation in a long-term affair with Albert Edward, and the aphrodisiacal smell of musk must have been very appropriate when he came to visit her.

Sagan's comments on this situation are not recorded, but he probably thought it quite chic to be cuckolded by *le Prince de Galles*. The French aristocracy had not entirely recovered from the lure of Versailles, and although at first they mocked Eugénie and Louis Napoleon for their parvenu court, they had taken to it like ducks to water, whirling in their crinolines around the romantic Empress and her amiable, unfaithful husband. The 1870 war had ended all that, and royal romance now had to come from England.

When the Prince of Wales visited Mello the servants and everyone else behaved exactly as if Louis XV was honouring Madame de Pompadour. Coachmen, butlers, cooks, flunkeys, footmen, gardeners, stonemasons, market gardeners, butchers, poulterers, ladies' maids, housekeepers, floor polishers, scullions went into frenzied activity.

Of course, a veneer of decorum was observed in the sense that the religious susceptibilities of the lower classes must be considered. When, after that nine-year interval, Jeanne de Sagan was bearing that second child, her affair with the Prince of Wales had become well known so that it was considered proper to stage a brief reconciliation with her husband. The Sagans both knew what good manners demanded, but neither felt it imperative to keep up appearances for long. Back went the dandy to his witticisms and his infidelities, and his wife to her perfumes and other interests.

It was around 1875 when the eldest Sagan boy (who was brought up with the son of the Comtesse Edmond de Pourtalés) was fifteen years old that this youth, the heir to a most illustrious French title, developed violent feelings concerning his mother's love affair. I cannot discover if he knew or had suspected it for a long time or if he acted impulsively on the shock of discovery. Whatever triggered off his brainstorm, the following occurred.

The Prince of Wales had come to spend the day at Mello and this poor young Hamlet, on entering his mother's boudoir, saw His Royal Highness' clothes on a chair. Outraged, he snatched them up and ran out of the long french window to hurl the bundle into the great water fountains. When the Prince emerged from his lady's bedroom it was to find his sopping apparel being rescued from the goldfish by hysterical servants. Understandably the Prince was annoyed—he had to drive away in borrowed, too tight trousers —but he took it bravely as an Englishman should. After all, when Frog he would a-wooing go, dangers must be faced. It was Jeanne de Sagan and her husband who felt they could never forgive their son. The boy was banished to some grim monastic school, a sort of reformatory, and scarcely ever spoken to by his parents again. Many years later, when he had become Duc de Talleyrand-Périgord, he would marry Anna, the daughter of Jay Gould of New York, but they found little happiness together. Both individuals had had odious parents and perhaps the poison had seeped deep. The interest of this sad story lies in the revelation of what people thought *mattered*.

6

The Duchess of Manchester
and Harty-tarty

AWAY BACK IN 1851 the rather wild young man who was to become
seventh Duke of Manchester had been sent by his father to Hanover
to study German and improve himself generally. It was apparently
generally conceded that room for improvement existed. No sooner
had the twenty-eight-year-old Viscount Mandeville, as he then was,
arrived to stay with Count von Alten than he fell in love with his
host's very beautiful daughter, Louisa, whom he had once seen on
the Riviera. Hoping that a happy marriage might be as stabilising
as a dose of German grammar, the old Duke agreed to his son's
choice, the marriage took place in July 1852 and the astonishing
Louisa von Alten immediately took her place as a leader in English
society. To her increasingly extravagant husband, who succeeded to
the dukedom in 1855, she bore five children and for a time they
appeared to be well suited. Both Duke and Duchess relished gambling
for high stakes, and the 'fast Manchester House set' was exactly
what Victoria and the Prince Consort hoped their teen-aged son
would avoid when he grew up.

Despite the cool eye cast on her by the Queen, Louisa continued
to entertain exactly as she wished, and she created style. As a
young married woman she vamped Lord Derby, and while under
her spell this 14th Earl signed a promise that, in what he considered

the unlikely event of his becoming Prime Minister, he would recommend her for the office of Mistress of the Robes. When political changes swept Derby to the premiership, Louisa Manchester made him redeem that perilous promissory note. Eventually Queen Victoria learnt the story and such was her anger that she declined to send the Duchess an invitation to the Prince of Wales's wedding—an unprecedented rebuff for a former Mistress of the Robes.

Lord Clarendon in writing Louisa a long description of the wedding tried to soften the blow: 'If it can be any satisfaction to you, you may be sure that there is but one feeling of surprise and anger at your not being invited. . . . The Queen looked down from a lofty pew in a widow's cap more hideous than any that I have yet seen, but her mourning was a little enlivened by the star and ribbon of the Garter.'

But Louisa could survive the Queen's displeasure. She possessed riches, a noble name, splendid homes, wonderful looks, an acquiescent husband and iron determination. When the Prince of Wales married and stepped forth into society, he and his bride were charmed by this flamboyant older woman who was so particularly adept in the art of dominating ministers. No scoldings from the Widow of Windsor could keep Albert Edward and Alexandra away from Louisa's house parties at Kimbolton Castle in Huntingdonshire, or those magnificent gambling soirées at Manchester House which so shocked the Dukes of Queen Victoria's set, such as stately Abercorn and ponderous Marlborough. The young Prince and Princess of Wales simply could not find any character as exciting as Louisa. And indeed she would be the only Edwardian lady to capture *two* Dukes!

What was the Duchess of Manchester really like? Among many ambitious and beautiful women how did she succeed in cornering so many important men? How did she manage to dominate London so that every man with political or social aspirations stood in awe of her? There is one early description of Louisa. The incident takes place seven years after her marriage. Paper chases had become the fashion in a few 'very fast' country houses and in 1859 Lady Eleanor Stanley wrote: 'The Duchess of Manchester, in getting too hastily over a stile, caught a hoop of her cage in it, and went head over heels, alighting on her feet with her cage and whole petticoats remaining above her head. They say there was never such a thing seen —and the other ladies hardly knew whether to be thankful or not that a part of her underclothing consisted of a pair of scarlet tartan knickerbockers (the things Charles shoots in)—which were revealed to all the world in general and the Duc de Malakoff in particular.'

We now know about Her Grace's underwear, but the boldness of climbing a stile in a crinoline does not explain her ultimate power. How did she hold her position in society when for thirty years everyone knew she was the mistress of Lord Hartington and when many intelligent men referred to her in private letters as stupid? Louisa was staunchly Conservative, her lover the steadiest of Liberals, a man without the lightning brain of his colleagues, Gladstone, Rosebery and Dilke, but with slow accurate judgment. Of them all he could most surely put a finger on the weak spot in any argument. Louisa was immensely ambitious for him, far more ambitious than he was for himself. She prodded and drove and warned. She was determined that her Harty-tarty should become Prime Minister. When Gladstone first retired from leadership of the Liberal Party in 1876 she regarded the event with anxiety, writing to Disraeli: 'That gentleman is only waiting to come to the fore with all his hypocritical retirement.' If Gladstone should return to the leadership she guessed it would endanger Hartington's prospects of attaining the premiership. How shrewd she was! A few weeks later Gladstone published his sensational pamphlet concerning Turkish atrocities, the pamphlet which inflamed England's virtuous anti-torture, anti-rape, anti-massacre bias and eventually led to Gladstone resuming leadership. Louisa could then say, 'I told you so!' But Disraeli's official biographer neatly insists that it was 'less a case of Gladstone exciting popular passion than of popular passion exciting Gladstone.'*

On a few other occasions Louisa showed perspicacity, but Sir Charles Dilke, most lucid humanitarian of his time, whom many regarded as the obvious successor to Gladstone, continued to regard her political manœuvrings with contempt. One exceedingly likable trait in Louisa was her fearless loyalty to those she admired. When the Prince of Wales quarrelled with Lord Randolph Churchill, and announced he would enter no house which received him, Louisa maintained: 'I hold friendship higher than snobbery,' and H.R.H. had to realise he could not rule her. After Dilke made a speech in which he followed a line of reasoning unusual in 1877, criticising the Franco-German War and condemning the 'taking of territory' as 'bound to lead to more wars,' the Duchess requested him to call on her—for brain-washing apparently. In his diary Dilke wrote after this interview that the Duchess of Manchester tried very hard to pick up political information for Lord Hartington, 'but her own strong Conservative prejudices and her want of clearness of head made her by no means a useful guide, and in fact the wonder to me

* Monypenny and Buckle, *Disraeli* (6 vols.).

always was to see how Hartington's strong common sense kept him from making the mistakes into which she always tried by her influence to press him.'

In 1878 she sent Dilke a letter concerning the Rt. Hon. W. E. Forster, author of the Education Bill. 'Please back up Mr. Forster. I think he is quite right. Fancy to be chosen and proposed by a Committee, adopted by 300 idiots or geniuses, and to have to submit when you can stand on your own merits.' Dilke noted on this: 'A German Conservative Duchess was not likely to be able to understand the Caucus. Forster was her friend, going and sitting with her almost every day and chuckling over her politics with his extraordinary chuckle and playing cards with her at night.'

When in 1880 the Liberals triumphed, and Queen Victoria unhappily faced the prospect of losing her dear Disraeli, she asked him, as outgoing Prime Minister, what to do. He advised her to send for Hartington: '. . . in his heart a Conservative, a gentleman and very straight-forward in his conduct.' The Queen would gladly have overlooked his liaison with Louisa, but Gladstone made it clear that he had no intention of serving under Hartington, who had not been born when he had entered Parliament! So Louisa never experienced the triumph of seeing her man reach the first place, but Hartington served his country loyally for fifty years. He was Secretary for India, and twice Foreign Secretary. In the end he broke the Liberal Party over Irish home rule by standing for continued union with England. He might, perhaps, have become Prime Minister after Dilke had been smashed by the most extraordinary divorce case in history, but with his great personal heritage and his sense of pure duty Harty-tarty probably cared less than any other man who just missed the premiership.

During all these years of scheming and working and keeping her fingers in important pies everyone feared Louisa Manchester—feared her and coveted her invitations. Although she failed in her largest ambition, she learned how to make and break men. She wielded power and used it without pity. She had no women friends —the feminine sex disliked her—but she could hold her man. Once she got her manacles on the good-natured Harty-tarty she never let go. She must have kept him in unplatonic tow for over thirty years before she became widowed and was able to marry him, thus earning the nickname of the Double Duchess.

Early in the sixties she nearly lost him to the famous horsy courtesan Miss Catherine Walters, known as 'Skittles.' It is difficult to imagine the great Hartington, even when his blood was young and fiery, even in his cups, asking a tart to marry him, but Skittles was

special. Although born in the slums of Liverpool, and although Sir
William Hardman referred to her in a letter as 'a whore, sir, much
sought after by fast young swells,' Miss Catherine Walters was no
ordinary street girl earning herself a fortune. She had come to London and somehow learned to ride extremely well; the owner of a
livery stable mounted her on his showiest hack and allowed her to
drive a pony phaeton in Hyde Park. Dressed in a skin-tight riding
habit, with a top hat, she looked both well-bred and seductive, and
the coarse Liverpool swear words which slipped from this apparently angelic person added to her piquancy.

The young Marquis of Hartington had never been sent to a boarding school, his father hating the brutality of Eton, and a rather intellectual country education left him unsophisticated. Louisa's hard
eye had spotted his potentiality immediately and so had the soft
blue ones of Skittles. The Duchess tried to capture him, offering
invitations to her magnificent political entertainments, even asking
him to *tea* alone with her, to discuss government bills, but Hartington fell seriously in love with the twenty-year-old street girl who
was mesmerising Rotten Row. Lady Augusta Fane in her memoirs
passes on the description of Skittles cantering her chestnut hack up
the Row, wearing her one-piece riding habit which 'looked as though
it was glued to the rider and showed off her slim figure to perfection.' Lord Hartington was rich enough and powerful enough to
marry whom he wished, but he could hardly have become politically
eminent with such a wife, even if he had eventually installed her at
Chatsworth. When the affair grew overserious my great-great-
uncle Charles Powell Leslie hurried him away to America where
the two men inspected the raging Civil War in the role of tourists!
Hartington had time to reflect on the embarrassments to which his
physical tastes might lead him. Leslie, a friend who was hardheaded
though not hardhearted, counselled him gravely. On their return
Skittles was given a large Mayfair house, carriages, servants and
an irrevocable £2000 a year for life. Then Hartington again went to
tea with the Duchess. She behaved with perfect coolness, perfect
discretion, handed him his cup with a smile, merely asking: 'Is it
one lump or two?' as if he had only been away a week and she could
not quite remember. Then she discussed his political aspirations and
made no mention of Miss Walters—then or ever. Within a short
time she had become his mistress—and from Louisa there was no
escape.

It was a sad little Skittles who continued her career of devilment
—in London, Paris and occasionally in the hunting shires where she
could jump her bold-hearted horses with the best. She was the only

courtesan to hunt with the Quorn and be accepted by the Master, who could not restrain his admiration for her riding, but a whore could be lonely at times. Although Skittles was strict with her lovers in wintertime, saying that hunting and love-making did not agree, yet she could never enter the country houses whence the other hunt followers would return for jovial dinner parties—the ladies would have been outraged. Even Skittles' famous chestnut hack, whom she kept during the winter in the same stableyard as her hunters, had to be 'exercised at night to avoid scandal.'

The Comte de Maugny's memoirs note the impression made by Skittles when she rode in the Bois de Boulogne during her summer visits to Paris: 'What perfect taste she possessed! What elegance! What grace on horseback! What a grand air and what originality in her choice of accoutrements!'

To a certain extent she consoled herself with the exotic young poet Wilfrid Scawen Blunt, but Hartington had been her first love and certainly she was his. It had not just been the case of a brave girl from the gutter trying to catch a rich peer.

The Prince of Wales knew of and enjoyed the love affairs of his friends, and in 1876, when Louisa had determinedly made Hartington her property, H.R.H. devised one of his most famous practical jokes. During an official tour of Coventry the Prince instructed his equerry to ask the mayor to make certain the party inspected the bowling alley because Lord Hartington was so particularly keen on that game. When they reached the alley Hartington showed no particular interest, so the mayor innocently exclaimed: 'His Royal Highness asked specially for the inclusion of this alley in the tour in tribute to your lordship's love of skittles.'

Harty-tarty was an indolent if dutiful aristocrat, a magnificent, casual, likable man who enjoyed fox hunting and breeding race horses, as well as politics, who wanted to share the joy of his art treasures and who could not remember who his guests were—a man who loved animals and sport and not being bothered. Margot Asquith sketches him: 'He stood by himself and could have come from no country in the world but England. He had the figure and appearance of an artisan, with the brevity of a peasant, the courtesy of a king and the noisy sense of humour of a Falstaff. He gave a great wheezy guffaw at all the right things and was possessed of endless wisdom. He was perfectly disengaged from himself, fearlessly truthful and without pettiness of any kind. . . . His speaking was the finest example of pile-driving the world had ever seen.'

This was the man whom Louisa had eventually got all to herself—Dilke says he remained faithful to her as she to him, and the liaison should therefore be respected unlike that of Mrs. Ronalds and the Duke of Edinburgh. Where the Duke of Manchester came into all this is unclear, but maybe like many other men he wearied of his high-powered wife and was grateful that another man could divert her energies. 'Kim' Manchester was also keen on fox hunting and many political letters addressed to Louisa contain hopes that his collarbone and other fractures are mending. Occasionally her correspondents wonder if he is 'giving up the dangerous sport.'

Hartington is often on the dinner lists for Marlborough House— sometimes with Sir Charles Dilke and Countess de Grey, always with Louisa. He cared nothing about clothes. At Aix-les-Bains in 1888 he shocked Mr. Smith, the extremely correct Conservative leader, by dressing as a 'seedy shady sailor' and he wore the same old round hat at race meetings until twenty-four of his lady acquaintances vowed to band together and each send him a new hat. When created a Knight of the Victorian Order (he already held the highest of awards, the Garter), he merely complained to the Prince's private secretary that it made dressing for dinner so complicated. Women, race horses and fox hunting filled the mind of Lord Hartington, and, above all these, he cared for England. Slow, thoughtful and exact, he served his country all his life because he believed it to be his duty. As several of his brothers had married and produced sons, the need to get an heir for the great Devonshire possessions did not worry him.

There is a conversation of the eighties recorded by George Smelley in *Anglo-American Memories* which incorporates Hartington's personal philosophy. Hartington and the Prince were taking the cure at Homburg. 'Said the Prince: Hartington, you ought not to be drinking all that champagne. No, sir, I know I oughtn't. Then why do you do it? Well, sir, I have made up my mind that I'd rather be ill now and again than always taking care of myself. Oh, you think that now, but when the gout comes what do you think then? Sir, if you will ask me then I will tell you. I do not anticipate. The Prince laughed and everybody laughed.'

Two other anecdotes give a yet more perfect description of the man. Hartington, when asked what he considered the best answer to the usual American greeting, 'Pleased to meet you,' replied: 'If the fellow addressed me like that, I should say, "So you damn well ought to be!"'

And when a man entering his railway carriage put the question, 'Do you mind if I smoke a cigar?' Hartington serenely answered: 'No, my dear sir, provided you don't mind me being sick.'

Louisa had two sons and three daughters. She was a strict mother.

One of the girls once made a saucy joke and was ordered to her room for three days on bread and water. Louisa the younger, who became Lady Gosford, told my grandmother that they were brought up knowing they must all marry eldest sons and it never entered their heads they could do otherwise. Two earls and one duke eventually became their ration of the peerage. When as children we were marched to the drawing room to meet Lady Gosford we were instructed to notice her lovely gentle voice. In the nineteenth century all well-bred girls were taught to cultivate a low silvery timbre, and never in stress or anger might the tone be allowed to rise. And although we were frightened to death of old Lady Gosford we can still recollect that soft controlled voice. Thus one can visualise the picture of the Manchester schoolroom with the French mademoiselle, the German fräulein and the over-all sense of restraint.

The odious Countess of Cardigan (wife of that insufferable leader of the Charge of the Light Brigade) states in her *Recollections*, 'I often used to meet Louisa, Duchess of Manchester, in the country. At that time she was in the freshness of her somewhat opulent German beauty, but we were never intimate, and have always disliked each other.' No one else dared be thus frank. Throughout the late sixties and the seventies and the eighties, when she was entertaining at Kimbolton Castle and giving house parties for the Prince and Princess of Wales, while Hartington kept his hunters in her stableyard, it is difficult to get more than a profile of the unique Louisa. Then, as my father searches in his cupboards, out falls a letter written to him in 1920, a month after the eighty-year-old Skittles had died. The letter comes from Bernard Holland, Devonshire's official biographer (who is not quite accurate, however, concerning Louisa's first casts for Harty-tarty):

2 Sept. 1920.

Dear Leslie—Thanks. I think that Skittles must be in a low circle of Purgatory by now. She survived the late Duke of D. who always made her an allowance. On his death the question arose whether the present Duke should continue it. The Duchess did not like this proposal—however I believe that it was done. She had entangled Hartington, in a sleepy mood, into a promise of marriage. This was of course before he knew Louisa who was rather a Skittles in higher life—to whom he was pretty faithful. Lady Greville told me the other day that when Greville was telling Hartington that he ought to marry a certain young lady of whom his family approved he said, 'I would marry at once if I was *certain* that the Duchess of Manchester was unfaithful to *me*.' The old Whigs were worse than the old Tories in such morals. An old man once said to me, 'No one knows how beau-

tiful a woman can be who did not see the Duchess of Manchester when she was thirty.' But she was not at all like that
when I knew her at about sixty or fifty.

Louisa must have been tough and determined, for during all this
period, as may well be imagined, the mamas of upper-crust society
were eagerly parading their daughters in front of Lord Hartington.
It must have been very galling to see the greatest of English catches
hooked first by an equestrian tart and then by a steel-nerved Duchess several years his senior. The knowledge that Louisa, who had
been anything but a faithful lady in the past, never played him false
evidently meant so much to Harty-tarty that he could forswear
the young girls of the world for her sake. My father remembers,
when he was a very little boy, his American mother coming to the
nursery all dressed up and saying in awe-struck tones: 'Tonight I
am going to the Duchess of Manchester.' No one dared attack
Louisa, but only Margot Asquith, who usually enjoyed pulling people to pieces, seems to have actually liked her. In her memoirs
Margot comments: 'A woman whose social ascendancy eclipsed
that of anyone I have ever seen or heard of in London society.'
Margot, who detested Lady Londonderry, goes on to call Louisa
'the last great political lady in London society as I have known it.
The secret of her power lay not only in her position—many people
are rich and grand, gay and clever, and live in big houses—but in
her elasticity, her careful criticisms, her sense of justice, and her
discretion. She not only kept her own but other people's secrets;
and she added to considerable effrontery—intrepid courage and real
kindness. She was powerful enough to entertain both the great political parties which few can do. You met everyone at her house,
but she told me that before 1886–87 political opponents hardly ever
saw each other and society was much duller. I have heard her re-
prove and mildly ridicule all her guests both at Compton Place and
at Chatsworth, from the Prince of Wales to the Prime Minister.
I once asked her what she thought of a certain famous political
lady, whose arrogance and vulgarity had annoyed us all, to which
she answered: "I dislike her too much to be a good judge of her." '

One evening many years later, when Margot was talking alone
after dinner with the Duchess, Louisa suddenly said: 'Margot, you
and I are very much alike.' Surprised, Margot asked her where the
resemblance lay. 'We have both married angels; when Hartington
dies he will go straight to heaven,' pointing her first finger upward.
'But when Mr. Gladstone dies . . .' Down, down, down, she pointed.

The virtues which Margot attributes to the Duchess—kindness,
elasticity, sense of justice—have been noted in no other memoirs,

but the existence of the last two emanate from the letters which Lord Clarendon wrote to her.†

Certainly Louisa was a marvel of discretion and there may well have been something in dynamic young Margot which conjured up a gentler side in her nature. Indeed the earliest description of her in my grandmother's letters (1881) mentions her kindness at a hunt ball, helping her to stick her hairpins in firmly before the quadrille, so maybe Louisa rather liked unmarried girls who could not possibly be rivals and looked up at her with awe.

When in public Louisa and Hartington invariably addressed each other by their formal titles. Only one occasion has been recorded in which the Duchess forgot herself. This was in the early eighties at a house party given by the Duke of Portland at Welbeck. The Duke's mother overheard Louisa, who was sitting at a writing desk near to Lord Hartington, say, 'Harty darling, stand me a stamp.'

After twenty years of clandestine nightly meetings it must have given them quite a shock to realise they had to walk to their apartments together in front of the servants!

Sir Charles Dilke wrote of the Duchess' 'stupid influence' on Hartington, who was his colleague in the Liberal Party, but Dilke was a republican-minded radical and would not have been impressed by Louisa's grandeur, nor did he care for playing cards which she so enjoyed. The Double Duchess makes a curious study. Quite how did she do it? She, a foreigner, whose fast ways and general influence on society shocked Queen Victoria, who made a cuckold of one Duke while keeping another faithful—or almost. Some called her hard and many called her stupid, but she could hold her lover against courtesans and debutantes alike. Louisa can be classified as the most feared and the most successful woman of her time. And a faint impression of her personality emerges from one of Lord Clarendon's letters: 'How *can* you say that you write unintelligibly when you must know how quaint and piquant your style is—the charm of a letter is to be like the conversation of the writer and that is just what your letters are.'

'Were it not for imagination, sir, a man would be as happy in the arms of a chamber-maid as of a Duchess,' said Dr. Johnson. But not, maybe, if the Duchess happened to be Louisa Manchester.

† A. L. Kennedy, ed., *My Dear Duchess.*

7

The Aylesford Case

IF ONLY QUEEN VICTORIA had taken her eldest son into her confidence, taught him the importance of discretion, and allowed him access to state papers, he might have felt less frustrated and kept his grosser appetites under control. The Prince and his younger brother the Duke of Edinburgh opened themselves to cool rebuke when they asked the young Lord Rosebery to lend them his London house for gambling parties and rendezvous with actresses. Albert Edward was learning by degrees that, however much he had altered the moral outlook of society, it was generally safer, if less interesting, to conduct physical amours with 'actresses,' the word then implying more than footlight fame.

The Mordaunt case had taught him the dangers of writing amiably to ladies, and now came another hard lesson. It may be noted that in both the Mordaunt and Aylesford cases, which caused the heir to the throne so many sleepless nights, there is no reason to suppose that he had an affair with either lady. He had simply been unwise enough to write complimentary notes, and then unexpected events brought these ordinary pleasant letters into the battle arena.

In October 1876 the Prince of Wales started out on an official tour of India. The summer had seen much dispute concerning expenditure and also his choice of a suite. Among the eighteen men he listed were Prince Louis of Battenberg, R.N., and Lieutenant Lord Charles Beresford, R.N., as A.D.C.s, Lieutenant Colonel Owen Williams, who commanded the Blues, as equerry, and the Duke of

Sutherland, Lord Carrington and Lord Aylesford as personal guests. Queen Victoria wished for 'some more eminent men' and objected to Lord Charles Beresford and Lord Carrington in particular. Disraeli only got the Prince's list passed by promising to caution these two gentlemen against 'larks.' From Paris, Carrington wrote to his mother: 'No jokes, or any approach to them. . . . No news—all well—no whist and no sprees, or bear fights, or anything!'

In India the Prince made a magnificent impression on all classes. The maharajas revered his sporting prowess and the lesser species were impressed by his naturally liberal outlook. To Lord Salisbury the Prince wrote angrily protesting against the 'disgraceful habit' of some British officers in referring to Indians as 'niggers.' For nearly five months he travelled the subcontinent, shooting elephant, tigers and cheetahs, attending state receptions, receiving the great princes and chatting with murderers in prison.

Finally he reached Nepal, where the ruler put one thousand riding elephants and ten thousand soldiers at his disposal. It was on February 21 that the Prince, having shot six tigers from the back of an elephant, returned to camp to enjoy his usual hot bath followed by dinner in a lavishly furnished tent and found an atmosphere of constraint had descended on the all-male party. 'Letters!!!' was all the Prince recorded in his diary, but the word bore an ominous tone.

Since leaving England the Earl of Aylesford had written many affectionate, humorous letters to his wife Edith, describing amusing incidents on the tour, and right up to February 15, 1876, these letters start 'My darling' and end 'Your most affectionate Joe.'* It is obvious that Sporting Joe had no inkling that his wife might during his absence carry on an affair with Lord Blandford, the eldest son of the Duke of Marlborough. Although he had a crude reputation for racing, gaming and whoring, this noble Earl was obviously very much in love with his wife Edith.

Lady Aylesford was a sister of the Prince's very close friend, Colonel Owen Williams, who came of an old Welsh family. Five of Williams' six sisters had married into the peerage and were about to attack their brother on the subject of Edith's delinquency, but Colonel Williams had received no knowledge of the erupting volcano when he left the Prince's camp a few days before to rejoin his wife, who was mortally ill.

Within hours of Lord Aylesford sending a last letter to 'My darling,' a letter which notes sadly that he has only received five

---

* These letters have been preserved by Edith's great-niece, Mrs. Edward Phillips, and two have been published in *Companion* I of *Winston S. Churchill* by Randolph S. Churchill.

letters in five months, the mailbag arrived which contained a hysterical screed from Edith informing her husband that she was going to elope with Lord Blandford (married to the Duke of Abercorn's daughter Bertha and the father of three children). Lady Aylesford had borne Joe two daughters but no son and heir, or the disaster might not have reached such proportions. Sporting Joe, who had been chaffed for being 'the only one that hardly ever has any letters when the bag is opened,' was stunned. His darling wife going off with that Churchill cad! He poured out his fury to the Prince of Wales, who counselled him to return to England and pour oil on troubled waters, etc.

Lord Aylesford, 7th Earl, climbed into a howdah and vanished in the direction of the nearest railhead. This was the last the royal party saw of him and there is nothing more melancholy, majestic and uncompromising than the hind view of an elephant. 'He has gone home broken-hearted at the disgrace,' wrote Carrington, 'and the misery it all entails is terrific.' Carrington was correct. The story of the Aylesford scandal has been fully related, and yet how difficult it still is to unravel the psychological stresses which drove the pretty, foolish, vulnerable Edith to post off the letter which ruined her life, her children's lives, and eventually her husband's life.

The outraged Joe endured a six-week journey back to England during which time his indignations grew. A famous man to hounds, one of those heavyweights who by sheer artistry and skill could ride light when galloping over the big shire fences, he had never been altogether light-handed with his wife. She was four years older than he, maybe more sensitive, but hardly more intelligent, as her actions and changes of policy show.

Reading Joe Aylesford's jolly, unsuspecting letters up to February 15, one has to feel sympathy with him, but the immediate telegram he sent to his mother, the Dowager Lady Aylesford, after his wife's revelations lack pity: 'Send for the children and keep them till my return. A great misfortune has happened. Am writing by the mail.'

And a few days later Edith wrote to her mother-in-law:

Dear Lady Aylesford,
    By the time this letter reaches you I shall have left my home for ever. . . . I do not attempt to say a word in self defence, but you can imagine I must have suffered much before I could have taken such a step: *how* much it would be impossible to tell you . . . you do not know, you cannot know, how hard I have tried to win his love, and without success, and I cannot live uncared for. I do not ask you to think unkindly of your son;

I know you could not do it, but for God's sake be kind to the
children, and do not teach them to hate their wretched mother,
let them think I am dead, it will be the best. . . .

This emotional outburst ignores the affectionate letters written
by her husband up to the very last moment. He obviously loved her
in his way, but Sporting Joe drank hard and gambled away his
money and was more popular with men than women—he may well
have been an inconsiderate husband, and no lover at all. Certainly
the way he had with a horse was not his way with a woman.

The hard fact remains that when the Prince had invited Joe to
India, Edith, who was already in love with Blandford, pressed him
to accept and took immediate advantage of his absence by going to
Packington Hall, one of the Aylesford country houses, where it
would be easy to meet her lover. Blandford moved his hunters to
the village nearby and rented accommodation. All that winter he
visited his lady love at night, leaving tracks in the snow to an un-
used doorway of which she had given him a key. The servants
knew, the stablemen knew, the village knew—and naturally the
whole county soon knew.

By the time Lord Aylesford reached England he found the Marlborough family wildly trying to persuade Blandford—not to give
up Edith, which they knew would be impossible—but to abandon
the idea of eloping. Blandford's brother-in-law, Marjoribanks, erred
when he wrote the Duke of Marlborough: 'I don't think anything is
very generally known as yet, only the following people are aware
of everything. The Duchess of Manchester, the Princess of Wales,
the Charles Kerrs and Huntington and Lords Alington and Lansdowne.'

Everyone knew by early March when, with Joe demanding a duel
and a divorce, it became obvious that a major scandal was about to
break. Society realised how harmful such a divorce case would be to
its own structure and to the Prince of Wales, whose close friendship
with Blandford, Aylesford and Edith's brother Colonel Owen Williams was well known. More embarrassing, the Prince had seen a
great deal of Edith in the past and had flirted casually with her as he
did with all pretty women, and then written her a few jolly notes.

We can never know quite how Edith's mind worked in the month
after she wrote her husband that she was about to elope. Maybe her
five sisters exerted influence; certainly her brother Owen remonstrated with her.

While Aylesford proclaimed in the clubs that H.R.H. had called
Blandford 'the greatest blackguard alive,' Edith showed her lover
the Prince's letters and he placed them in the hands of his younger

brother, the impetuous, hotheaded Lord Randolph Churchill, who said that, instead of insulting Blandford, the Prince, who had once liked Lady Aylesford, should order Joe not to divorce her.

In a burst of unjustifiable temper Randolph and Lord Alington accompanied Lady Aylesford when she called on the Princess of Wales at Marlborough House to tell her the whole story and mention the nasty fact that, if Aylesford did sue for divorce, her husband's letters might be published and that in this eventuality the Prince 'would never sit upon the throne of England.' Alexandra was enormously distressed and could not assess the extent to which these thoughtless letters might be dangerous. When Queen Victoria heard of this visit she wrote her son: '10th March 1876. . . . What a dreadful disgraceful business about Lady Aylesford and Lord Blandford! And how unpardonable of Lord Alington to draw dear Alix into it! Her dear name should never have been mixed up with such people. Poor Lord Aylesford should not have left her. I *knew* last summer this was going on. Those Williamses are a bad family. . . .'

Ponsonby, the Queen's private secretary, wrote to Knollys, the Prince's private secretary: 'Lord R. Churchill who had been a very intimate friend of the P. of Wales and Pss also spoke to Her R.H.'ss about it—and afterwards threatened to publish letters from the P. of Wales to Lady A. if H.R.H. did not prevent Aylesford bringing an action for divorce. The letters are said to be innocent but containing chaff which might be mis-interpreted.'

The Prince of Wales reached Cairo fatigued. The last month in India had been particularly exhausting and his nerves were on edge. On leaving Nepal the Prince had warned the ruler, Sir Jung Bahadur, not to expect a warm welcome in England if he allowed his daughter to commit suttee on her husband's death. Sir Jung contrived to prevent her incineration, but, when he was murdered soon after, his own three widows all threw themselves on the funeral pyre after the senior widow had written courteously to the Prince announcing their intentions. He knew the Indian tour had been a triumph, but the snobbism of suttee was more than a Prince of Wales could conquer.

It is hardly surprising that H.R.H. lost his temper on hearing that his wife had been approached during his absence, and at the same time receiving a telegram from Lord Randolph Churchill asking him to prevail on Aylesford to drop the divorce. The Prince behaved admirably. It was all to his advantage to stop a scandalous divorce case, but he stoutly refused to interfere in anyone's private affairs. However, he was so incensed that he unwisely sent Lord

Charles Beresford back to England to challenge Randolph to a duel on his behalf.

The Churchills were an unkind breed. Randolph asked Lord Falmouth to be his second and then sent a wounding note to the Prince saying he must realise that a duel was out of the question (the Prince Consort had banned them). This insult, insinuating that H.R.H. had issued the challenge because he knew it could not lead to action, was handed by Charles Beresford to the Prince at Malta on April 9, 1876.

Almost the last person to learn of the drama was Blandford's wife, an elder sister of Lord Ernest Hamilton. Known to her own family as Goosie, she had during the last year scarcely noticed her husband's affections waning—perhaps because he gave her so little. Indeed, she had infuriated Blandford by copying Edith Aylesford's much-admired dresses and at the height of the crisis she pathetically tried a joke. To brighten her husband's gloomy face at breakfast she placed a little celluloid baby on toast instead of his poached egg. Blandford lifted the cover, choked and fled.

While brainstorm letters swept across England, the Queen's and the Prince's private secretaries scribbled notes marked *very private*, Blandford (who had promised not to see Edith for a year) wrote to his brother Randolph from Belgium: 'Poor little E. I telegraphed her from Brussels. I enclose you a letter for her. Please post it at once. . . . If A. thinks he is going to put off settling anything, so soon as H.R.H. turns up, I come back without fail. Goodbye old boy, many thanks to you for all the bother you have—I must say though with Edith that it is not worth all the trouble to avoid the Divorce Court. . . . One thing strikes me. If A. leaves matters as they are between him and Edith I shall only wait till H.R.H. comes back to appear on the scene and then if A. tries to lick me I shall do my damnedest to defend myself and afterwards if I am all right, I shall lick H.R.H. within an inch of his life for his conduct generally, and we will have the whole thing up in the Police Court!!'

This was *not* the way the Prince liked his friends to behave.

Queen Victoria, following the affair in detail, supported her son and passed judicious comments. She accepted unreservedly that the letters to Lady Aylesford were innocent, '. . . but the publication of any letters of this nature would be very undesirable as a colouring might easily be given and injurious inferences deduced from hasty expressions. The Queen, therefore, regrets that such a correspondence, harmless as it is, should be in existence; but Her Majesty thinks it quite right that His Royal Highness should not interfere in Lord Aylesford's affair in consequence of this threat. . . .'

One had to admire the Queen. She did not look for the easy way out but for the *right* thing to do.

While Lord Hardwicke (the Prince's dandy friend who had perfected the top hat) argued with Aylesford, Prime Minister Disraeli sought to inculcate repentance into Lord Randolph, whom he had known since boyhood. The Duke and Duchess of Marlborough, staid old friends of Queen Victoria, were appalled at the turmoil which their two sons had brought about and by May 11, 1876, when the Prince reached England, the whole of society, which constituted an entity with mutual interests, knew exactly what had occurred. The Prince requested Princess Alexandra to see him '*first* and *alone*' before disembarkation, while his brothers and children waited at Portsmouth. Evidently he wanted to give the Princess *his* version and hear *her* story before accepting anyone's advice. Then they travelled to London by special train and drove in a procession of carriages to Marlborough House. However harassed and exhausted, the Prince and Princess of Wales would put up a good show. Within an hour of their arrival home they set forth to attend a gala performance at Covent Garden Opera House. It was a brave decision to face the public and allow an immediate opportunity for demonstration. The Prince and Princess were rewarded when the audience rose to its feet to give them a standing ovation before the start of every act, as well as at the end, of Verdi's *Ballo in Maschera*.

On the following day Lord Hardwicke drove to Marlborough House with the news that Aylesford, 'not wishing to create public scandal and mischief,' had agreed not to divorce his wife.

So, although the Prince refused to intervene, the pressure of society had caused Sporting Joe to act in accordance with its wishes. It seems a little hard that when, a few years later, after ranching in Texas, Aylesford wanted to marry someone else and did ask for a divorce, the Queen's Proctor should have stopped the case, because his own life was not blameless.

Lady Aylesford had to face the fact that she was 'out of society forever.' Having lost the custody of her daughters, she lived in the country or travelled abroad with Lord Blandford. In 1881 she bore a son who was rather stingily given half his father's name—Spencer, instead of Spencer-Churchill. He spent much of his boyhood at Blenheim, a mysterious wraith in that great dumping ground for children.

No photographs of Edith seem to exist, although Blandford certainly possessed some, for in one of his letters to her he criticises the buttons on her dress as a little vulgar! Blandford was certainly deeply in love with Edith Aylesford. Long, angry letters to his father survive: 'You have displayed to me an untold cruelty of intention. What can it affect you who I marry and who my children may be? In what manner do they come into the circle of your life? What matters it in the future of our things? For what considerations of a worldly character have you thought fit to step in to sacrifice my whole life?'

This is how Blandford wrote to the old Duke, but it may here be recorded that *his* eldest son (who became 9th Duke of Marlborough) said that he never received a kind word from his father and was 'entirely crushed.'

We have to guess at the characters of Blandford and Aylesford from the telling phrases of people who knew them. Owen Williams remarked to his brother-in-law, 'Aylesford is already so unsavoury that it will not do for him to appear in the Divorce Court.' And the Queen said to Ponsonby: '. . . Tho' I never believed it, some people said it was Lady A. the Pce admired—as Lord A. was too great a fool to be really agreeable to the P. of Wales.'

So he was unsavoury and a fool—but his letters to his wife reveal an affectionate humorous disposition. And—not that it counts for much in affairs of the heart—among horsemen he was the 'greatest of the heavyweights,' a man who could ride with hands of gossamer. There is something very sad in a description by a cowboy of him some years later when drink and disaster had got him down. He was ranching in Texas and had won the title of the 'Judge' among tough customers. 'The Judge would open a bottle of whisky for any cowboy who dropped in. He doesn't stop at one neither; I've been to the ranch many a time to stay all night, and woke up in the morning to find the bottles lying around thick as fleas, the boys two deep on the floor snorin' like mad buffaloes and the Judge with a bottle in each hand over in the corner.'

Blandford was very different: a high-strung, brilliant scientist, a man with a good brain which shines through even in the furious fifteen-page letters he wrote to his father in the autumn of 1876 when the tempests of his emotions were at their height. Moreton Frewen, who knew him well, describes his 'entrancing conversation' and 'the universality of his genius.' In a private letter to his wife Moreton wrote: 'Was ever man more agreeable? Nor had anyone such charm of voice?' And he was obviously able to show Edith Aylesford that he cared for her while boisterous Joe cared but could not show it.

Blandford now fell out not only with his father but with his brother Randolph, who was receiving the execration he deserved for having approached the Princess. Randolph's wife Jennie, however, stood by him staunchly. 'My dearest, darling R. . . .' she wrote, '. . . you ask me what I think of your father's 2nd epistle. I think it very bad. He is quite willing that you should do all in your power to prevent Blandford from disgracing himself and his family —but is not at all willing to take upon himself any of the responsibility or any of the *désagrément* which must arise from being at open war with H.R.H. But my dearest there are few as generous as you and not many brothers would risk what you are risking for one so worthless as B though he is your only brother.'

So there is another opinion of Blandford! But Jennie found him congenial later.

It was high time for the young Churchills to take a holiday out of England. They sailed for America to stay with Jennie's father, Leonard Jerome. Meanwhile the Prince of Wales, pressed by Queen Victoria, reluctantly agreed to accept an apology from Randolph on condition it was dictated by the Lord Chancellor.

An abject apology was drawn up and shown to the Duke of Marlborough by the Queen before being despatched. Jennie and her American father were not able to reach the same pinnacles of outraged feeling as English people and they sought to cool Randolph's fury when in August he received this document and realised he had no way out. Slightly appeased by the irony of signing an apology at Saratoga where the beaten British General Burgoyne had once insisted he signed a *convention* and not a *capitulation*, Lord Randolph could not resist adding a postscript which rendered the apology unacceptable as far as the Prince was concerned.

When the Churchills returned to England that winter it was to find that, although Queen Victoria did not wish entirely to exclude them from court festivities, the Prince of Wales had let it be known that he and the Princess would boycott any house they entered. It is interesting to note the power the Prince of Wales could wield. Only two people flouted him—the unique Louisa, Duchess of Manchester, and John Delacour, a close friend of Randolph, who when reprimanded by the Prince answered: 'I allow no man to choose my friends.'

The atmosphere remained so hostile that the Duke of Marlborough, who was not at all well off compared with other dukes, decided he must hold a sale of art treasures at Blenheim and accept the exceedingly expensive post of Viceroy of Ireland. Queen Victoria wished to help out her old friends in trouble and there was nothing for it but, as Disraeli put it, '. . . the dignified withdrawal of the family from metropolitan and English life.'

On December 9, 1876, the Duke and Duchess of Marlborough

were received by Queen Victoria at Windsor prior to replacing the
Duke and Duchess of Abercorn (Goosie's parents) in Dublin. Her
Majesty wrote: 'The Queen pitied them. They looked so *distressed,
wretched,* and the poor Dss especially, who could scarcely restrain
her tears.'

It would be eight years before the Prince spoke to the Churchills
again. Then, in March 1884, pressed by the Queen and well aware
of Lord Randolph's rising reputation in the House of Commons, His
Royal Highness consented to attend a dinner given by the Attorney General where the guests included Mr. and Mrs. Gladstone and
Lord and Lady Randolph Churchill. The meeting passed off well,
but another two years elapsed and Lord Randolph had become Secretary for India before the Prince could bring himself to enter the
Churchill home. On this occasion Blandford also attended, and
Jennie, the bewitching Jennie, was thirty-two—approaching the
age at which the Prince really appreciated his lady friends. The
date was May 16, 1886, and it proved her most successful dinner
party because so much was at stake.

Within the next six months an absolutely new and very close relationship would grow up between the Prince and Lady Randolph
Churchill. Disraeli was not right in inferring that the Prince was
chiefly taken by success; it might catch his attention but what really aroused him was disaster. When at this stage Randolph looked
as if he was going to be the youngest of Prime Ministers, the Prince
seemed relieved that the long quarrel had been patched up and he
certainly rejoiced in the fact that he could enjoy Jennie's company.
But it was when Randolph lost office that he showed true friendship, and whatever his relationship with the irrepressible Jennie, it
was in her days of distress that his kindness poured forth and he
took most trouble.

8

~

Mrs. Langtry, Lady Dudley and Lord Rossmore

TOWARDS THE END of the seventies the Prince, who was now approaching forty, openly conducted affairs with several famous ladies. These included Sarah Bernhardt and Mrs. Edward Langtry—one known as the greatest actress of all time and the other as the greatest of 'professional beauties.' This term meant that photographers could earn money by selling likenesses of the lovely faces dominating the Prince of Wales's set—not that the ladies were paid for posing as models are in our day.

Photographs of Mrs. Cornwallis-West, known as Patsy, who came from a top-notch Irish hunting family, and Mrs. Luke Wheeler were displayed in shopwindows and sold to the masses who vicariously enjoyed the royal goings-on. They were, in fact, the first pin-up girls and a great deal of money could be made by a lucky photographer.

Patsy Cornwallis-West is long forgotten and how furious she would have been if she could have guessed that her chief claim to fame would eventually lie not in her own good looks, which caught the Prince's eye, or her success in marrying her two daughters to the rich Prince of Pless and the almost as rich Duke of Westminster, but in the plain fact that her unkindly treated son would someday become Winston Churchill's stepfather! Mrs. Wheeler is also remem-

bered only by her own family, but several of them have told me
how angry her husband became whenever the Prince tried to mo-
nopolise this lovely creature on the Scottish moors. Maybe she
managed a tête-à-tête tea, but maybe not, for teatime was becoming
a famous hour for amorous dalliance.

It was, as I have mentioned previously, considered good manners
for a gentleman to carry his top hat, his walking stick and his
gloves into a lady's drawing room when on an afternoon visit. It
would have appeared overcasual to hand these to the footman in the
hall, thus giving the impression of the intention to stay some time
on a prearranged invitation. Certain French diplomats retained this
habit right up into my lifetime, politely behaving as though they
had just popped in for a moment while out for a walk. The courtesy of the habit is obvious—to leave hat and cane and gloves in the
hall as if certain of being received could be considered presump-
tuous. Once the hat and cane had been placed on the floor, however,
there was no time limit to the conversation. Yet the costumes in
which our heroines produced themselves must in themselves have
been a certain safeguard. The Victorian steel corset, a veritable
ceinture de chastité, had been replaced by the longer Edwardian
whalebones. My grandmother told me that it was considered 'improper and fast' not to wear corsets at this hour of relaxation, a fact
which fills one with suspicion. Lillie Langtry was famous for refusing to tight-lace—which must have made her even more attractive
amidst all those ridiculous creaking hourglasses, but let us admit the
old fogies were practical when denouncing an uncorseted regime.
When laced up, it must have taken a long time and much dexterity
for even the most pliant ladyship to, in the term of the day, 'con-
cede the ultimate favour.'

The life of Mrs. Langtry, the 'Jersey Lily,' has been much
written up. She arrived from Jersey with a meek, weak husband
and no money. The first mention we find of her is in a letter written by Lord Randolph Churchill to his wife Jennie: 'I dined with
Lord Wharncliffe last night, and took in to dinner a Mrs. Langtry, a
most beautiful creature, quite unknown, very poor, and they say
has but one black dress.'

She did not remain unknown for long. A short time after this
Moreton Frewen, the handsome young sportsman-adventurer who
was to become Randolph's brother-in-law, also met her at dinner.
Arriving late, he was covered with confusion as he entered the dining room and found that he was to sit next to a lady he had recently
heard spoken of for her wonderful profile. Lillie turned her blue
eyes straight on him. 'What are your spiritual beliefs?' was her

opening gambit. Frewen, being at that time obsessed by fox hunting and fortune-making, was taken aback and could not think what
to answer. But when she invited him to tea in her little house in
Norfolk Street he accepted with alacrity. 'Too small and slight of
throat and neck, little Greek head all perfect, but I felt that I required direction.' Frewen was a famous judge of horseflesh where a
good strong neck is important. 'It has always seemed to me that in
Beauty's domain the beauty of a horse ranks very high . . .' he
wrote.

What he meant by needing 'direction' is not very clear, but he
seems to have got it. For a month or so, while the story of her
beauty travelled through London, Moreton and a younger friend,
John Leslie, were frequently invited to tête-à-tête meetings. They
attended her teas separately, but together they tried to teach her to
ride, for it was an essential part of the smart routine to ride in Hyde
Park. Mrs. Langtry had never been on a horse in her life and when
hoisted on to the quiet hack Frewen had selected for her she fell in
a dead faint on his first step forward—or at least she pretended to,
said my grandfather, who caught her! However arduous the attentions of these two young bachelors, they were soon ousted by the
Crown Prince Rudolph of Austria, and although Mrs. Langtry
continued to use the penniless good-looking Frewen as escort when
she felt the need, he knew his day was over.

Her big moment came on May 27, 1877, when Sir Allen Young,
the arctic explorer, invited her to late supper in his house, where it
had been arranged that the Prince of Wales should meet her after
the opera. The result was all that could have been expected. Mrs.
Langtry became the Prince's first openly recognised mistress.
Within a month crowds began to collect whenever she appeared,
with or without the Prince of Wales. The riding lessons with her
two young beaux proved very useful, for she could soon trot along
beside the Prince in Rotten Row on Redskin, the superb chestnut
hack which Moreton Frewen had given her before going off to lose
his and his friends' fortunes in Wyoming, and, indeed, to earn the
sobriquet of 'Mortal Ruin.'

From her small house in Mayfair, Mrs. Langtry moved to Hamp-
stead, where she bought a mansion called Leighton House in Alexandra Road which still contains her drawing room festooned with
moulded cherubs, a rare pre-Raphaelite stained-glass fanlight, and a
delightful domed, velvet-hung room with a mural of the British
Raj. From the front door a glass canopy led to the street which
made surreptitious visiting easier, but, of course, gentlemen had to
cross the pavement in full view, and behind the moveless lace cur-

tain of every house in Alexandra Road all breath would be held when the Prince's landau stopped.

Sometimes he used hansom cabs when calling on ladies, but the cabbies always recognised 'good old Teddy,' and as no embarrassment existed in his own mind, H.R.H. usually allowed his own conveyance to wait at the door.

Margot Asquith in *More Memories* gives a vivid account of Lillie in her heyday:

'Mrs. Langtry was new to the public and photographs of her exhibited in the shop windows made every passerby pause to gaze at them. My sister, Christine Ribblesdale, told me that she had been in a London ballroom when several fashionable ladies had stood upon their chairs to see Mrs. Langtry come into the room.

'In a shining top-hat and skin-tight habit, she rode a chestnut thoroughbred of conspicuous action every evening in Rotten Row. Among her adorers were the Prince of Wales and the Earl of Lonsdale.

'One day when I was riding, I saw Mrs. Langtry—who was accompanied by Lord Lonsdale—pause at the railings in Rotten Row to talk to a man of her acquaintance. I do not know what she could have said to him, but after a brief exchange of words, Lord Lonsdale jumped off his horse, sprang over the railings and with clenched fists hit Mrs. Langtry's admirer in the face. Upon this a free fight ensued and to the delight of the surprised spectators, Lord Lonsdale knocked his adversary down.'

This adversary was Sir George Chetwynd, who had complained that she ought to be riding with *him*. The angry pair were separated by the Duke of Portland and Sir William Gordon-Cummings.

'The "Jersey Lily" who received this nickname from Millais' picture of her holding a lily, had Greek features, a transparent skin, arresting eyes, fair hair and a firm white throat. She held herself erect, refused to tighten her waist, and to see her walk was as though you saw a beautiful hound set upon its feet. . . . The Princess of Wales, the Empress of Austria, Lady Dalhousie, the Duchess of Leinster, Lady de Grey, Lady Londonderry, Mrs. Cornwallis-West, Mrs. Wheeler [etc., citing conspicuous Amazonian belles], dazzled every London drawing-room. But with the exception of Georgiana, Countess of Dudley, no one in my life time has excited the same excitement and attention as Mrs. Langtry.'

There was, however, an increasing amount of adverse publicity when Mrs. Langtry bore a daughter and rumours of a possible divorce sullied her reputation. The houses which had been open to her as the Prince's mistress closed at the imminence of scandal. Her photographs sold by the thousand, but Mrs. Langtry found herself in a precarious financial situation. She hid this fact and Margot Asquith could write long after: 'I have seen great and conventional old ladies like old Lady Cadogan and others standing on iron chairs in the Park to see Mrs. Langtry walk past.'

As she had not been born and brought up a 'lady,' and as she had guts and talent and no inhibitions, it was not difficult for Lillie Langtry to go on the stage. After acting in a charity performance of *She Stoops to Conquer*, drawing what *The Times* called the 'most distinguished audience ever seen in a theatre,' she joined a professional company and early in 1882 she appeared in a comedy called *Ours* at the Haymarket Theatre. The Prince of Wales backed her venture to the hilt. He *never* let his friends down when things went wrong for them. Having written to his son Prince George about Mrs. Langtry's successful debut, he travelled up three times from Sandringham to see her act. The dates, noted punctiliously in his engagement diary, are January 28, February 13 and March 15. The Prince's interest, of course, helped the box office, and when certain of her play's success Mrs. Langtry gave a midnight supper party which the Prince and his cousin the Duke of Cambridge attended.

If some doors had shut in Mrs. Langtry's face, others soon opened and in her new theatrical world the acclaim grew. During the following winter Lillie Langtry toured America and considerably increased her personal triumphs with gentlemen. She made no effort to appear virtuous and did not care if she was accepted socially or not. Jennie's father, Mr. Leonard Jerome, could not consider bringing her to his Puritan wife's home, but he took her out driving in his carriage and introduced her to Freddy Gebhard, a wealthy young man about town who had pestered Jerome's youngest daughter, Leonie, to marry him.

Freddy made rather a fool of himself, keeping Mrs. Langtry in a luxurious apartment in West Fifty-third Street, where the 'fast set' attended lavish supper parties, accompanying her publicly and showering her with jewels.

The result of the American tour was as anticipated. Mrs. Langtry amassed a fortune and was then able to reinstate herself in London, patronise the Turf, and marry Sir Hugo de Bathe.

When she sailed back to England in the spring, old Leonard Jerome wrote his wife with amusement, 'I am going to see her this afternoon by special invitation!' Then, referring to Moreton Frewen, now his son-in-law, he adds: 'He sails tomorrow in the *Etruria* along with this letter and Lillie Langtry.' Let us hope that she was content to leave the newly married Moreton alone, for as well as courage Mrs. Langtry possessed certain propensities which did not become an older woman.

Three years later, in 1886, Frewen wrote to his in-laws: 'Everyone thinks Mrs. Langtry grown fat but pretty. Redskin is dead of staggers.'

He mourns the poetry of the horse more than the overblown beauty of that Jersey flower.

When we look at photographs of Mrs. Langtry today the famous straight Greek nose leaves us unmoved—we who have been reared on the cheekbones of Greta Garbo and Marlene Dietrich, faces which must surely fascinate through the centuries. Lillie had more than looks, however. She developed a psychological technique which at the time bowled men down like ninepins. My grandfather told my grandmother, and my grandmother told me, that when a young gentleman arrived for tea in her Norfolk Street house she would wait until they were alone, fix him with her huge blue eyes and appear to swoon, the idea being that the charm of his person had rendered her senseless. A lady in this state has to be held, supported on the sofa and perhaps her clothes loosened. Of course, there may have been some mugs who rang for help, but on the whole this appeal to male vanity worked marvellously. There she lay, beauty helpless and limp in their arms, until flickering eyelids and sighs made it clear that she was not actually going to die. Men are conceited creatures and these vapourings completely addled their wits. She did not have to faint to get the Prince of Wales, of course. He was never bashful.

The Prince's relationship with Sarah Bernhardt, who fascinated him as she did many other gentlemen, is not well documented, but there is an amusing account by Sir Charles Dilke, who attended a midnight supper party which the Prince had asked Ferdinand de Rothschild to give in order that the great Sarah should be presented to the Duc d'Aumale. A few grand English ladies went because the Prince wished it, but Dilke described the frost that settled: 'It was one thing to get them to go, and another to get them to talk when they were there; and the result was that, as they would not talk to Sarah Bernhardt, and the Duc d'Aumale was deaf and disinclined to make conversation on his own account, nobody talked at all, and a reign of the most absolute and dismal silence ensued.'*

Now perhaps is the moment to bring in Lady Dudley, who came of an entirely different strata to Mrs. Langtry and who held a close

* S. Gwynne and C. M. Tuckwell, *Life of Sir Charles Dilke.*

acquaintanceship with the Prince for many years. 'Midnight supper, Lady Dudley' is a frequent entry in the Prince's engagement diary.

Georgiana, Countess of Dudley, is, along with Louisa, Duchess of Manchester, the lady most frequently referred to in memoirs as 'the most beautiful woman in England.' Their photographs leave one wondering why. Two other women have been described to me by men who actually saw them as 'the most beautiful woman I ever saw'; they are Anna, the half-American Duchess de Mouchy, and the wholly American Lady Randolph Churchill. Photographs of the latter reveal a face lovely in our or any age. The Amazonian Georgiana, Countess of Dudley, looks like a handsome lady colonel, but her story may explain the grimness of that stare. Of her, Lord Ernest Hamilton writes: 'Lady Dudley's looks were of European fame, and I can still remember when riding in Rotten Row, joining the crowd that collected in front of her barouche to see the lovely Countess of Dudley. She did not ride but sat erect with the indifference of an Oriental, under a brown holland umbrella which she held over her elderly husband.'

The 1st Earl of Dudley was one of the richest men in England, for his wide acres contained collieries, but he suffered from mysterious glooms. In his youth he had made one most unfortunate marriage to a young lady whom he had courted for a long time. She suddenly accepted his proposal and he later discovered that she was in child to another beau who had thrown her over. Dudley terminated the marriage and disowned the child, who died at birth with the mother. Many years later, when he was forty-eight and more circumspect, Dudley chose his second wife from the five statuesque daughters of Sir Thomas Moncreiffe of that Ilk, a Scottish baronet of ancient lineage. Georgiana was over twenty years his junior and one of her great-nieces tells me that the only instruction Lady Moncreiffe gave her girls when they left the Highlands to enter London society was 'NEVER comment on a LIKENESS.' This was a tactful rule to remember when admiring Edwardian babies.

Wilfrid Scawen Blunt's diaries record that Dudley was a strange fellow unpopular with men, but that he formed a high opinion of Dudley's character in the role of a middle-aged husband with a young bride, 'though it was anything but a love-match at starting (for she was in love with another man, Lord Tyrone who had failed to marry her) and she took Dudley as a *pis-aller*. He was so assiduous and tactful that he succeeded in gaining her full devotion and eventually she bore him sons and daughters not a few, and remained through life attached to him, although he was unfaithful to her.'

This seems hardly fair, but then Blunt adds that Georgiana Dudley was 'a lovely girl, tall and framed like a goddess, but with an unlovely voice.' Maybe she had reason to unmelodiously lament, for during the twenty years she was Dudley's wife and bearing him many children he gave her little freedom and their tastes differed. Lord Dudley was highbrow and musical. Young musicians and composers would call at Dudley House to ask for his advice and patronage and the concerts he gave there were extremely high class. Whereas his much younger wife had quite other tastes. She enjoyed the bawdy singing of Lord Hardwicke, and Lady Augusta Fane writes: 'I can still see him sitting in Lady Dudley's boudoir, playing on the guitar and singing "A little more ginger, ginger, and a little more ginger now," and other popular airs, to an admiring audience.'

Long after Hamilton's appraisal, Margot Asquith would note: '. . . Where Georgiana, Lady Dudley, drove there were crowds round her carriage when it pulled up, to see this vision of beauty holding a large holland umbrella over the head of her lifeless husband.'

What a relief it must have been when that umbrella could be folded up for good. The old Earl died in 1886 aged seventy—no great age, really, but a terrible age at which to have to be propped up in public by a 'vision of beauty.' Georgiana thus became widowed in her early forties, which was considered the most alluring time for women. Edwardian hostesses did not need to worry about wrinkles and plumpness, it was their conversation that counted. Ripe figures were popular, ripe minds essential.

Dudley House still stands in Park Lane. I went to a dance there as a girl when many old people could remember *the* Lady Dudley. Of course, she inherited a great fortune, and this was needed to entertain as she did in the eighties and nineties. After all that umbrella-holding she deserved to be the one whom the Prince chose to sup with on the happiest day of his life. This was June 3, 1896, when H.R.H. won the Derby with Persimmon to tumultuous applause. After the usual dinner at the Jockey Club, Albert Edward, so his engagement diary records, went on to 'midnight supper with Lady Dudley.' In the Watts Gallery near Guildford, England, there is a very attractive painting of her which the Prince once tried to buy but Mr. and Mrs. Watts were very prim and disapproving of such 'goings-on'; the artist refused to sell.

Perhaps Georgiana's lavish spending dug too deeply into the Dudley substance, for a letter of Moreton Frewen's to his wife tells of their friend Millie Sutherland (Duchess of Sutherland) going to Windsor Castle 'to dine and sleep and the old Queen would pump her about the family row! Kept them waiting till nine-fifteen for dinner and kept them all standing afterwards for fifty minutes. Rather doubtful entertainment. The Dowager Lady Dudley has sold those two rows of pearls to Lord Burton for £17,000 and there is likely to be quite a row as her son claims they are heirlooms.'

Frewen became a close friend of Georgiana's son, the 2nd Earl, who brought his own wife, blazing with Dudley jewels, to Dublin when he became Viceroy. The famous pearls were scarcely missed.

Once again a casual line in personal letters shows up characteristic tendencies. Lady Randolph Churchill, writing to her sister concerning the rumour that the widowed Countess of Dudley intended to marry Lord Rosebery, remarks: 'I never feel I can care for a woman whose children don't like her.'

More amusing still is Leonie's recollection of Jennie's tiff with the Prince of Wales because he had written teasingly after she discovered her handsome Major Caryl Ramsden embracing another woman: 'So grateful for your sympathy—as your Royal Highness knows exactly *how* it feels after being jilted by Lady Dudley!'

When the famous Georgiana had other fish to fry she would not hesitate to drop a friend—even the Prince!

Things I Can Tell, the memoirs of Lord Rossmore, our nearest neighbour in Ireland, is a volume heavily annotated by my great-grandmother; starting with a swipe at the title, which she changes to 'Things I Should *Not* Tell.' He is the sole Edwardian who actually relates stories in print concerning his own escapades which in the parlance of the time were 'roguey-poguey.' 'I remember once I was invited to a country house where a lovely lady I greatly admired was also a guest. We were delighted to meet in this accidentally-done-for-the-purpose manner and we arranged to have a *tête-à-tête* later to look at the stars. Well, I must have dropped off to sleep because I was horrified to find it was three a.m. when I set out down the ghostly corridor to keep my appointment. I padded along and turned down the passage which led to the room where we planned to meet, but when I got there I noticed a man sitting on guard outside.

'He viewed me with lowering brow and then I grasped the fact that as he had not been asked to star-gaze he was determined to see who had.'

Lord Rossmore pretended not to notice him and walked on to the bathroom where he took an early tub while inwardly cursing the spoil-sport.

After this we get a long recital concerning a very complicated tea party. Lord Rossmore tells us that a certain husband, having discovered love letters to his wife, had made the sender promise not to see her again. Some time later Rossmore went to tea with another lady in her sitting room at Claridges and found the forbidden one also there. 'Hello, fancy seeing you!' he exclaimed somewhat lamely. 'Well, as I am here suppose you give me a kiss,' was the rejoinder. 'Oh certainly not, I'd better leave trouble behind me.' Lord Rossmore turned for the door but the flirtatious one turned the key, dropped it down her bodice and started to chase him round the room, overturning the furniture. The hostess screamed with laughter until knocking reminded her the Prince of Wales was coming to tea. They had to unlock the door and after letting His Royal Highness in to view the shambles both ladies disappeared. 'I thought H.R.H. looked rather down his nose . . . for he knew all about the affair with the lady, and had complimented my sister on the discretion I had shown in having avoided further complications. However with his usual tact he made no allusions to what he knew, or to what he now saw, but chatted on general topics until the reappearance of my hostess.'†

Another story of the amorous tea hour concerns a husband whose kind friend informs him that his wife has a lover and is even then 'having tea with him.' Indignantly he marches around to the other man's flat and asks for his wife. 'Lady Blank is not here,' says the servant with a sphinx-like expression, but then he caught sight of his wife's umbrella in the stand. Seizing it, he snapped it through the middle, loudly exclaiming: 'There now—let's hope it will rain!'

Lord Rossmore's guileless descriptions grow riveting when he gets on to himself and his father-in-law, the rich Mr. Naylor (who was to cut him off without a penny for spending thousands, if not millions, of his wife's money on building roads, hills and lakes in his already hilly, lake-dotted Irish domain): 'Mr. Naylor was a very bad judge of character, I think, for he never appreciated me. He

† An artless letter from the unmarried Leonie Jerome to her eldest sister reveals who this lady was: Mrs. William Cornwallis-West, the mother of George, who would become Winston Churchill's stepfather! My grandmother is describing her first hunt ball at Melton Mowbray in 1881. Among the guests is Patsy Cornwallis-West, at that time a close friend of the Prince of Wales, who arrives late for dinner in her travelling clothes. 'She really is lovely. She had on a stamped velvet cloak, the satin part red and the velvet part black and a black velvet beret—poor thing she looked so ill—but so pretty. . . .' Next day, when Mrs. Cornwallis-West has departed, Leonie learns more about her: 'It seems she came to the ball expressly to see Rossmore—as she had just arrived from Cannes, but Rossmore promised Mr. West never to speak to her again et elle a beau faire he won't—so she only stayed one hour and then went back to the Lodge—She makes such fun of her husband—calls him old Custos (he is Custos Rotolorum of a county) or the High Cocholorum! But isn't she lovely!'

hated the Irish "like fun," in truth he detested most men and especially those who came after his girls.'

The truest vision of an Edwardian swell and his 'gentleman's gentleman' appears in the little story concerning Lord Rossmore's Irish manservant Menally, who entertained as high an opinion of himself as his master did. Menally was temporarily installed in a relation's household, and within a short time the head housemaid angrily announced that she and the other maids wished to give notice. 'But why?' asked their mistress. 'Menally went into the housekeeper's room last night and said to her in his 'aughty manner, "When Lord Rossmore and I were in the Guards, we two were the handsomest men that ever walked down Piccadilly, and all the women said so; they *was* women and no mistake—But as for the crowd in this house, I wouldn't give a cuss for the lot." '

9

The Prince Matures

As THE SEVENTIES MERGE into the eighties and the Prince of Wales passes the age of forty, we might run through the London *mise en scène* with Lord Ernest Hamilton—youngest of the Duke of Abercorn's fourteen children. Now a man about town, Ernest joins the throng of younger sons who are invited everywhere but seldom placed next to the daughters of ambitious mamas, for they are not *partis*. Lord Ernest recollects: 'In London tall hats and long-tailed coats were always worn. Men rode in tight blue overalls, Wellington boots and spurs, tall hats and tail-coats.' The Prince of Wales had yet to give the death blow to the tall-hat brigade by appearing on horseback in Rotten Row wearing a Homburg hat. Immense importance was attached to clothes. 'Every man had attached to him a highly paid scoundrel—maybe a foreigner—which was considered *chic*—called "his man." He would look up trains, take the tickets, pay his bills.'

We think of the Prince of Wales as arch practical joker, but in country houses lesser jokes were considered a feminine perquisite. 'Applepie beds, holly leaves in pillow cases and soap suds in place of whipped cream, received roars of laughter, but the jokes were always perpetrated by maidens on men.' Out in the ordinary world, however, practical jokes could be played on anyone and were considered particularly funny when perpetrated by lords. This standard of humour is admiringly recorded by Lady Augusta Fane when she went to Goodwood Races and took a house at Bognor, near that rented by Lord Worcester, heir to the Duke of Beaufort. 'Lord Worcester especially was very fond of practical jokes. One dark evening he tied cords across the main street, then blew a policeman's whistle and shouted "Stop thief" at the top of his voice. Out of the houses rushed the inhabitants, round the corners came the local police, and down they went over the cords, everyone cursing everyone else, whilst Lord Worcester retired to the front windows of his house holding his sides with laughter!'

The middle classes strained hard after gentility, and certain words then in use have taken on new senses today. For instance, 'cad' and 'snob' were much used, but snob then merely meant a man who worked for his living. 'Bankers were snobs, brewers were snobs, everyone in fact who in the secrecy of low commercial retreats busied themselves with accounts and figures.'

A solicitor or a doctor was a snob and not a gentleman. A cad was lower than a snob—farm hands and bricklayers were cads and not snobs. The terms were not derogatory, they simply classified. By 1900 a snob was jeered at as a chaser of royalty or titles, and a cad was any man who did not play fair.

Of his own heart-stirrings Lord Ernest writes tenderly: 'After dinner in country houses there would be dumb crambo or charades or music, and so fairly early to bed, with the men standing in a cluster under the chandelier at the foot of the grand staircase, while the maidens tripped up to their bowers, holding their long cylindrical bedroom candles at an untidy angle, the while they whispered reluctant "goodnights" over the banisters.

'The picture stirs certain memories which are locked away in an enchanted casket. The key is a key of gold, but it is a key that does not turn at the bidding of any fingers, and the lid remains and ever will remain closed down.'

How many unrecorded love affairs there must have been—recorded, that is, only by glances and a few words over many years. Love letters tied with satin ribbon they all had—and what a lot of trouble these were always causing. But to throw away a well-written love letter is beyond the capacity of any woman. Husbands did well not to go routling in their wives' caskets.

And hostesses might do well not to show guests around the less frequented rooms late at night. My grandmother won her reputation for keeping her head in a crisis when one night she accompanied the lady of the house and several young people to look at a certain picture in the library during a dance. On opening the door they perceived the shocking sight of a lady and gentleman in full evening dress sitting together on the floor in front of a dying fire.

Two guilty faces looked up speechless and the young girls were swept from the room murmuring, 'But what are they doing?' My grandmother immediately interjected: 'Mending the carpet—so kind.' Such was the conviction of her reply that it closed the subject completely.

A brief glance at the men whom the Prince of Wales chose as his special cronies shows that the quality which attracted him most was vitality. I will not touch on his clever foreign friends—the Portuguese Ambassador Marquis de Soveral, or Sir Ernest Cassel, who looked after him financially, or Baron Hirsch, who, encouraged by Edward, sent £10,000,000 to help found a Jewish national home by creating vast agricultural settlements in the Argentine, or the exotic Jewish families of Rothschilds and Sassoons who bought great country estates and took to sport like the English. These vibrating outsiders, unique to any court in Europe, require a volume to themselves. I will merely sketch the English gentlemen in the Prince's entourage, leaving to a later chapter Lord Esher, the one whom, in schoolboy parlance, I would call the Prince's 'best friend.'

Lord Hartington, who was a Liberal Member of Parliament until 1890 when he became 8th Duke of Devonshire, remained an intimate friend for some forty years and accompanied H.R.H. to many functions, as well as entertaining him at Chatsworth when that great house became his home.

Another close friend of the Prince of Wales, Christopher Sykes, has been immortalised by his nephew and namesake in *Four Studies in Loyalty*, but the sycophantic Sykes, who beggared himself in efforts to amuse his royal master, was not really the type to attract the Prince, who was fascinated by action and success.

I like the arrogant dictum of Hugh, Earl of Lonsdale, who spent four years in the lowest class at Eton: 'I can always tell everything I want to know about a man by the way he sits on a horse.' At the start of his career the Prince obviously lacked this gift. Several male acquaintances led him on and let him down. The officers at the Curragh got him into trouble they did not share. Aylesford and Randolph Churchill had hurt him to the quick, the Dukes of Sutherland and Manchester were wild gamblers and this drew disapproval on the Prince's set, for middle-class England distrusted gamblers more than profligates. They could forgive weakness for the feminine sex, but not winter trips to Monte Carlo casinos.

The most colourful figures among the Prince's early men friends were the Beresford brothers, who were my grandfather's first cousins. Charlie Beresford's mother, Christina Leslie, was so roughly handled by her husband, that fox-hunting thug, the Rev. Lord John

Beresford, that she threatened to leave him, and her Leslie brothers set forth to help her. But as they arrived, John's elder brother, the Marquis of Waterford, broke his neck while out hunting. (Incidentally, he was wearing a huntsman's cap, not a top hat, and this accident quite unwarrantably caused velvet caps to go out of fashion and be called more dangerous than the far frailer top hat.) The Leslie brothers now thought twice about the benefits of a 'separation.' Eventually they persuaded Christina to accept the glories of being a Marchioness in magnificent Curraghmore. Her three younger sons all made names for themselves: Bill by winning a V.C. when he rode back with one soldier through a hail of assagais to rescue a wounded trooper in the Ulundi campaign; Marcus, training the Prince's horses and three times winning the Derby for him; and Charlie as a dashing sailor. Christina seemed to have made up for her own ill treatment by beating her brood fiercely. Charlie always swore that he carried permanently the mark of the gold coronet on his mother's hairbrush on his backside, as a steer carries a brand.

The Beresford boys were all superb horsemen. Marcus had the most delicate hands on a horse's mouth, Bill the quickest wit, Charlie was the biggest and toughest and incorrigibly fond of the ladies. He married a woman ten years older than himself and was consistently unfaithful. To entice him back, Lady Charles rouged her face and piled false hair on top of her own. The only compliment she received after such efforts was to hear Charlie remark as she descended the stairs for dinner: 'Here comes my little freshly painted cutter.'

However this may be, Charlie had a distinguished naval career, went with the Prince on the most amusing excursions, sailed with him in his yacht at Cowes (where my grandmother said he behaved outrageously and she had a fearful battle keeping him at bay in her cabin, but she laughed when she recounted this). Wherever action occurred Charlie got there. Of course, what he needed with all that energy and physical courage was a war.

The chance came in July 1882 when Colonel Arabi led a nationalist revolt in Egypt against the situation imposed on the country by Disraeli, who had cunningly acquired the Khedive's shares in the Suez Canal and imposed financial control over the bankrupt Egyptian treasury. Mr. Gladstone had castigated Disraeli's coup, but later when he found himself Prime Minister, and Arabi repudiated the European shareholders and established military dictatorship, the Grand Old Man found himself forced to order the British Navy to bombard Alexandria.

In England a violent cleavage of opinion erupted. It was that sort of war. Lord Randolph Churchill was appalled by the idea of 'fighting for shareholders,' while Lord Charles Beresford, who had lost his seat in Parliament and was commanding the gunboat *Condor* in the Mediterranean, wrote heated letters to the Prince of Wales calling for immediate action and asking the Prince to use his influence with the government to allow a shooting war. The Prince did his utmost to persuade the government to employ force and showed the Foreign Secretary some of Charlie's letters, which revealed his private efforts to inflame a press campaign. To the Prince's annoyance, Lord Granville handed this information to the First Lord of the Admiralty, who, disapproving of naval officers meddling in politics, proposed immediate arrest and court-martial. While the Prince strove to save Beresford, Colonel Arabi was mounting guns in Alexandria Harbour which threatened the British ships, and a mob looted the city. On receiving no reply to an ultimatum ordering work on the guns to stop, the British fleet opened fire on July 11, 1882, and Lord Charles Beresford had the chance really to enjoy himself.

As boatloads of refugees departed, three battleships anchored in Alexandria Roads, while six small-gun vessels, including Beresford's *Condor*, waited for the opportunity to attack.

Charlie was adored by his sailors, who worked themselves into a fever pitch of excitement. 'Now, my lads,' he cried, 'if you will rely on me to find the opportunity, I will rely on you to make the most of it!'

When at dawn the admiral on his flagship *Invincible* gave the order to attack, Charlie pushed up little *Condor* so close to the shore batteries that the enemy guns could not depress sufficiently to fire at him. Thus he was able to silence them from close range.

On the bridge of the *Invincible* the admiral exclaimed: 'Good Lord, she'll be sunk,' but off went *Condor*'s guns again and again. From the flagship went the famous signal, 'Well done, *Condor*,' and the battleship sailors burst into cheers as the little gun vessel finally crept back.

Charlie returned to England a hero and was offered several safe parliamentary seats. Although the Battle of Tel-el-Kebir afforded army officers other opportunities to display bravery, none of them had the chance to do anything quite as spectacular as the captain of the *Condor*. A lot of 'good fellows' felt envious and wondered if they really liked Charlie quite as much as they had before. There were not enough dangerous tasks to share out among the exuberant, ambitious warrior types of England, who knew real chagrin when Egypt capitulated within two months.

The Prince of Wales, who resented bitterly the fact that he had never been properly trained and could not accompany this military venture with his younger brother, the Duke of Connaught, who commanded the Guards Brigade, swallowed his personal feelings and gave a warm welcome to the returning warriors. In the following summer he invited Lord and Lady Charles to accompany him to Baden, along with Christopher Sykes and the Duchess of Manchester. It was, at this moment, considered expedient to keep Charlie B. out of England because of his affair with Lady Brooke.

Charlie's social habits can be deduced from the story in Chapter 1, but apart from his inability to refrain from questing after ladies and his firm belief that no woman says 'No' *forever*, he was really a man's man. In that world of inane practical jokes Charlie's showed up amusingly. With a gang of friends in navvy clothes he tore up the roadway of Piccadilly, put down warning signs and left it closed to traffic for three days. Funnier then than now, for Piccadilly was lined not by shops but by large aristocratic mansions. Then he won a bet that he would not walk down the centre of Rotten Row amidst the horses at the fashionable hour by dressing as the man who followed the watering cart. Queen Victoria had requested him to refrain from 'larks' on the Indian tour, but Her Majesty could not have guessed at the lengths to which Charlie was prepared to go when he took a whim. And she disliked his bear-fighting. When the Prince wagered that Charlie could beat Lord Suffield in a wrestling match and won his bet, the Queen felt that he was, on top of his other faults, a sad inducement to gambling.

Apart from the men friends chosen by the Prince for his own pleasure, he naturally saw a great deal of his country's statesmen and especially of the Prime Ministers, Disraeli and Gladstone. They have been meticulously portrayed, and so have the later young Prime Ministers, Rosebery, Balfour and Asquith. Lord Salisbury, who led the government for much of the late Victorian era, will soon be re-presented for modern consumption.

There is an amusing letter by Sir Charles Dilke of a dinner he attended in 1878 where Schouvalof, the multilingual Russian Ambassador, did imitations of people he had watched in the recent Congress of Berlin: 'He described almost every member of the Congress, standing up at the table, speaking English when he did Lord Beaconsfield, and mimicking the Prime Minister's grave manner with absurdly comic effect. At last he came to Lord Salisbury who, according to him, spoke bad French. He made Lord Salisbury coin an extraordinary phrase, at which he himself [Schouvalof], all the Frenchmen, and Gortschakof shrugged their shoulders. Lord

Salisbury turned fiercely round and asked what was the matter with it, to which Saint-Vallier replied that "there was nothing the matter with it except that it was not French." "Not French?" said Lord Salisbury, and he rang the electric bell by the button in front of him and when the door opened, holding up his hand to show the messenger who had rung, said, "Fetch Mr. Currie." Philip Currie appeared at the door, whereon Lord Salisbury read his phrase to him and said, "Mr. Currie, is that good French?" to which Currie replied, "Excellent French, my lord," whereupon Lord Salisbury turned to our French colleagues and said, "There!" '

Curzon called Salisbury 'that strange, powerful, inscrutable, brilliant, obstructive, deadweight at the top.' Sir Ian Malcolm in a forgotten volume called *Vacant Thrones* writes:

'I was brought up, in the best tradition of an old Tory family, to think as badly as possible of Mr. Gladstone and to believe that nothing but a double dose of Lord Salisbury as Prime Minister and forty years of resolute Government would produce tranquillity in Ireland and restore to Great Britain the prestige which she had lost between 1880 and 1888.

'It was in July of 1889 that I first saw a Prime Minister of England. I had just come down from Oxford, and was walking through St. James's Park when I noticed a tall, heavy, bent and bearded figure standing against the railings and gazing at nothing in particular. He was dressed in a roomy black frock coat and wearing a somewhat ragged tall hat; he gave me the impression of an Atlas in Modern Dress, bearing upon his shoulders the weight and the cares of a world wide Empire. Of course I had realised who he was, for his photographs and caricatures in the newspapers had made Lord Salisbury a familiar figure to the public; and I followed him in distant reverence as far as the park entrance into the Foreign Office.'

To work under Lord Salisbury was an education in consideration for others. His admiring junior describes the minutes appended to despatches in red ink for the guidance of subordinates, many of which revealed foresight and wisdom: 'There was a question of a Missionary Society sending some of its devoted evangelists into a dangerous and remote part of China to which it was most inexpedient, in the circumstances, that they should proceed. Short of absolutely forbidding them to undertake this perilous journey everything had been done by the Foreign Office to dissuade them from so doing.' Lord Salisbury's intense interest in foreign missions was widely known, but the following minute, written in his own beautiful script, showed his horror of punitive expeditions: 'It is all very

well to have the Gospel of Christ in your head, but your influence
will be greatly diminished if you must be followed by gun-boats at
your tail.'

The expedition was deflected elsewhere.

According to all gossip-writers, he was faithful to the hard polit-
ical-minded Lady Salisbury.

Writing of Lord Salisbury's two periods of office, Sir Ian Malcolm states: 'I do not suppose that during the whole of that time he
would have claimed, or that anyone would have claimed for him,
the attribute of "popularity" in the sense which we give to that word
today. He was too reserved to be popular in that sense; indeed he
might have mistrusted himself, as well as those who offered it to
him, if he had achieved it. But he was more than popular, he was an
institution in the country; one whose speeches and despatches were
treated with respect by all parties, whether they agreed or disagreed
with him.

'Lord Salisbury at Hatfield was, to all except his family, the same
strong cloistered personage that he was in London. . . . It was rare
to meet him out of doors, his only forms of exercise were pounding
along the park paths at Hatfield on a pre-historic tricycle or going
for short but perilous expeditions in a very elementary motor-car
driven by steam. Undoubtedly his strength was to sit still; to read
and wrestle with his subject; to discuss it little, if at all, with anybody else; to come to his own conclusions and then to act upon
them. . . . The Prime Minister talked to his children as if they
were his contemporaries whatever their age. Every member of the
family said what they chose but even the youngest had to take full
responsibility for his own words.'

Lord Salisbury studied his rivals seriously. Of Louisa's Whig
Duke, he said: 'I really must learn to play bridge. If I don't I shall
never know Devonshire.'

And of Cecil Rhodes he remarked astutely: 'It seems to me quite
extraordinary that such a man, who never travels, should have found
out all the places in South Africa where an Englishman can breed,
reserved them for Great Britain and rejected all the others!'

Salisbury spoke as a statesman sure of himself: 'Those who have
the absolute power of preventing lamentable events, and, knowing
what is taking place, refuse to exercise that power, are responsible
for what happens.'

His calibre is demonstrated by Malcolm's story of an incident
which brought war very near, when Lord Salisbury was entertaining
Princess Christian at Hatfield. 'It was a brilliant scene, a splendid
old-fashioned Yule-tide festival. About the middle of dinner, a foot-

man brought an "urgent" Foreign Office Box containing a despatch. Lord Salisbury unlocked it and read the contents. He apologised to the Princess who said she hoped it brought no disagreeable news.

' "No not very. It is only to tell me that the Germans have sent two men-of-war into Delagoa Bay."

'One can imagine how a novelist might have dealt with the situation. He would have depicted an embarrassed silence, then general consternation, then the incontinent break-up of the feast; the ordering of a special train to London, and the hurried departure of the Secretary of State. Instead of which Lord Salisbury quietly re-locked the box and said casually to Her Royal Highness with a shrug of his massive shoulders: "What cheek, Madam, what cheek!" and the banquet went blithely on.'

10

Edwardian Males

SPARKLING DISRAELI, magnificent Gladstone and careful aristocratic Salisbury were the Prime Ministers with whom for forty
years the Prince of Wales had to struggle to obtain information
concerning affairs of state. The Princess of Pless thought it sharp-
ened him to be forced to be an observer, but it hurt at the time.
He was naturally much closer to the younger ministers; to Hartington, who would listen to a brilliant argument and then slowly, quietly, put his finger on the weak spot in the logic; to the fascinating
Lord Rosebery, who was briefly Prime Minister in 1895; and later
on to that extraordinary Lord Esher who has been called his Grand
Vizier. The literary, philosophical Arthur Balfour he never liked,
nor did Balfour, when he became Prime Minister, feel that he could
control King Edward.

The weighty character of Lord Salisbury is quickly felt on reading the incidents penned by Sir Ian Malcolm and the quality of
Lord Rosebery reveals itself in his books, most especially in the
slim volume he wrote about his friend Lord Randolph Churchill—
all the tenderness and sensitivity of Rosebery as a human being lie
in these pages. He is writing about another man, not himself, but
when we put that book down it is Rosebery that we know.

In that world where men had the advantage over women in almost every respect one has to pause in admiration of kindness. It
was 'the thing' for a young gentleman to keep a mistress of his own,
it was not 'the thing,' for medical reasons, to pick up women casu-

ally. The 'call girls' of the time were hungry and desperate. Lord Carlingford noted in his 1886 journal, after walking home through Mayfair after a dinner: 'Strange to walk through scores of women silently offering their bodies to the passer-by.' There were few ways in which a woman could earn her living and all of them disagreeable. Mr. William Whiteley, of the store which still bears his name, not only overworked his employees but seduced the shopgirls and abandoned them when he had got them pregnant. His illegitimate son by one of these poor creatures grew up so full of hatred for his father that he eventually shot him dead in the store. I have asked assistants if they knew the exact spot where this occurred (for the interior remains unchanged), but I am met with blank stares. This little bit of history plays no part in advertising schemes.

While glorifying the seductive powers of women in that age of bustles, bosoms and huge beflowered hats, one may pause to wonder what good all these trappings did when a love affair went wrong. Today the lovelorn miss, clad in jeans, drives off across Europe in a jeep with a party of men friends and has forgotten her woes after the eighth puncture. But in those days a woman had just to sit and think about it.

Charlie Beresford—that dreadful great-uncle Charlie—who caused such havoc among the ladies, told my grandmother that he enjoyed making women cry—'It was such fun to hear their stays creak.'

That was what men were like. Charlie was no worse than many others. He just took what he wanted. Faithful husbands could be monstrous too. One of the badly treated beauties whom I knew quite well as a child was Priscilla, Countess Annesley, whose much older husband my gentle grandfather always referred to as 'that brute.' The 4th Earl Annesley had died before I was born, so I can offer no juvenile opinion, but he was apparently an ogre to Priscilla —who was magnificently lovely in the Edwardian tradition, with a straight Greek nose like Mrs. Langtry's, and even in my day she used to turn it purposely sideways when talking so that one could see the line of her profile.

Priscilla was Irish, and her mother had been proud to flaunt the girl around Dublin until she got engaged to three men simultaneously. This enraged them and, forced to make a decision, she chose Annesley, presumably because he was an earl. Lord and Lady Annesley lived at Castle Wellan, County Down, not very far from Castle Leslie, and when her husband was too odious Priscilla used to take the train to our small sham Gothic station and arrive at Castle Leslie in tears. My grandmother loved her and my grandfather comforted her so well that Lord Annesley grew furiously jealous. What a relief it must have been when he departed to that other world where tyrant husbands get their deserts.

From then on my uncle Seymour tells the story. He was an observant little boy: 'Oh the wonderful Titian red hair and the swish of silks! Priscilla Annesley, widowed, surrounded by lovers such as the randy Lord Kintore, all hovering around with Perfect Edwardian Gallant Manners, jumping to open doors, sending little ivory boxes indiscreetly engraved which were kept at first in her boudoir but seeped gradually into guest rooms. As a small boy visiting her I found myself in a room cluttered with artifacts; sentimental bibelots had even got under my pillow—'*A toi toujours, 1893*' I read; *Souvenir de Deauville, A.R.*—I wondered who A.R. could be—and many other initials. William Waldorf Astor wanted to marry her but Priscilla had had enough of husbands. Widowhood suited her. . . . Dear, dear Priscilla with her ladies' maids and Cachet-Faivres and green leather bags all full of secret love letters. She had such marvellous unpractical feminine appeal.'

Everyone loved the Countess Annesley, including her servants, and she could smartly tell a story against herself—such as this: when walking at the races, very pleased with her new gown, she overheard her groom's voice calling to other employees: 'Come and watch the strut of her ladyship.'

My grandfather was, of course, in love with Priscilla. This was understandable. But he remained a very discreet gentleman, and although he was often on the edge of great scandals he managed not to get involved himself. Mrs. Langtry had seduced him when he was a young man, but then along came Crown Prince Rudolph of Austria and then the Prince of Wales. 'She had no time for lieutenants after that.' In Jubilee Year, 1887, when the Crown Prince represented his father the Emperor in London, Rudolph was put in charge of the attaché Count Charles Kinsky who, very unkindly playing on Prince Rudolph's nervous system, teased him about brigands in St. James's Park and other imaginary dangers. Actually, there were complications behind the scenes. The rich Baroness Vetsera had hopefully brought her sixteen-year-old daughter Marie to London for the season and was paying for the gorgeous Worth dresses worn by Countess Larish, the Empress Elizabeth's niece. But her social climbing was fraught with difficulties. The Austrian Ambassador in London would not receive the Baroness, and although it was much easier to obtain palace invitations in England than in Austria if one was not very aristocratic, the Baroness found that she could not edge her way into the Prince of Wales's set.

Charles Kinsky, who was a great friend of the Larish family, found his diplomatic skill tested to the utmost as he shepherded Baroness Vetsera and her teen-age daughter around London. Marie was not yet 'out,' but her mother wished her to be seen by English society. The girl was apparently enchanting, although not exactly pretty.

In a not very easy moment at one of the smaller dances to which the Vetseras had been invited Kinsky came up to my grandfather —then aged twenty-nine and three years married—and said: 'Look here, old chap, this girl's mother is plaguing me and I can't find anyone for her to dance with. You know all the Guards officers, do try.' So my grandfather bowed to Marie (rather mousy, he called her) and invited her to dance. But it was one of those evenings when none of the young men who would be just the thing seemed to appear. My grandfather found himself saddled with the shy creature for the entire evening—and considered her very 'heavy going.'

Two years later, when Marie Vetsera and the Crown Prince Rudolph were found shot at Mayerling, my grandfather wished he had taken deeper note of 'the little mouse.'

There is a revealing little book published in 1885 which has lain about in the top story of Castle Leslie for eighty years called *Society in London, by a Foreign Resident*. The anonymous writer, a French diplomat, has dared to say exactly what he thought at the time. 'The Prince of Wales is in 1885 very different from what he was in 1878. The *vie orageuse* is over and forgotten, or remembered only and only looked at through the mellowing medium of middle age.'

How wrong the author was! During the next year the Prince started the greatest physical passion of his life, while his tranquil but hardly platonic relationship with Mrs. Keppel, most admirable of kings' mistresses, would not begin until 1898. The *vie orageuse* was not over at all, merely getting better organised in the company of more gracious women.

Foreign Resident goes on to describe divers excellent tendencies cultivated by the Prince of Wales—the curtailment of the menu, 'the introduction of the cigar after dinner when the ladies had retired and the economy of wine which it promotes, the diffusion of a taste for music and the theatre; the personal as well as the professional welcome accorded to theatrical and operatic artistes in society etc., etc.

'In his attitude, then, to English society the Prince of Wales at the age of forty-three years is a benevolent despot. He wishes it to enjoy itself, to disport itself, to dance, sing and to play to its heart's content. But he desires that it should do so in the right manner, at the right time, and in the right places.

'Although the Prince honours with his company hosts of every degree, you could scarcely imagine how many excellent persons there are, the one unfilled ambition of whose existence is to be invited to the Royal Highness's table.'

The writer must have lived on the fringe of upper-crust society. He advises: 'Never attempt to be amusing: never venture into an anecdote. . . . The social genius of the English race is solemn. Look at the exquisites whom one will encounter in London theatres and clubs, known till recently as "mashers." They are ripe for any folly or dissipation, but their physiognomy is severity itself. . . . They might, when they are not exchanging improper innuendoes with each other, be mutes at a funeral.'

If husbands and wives get 'a little mixed up,' remarks this foreigner, 'duels do not ensue because the dominating idea is not the cultivation of virtue, but the prevention of scandal. . . . The real significance of this interesting phenomenon is the extreme sensitiveness of the ladies and gentlemen prominent in London society to the public opinion of their inferiors . . . and society regards as, in some sort, an enemy and a traitor to itself, the man or woman who puts it openly to blush.'

Knowing how the brothers ended, it is rather sad to read *Foreign Resident*'s opinion of Blandford, now 8th Duke of Marlborough, and Lord Randolph Churchill in 1885. 'The Duke of Marlborough has material in him for half a dozen reputations. He is chemist, mathematician, traveller and linguist. . . .' Blandford, having shed the unfortunate Edith Aylesford, had now married a kindly rich American widow whom he was deceiving with the glamorous nymphomaniac Lady Colin Campbell, whose naked picture by Whistler would eventually be torn to shreds by his outraged wife. (A pity, for today's museums are short of Whistlers!)

Then, never guessing at the secret tragedy, he writes: 'The most attractive figure among the young members of the Conservative Party is beyond doubt that of Marlborough's brother, Lord Randolph Churchill. With his audacity, his *insouciance*, his impetuosity, his vehemence and his occasional coolness—in a word, with his fresh and vivid personality, he stands out in delightful relief from the humdrum mediocrities by whom he is surrounded.'

Sweeping through the Liberal statesmen, we learn that Lord Hartington is *of* London society, Mr. Gladstone is merely *in* it. 'One of my compatriots,' writes *Foreign Resident*, 'once fairly summed up the air and demeanour of this distinguished nobleman when he said to an English friend, "What I principally like about your Lord Hartington is his you-be-damnedness." He has *hauteur* but he has not insolence—for insolence implies something which is ill-bred or under-bred. . . . He says little and presents to most people the front of an impenetrable reserve. . . .

'Is he a popular man? On the whole, yes. First because he is a lord, the heir to a great dukedom, and Englishmen love a lord. Secondly because he is fond of the turf, a man of pleasure, with a dash of libertinism in his composition, and Englishmen like to feel that their leaders have the same passions as themselves. Lord Hartington has never resisted feminine influence with relentless obstinacy, and a few venial escapades of his youth are fondly remembered by his countrymen and endear him to their heart.'

Everyone knew of the liaison with Louisa Manchester and respected it—except the unwise adder-tongued Sir William Gordon-Cumming, who would pay heavily for his public sneers. Harty-tarty and his beautiful auburn-haired Duchess knew how to conduct themselves.

Foreign Resident evidently knew of all the famous attachments. Referring to the ladies who were able to carry on long-term affairs, he thinks they must be 'absolutely sure of their positions, and must have the art, which only natural powers can develop, of never violating appearances or offending decorum. It is the rarest thing in the world for any one of these to make openly a *faux pas,* and the penalty for such a blunder is usually ostracism for life. Place for penitence there is none.'

Despite the impropriety of going on the stage, feelings were, due to the Prince's interest in the theatre, beginning to change. In 1885 actresses began to be *invited out to dinner!* 'The actress in society is as powerful as the best substitute which London can offer for the *grande dame,* and—which explains her popularity—she is infinitely more amusing.'

Foreign Resident ends his book with an explanation 'for those who are not Englishmen' of why duels do not exist in England. 'This is to a large extent because there exist in London society social tribunals, before which there can be tried questions that in France we settle in the Bois de Boulogne. Club committees are in effect courts of honour, and the organised public of London society can visit any grave offence against it with penalties as severe as the bullet of a pistol or the thrust of a rapier.'

These observations were made by a Frenchman—one who was in the know to a certain extent only. But that he picked up so much gossip accurately gives an idea of the perils attendant on love affairs in high society. As when riding over the fences and ditches of the shires, nerve and style were essential.

The retribution attendant on putting society 'to the blush' was clearly demonstrated after the Shrewsbury scandal of 1880. Mr. Edward Miller-Mundy, described by his great-niece as 'the most elegant man I've ever seen and at that time supposed to be the richest commoner in England' had married in 1872 Ellen, a beautiful granddaughter of the 7th Lord Byron. She possessed not only a lovely face but superb legs and these unmentionable appendages seem to have been mentioned somewhat freely in her circle. To gild his lily, Mr. Miller-Mundy ordered special silk stockings in various colours to match all her shoes and dresses. Ellen had been married for seven years and had one small daughter, when she met young Lord Shrewsbury, Premier Earl of England, whose ancestors' exploits occupy five pages of *Burke's Peerage*. The greatest of these had sustained the cause of Henry VI in battle after battle until his very name 'became a terror to Frenchmen.' He was once captured by Joan of Arc, but after being exchanged, the King created him 1st Earl of Shrewsbury in 1442, and Shakespeare vaunts him with six lines of other titles. Unfortunately the twenty-year-old 20th Earl tended to obey literally his family motto: *Prest d'accomplir.*

On the night of the great Miller-Mundy ball in their St. James Square mansion, he persuaded the hostess to elope. It must have been late when Mrs. Miller-Mundy crept away from her waltzing guests to arrange a long line of rainbow-coloured shoes and stockings across her bedroom floor to the note saying she had flown. She could hardly have travelled to the Continent in her ball-gown, so a lady's maid with packed trunks must have met her en route. For several weeks London society (headed by Shrewsbury's sister, the powerful Marchioness of Londonderry) waited appalled while Edward Miller-Mundy and his brother pursued the wicked couple in Paris. Entreaties proved vain. Eventually there seemed no alternative to a divorce. Ellen never saw her daughter again; a guilty mother could not claim custody. The Decree Absolute came through in 1882 and for some reason Mrs. Miller-Mundy and her lover were married twice, on June 21 and on July 26. It was only just in time. Their son Viscount Ingestre was born on September 8.

These legal proceedings and above all these dates were noted with bated breath by those referred to by *Foreign Correspondant* as 'inferiors.' Henceforth Shrewsbury, while neglecting his lady, enjoyed the rollicking mode of life open to a nobleman of huge fortune. Racing, polo, fox hunting and gay living atoned for banishment from court. A whole world of male pleasures remained open.

For his Countess it was different. No invitation to a great house ever arrived. Women who had been divorced stepped out of society forever. She lived on, until the age of ninety, in an England of closed doors.

11

The Irish Version

WHILE THE GRANDEES of England flocked to London for the entertainments of May, June and July, the Irish country gentry enjoyed a merry routine of their own. Officially the Dublin season lasted from Christmas to St. Patrick's Day on March 17, but evening parties started with fox hunting in November.

In Dublin, the most perfect Georgian city in Europe after Dresden, lay a charm and gaiety which poverty did not darken as it darkened English cities. The Irish, basically a gracious and joyous race, made the most of all the goings-on during the winter months whether they were of Celtic, Danish or Norman descent or bred of the later Protestant invaders, many of whom were, after a few centuries, inclined to become 'more Irish than the Irish.' It took very little money to enjoy the special delights attending the Dublin winter, where the Meath countryside, with its banks and ditches, lay to one side of the city, so that if frost did not harden the ground it was possible to dance till dawn and then go fox hunting till sundown. During these winter months the Viceroy entertained magnificently in Dublin Castle and there were private balls every night in those elegantly proportioned houses of Merrion and Fitzwilliam squares which are now so admired by architectural societies.

The Viceroy of Ireland always spent the summer months in Phoenix Park inhabiting what is now the President's house. In the winter he and his family would move into the medieval discomforts of Dublin Castle to represent Queen Victoria and hold court. By curious custom the Irish Viceroy had to kiss the debutantes presented to him. 'Lucky fellow,' remarked the Prince of Wales, to whom no such benefits accrued at the Queen's drawing rooms. But sometimes the Viceroy happened to be a grim old patriarch who did not appreciate these occasions, when some fifty blushing country maidens had to rise from their curtseys to receive a kiss, while frantically trying not to trip over three feet of train. One hears that rouge was anathema but in the eighties there came a vogue for powdered noses and Lord Spencer, who was then Viceroy, happened to possess a long red beard. As he was nuzzled by one terrified miss after another, this grew whiter and whiter until he had to retire from the dais to be de-powdered.

An enchanting account of an Irish girl's debut into viceregal Dublin comes from Daisy, Countess of Fingall, in *Seventy Years Young*. 'My frock had come home, and if one should possess in time the wardrobe of the princess in the fairy tale, no other frock would be the same as that first ball dress for one's first ball. . . . When I was dressed I stared at myself in the long solemn mirror. I stared at a stranger whom I saw for the first and last time. Never again can one see oneself in one's first ball dress.'

So she steps into that grown-up world where she will break an outrageous number of hearts. Born of old Irish Catholic stock, Daisy had been brought up in the West of Ireland. Her father, a magistrate, administered justice in his house near Moycullen on the outskirts of the Connemara mountains. Her childhood was more magical than could be possible in England, for the peasantry had a richness of mind and of phrase that did not exist anywhere else on earth. Daisy and her sister would pay visits to cottages. 'God save all here,' they would say, standing in the doorway, blinking for a moment in the turf smoke, and the answer would come: 'God save you kindly.'

Daisy Burke was completely Irish in the sense that her tribe had come to Connaught with the Norman conqueror Strongbow in the twelfth century, and her father belonged to the land as completely as those Celts who had driven away a smaller people in the dawn of history. While Lord Clanricarde, the head of the Burke tribe, could write from London to his agent on a postcard he knew would be read in the village post office, 'Tell the people that they need not hope to intimidate *me* by shooting *you*,' Daisy could write of her own father in the West: 'Everything that the landlords had then, they shared with the people. I am speaking of the good landlords, of course, not of the absentees, whose sins were to be paid for by all of us. My father remembered the people dropping by the roadside on their way to the Big House for help, the "coffin ships" going out from Galway Bay. Those emigrants who reached America alive were to establish a race sworn to implacable hatred of England. He remembered the smell in the air that foretold the blight, and sometimes when he stood looking at the land without seeing it, he would lift his head, sniffing for a warning, which he would understand if it were to come again. . . .'

What would be the 'education' of the daughters of an impecunious Irish magistrate? A governess came for a time, of course, but the girls learnt more when helping their mother in her amateur dispensary which the people preferred to the energetic new doctor. 'All the gossip of the neighbourhood was spread and discussed while the women waited. . . . The rich, sonorous Irish tongue filled the air, which was warm with it.'

Later, when their father's sight failed, the girls travelled with him through France and by the time Daisy 'came out' in Dublin she had learnt to speak fluent French. Along with the rest of the merry penniless gentry who flocked from their country homes but could not afford to rent a house for the season, the Burke family stayed in a hotel, Buswell's Hotel actually, which still exists. Bouquets from admirers arrived daily for the girls and the hotel servants joined in the excitement, complimenting guests as they swept off to dances. 'Sure, Miss Daisy, it's what they say, you're mowing down the military,' exclaimed a housemaid as little Miss Burke stepped forth in her white dress that had cost all of £5.

In this festive atmosphere marriage proposals abounded and Daisy Burke accepted her first. The twenty-four-year-old Lord Fingall, who had recently succeeded as 11th Earl, was supposed to marry money to keep up Killeen, a huge, rambling castle where his family had lived for eight hundred years. But he spied Miss Daisy Burke shopping in Grafton Street and that was that. She would not give an immediate answer to the little note he slipped into her bouquet, but 'at the next Ball we danced together, he begged me not to keep him waiting any longer. . . . I thought how nice he was and what fun it would be to live at Killeen. And I probably thought that it would be fun to marry an Earl too. And of course, it was exciting to get engaged in one's very first Season. So I said, "I think I would like to, awfully!"'

It was as simple as that. But marriage did not mean that one could not continue to mow down the military. She was still at it, I think, when I knew her some fifty years later.

As the wife of the State Steward, young Lady Fingall faced duties which included leading off the ball with the Viceroy in the state quadrille, but this came easily. 'Dancing was life to me.' Less easy was fox hunting, for she had been brought up to ride over mountains, not to jump huge ditches, and her horse Lifeboat frightened the wits out of her. 'His name was reassuring, but that was all. How I used to pray secretly, as we trotted gaily down the road, that they might not find [a fox]. I dreaded the note of the horn which meant that we must leave the pleasant harbour between the hedges for the terrifying open sea of the country.'

Sometimes Daisy admits she went rather well on the mounts provided by her husband, so that countrywomen said, 'That little woman will kill herself.'

The day would end with a 'hunter's tea' of bacon and eggs and scones in one of the inns where carriages assembled to take the riders back to Dublin while the horses remained stabled for the night. 'Exquisitely weary and sleepy, we stumbled out into the yard, put on our warm coats and got into our various vehicles. . . . Sometimes by the time we drove through Phoenix Park and approached the lights of Dublin I was fast asleep in my corner of the carriage and already dreaming of the dance that night.'

Few memoirs of the period describe the writer's husband; it could have been considered bad form, but Lady Fingall's rippling pen shows up a home-bred Irish peer. 'Once a discussion arose at a dinner party at Killeen as to what constituted a gentleman. When everyone else had spoken, Fingall, who was never first except in the hunting field, came in: "I think," he said slowly, "that any man is a gentleman who tells the truth and takes a bath every day." He was fanatically truthful. Often my wild tongue used to distress him and he would protest, "I think your ladyship exaggerates."'

Daisy Fingall describes a sightseeing trip in the eighties. 'We women were still pleased with our bicycles and ourselves in our neat tweed suits, specially designed for that occupation, and little jaunty hats planned not to catch the wind. In the vicinity of Foxford, an old man stood still and stared, then crossed himself solemnly as I flew by!'

And when one of Lady Fingall's ardent admirers, Sir Horace Plunkett, pioneer of efficient Irish farming, imported the *first motorcar ever brought into Ireland*, Daisy and Lady Mayo and the famous Father Finlay were photographed in it. 'Our hats, including Father Finlay's clerical one, are tied on with enormous veils!

'Then Plunkett thought of helping the poor by loosing Swiss goats in the West where there were enough goats already. These were livelier and better goats and even more destructive. They ate everything before them, hedges, gardens, bark of trees and clothes when they were hung out to dry. They climbed on the tops of cottages and ate thatch on occasion!'

Ireland was then undergoing a puritanical period when country dancing and company keeping was frowned on by the Catholic priests. A little story which really needs Lady Fingall's twinkling eyes for the recounting is in her memoirs: 'We had our own private chapel at Killeen, but we went to the parish church to set a good example. In the days of bustles and fringes, the new young curate began his sermon thus: "I have not been four weeks in the parish, and I have already discovered that the besetting sin of this parish is vanity—above all among the women. Now take notice once for all, that I refuse absolution to any female wearing curls in front or wires behind." I had no fringe in front, but I felt a guilty waggle of my "little piece of whalebone behind"!'

When she was nineteen Lady Fingall was allowed her first London visit. 'It was May and London of the 'eighties. All the houses had bright newly-watered window-boxes. There were flowers everywhere and sunshine and jingling hansoms. With my return to Killeen drawing near I had shopping to do. The London shops were thrilling to a girl of nineteen. I drove in a hansom by myself, much enjoying this emancipation. One morning when I was going on to lunch at the Berkeley, I took a hansom driven by a charming and good-looking young man. He was a paragon among the hansom drivers. Such courtesy, such delight in rendering me service! I could not part from him at the door of the first shop and told him to wait for me. And when I said Busvine (for an alteration to my habit) he needed no address. Nor for Hodgkinson's to buy hunting ties and silk handkerchiefs. Nor for the dressmaker to whom we all went in those days, in Dover Street. He seemed to know where one wanted to go almost before one knew oneself. So I kept him for the morning, recklessly. And when all the shopping was done, it was time for lunch and we drove to the Berkeley. As I paid him I said, "I would have liked very much to have kept you, but I'm afraid I can't afford it." He took off his hat with a low bow: "That's just what I was thinking about *you*, Miss."'

Although the Earls of Fingall had retained the Catholic faith, Daisy's husband had an official post in the Viceroy's court and the official Protestant rulers were soon at her feet, George Wyndham, the Chief Secretary, among them. She was charmed when someone said to her, 'I can always tell when you have entered the ballroom. I see the Chief Secretary's face light up.'

A story went the rounds that when the Pope was asked how he influenced Ireland His Holiness answered: 'Through the parish priest at Dunsany who talks with Lady Fingall, who talks with Sir Horace Plunkett, who tells Mr. George Wyndham the Chief Secretary what to do.' Well, all's fair in love and war and in those days there was precious little war to keep gentlemen's minds off the other thing.

12

Lady Londonderry and Lady de Grey

THE STARK STORY of Theresa, Marchioness of Londonderry, and Gladys, Countess de Grey, was recounted by my grandmother when she took me to Covent Garden Opera. She used to point out the box which had belonged to the Lady Londonderry of her time. There she would sit, proud and upright, receiving her friends during the intervals, scanning the auditorium through lorgnettes. After Louisa Manchester she was the most important political hostess of the day; haughtily gracious, a little intimidating. Occasionally her husband might appear in the same box, casually choosing a chair which was not next to hers, but usually he sat in the stalls.

The 6th Marquess of Londonderry was the grandson of that redoubtable Frances Anne of an earlier chapter, and a nephew of the Duchess of Marlborough who was the mother of Lord Blandford and Lord Randolph Churchill. He had been raised in the noble tradition of a great family of statesmen, taught to serve his country, to run huge estates and to conform to the highest code of honour. He owned Wynyard in the North of England, where much of his land contained collieries (enlarged and even more flourishing than in the day of Frances Anne), and Mountstewart, a beautiful eighteenth-century house in Ireland where the family furniture included pieces such as the desk at which the Congress of Vienna had been signed.

A man bred to such inheritance would be schooled from boyhood to certain ideas of responsibility and behaviour. An English gentleman did not let people down.

In 1875 when Londonderry was twenty-three he married the Lady Theresa Chetwynd-Talbot, daughter of the 19th Earl of Shrewsbury—a suitable young girl, brought up according to aristocratic habit in her father's great country house, educated on the top floor by governesses and taught to ride by grooms. It was *un mariage arrangé* in the sense that both families approved the match. Within four years Lady Londonderry had borne two sons and a daughter. Within ten she had fallen in love with another man. This was Mr. Harry Cust, cousin and heir of the Earl Brownlow, the lady killer of the century, to whom a later chapter is entirely devoted. At Eton College his tutors had thought that his first-class mind would probably lead to the premiership, but throughout his twenties he lived in London, allowing women to fall in love with him, writing them poems, frittering his immense talents. When Lady Londonderry, who was slightly older than himself, joined the list of his conquests, he kept her love letters.

Men can be as vain as women in regard to missives which praise their worth, and out of foolishness or conceit or the desire to re-read at leisure Harry kept these letters which he must have known should not be preserved, for in the thoughtlessness of passion Lady Londonderry mocked her husband. Not only did young Mr. Cust keep these letters, but he left them lying around, or in some way available to the jealous searching of another married woman who was in love with him.

This was the Countess de Grey—tall and dark, a proud black swan who according to a contemporary 'made any woman near her look pale.' A sister of the Earl of Pembroke, Gladys Herbert had first married the 4th Earl of Lonsdale, who died two years later, leaving her with one daughter. Lord Lonsdale, a curious introverted man (very different from his brother Hugh, the famous Sporting Earl), does not seem to have appreciated the activities of his young wife, for, on departing for a long yachting trip, he wrote to his agent: 'You will see that I have allowed people to stay at Lowther because, when I come to think matters over, I believe it is better not to give my Lady the excuse that she should go and stay at *all sorts of fast houses*, because I would not allow her friends to come and stay at Lowther.' When, a few months after writing this, Lonsdale died suddenly, his pleasure-loving Countess was in the South of France and Lord Rosebery's diary recorded that Lord Lonsdale had been taken ill, *not* in his usual London abode, but 'he is dying in the house he took to give actresses supper in. His wife does not leave Monte Carlo till tomorrow night.' For the sake of respectability the body was smuggled sitting up in a cab from 30 Bryanston Street to the Lonsdale mansion in Carlton House Terrace.

Two years later Gladys met the Earl de Grey, the best shot in England and eldest son of the 1st Marquess of Ripon, Viceroy of India. He saw her at a country house party and proposed almost immediately. Little has been recorded concerning Lord de Grey except his prowess with a gun. He never wounded a bird—he was so accurate he always hit them in the head—and even at his own shooting parties at Studley Royal he took the best stand for himself. Presumably he imposed less onerous restrictions on his bride than had her former spouse. They attended country house parties together. No children were born of the marriage, and Lady de Grey had *many* interests.

Exactly how Gladys de Grey managed the complicated act of entering the house of a bachelor well known for amorous activity unobserved is not documented, but she certainly had some secret entrance which may, indeed, have been also used by Lady Londonderry. A man who received great ladies in private must have devised a discreet method of entry and exit and Mr. Cust may have injudiciously handed out several sets of keys. However that may be, the Countess de Grey always pursued her romantic inclinations with the determination of an Indian brave on the war path.

When Gladys grew jealous of Lady Londonderry she did not hesitate to rifle through Harry's desks and cupboards. Considering the force of those passions which Harry Cust knew he aroused, and, indeed, enjoyed arousing, it is astonishing that he could have left such dangerous effusions lying around. Maybe they were locked up, maybe Lady de Grey picked the lock—we know only that she found and made use of her rival's letters.

The nobly bred Gladys then showed a temperament suitable for a Euripides play. For a time she kept the letters under her pillow and read excerpts aloud to her friends—including my grandmother, who was shocked and told my grandfather, who to the end of his life would fulminate about this 'dishonourable act.'

Then Lady de Grey concocted the ultimate revenge. She tied up the letters in a sealed package, placed it in the hands of a footman and sent him off to Wynyard with firm orders that he was to place it in the hands of Lord Londonderry himself.

One can imagine the kindly, intelligent Londonderry, a gentleman of the old school, pacing his terraces; the sudden announcement of a manservant with an important missive; the puzzled recipient opening the packet and seeing letters in his wife's handwriting; the slow wounding as he read each sentence; the pain; the mortal blow to pride; the slow adamant decision on how to act.

Lord Londonderry rewrapped the letters, enclosed a note, 'Henceforth we do not speak,' and rang for a servant. The parcel was placed on Theresa Londonderry's dressing table.

My grandmother told me this story in detail, but as I seek to re-enact it there are gaps. Was it evening or morning? Did Lady Londonderry come to her room to dress for dinner and find the package? Did her maid notice anything strange in her expression as she opened it? Did her hands tremble as she sat down at the long table opposite her husband?

We cannot know the heartbeats or the tears. These were hidden. But we do know that until he died over thirty years later Lord Londonderry never addressed a single word to his wife except necessary announcements in public. The details of this drama became known to English society, which watched with mingled approbation and horror. This was how a great gentleman should behave when betrayed and yet—and yet . . . The impassive face of Lord Londonderry while his wife sat in her splendid jewels (those jewels the Tsar had given to the former Marchioness, Frances Anne); the dignified pair receiving at their political receptions at Londonderry House (always standing a little apart); the arrivals by separate carriages at balls or at the opera—all this, with the knowledge of silent unforgiveness, chilled even materialistic Edwardian society which paid such homage to outward form.

When in 1915 Lord Londonderry lay dying, his wife sent a servant with a note begging him to see her. The answer was 'No!' Three years later when Gladys Ripon was dying she sent her enemy Theresa a telegram asking for forgiveness. The answer again came 'No.' Could Balzac invent a story more jagged, more human? What did contemporaries dare to write about these terrible enemies? Glancing through the autobiography of Margot Asquith (annotated by my grandmother), I find this about Lady Londonderry: 'She was a beautiful woman, a little before my day, happy, courageous, and violent, with a mind which clung firmly to the obvious. Though her nature was impulsive and kind she was not forgiving. One day she said to me with pride: "I am a good friend and a bad enemy. No kiss-and-make-up about me, my dear!" I have often wondered since, as I did then, what is the difference between a "good" and a "bad" enemy?

'She was not so well endowed intellectually as her rival Lady de Grey, but she had a stronger will and was of sounder temperament.

1. Albert Edward, Prince of Wales, in 1864

2. Albert Edward, Prince of Wales, in 1870

3. The Marquess of Hartington ("Harty-tarty"), later
the 8th Duke of Devonshire

4. Louisa, Duchess of Manchester, later the Duchess of
Devonshire

5. Lord Charles Beresford

6. Georgina, Countess of Dudley

7. Mrs. Langtry

8. The Marchioness of Londonderry (by Sargent), who wrote indiscreet letters

9. Gladys, Countess de Grey (by Sargent), who found them

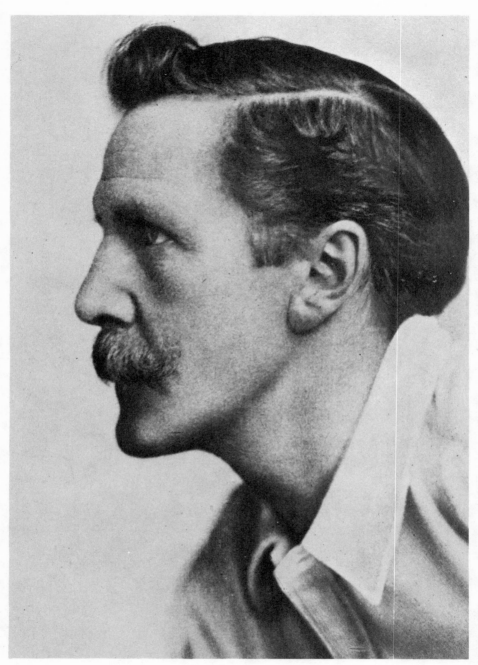

10. The Hon. Harry Cust

11. H.R.H. the Duke of Connaught and Leonie Leslie. Dublin, 1902.

12. Alexandra, Princess of Wales

13. H.R.H. Princess Victoria

14. Lady Randolph Churchill (Jennie Jerome)

15. The Marquis de Soveral

16. H.R.H. the Duchess of Connaught

17. Lord Ribblesdale

18. Lord Esher

There was nothing wistful, reflective or retiring about Lady Londonderry. She was keen and vivid, but crude and impenitent.'

Very few descriptions of Lord Londonderry exist. Daisy Fingall comments on the days when he was Viceroy in Dublin: 'When Lord Londonderry came to Dublin Castle he hurried up the dinners. He hated food and he instituted short meals instead of the immensely long ones to which we had been accustomed. I believe half an hour was the time allowed for dinner and the occasion was a poor one for a gourmet. A footman stood behind nearly every chair and plates were often whipped away from the guests before they had finished. . . .

'One night I sat beside a Lord Mayor at a State Banquet. The Lord Mayor, who, no doubt, had been looking forward to his Viceregal meal, was a slow eater and talker and while he had his head turned towards me the footman took away his plate and he was left looking in some surprise at the empty one put before him for the next course. When he was offered cold ham his endurance gave out and he expressed his feelings to me: "I don't call this a dinner at all," he said, "I call it a rush," and, eyeing the ham disdainfully, "cheap, too." '

Lady Fingall, who like everyone else must have known about the Londonderry situation, expresses her view that Lord Londonderry, while not being exceptionally clever, always 'did the right thing by instinct.' She writes this casually as if she did not realise it was the greatest tribute which could be paid to a man.

When describing his lady, Daisy Fingall proceeds cautiously: 'She was Theresa Londonderry when she wrote a stern letter, "Nellie" to her friends. She was most beautiful then, although not in her first youth. If she had had a little more height she would have been wonderful to look at, but she was too short for her regal beauty and rather square in figure. Hers was a most dominant personality. She had the proudest face I have ever seen.'

A glance at her portrait by Sargent shows an expression of that extraordinary self-confidence which must have indeed been needed to confirm a woman's determination to continue dominating society through those years, as if nothing had happened—only communicating to her husband through servants, never able to catch the eye of the man at the end of her long dinner table—and this after bearing him three children, and knowing his love and the hurt she had done him.

She liked to dominate other people. She was not afraid. 'In love with love,' comments Daisy Fingall. 'She was deeply interested in the love affairs of her friends, and very disappointed if they didn't take advantage of the opportunities she put in their way. She used to say to herself: "I am a Pirate; all is fair in love and war." She had a private understanding with the Almighty as to what people in her position could or could not do!'

Perhaps the verdict of Lady Fingall's personal maid hit a truthful note: 'Very pompous.' But Theresa Londonderry must have had *something*, for when the Shah of Persia came to England he wanted to buy her!

Women, especially musical ones, liked Lady de Grey and many pretty descriptions of her exist. Lady Augusta Fane, who was a debutante with her, wrote in her scatty memoirs *Chit-Chat:* 'Gladys had a character and a broad outlook on life. She had, however, an overwhelming curiosity to know everything and experience every sensation, and this inquisitiveness led her into dark places and amongst undesirable people, but, fortunately, it neither altered nor debased her mind.'

Then from Margot Asquith's autobiography (published 1920) tumble a dozen letters she wrote at various times to my grandmother, who, like Margot, could not resist the charm of Gladys de Grey. One of these letters written soon after Lord Londonderry's death is revealing. Proud 'Nellie' had tried to snub Prime Minister Asquith's wife over Home Rule for Ireland which Asquith was determined to enforce, but there is more than political bitterness in Margot's outburst:

10 Downing Street

Darling Leonie,

If you know Nellie Londonderry you can tell her I am *deeply* hurt and even profoundly shocked that she should not have jumped at the opportunity I gave her when Londonderry died to be nice with me. *Never* again ought a woman like Nellie to go to the Communion Service at St. Paul's and dare say that she is at peace with all men when I am kneeling a little further down (before the same altar praying to the only and same God). I wrote her a simple and very dear kind letter expressing what I felt of sympathy for her—saying that of course the Past would always be the past as far as we were concerned—No woman could have got a nicer letter.

How easy for her even if she still wants to give way to a naturally vulgar revengeful nature to *acknowledge* my letter but she never has written *one line*. (These kind of animals ought to be drowned at birth)—they keep up a low standard of social sweetness and perpetual offences which no one tolerates in a nursery.

But Nellie Londonderry was a tigress prowling through not a nursery but a very sophisticated jungle!

And here is Margot's opinion of Gladys de Grey, whom she refers to as a 'social antagonist of Lady Londonderry'—(these Asquith memoirs were considered indiscreet!): 'Apart from her beauty, she was the last word in refinement, perception and charm; but there was something unsound in her nature and I heard her say one day that the cry of the cuckoo made her feel ill. . . . When anything went wrong with her entertainments—cold plates, a flat *soufflé* or someone throwing her over for dinner—her sense of proportion was so entirely lacking that she would become almost impotent from agitation and throw herself into a state of mind only excusable if she had received the news of some great public disaster.'

Every Edwardian memoir describes the tall, dark Countess de Grey, later Marchioness of Ripon, whose swanlike beauty could hush a ballroom, and her artistic instinct which led her to be the first great patroness of Covent Garden Opera, but only Margot's book mentions the cuckoo. What did Gladys hear him say— 'Cuckoo—cuckoo. It was *you*—It was *you*'?

13

Tranby Croft

To ROYAL CIRCLES the nineties presented a decade more irritating than naughty. The Prince had entered his fiftieth year—square, gracious, as fond as ever of good food and lovely ladies, though in a more thoughtful fashion. He was now to know the great passion of his life—indeed Lady Warwick assumed this status in the lives of other gentlemen but it was her affair with the Prince which singled her out in popular view as England's *grande amoureuse*.

Much has been made of the Prince's excursions into the world of demi-mondaines, but although like other royal personages he occasionally visited the most famous of Parisian establishments, one might as well say he was obsessed by circuses because he once watched a tightrope artist. Every kind of *show* was put on for the Prince of Wales *wherever* he went, and when such individuals as Mistinguett and the famous courtesan Emilienne d'Alençon wrote their memoirs it became natural to garnish the pages with royal anecdotes, and seek to convey the impression that they had in their time knocked *le roi Edouard* for six.

Naturally, the demi-mondaines of Paris were at his disposition. There could have been few Frenchmen who would not have been pleased to lend a mistress to England's heir for the afternoon—it would make such an amusing story at dinner. And several fantastic cocottes dominated Paris at this time. Apart from Emilienne there was La belle Otéro, a Spanish dancer who had lassoed several Russian grand dukes and been recompensed by diamond necklaces which had once graced the necks of Marie Antoinette and the Empress Eugénie. A different type of houri—delicate as porcelain, called indeed *la reine d'ivoire*—was little Liane de Pougy,* a girl from Provence who decided to make her name at the Folies-Bergère clad in simple, clinging—*very* clinging—black. Timing her first appearance to one of the Prince's visits to Paris, she sent him a note: '*Monseigneur, je vais faire mes débuts à Paris. Je serais consacrée si vous daigniez venir m'applaudir.*'

This artless invitation appealed to the Prince, who attended her first night with a number of enthusiastic men friends. Liane was made. Henceforth Parisian milliners and dressmakers vied to create her costumes and every top-hatted gentleman who wanted to show what a dog he was tried to inveigle her into lunching or dining with him in public.

An episode recorded by Yvette Guilbert in *Chanson de ma vie* gives the impression, if it is exact, that the Prince could be over-familiar with Parisian vedettes. She describes a supper party which the Prince asked Sir Arthur Sullivan to give for her in London. The Prince and his brother, the Duke of Connaught, and his cousin, the Duke of Cambridge, attended. According to Mademoiselle Guilbert, the Austrian Ambassador paralysed guests by loudly talking about the Prince's reactions when La Goulue, the famous red-stockinged dancer of the Moulin Rouge (immortalised by Toulouse-Lautrec), had welcomed him to the music hall with a shout of ''Ullo, Wales!' The Prince had roared with laughter and ordered champagne for all the dancers and the orchestra.

The demi-monde went into ecstasies whenever royalty peered in at the door. But the Prince's real interests lay with women he could talk to. His old French friends, the Comtesse de Pourtalés and the Duchesse de Mouchy and Madame Standish as well as the Princesse de Sagan, continued to entertain him privately on all his visits to France. He would not have dreamt of visiting the realm without dropping in for a gossip; and all their children and in time their grandchildren had to be marched into the drawing room to be presented. As the enquiring grey-blue eye passed over the squirming figure a pudgy finger would be extended to the little ones. Older boys and girls bowed or curtseyed and stood at wide-eyed attention before scurrying back to the nursery.

The fact that he immensely admired talent, especially theatrical talent, did not mean that the Prince went to bed with every actress

* Liane de Pougy alone among the great courtesans made a grand marriage. She was quietly happy with the Prince Ghika, nephew of Queen Nathalie of Greece. When widowed she became a nun.

whom he congratulated. Certain French books make much of the Prince's association with Jeanne Granier, a delicious, extremely talented actress. On one occasion when His Royal Highness was a guest of the French President he did walk across the foyer of the Théâtre Français to where Jeanne was standing with a group of friends, to kiss her hand and openly exclaim: 'Mademoiselle, I remember applauding you in London where you represented all the grace and spirit of France.' However, this is no indication that she automatically became his mistress. Jeanne Granier blushed with pleasure at the compliment and Edward's remark was repeated throughout Paris, where it made him extremely popular at a moment when England was being much criticised on account of the Boer War.

However felicitously the Prince bestowed compliments on Parisian actresses, it was not the vedettes who held his thoughts in the nineties, but the special blend of passion and breeding that he found in his young lady love Daisy, wife of Lord Brooke, eldest son of the Earl of Warwick. Her long, eventful story demonstrates so perfectly the entire Edwardian era that I have had to set her apart for a special chapter, but we must note her entrance into the procession of Edwardian romantics at this time. Indeed, she should head the lot, but I will only state here that she became the Prince's mistress in about 1889 when she was twenty-nine and the Prince was forty-eight. Her impact helps to form the background of the Tranby Croft scandal in September 1890.

The story of Tranby Croft has been told and retold. The only new sidelights are the remarks of my grandmother (who detested Sir William Gordon-Cumming) and the letters written to me personally by that very charming lady Mrs. Cecily Muir, who was Sir William's youngest daughter.

A gaming scandal is not perhaps pertinent to a book devoted to romance, but as all country house parties were permeated by the special atmosphere of accepted love affairs, Tranby Croft gives a typical backdrop.

The Prince of Wales had for the first time agreed to stay for the Doncaster Races with Arthur Wilson, a rich shipowner. It was the smart thing to entertain His Royal Highness and this visit marked the culmination of social ambition for the Wilson family. In other years the Prince had visited his devoted old friend Christopher Sykes—lightly described by his great-nephew as 'a snob, I fear, even by the standards of those snobbish days.'

For the St. Leger Stakes in September the 'great Xtopher' had always entertained the Prince 'not only with the maximum of comfort and splendour but in strict accordance with his idiosyncrasies.' Mr. Sykes's Yorkshire house had for ten years or more seen 'a succession of sumptuous entertainments . . . while the scene is crowded with great names.' But now poor Christopher Sykes, whom the Prince thought it so comic to souse with his own brandy, was facing bankruptcy and his sister-in-law Jessica Sykes told the Prince frankly that Christopher's dilemma was entirely due to magnificent London dinners and huge Yorkshire house parties which he ceaselessly gave to please his lord and master.

The moment the Prince *realised* his friend was in financial trouble he had called a halt to such commands and contrived to gather sufficient funds to avert the bankruptcy court. But by 1890, when Christopher Sykes was sixty years old, he could no longer afford to entertain the Prince at all, so the Arthur Wilsons took over with delight, and Mr. Sykes and Colonel Owen Williams, old friends of the Prince, were automatically invited. So was Lady Brooke and her husband, but at the last moment Daisy had to cancel because of the death of her stepfather Lord Rosslyn in Scotland. So the party lacked the allure of her presence. As the Prince now preferred baccarat to dancing, tables and counters had to be laid on. The sums won and lost were not enormous, but some people found gambling a bore and hated to lose anything whatever.

I once asked a very old man who had attended some of these parties if he believed Sir William Gordon-Cumming had truly cheated, and he laughed. 'Of course he cheated. We all did. It was such a nuisance being made to play and lose money, and I and a lot of the other young men longed to be dancing instead. But Cumming cheated *too much* and he had a lot of enemies.'

The Duke of Portland in his massive memoirs gives Gordon-Cumming a write-up which fits him exactly into the exotic Edwardian scene: 'I knew Bill Cumming very well, and for a long time liked and admired him, both as a gallant soldier and as a fine sportsman. . . . A friend of mine who went on an expedition (tiger shooting on foot) with him was loud in his praise of Bill's sportsmanship, bravery and unselfishness . . . but he had one serious failing: he could not play fair at cards. . . . In the days of duelling, it would have been a brave man who accused Bill of any such thing, as he was a dead shot with a revolver or a pistol. If England had always been at war, or if Bill had always been in pursuit of big-game, everyone would have thought, quite rightly, that no better soldier, or finer fellow in every way, ever existed.'

Alas for a man who needed England *always* at war to keep him happy. On the second day of this unfortunate house party his host and four others went late at night to Gordon-Cumming to say they had all seen him cheat. They accused him of repeatedly looking at his cards and then sliding the counters about, a trick known as *la pousette* in Monte Carlo. He was to sign a paper swearing never to play cards again. Gordon-Cumming refuted the allegation but agreed to sign the paper to settle the matter if they all swore to secrecy. When the Prince was informed of the incident he unwisely added his name to that of the witnesses.

Early next morning Sir William left Tranby Croft, and the Prince moved to the 10th Hussars' Mess in York for the last day of the races, which was a terrible blow to the Arthur Wilsons' social aspirations. They realised His Royal Highness would never enter their house again.

Next day, the Prince asked Lord and Lady Brooke, who were on their way to Scotland for the funeral of Lord Rosslyn, to step off at York Station to see him. There he related the story and Daisy became known as 'the babbling brook' when the scandal leaked out. But this was not due to *her* indiscretion. The other men involved had already told their ladies and Doncaster race-course knew the story even before the Brookes. The secrecy which had been promised Gordon-Cumming had not been given and on returning to London he was cut in his clubs. Among his most powerful enemies was Louisa Manchester. Had he not once said out loud, 'Harty-tarty, when are you going to make Louisa an honest woman?'

Three months later, in January 1891, the Prince was attending a house party in Norfolk when he learnt that Gordon-Cumming was bringing a libel action against his original accusers. This house party included Lord Hartington, Daisy and 'Brookie,' Lady Randolph Churchill and her beloved Charles Kinsky. Daisy Brooke and Jennie Churchill were close friends and the Prince poured out his woe to them. Jennie had known Gordon-Cumming for sixteen years; he had been in love with her and then with her sister Clara, who had considered marrying him but wrote her mama she could not love him and besides he was 'so poor.' Maybe his second reflections resembled her own! Anyway, he later showed unforgivable rudeness to poor little Leonie, the youngest Jerome sister, marching up to her in Hyde Park and saying: 'Over here husband-hunting?' To cap this insult, he had pounced on her 'in a corridor at a house party' soon after she married Jack Leslie, and when she broke away, he said, 'Silly little fool—all the married women try me.' I quote this story in her own words because it so clearly shows the kind of man he was—all right tiger shooting with other chaps but nasty to have around. After such encounters my grandmother's views must have been prejudiced, but she also told us she had noticed Gordon-Cumming cheating at cards in Jennie's house, and when she told Randolph he said: 'Keep quiet about it. We won't have him here again.'

If, as my old friend said, everyone cheated a bit at that enforced baccarat in country houses, then Gordon-Cumming was just unlucky. But the weakness was dangerous for a Guards officer. And he was arrogant and had injured the feelings of many, as well as the redoubtable Louisa. Now no man stepped forward to call him friend and the Princess of Wales's terms for him were 'worthless creature' and 'vile snob.' Queen Victoria always stood by her son when he got into trouble and great efforts were made to prevent this libel action from reaching the courts because it would mean the revelation of the Prince's signature and involve him in an unsavoury gambling quarrel.

For six months the Prince fretted himself ill over the impending court case. When it finally occurred in June 1891, and the heir to the throne was subpoenaed as a witness, the impression made on the nation was appalling. Queen Victoria wrote to her eldest daughter: 'This horrible Trial drags along, and it is a fearful humiliation to see the future King of this country dragged (and for the second time), through the dirt, just like anyone else, in a Court of Justice.'

The Solicitor-General, Sir Edward Clarke, who represented Gordon-Cumming, was extremely offensive to the Prince, but he lost the case against the five witnesses of Tranby Croft. Sir William was dismissed from the Army and expelled from all clubs, but it was on the Prince that the country turned its wrath. And, of course, the Kaiser could not resist writing protesting to Queen Victoria that his uncle, who held the honorary rank of a colonel of Prussian Hussars, should become involved in a gambling quarrel with men young enough to be his sons.

'The Press have been very severe and cruel because they know I cannot defend myself,' wrote the Prince to his sister, and then, revealingly, to his son Prince George: 'Thank God! the Army and Society are now well rid of such a damned blackguard. The crowning point of his infamy is that he, this morning, married an American young lady, Miss Garner (sister to Madame de Breteuil) with money!'

The Prince had other interests—Lady Brooke and his new racing yacht *Britannia*. Gradually he would recover from the blow, and unpopularity, the sleepless nights, the sense of being ill used, but for the Gordon-Cumming family living in that great mansion Gordonstoun (which in time became a school for Prince Charles, Edward's great-great-grandson!)—what would the next forty years bring for *them?*

A recent letter written to me by Mrs. Cecily Muir (Sir William Gordon-Cumming's youngest daughter), reflected her feeling that I had referred unfairly to her father in my biography of Lady Randolph Churchill: 'No one knew the truth re Tranby Croft. If Papa was guilty, which it looks like on paper, Edward Clarke, who defended him, sent for me before he died and assured me he was innocent. I wonder if Leonie tried to protect Jennie from Papa, he being so awfully in love with Jennie? Hence Papa being beastly to Leonie. . . .

'I suggest you add this footnote to new editions of *Jennie:* "Sir William Gordon-Cumming was made an outcast after the case. The Prince of Wales said that anyone who spoke of him would never be asked to Marlborough House again, also no Army or Navy Officer was to accept invitations to shoot at Altyre or Gordonstoun."

'We never knew "the county" and Papa was blackballed from every Club however humble. So the vengeance was thorough.'

This is the true end of the story depicted with pathos and exactitude. We see the children of that handsome rude Sir William and his loyal adoring wife growing up completely isolated on the forty thousand acres of Scottish moorland which was their kingdom. They must have wondered as they grew older why they and their parents were surrounded by invisible walls. Gradually they would learn the story. At least they had ghillies and farm folk to talk to and a most beautiful wilderness to play in, crofters being kinder than the Marlborough House set!

14

Ideas of Fun

'IT HAS BEEN for years a diversion to me, and a study in social stratagem, to watch certain foreign hostesses, now firmly established in Edward's favour, approach London, the Mecca . . . by such routes as *hotels* in Paris, *villas* on the Riviera, *chalets*, in Switzerland, or *palazzi* in Venice,' wrote the anonymous widow of a diplomat in her *Intimacies of Court and Society*. This diversion was shared by many others.

Throughout the nineties the working classes drew real enjoyment from the goings-on of the Prince's set. Their own poverty did not seem connected to royal escapades. Because Queen Victoria sat glooming in a black dress, it did not make them less hungry. Edward's magnificence stimulated trade, gave work and cheered up gossip in the pubs. The middle classes might frown, but the ordinary Englishman, emerging from some dismal cellar to look for work, felt like the young Charlotte Brontë: 'I like high life, I like its manners, its splendours, the beings which move in its enchanted sphere.'

Britannia, the 300-ton racing cutter, now the joy of the Prince's heart, outclassed all her rivals for four years. The Prince could take several friends with him as well as the crew of twenty-eight and in her first year, 1893, she won thirty-two prizes in forty-three races. But behind the scenes Edward suffered maddening pinpricks from his nephew the Kaiser. Since 1889, when he had been snubbed in St. Petersburg, Wilhelm had taken to visiting England frequently.

Sympathising with the Prince, the German chargé d'affaires, Baron von Eckardstein, in his *Ten Years at the Court of St. James*, writes: 'It was the Kaiser's annual August appearance at Cowes that seemed most to get on his nerves.'

As soon as *Britannia* had shown her speeds Wilhelm wanted to pit his own racing yacht *Meteor* against her. One day in 1893, the *Britannia* and *Meteor* set off to race each other around the Isle of Wight. In the afternoon the wind dropped and amidst flapping sails the Prince signalled his nephew that Queen Victoria, who was giving a dinner in Wilhelm's honour, would be highly displeased if they were late. 'Prepare abandon race and return by train,' signalled the Prince. 'Race must be fought out,' replied the Kaiser. Breezes died and they finally reached Osborne at 10 P.M. as the Queen and her guests were leaving the dining room. The bumptious grandson apologised bravely while the son hid behind a pillar!

The awe which Queen Victoria inspired in her middle-aged children caused even her eldest daughter to quail when, as Empress of Germany, on visits to England she had to take precedence of her mother. Eckardstein noted: 'One could see how difficult she found this by the embarrassed way she edged herself sideways through the doors.'

In 1895 the Prince of Wales said to Eckardstein, 'The Regatta at Cowes was once a pleasant holiday for me, but, now that the Kaiser has taken command there, it is nothing but a nuisance. Perhaps I shan't come at all next year.'

And in the next summer Edward saw his pleasure ruined, for the Kaiser appeared with a new boat, *Meteor II*, specially commissioned to outclass *Britannia*. With sadness the Prince realised he could not afford to continue this family competition. He sold *Britannia* and never participated in yacht racing again.

Eckardstein was an immensely greedy man and there was one famous incident which he did not put into his diplomatic memoirs —indeed, he may never have realised that he was the cause of a long sad wait. A certain gentleman, worried about which door to open on his night perambulations, had asked his lady to put the sandwiches (which were placed by each bedside in case of sudden hunger after the five heavy meals of the day) outside *her* door. Unfortunately Eckardstein passed that way, could not resist a tasty mouthful, and ate them. When Romeo came tiptoeing along the corridor he saw an *empty* plate and, fearing that it was intended as some kind of warning, fled.

No volume offers more comic descriptions of the nineties than Mrs. Hwfa Williams' reminiscences, *It Was Such Fun!* The book is not intended to be funny. On the contrary, Mrs. Williams, who married a younger brother of the Prince's friend Colonel Owen Williams, and who was therefore a sister-in-law of the unfortunate Edith Aylesford and of the Countess of Cowley and Duchess of Wellington, recounts her Edwardian stories with breathless enthusiasm. She was first presented to the Prince in 1887 when only fifteen. Then she came out and married into the important Welsh family whose only black sheep was Lady Aylesford.

Mr. Hwfa Williams was, like his brother, an intimate friend of the Prince of Wales and we learn that 'It was a real stroke of genius that led Hwfa to think of turning Sandown Park into a race course.' Brother Owen had bought this fine country estate and couldn't imagine what to do with it, till Hwfa had the idea of making a racecourse near London. 'So careful was Hwfa in arranging even the smallest details of Sandown Race Course that he even invented a pencil to fix on the race-cards. King Edward and Queen Alexandra graciously accepted the first two of these and they were soon in general use.' Triumph!

I had always heard of the Prince's incomprehensible family jokes with Hwfa Williams. His Royal Highness called him 'Squirrel' and shook with laughter whenever he did so. This book explains why.

'One night, returning alone from Louisa Devonshire's Derby Night Ball (the Prince always came on to this after the Jockey Club dinner in Marlborough House), Mr. Williams found the second footman, whose custom it was to sleep in the pantry at the front of the house, had gone to bed at the back. As the clanging bell did not penetrate to those quarters Hwfa tried to climb up to the balcony, fell onto the area railings, was finally rescued and had to spend three weeks in bed.' Ha, ha! What a joke. The Prince would heave with merriment and Squirrel he remained henceforth.

Another way of triggering off guffaws of laughter was to use the word 'indy' for indigestion. This is a curious little tale. One night Mr. Hwfa Williams was walking down the Mall when a lunatic suddenly shot him in the leg. He was carried home where he began to suffer terrible chest pains which the doctor called indigestion. The Prince then sent his own doctor, who diagnosed double pneumonia and removed a large blood clot which had travelled from the knee into Hwfa's mouth—an unusual occurrence which caused the medical profession to beg for 'the legacy of his body after death.' But Mr. Hwfa Williams lived many another day to hear the royal bellow of laughter at the query: 'A little touch of indy perhaps?'

'The greatest amusement was to hear him chaff the poor old

blind Duke of Mecklenburg . . . the Duke was full of fun and enjoyed the Prince's teasing as much as anybody. The Duke's great
friend in those days was Helen Henneker. She was celebrated for
her wit but alas she was colossally fat. One day, just to tease them
both, the Prince took the Duke's hand in his and laying it on
Helen's arm said: "Now don't you think Helen has a lovely little
waist?" For a moment the Duke looked bewildered and a little
embarrassed, but a roar of laughter, in which no one joined more
wholeheartedly than Helen, made him realise that it was just another of the Prince's jokes.'

Then 'Another old friend the King delighted to tease was "dear
old Christopher Sykes." He was a very dignified figure, extremely
tall, and with a very charming but solemn appearance. King Edward
used to say: "Come here, Christopher, and look at the smoke coming out of my eyes." When Christopher's eyes were fixed on him,
His Majesty would playfully pretend to burn his hand with his
cigar. It sounds rather brutal, but Christopher knew what was
coming as the joke had been played on him so often.'

As a great treat the Prince occasionally took Mrs. Hwfa Williams
out in *Britannia,* and, oh dear, what she suffered in a choppy sea.
'With his usual geniality the King insisted upon my drinking
champagne, which I hate. To complete the fare hard ships biscuits
were served.'—But, 'What fun it was!'

Louisa Manchester pounced on Mrs. Williams as a travelling
companion and off they went to Nice. It was a nightmare journey
because the Duchess scorned sleeping berths. She sat bolt upright
all night sleeping soundly while wretched Mrs. Williams longed
for the dawn.

From the Hotel Splendid expeditions into the mountains were
organised by Lord Hartington. 'Off we would go with donkeys.'
But the Duchess proved craven, and, panting, she begged for a
halt: 'Really, you don't have an eye for the lovely view.'

When in 1897 Louisa, now Duchess of Devonshire, gave her
famous fancy-dress ball Mrs. Williams was all set to go. She had
been rehearsing quadrilles with her selected partner, and then, two
days before the ball, her sister-in-law Edith Aylesford (inconvenient
to the end, poor dear) went and died. So she had to spend the
evening with Lord Mildmay, who was also in mourning, up at a sky-
light on top of the staircase. 'Never shall I forget the heat we endured as we stood at our observation post. We stayed there till
nearly four in the morning, abandoning it only for a few minutes
to creep down the back staircase to get something to eat!'

One person was deliberately *not* invited to this famous ball, and that was little Lady Fingall, who could have much enjoyed it. Louisa's jealous nature had been provoked when Daisy first went to Newmarket Races. Very few women attended those and each had to come with a member of the Jockey Club (probably the most exclusive club in the world). In the enclosure there happened to be a special bench for the Prince of Wales, and Daisy in all innocence sat down on it. Louisa Manchester swept up glaring, but did not explain the offence until Lady Londonderry came up: 'Come away, my dear, this is no place for you.' Daisy dissolved into tears of embarrassment, but next day the Prince walked up to her laughing and insisted she sit on the bench beside him. Louisa never forgave her for getting this attention.

As Christopher Sykes and the Arthur Wilsons were 'out' for Doncaster Races, the Prince stayed with Lord and Lady Savile of Rufford Park, and the Hwfa Williamses accompanied them and travelled on to Scotland on the royal train. 'What a lovely journey that was! How I should like always to travel on a train like that! I forget what time we left Rufford but it was too early to have breakfast and we now had a really luxurious one served. . . . His Majesty was in the best of humours. . . . He poured out tea and coffee himself!

'How all the ghillies adored King Edward! He would take tea with the one old ghillie in his lodge. "Now then let's have some of that poisonous whiskey of yours."—"Och yer Majesty, ye ken well that I wadna poison ye. . . . But a' the same take a wee drap o' poison."'

Mrs. Williams fell, tore ligaments in her foot and the King took her on his special train to London where she had to spend six weeks in bed at Claridge's Hotel. 'I found it quite fun lying in bed and receiving a constant stream of visitors.'

Mrs. Williams gave guileless descriptions of one of the big pheasant-shooting parties for which England was famous. Only the best shots were invited and they were not expected to wound birds. Dogs swiftly retrieved any that were not dead. Although the carnage was fearful mathematically, the actual suffering incurred would probably be far less than that incurred by mediocre shots. But what a ghastly form of house party entertainment for the ladies who had to hang about all day! Mrs. Williams went to a smart party at Lord Nunburnholme's Warter Priory near York. 'Only a few of the men used to come down to tea during the week of the big shoot, as it was really most exhausting work at the stands. I remember at one stand over 1500 head of pheasants were killed. Lord Howe, Lord de Grey, Harry Stoner, Bertie Willoughby

and Bertie Tempest were at this stand; the birds flying very high
and it was really most tiring work to shoot them; but with four
guns apiece they brought down this enormous bag. Naturally
in these conditions, with the birds flying so high, they were tired
out when they came back and many had splitting headaches.'

There was a large round table in the hall of Warter Priory.
'After shooting we used to gather round it for tea in our many-
coloured tea-gowns. . . . What teas those were! Most of the men
would go upstairs to rest until dinner-time, as so many of them
had headaches after so great a shoot, while we ate hot buns and
jam with delicious cream from the Nunburnholmes' herd of pedigree Jerseys.'

A masculine description of Lord Dudley's famous shoot at Him-
ley near the collieries comes from Moreton Frewen (who had
married Clara Jerome). He was a first-class shot and the keepers'
pet.

'I found myself playing up to an alarmingly critical gallery. The
coverts on one side are hemmed in by coal pits, and scores, perhaps even hundreds of miners had collected behind the guns, bet-
ting on the shots, full of vociferous approval if the performance
was good.'

Moreton noticed that the man next to him, unable to take the
strain of playing in front of a critical public, began to miss.
Noticing this, the head keeper quickly moved him to a hidden
butt and brought up a crack shot to take his place. 'Happily
both he and I shot our best and the crowd was in a few minutes
sympathetic and approving.'

The best shots in England were Prince George (later King
George V) and Earl de Grey. The Prince of Wales did not much
care for shooting, but he used to go to De Grey's shoot at Combe
Court where Gladys would sit in the butt with him cuddling her
white chow.

Far more entertaining for H.R.H. were the tremendous house
parties given at West Dean Park in Sussex by Mrs. Willie James. An
August 1896 letter from Moreton Frewen, who was staying in what
he describes as a colossal party at West Dean, recaptures the atmosphere of these. At one in the morning twenty-three of the
guests set off on bicycles to see the sunrise from the downs. They
pedalled away until 4:30 A.M. Mrs. Willie, wearing 'next to no
clothes,' was saved from pneumonia by donning a gentleman's
swallow-tail coat.

King Edward is spoken of with reverence still among villagers
around West Dean. Their grandsires enjoyed the royal visits, it

gave them something to talk about. Many of the hostesses who entertained the King bore children who resembled him, but this may be due to psychological reasons. People grow to look like the dogs who constantly occupy their thoughts.

No book about the Edwardians can refrain from quoting Hilaire Belloc's lines which Vita Sackville-West remembered for Sir Philip Magnus when he was writing the life of Edward VII.

> There will be bridge and booze 'till after three
> And, after that, a lot of them will grope
> Along the corridors in robes de nuit,
> Pyjamas, or some other kind of dope.
> A sturdy matron will be sent to cope
> With Lord ——, who isn't quite the thing.
> And give his wife the pleasure to elope,
> And Mrs. James will entertain the King!
> Envoi
> Prince, Father Vaughan will entertain the Pope,
> And you will entertain the Jews at Tring,
> And I will entertain the larger hope,
> And Mrs. James will entertain the King.

15

{~}

The Countess of Warwick

IF A SINGLE EDWARDIAN romantic can represent the whole epoch, then Daisy, Countess of Warwick, must be chosen. She cannot be called typical of her class because both her indiscretions and her compassion were unique, but for nine years she dominated the Prince of Wales and every facet of the time is revealed by a study of this fascinating, seductive, generous-hearted, dangerously impulsive English beauty.

Daisy would have caused havoc in any court in any age, but only amidst the crumbling prejudices of Victorian England, with the amoral Prince in charge of society, could she have blossomed into such a complete and uninhibited character.

In that century of terrible poverty, industrial hells, depressed agriculture and splendid upper-class life, Miss Frances Maynard, known as Daisy, was born an heiress. Her father died before her grandfather, the last Lord Maynard, who left his fortune and his lands to the little girl who, had she been a boy, would have inherited his title.

Two years later Daisy's mother remarried. As Countess of Rosslyn she produced five children and, because Lord Rosslyn's home lay in Scotland, Daisy and her younger sister, step-brothers, and step-sisters were brought up almost entirely at her own home, Easton Lodge, in Essex. In this dream world, where the rambling mansion lay in a thousand-acre park with great oaks and herds of deer, the children knew bliss.

Until they were grown up the girls were never allowed pretty dresses for fear of encouraging vanity, but from earliest days 'Miss Daisy,' toddling, driving or riding, must have heard the estate workers refer to her as their future mistress. Lord Rosslyn, a strict but kindly Victorian father, saw that all the children learned to ride well. Daisy's young life revolved around her dear white pony; she knew far more about horses' legs than feminine fashions, and would someday write: 'As I had my first pony when I was five, I can scarcely remember when I could not ride, and my step-father had such confidence in our fearlessness that he used to let us children ride his young thoroughbreds that were unfit to race and showed temper.'

According to the usual custom, the girls were educated by a governess, in this case a sensitive young woman, the illegitimate offspring of aristocratic parents who could find no other niche. She taught her charges to speak French and German without accent by making them recite long passages from Racine, Corneille, Molière, Goethe and Heine—stiffer medicine than was usually meted out to girls. The boys had Greek and Latin drummed into them and were then sent off to be whacked at boarding schools.

In 1875 Disraeli received an interesting report from his secretary, a house guest at Easton Lodge: 'The heiress Miss Daisy is growing into a fine young woman. She is now fifteen, so that she will not for three years be the talk of London. Munster says her fortune will be much over £30,000 a year. Whatever it be, I see she will bestow it upon who so ever *she* chooses—and turn out a *maîtresse femme*.'

In the following year Miss Maynard was spotted by young Lord Brooke, eldest son of the Earl of Warwick, who fell in love at first sight, but when he asked Lord Rosslyn if he might mention this to Daisy the answer was a stern 'No,' for Lady Rosslyn had great ambitions for her eldest daughter. Queen Victoria, most practical of matchmakers, had recently decided that it was uneconomic to keep marrying off her children to penniless German royalties who needed large settlements. Having chosen Lord Lorne, son of the Duke of Argyll, for Princess Louise, she was contemplating an English heiress for her youngest son Prince Leopold, Duke of Albany, and descriptions of little Miss Maynard had aroused the Queen's interest. Lady Rosslyn preened her maternal plumes—this would be a great match.

In December 1879, before Daisy had actually been presented at court, Lord and Lady Rosslyn were commanded to bring the girl to dine and sleep at Windsor Castle. After dinner Queen Victoria asked her a few questions: 'I was agonisingly shy in the presence of this mysterious Queen. . . . But self-consciousness was my usual state of mind in those days,' Daisy would write.

For her eighteenth birthday a dance was held at Easton Lodge, and Lord Brooke, grateful at being allowed to attend, promised not to propose marriage while determinedly reiterating his hopes. In the following spring, when Daisy Maynard was enjoying her first season, Queen Victoria and Lady Rosslyn brought marriage negotiations to a climax. Miss Maynard was taken to stay at Prince Leopold's country house and there the eighteen-year-old girl firmly refused his offer, apparently to his relief. A few hours later, while walking under an umbrella with the equerry, Lord Brooke, she happily accepted the second marriage proposal of the day.

Queen Victoria insisted on an immediate decision, 'and not allow the matter to be hanging on,' but she could not help feeling displeased.

Daisy was now eager for the freedom of a married woman which would enable her to escape maternal restrictions and to run her own estates, but months had to pass while old Lord Warwick argued finances with Lord Rosslyn. The great family of Warwick was not particularly well off and the bridegroom received only a modest allowance. Eventually, a year later, the most splendid of marriages took place at Westminster Abbey with royal guests in front and merry tenants and retainers, brought up from Essex by special train, behind. The Prince of Wales, Prince Leopold and the Lords Warwick and Rosslyn signed the register and after some difficulty with the horses the Warwick state coach drew bride and groom to the reception. Then came the usual long-drawn-out secluded honeymoon. Daisy's schoolgirl sister Blanche wrote touchingly on the first night of separation: 'Mamma and I have been having dinner together upstairs and talking of you, dearest, and we could not help howling a little, but I know darling, how happy Brookie will make you. . . .'

In the following September Daisy suffered a miscarriage, but a year later she bore a son and heir, and two years later a daughter Marjorie. Lord Rosslyn kept busy writing long homilies on the importance of keeping married love going 'as the one thing that grows deeper and holier as death draws near.' Unfortunately, Lord Charles Beresford and Major Joe Laycock would draw near long before death.

During the first few years of their marriage Daisy and Brookie lived in the traditional aristocratic manner, entertaining gaily at Easton Lodge for the hunting and shooting, or trailing to the great houses with maids and valets for those vast shooting parties

which seemed so important, but the lively, intelligent Daisy soon
tired of these, which were entirely arranged for the men, and
she found other people's houses cold and uncomfortable. Fox hunting was her joy, and while Brookie continued to shoot throughout
the winter months, she could remain with her hunters in Essex or
travel to the best shires or to Ireland.

Now that she was her own mistress she decided to learn to
drive a four-in-hand at Easton, with two top-hatted footmen
perched behind her. 'Miss Daisy,' now 'her ladyship,' was the pride
and delight of the estate, even if, as Elinor Glyn complained, the
ponies went much too fast or else not at all. Although they appeared to be slipping into the fast Marlborough House set, the
Brookes were a devoted young couple—only their sports diverged.
Lord Rosslyn could write unctuously: 'Surrounded by all the clever,
the pure and noble-minded, unselfish and careless about your own
little hobbies, you preside over a society that is without profanity
and religious without intolerance. . . . For work, have you not
your poor, your hundreds who depend more or less on you—your
servants and domestic affairs . . . and as appears probable many
children of your own to educate?'

Yes, all that, but Daisy could not just unthinkingly accept her
situation. She would discover herself to be quite unlike others of
her class.

The dazzling social round in which Lady Brooke found herself
caught up palled rather quickly. Yet adulation is pleasant to the
young, especially after a strict upbringing. 'From the beginning
of our life together my husband seemed to accept the inevitability
of my having a train of admirers,' she would write, and Lord
Brooke emerges as a typical English sporting gentleman who
could love his wife and yet care more about his shooting and
fishing than her sidelong glances.

Each year Queen Victoria would command Lord and Lady
Brooke to Windsor for dinner and to spend the night. On one
occasion when it was not possible to get her husband back from
an Irish salmon river in time Daisy had to go alone. However,
she determined to return to Essex next morning in time to go
out hunting, and then to watch one of her horses run in a race.
To the horror of the equerries Lady Brooke desired to rise at
6 A.M. and then drove off to Windsor Station booted and spurred
and wearing her scarlet hunting coat (permitted to a few women
who rode to hounds extremely well). 'Very fast—very fast,' was
Queen Victoria's comment, and she must have sighed with relief

that this particular young woman had not become her daughter-in-law.

For several good reasons Daisy preferred entertaining in her own beloved country home to trailing around to other people's houses. She liked to pick her own guests, order her own meals, enjoy the company of her numerous animals and run her own affairs. During the winter months, when Lord Brooke with valet and loader continued his peregrinations from one famous shoot to another, his wife remained in Essex fox hunting. She rode with dash and skill and imparted a touch of glamour to all she touched. Yet she was a child still—one who had suddenly had this world spread before her, with eager friends cajoling and praising.

During those early years the names of Lord and Lady Charles Beresford often appear in the Easton Lodge visitors' book, and as we have already met my great-uncle Charlie, we can guess the impression he tried to make on an impulsive young woman whose husband was often away. Much older than Daisy, a masculine type, who had made his name in naval combat, Charlie B., as he was known in the service, was bound to catch this girl's imagination. Reared in Ireland, he rode to hounds with boldness and flair. He was experienced in driving a four-in-hand and could instruct Daisy in that art; when her own tandem ponies played up, Charlie's immense paws would close over the little gloved fingers to teach the gentle tugging of each rein so that each horse's mouth received a separate message. The co-ordination, the speed, the slight danger would bring a flush to Daisy's cheeks, a frown to her lovely straight brow and maybe a lip would be bitten in concentration.

The result was inevitable, and Lady Charles's face grew sourer and sourer. Within five years of her marriage little Daisy Maynard, the innocent debutante, the one Queen Victoria had wanted for her delicate hemophiliac son, was gazing with admiration at that splendid reckless sailor who was such a close friend of the Prince of Wales and so difficult for the fair sex to argue with.

During 1884 Lord Charles was away in Egypt organising transport steamers through the Nile cataracts to relieve General Gordon in Khartoum. After the Battle of Abu Klea, at which all the naval officers except Beresford were killed, Charlie nonchalantly agreed with an army comrade that it would indeed 'be hard to die without knowing who had won the Derby.' He then managed to rescue Sir Charles Wilson's advance detachment, left in isolation after Khartoum fell, and this dangerous operation, brilliantly performed under enemy fire, won him the C.B.

In July 1885 the hero returned and Lady Brooke, who like a diligent wife was producing for a third time, gave a celebration with fireworks at Easton Lodge to the amazement of the villagers and delight of the county. Five months later when she bore a son, the Brookes proudly named him Charles. This child died in infancy, and thirteen years would elapse before Daisy had another baby. During that period she would disastrously quarrel with Lady Charles Beresford and drive a deep furrow through the Prince of Wales's heart.

The cause of her troubles lay in Daisy's temperament. She was reckless and tempestuous as well as beautiful; when she fell in love she threw caution to the winds. My grandfather, who had admired her since boyhood, was present on the night when Daisy learned that the forty-year-old Lady Charles Beresford (who had produced one daughter ten years before) was pregnant. As Mina Beresford's virtue could not be doubted, this meant that Charlie, having sworn to be true to Lady Brooke, had embraced his wife. Like an outraged child, Daisy accused him of *infidelity!* Tantrums, tears, smelling salts! Nothing could persuade her that Charlie had not behaved disgracefully. He was *hers!*

In January 1889 Mina Beresford—claiming that her absent husband had requested her to read his mail—opened a letter addressed to him in that well-known flowing hand. Soon after this the Prime Minister, Lord Salisbury, received a furious screed from Lady Charles explaining how she had opened Lady Brooke's letter and saying that in it she read that 'I had no right to have a child by my own husband.'

When Charles returned to London, Mina did not tell him she had intercepted Daisy's letter and placed it in the care of Mr. Lewis, the well-known solicitor. She merely asked her husband to take her to the South of France for 'health's sake.' Maybe she wanted to stir up trouble and a confrontation might do this. Maybe she just wanted to taunt Daisy with her pregnancy. The Beresfords resided only two miles from Lady Brooke's villa. Accounts now differ. Mina said that Daisy chased her husband; Lady Brooke said that Charlie chased *her.* The charm of springtime on the Riviera certainly evaporated, but not until she had returned to London was Daisy notified by solicitor Lewis that he held her most damaging letter.

In the moment of bewilderment and shock, to whom could Lady Brooke turn? As the Prince and Princess of Wales had stayed at Easton Lodge and he had always seemed most affable, she thought that help might lie in that quarter. After all, the Prince was Charlie's great friend and he might be able to retrieve that letter which she now so regretted writing. Flustered, but prettier than ever, Daisy called at Marlborough House and poured out her woes to the Prince. He reacted nobly by driving after midnight to the home of Mr. Lewis, who, flattered by the drama of finding the heir to the throne on his doorstep, took the unprofessional step of showing him the letter. The Prince admitted surprise and shock but resolved to continue his efforts. Calling on Lady Charles, he begged her to surrender the letter. Mina detected his uneasiness and realised her power. Her desire was to destroy Lady Brooke's position in society, and a second call from the Prince further inflamed her. H.R.H. then hinted that if Lady Charles kept this letter he really could not continue to invite her to Marlborough House, and her own position in gay society would be imperilled.

According to her own hysterical letter to Lord Salisbury, Lady Charles now realised the Prince must be 'under the influence of the lady,' for 'he was anything but conciliatory to me . . . still of course, undeterred by these threats, I refused to return the letter for obvious reasons.' H.R.H. had to inform Lady Brooke that he had failed in his mission. Filled with tears, those blue eyes appeared more seductive than ever, and when a lady is in trouble a Prince's shoulder is as good to weep on as any other. Before he had in any way improved the situation, the Prince of Wales found himself deeply in love, not just attracted but genuinely moved with deep emotion, and as she could hardly seek sympathy from the patient Lord Brooke in this dilemma, Daisy began to return his affection.

At this stage of the proceedings Lady Charles was brought to bed of a girl, from which brief happening she arose in wrath to discover that she was indeed being left out of all the best parties. Charlie B. wisely disappeared to command the cruiser *Undaunted*, but before leaving he called on Daisy and to his annoyance found the Prince in her boudoir. A jealous scene resulted. There was an unfortunate push and the Prince sat down heavily and unexpectedly on a sofa. This was lèse-majesté and Charlie knew it. He went off to sea angry with Daisy, Mina, himself and his Prince.

Lady Brooke now found herself in a new situation and could hardly forbear enjoying such complete supremacy over her defender. During the racing season she travelled with the Prince in his special train and sat, looking delicious, in the royal box. H.R.H. started to spend long weekends at Easton Lodge and the great houses were requested always to invite Lord and Lady Brooke when the Prince would be present. It was exceedingly enjoyable and Brookie took it all in good part, for he found it very difficult to be cross with Daisy for long. In fact he told my grandfather that he would rather be married to Daisy, with all her peccadilloes, than to any other woman in the world, however virtuous.

Meanwhile Admiral Lord Charles suffered an avalanche of grumbling letters. Why did he not return to threaten the Prince with reprisals for leaving his wife out of the best parties while Lady Brooke had it all her own way?

In September 1890 there occurred the Tranby Croft disaster and in the following summer H.R.H. had to suffer the humiliation of appearing in the witness box. The Princess of Wales, who stood staunchly by her husband whenever scandal threatened, deliberately invited Lady Brooke to Marlborough House, a proceeding which still further enraged Lady Charles, who wrote more screeds to poor Lord Salisbury about the Prince: 'Having as he thinks shielded himself and his friend behind his wife! he has cast all sense of decorum to the winds and probably prompted by the now victorious lady, who thinks that during Lord Charles' absence I am defenceless—he has now proceeded to boycott me in the most open manner.'

Pained and irritated, Lord Charles sat down in his cabin to write a letter to the Prince which might appease Mina: 'I consider that from the beginning by your unasked interference and subsequent action you have deliberately used your high position to insult a humbler by doing all you can to elevate the person with whom she has had a quarrel.'

This letter he sent not to H.R.H. but to Mina, who sent it on to the Prime Minister with a long ungrammatical splutter of her own. That wise old statesman, instead of forwarding such a missive, strongly counselled restraint.

All might have been well. It looked as if a peaceful termination of this uncomfortable affair was in view, but then Lady Charles's sister circulated an anonymous pamphlet, *Lady River*, which contained in full a copy of Daisy's original letter. So now all London knew that Lord Charles had deceived his lady love with his wife and it found the situation humorous.

But not so the Beresford family. Lord Marcus, who managed the Prince's stud, wrote his brother: 'You bear a name which has hitherto been untarnished and to the glory of which you have been no small contributor. . . . That name, at this moment is in the greatest danger of being dishonoured. . . . This pamphlet is a tangible proof that honour and chivalry—qualities you prized so much, are no longer synonymous with the name of Beresford.'

But Mina continued in her determination both to dethrone Daisy and get herself invited to the entertainments of the Marlborough House set!

When Lord Charles arrived back in England that December, it was to find his wife determined to force the Prince to make Lady Brooke withdraw from court. H.R.H. stoutly refused to allow such a request to be made, but Daisy herself announced that she was perfectly ready to retire to the country.

During all this Charlie behaved extremely badly; the brave fighter could not stand up to his wife's nagging, and it is fairly obvious that, aggrieved at losing Daisy, he was now strongly motivated by sexual jealousy. With great difficulty Lord Salisbury, a Prime Minister who, unlike Disraeli, did not relish social dilemma, managed to prevent a major scandal from breaking, and eventually after Lady Brooke had for some time retreated to Easton Lodge the dangerous letter was returned to her.

What did Lady Brooke care about London society? Where she went the pick of the Prince's set would follow. Now she could entertain privately in her own little kingdom. The most coveted invitations in England were those to house parties at Easton Lodge marked: 'To meet the Prince of Wales.' And her tenants and estate workers—who adored her for her kindness to them—watched goggle-eyed as their own 'Miss Daisy' drove the Prince of Wales up her long avenue.

Easton Lodge house parties were carefully arranged to be amusing. A dozen or so picked guests would arrive, the rooms were full of flowers, the servants hurried delightedly through their preparations, the cook excelled himself. There was so much to do at Easton —riding or driving through the park, hunting or shooting in winter, returning to the long gold and white drawing room for tea, where the ladies would be fluttering like butterflies in gorgeous long-sleeved tea gowns, before the ascent to large chintz-curtained bedrooms each with books specially chosen by the hostess for a quiet hour of reading. Then came the great dress-up in tight-waisted, low-necked gowns for dinner. While in the basement muddy boots and clothes were being cleaned, upstairs the personal maids set diamonds in their ladies' hair. Everyone would be in bed by midnight—the ladies going up first with the candles and lamps to cries of 'Sleep well.' Lady Brooke always warned her visitors that the stableyard bell rang at 6 A.M. It might be useful just to know.

As the Prince came often and the railway station was quite a distance away, Lady Brooke indulged in the supreme extravagance of building a special little station for the royal train. It meant that H.R.H. could reach Easton quicker and the employees so appreciated a full view of the Prince of Wales. Their lady had caught a very big fish and they cheered her for it.

So the years passed—1891 to 1898—and although many stories concerning Daisy are hilarious, none prevent one liking her. Certainly my own grandparents and my great-aunt Olive, who all stayed at Easton Lodge during this period, talked only of Daisy's fascination—'You never saw a more perfect *grande dame* at the head of her dinner table.' And Olive would recount the story of a guest who, lent her favourite hunter, returned blanched at teatime to say he had broken its neck. 'How dreadful for *you*,' was all that Daisy said. Only later, alone with Olive, did she weep.

No one who knew Daisy Brooke could help loving her, even when she did things which my fairly staid relatives thought very naughty indeed. On the other hand, when Charlie and his termagant wife came to stay at Castle Leslie, no one could really like Mina. Mary Leslie nicknamed blustering Charlie the Red Admiral and his wife the Painted Lady, and my father used to swear that one of his earliest recollections was of Lady Charles Beresford peering into his pram and, when he reached up to grab what he thought was a butterfly, one of her eyebrows came off in his hand—a traumatic experience!

Throughout the years in which Daisy dominated the Prince, Lord Brooke acted as the perfect host.

He was a very charming man to meet and a diligent Member of Parliament. Although he had voted against Gladstone's Franchise Bill in 1884, Brooke would understand in time his wife's horror of agricultural misery, and when in December 1888 he was suddenly asked to stand as Conservative candidate for Colchester (the existing member having been killed in the manner appropriate to a country squire while out fox hunting), Brookie and his wonderful Daisy could plunge into the campaign with identical desires—to make things better for everybody!

At this period the Liberal Party was not noticeably more eager to do away with poverty than the Conservatives. Only the radicals fought to pass the ten-hour Working Day Bill and it was in fact individual Conservatives who struggled hardest to help the miners. The December polling day in this by-election dawned foggy and cold, but there was fun to be had, for Lady Brooke was gaily driving voters in a wagonette drawn by four horses. A jolly ride with that lady who could return quips and raise a laugh was as good a reason to vote Conservative as any other. Lord Brooke won the seat with an enormous majority and the Liberals were extremely annoyed. Such canvassing they deemed not quite fair, but Lord Brooke held the seat for many years.

Of course, he had his own interests apart from shooting and fishing. When Elinor Glyn came to live in Essex with her handsome, spendthrift, landowner husband she caused much interest locally and Lady Brooke took to her. The clever novelist would someday etch her neatly: 'No one who ever stayed at Easton ever forgot their hostess, and most of the men fell hopelessly in love with her. In my long life, spent in so many different countries, and during which I have seen most of the beautiful and famous women of the world, from film-stars to Queens, I have never seen one who was so completely fascinating as Daisy Brooke. She would sail in from her own wing, carrying her piping bull-finch, her lovely eyes smiling with the merry innocent expression of a Persian kitten, that has just tangled a ball of silk. Hers was that supreme personal charm which I later described as "It" because it is quite indefinable, and does not depend upon beauty or wit, although she possessed both in the highest degree. She was never jealous or spiteful to other women, and if she liked you she was the truest most understanding friend.'

To Mrs. Glyn's unsophisticated eyes the discreet amours countenanced at Easton Lodge were extremely exciting. 'It might be a lovely lady's own lover who was sitting beside her, but he would never lean on her or touch her arms to accentuate his speech, for all touching in public was taboo.'

In certain instances, however, Elinor Glyn lacked humour. When Lord Brooke made up to her she reported this indignantly to her husband, who merely remarked: 'Did he, by Gad—good old Brookie!' The red-haired, green-eyed siren found his amusement exasperating.

But now the harsh waves of history were lapping around the dream world of Easton. A grave agricultural depression was bringing misery to Essex villagers and despite the fact that they themselves were the kindest of landlords, forgoing rents and dealing generously with the cases of hardship which came their way, both Lord and Lady Brooke were coming to a realisation which reached few of their social status—that a vast world of suffering poor lay around them. Daisy had always felt a creeping unease when she rode back from her long day's hunting, healthily exhausted and exuberant, to see the weary figures who had been toiling in the fields all through her hours of pleasure. These inconvenient thoughts may have come to many others but they put them away. Daisy could not do so—pity and affection for her fellow creatures lay too deep in her warm nature. When she saw a harassed face she cared.

But what could she do about it? Rents could be excused, jellies sent to the sick, blankets to the aged—but this was mere charity. What could a rich woman who understood nothing about business really do to make the world a kinder, juster place? The Prince of Wales when he was alone with 'Beloved little Daisy' noticed her preoccupation. At first he found it yet more endearing, then he began to weary of all this fussing about the poor. Although the Prince had a kind heart and took his duties on the commissions which dealt with poverty extremely seriously, he could not venture into politics and he abhorred the word 'socialist.' There is a nice story of the Prince's hearty handshakes when he met workingmen. In 1889 a blacksmith who met him in a deputation remarked: 'It isn't everybody that education refines as it has him.' Naturally he tried to help Daisy's philanthropic schemes, but he had a lot of official work, and needed relaxation when off duty. Queen Victoria also favoured a leavening of the social structure, but could not impose her views. In 1892 she wrote firmly: 'That division of classes is the *one thing* which is most dangerous and reprehensible, never intended by the law of nature and which the Queen is always labouring to alter. . . .'

Perhaps women have softer hearts than men, certainly they are more aware of physical wretchedness. Racking her brain to discover some positive method of helping those within her immediate range, Lady Brooke organised a room at Easton Lodge where delicate village girls could learn needlework. This scheme proved immediately successful. Royal connections helped, of course. Princess May of Teck (who was to become Queen Mary) ordered her trousseau to be embroidered at Easton, after which it became the 'smart thing' to have thin white cambric lingerie hand-stitched in Lady Brooke's own house. As orders poured in, Daisy bravely rented a shop in Bond Street to deal with the expanding production. The rot of the times is revealed by the fact that her notice board, *Lady Brooke's Depot for the Easton School of Needlework*, aroused mockery and contempt. Underclothes indeed! So the Prince's lady has turned to *trade!* Soon London could hope to see a countess behind the counter.

Her critics could not see that she put heart into unfortunate invalids and invented work for those in difficult situations. Having no business experience, Daisy ran this venture at considerable cost to herself, but many frail girls were enabled to earn reasonable salaries. She was the only person of her class who did a damn thing! She hated subservience and strove to create work that was nothing to do with charity.

Then in 1892 Lady Brooke met W. T. Stead, the progressive editor of *Review of Reviews*, and his idealism and moral fervour stimulated her still further. Stead, an extraordinary character of unbounding energy, completely certain of bettering mankind, had perceived the potential power of the Prince of Wales and was involved in research for a character study. He learned from various sources that 'since the Prince had taken up with Lady Brooke, he had led a much better life. . . .' As the Brookes heavily discouraged gambling and drinking, and as they liked early nights after long days out of doors, there was indeed an improvement in the tone of the Prince's life. Easton Lodge activities may not have been moral but they were healthy.

In 1893 the Earl of Warwick died and Brookie succeeded. Now Daisy could entertain not only in her own home but in splendid old Warwick Castle. She was received with acclamation by tenants and townsfolk, but all the exquisite thirty-one-year-old Countess desired was to become a trustee of the dreaded workhouse! This was a novel position for a woman, but she got herself elected and in 1895 the inmates of that dismal establishment saw the Prince of Wales being led around by a lovely lady who really seemed to *care*. 'I did everything that was within my power to let him know the truth about such places as workhouses and prisons, and I told him all I knew of the lives of the poor he would one day govern.'

The following winter was a cold one and the poor suffered intensely as unemployment increased. In February, after a year of conventional mourning, the new Earl and Countess of Warwick gave a ball for four hundred guests attired in eighteenth-century court dress. Daisy's youngest half sister Angela writes: '. . . As one stood in the old hall, with its coats of arms and the men in armour, looking out across the river, the countryside decked in its glistening white mantle, the rich colours and fantastic costumes of the guests seemed enhanced by the romantic setting.' At midnight, trumpeters in cloth of gold marched through the hall blowing a fanfare to summon the guests to a banquet—minuets, waltzes, champagne—and outside the bleak countryside. But, thought Daisy—and she was incapable of hypocrisy—how lucky for everyone she was giving this ball; it aided employment.

Two weeks later, before her last house guests had departed, the Countess of Warwick, who made a point of ordering radical newspapers, read a harsh attack on herself in the *Clarion*, a Labour journal: '. . . Thousands of pounds spent on a few hours' silly masquerade; men and women strutting before each other's envious eyes, in mad rivalry of wanton dissipation. . . . Other men and women and children the while huddling in their ragged hovels . . .' etc.

Dazed by such a version of her glamorous ball, trembling with indignation at what she felt to be the injustice of these accusations, Lady Warwick took the first train to London. In Fleet Street she searched for the *Clarion* offices and, marching up the stairs, paper in hand, she found the editor, Robert Blatchford, sitting in a dilapidated office. A working-class man, bitter and fiery of temperament, he stared in surprise at the velvet-hatted beauty who swept in furiously demanding, 'How could you be so unfair, so unjust? Our ball has given work to half the county and to dozens of dressmakers besides.'

Her perturbation seemed so genuine that Mr. Blatchford, whose early life had been that of a badly treated brushmaker, found himself conciliating her while seriously explaining his views on the difference between productive and unproductive economics. Dressing up as Marie Antoinette and hanging your medieval hall with silver banners was *unproductive*, making pots and pans and houses and honest bread was *productive*. Daisy, her wonderful blue eyes fixed unblinkingly in concentration, sat through an hour of this. 'During the journey home I thought and thought about all that I had been hearing and learning. I knew my outlook on life could never be the same as before this incident. I reached home just as my wondering guests were going in to dinner, and when I joined the party I made no effort to satisfy curiosity and explain my odd absence. I was as one who had found a new real world.'

Yet what could she do about it all? Things were wrong, but how was Daisy Warwick to put them right?

For a time her busy social life continued. Within a year she had plunged into a defence of the Jameson raid which won her many enemies and the Prince had to help her draft a missive repudiating rumours that she had written an 'impertinent letter' to the Kaiser. Impulsiveness had once again landed her in hot water.

In the summer of 1896 she felt she had finished with London frivolities and 'the infinite fritter and waste and exhaustion of vitality involved in late hours and perpetual greetings in the market place.' Off she went to the peace of Easton Lodge where the woods around the house had been turned into a sanctuary for wild birds and animals, and where she had a little secret pleasure cottage called Stone Hall into which she could retreat with her favourite books—or people!

That winter she planned to help the world towards better things by introducing her moralising editor friend W. T. Stead to the Prince of Wales. There is always a comic element about Daisy's serious endeavours, and in this case she fell on her head while out hunting and had to supervise the all-important meeting while suffering from concussion. Stead asked her what subjects might please the Prince: 'I asked whether we could talk about South African affairs or my proposed character sketch of the Queen, and she said anything I liked.' Then Stead suggested talking about *her*. 'She laughed very much at this and said she had no doubt it would please him as much as anything. . . .'

Stead has himself written up this lunch at 77 South Audley Street: 'Lady Warwick advanced to meet him and made an extremely pretty curtsey, prettier than any I had seen before, then he came forward and shook hands. Then I made a small bow which I felt contrasted badly from the point of view of grace. . . .'

Stead, who was, after all, a terrific radical, and had gone to prison during his efforts to show up child prostitution, felt ill at ease throughout the meal. The Prince talked enthusiastically of Cecil Rhodes, who had greatly impressed him, in fact he had resigned from the Travellers' Club when Rhodes was blackballed. When the two men were left alone for coffee and cigars they could not really link up; they were too different—and yet Daisy could inspire each. When they joined her in the drawing room she was lying down under a quilt, nursing her bruised head. At this sight, Prince and journalist stopped dead. South Africa ceased to be on the agenda. Both men sat imploring her to give up the dangerous sport of fox hunting. 'But I so enjoy it!' She had the guilelessness and the pathos of a child. Men would do anything for her—great matters left their heads and all they knew was concern for an adorable woman. It was her own sex appeal that stymied Daisy's efforts as a world-shaker.

But no more determined lady ever existed. The shortest account of her activities through the next years gives one slight brain fever. As the chatelaine of Warwick Castle she entertained statesmen, temperance workers, trade unionists and the pick of her personal friends. Not only did she open bazaars, clubs and nursing associations, but she visited and reorganised them. She equipped a large house as a crippled children's home, she *invented* careers for women. As Lady Mayoress her Christmas duties at Warwick embraced trees for the workhouse, tenants, employees, postmen, children and school staff culminating in a servants' ball. Then the same programme would take place at Easton. And still she rode to hounds and still she dominated the Prince.

In March 1897 she suffered another bad fall, and to the relief of her friends she went off for a holiday in Paris with her sister Blanche (Lady Algie Gordon Lennox) and her half sister Millie (Duchess of Sutherland). But she continued to read political literature and to correspond with W. T. Stead about converting the Prince of Wales to her own advanced views. The effects of this particular concussion did not last long, for she was soon writing to Mrs. Stead: 'I get on my bicycle and speed away for a time for exercise and all sorts of adventures.' The Lady Warwick was beginning to be considered a dangerous radical, but she insisted on having her political cake and eating it too. When Louisa Devonshire gave the most famous fancy-dress ball of the century Daisy Warwick did not hesitate to wear that glittering Marie Antoinette costume which had made Mr. Blatchford scold. What good could it do the poor to leave it lying in a trunk? Daisy's activities in this year of the Diamond Jubilee, apart from ordinary affairs, include entertaining 2500 schoolchildren and 100 civic guests at Warwick Castle, making over one of her Essex farms to be a technical-agricultural-scientific school, and editing the memoirs of Joseph Arch, a former ploughboy who had become England's most forceful attacker of class.

While Lord Willoughby de Broke and other big landowners, who were coping with the depression in their own ways, wrote indignantly to the press about Lady Warwick's Agricultural Scheme for Women (she was feminist as well as socialist), and Mr. Stead begged her to take some rest apart from that forced on her by tumbles when out hunting, and her relationship with the Prince grew more evenly platonic, Daisy was approaching a period of terrible unhappiness.

Fate can be very unkind. Daisy Warwick would meet the great love of her life when she was thirty-eight, beautiful still but overvoluptuous, and he would be five years younger. It was her bad luck. The ages would matter, not very much, but a little, and had they been reversed she might not have lost him.

A recitation of Lady Warwick's good works would not allow one to expect time off for procreation, but after thirteen years she found that she was going to have a child. The Prince was not jealous. He realised that their affair was over and when she wrote hoping she could keep his friendship and that enemies had not turned the Princess against her, H.R.H. replied: 'My own lovely, little Daisy . . . She really quite forgives and condones the past, as I have corroborated what you wrote about our friendship having been platonic for some years. You could not help, my loved one, writing to me as you did—though it gave me a pang after the letters

I have received from you for nearly nine years! But I think I could read "between the lines" everything you wished to convey. . . . The end of your beautiful letter touched me more than anything—but how could you, my loved one, imagine that I should withdraw my friendship with you? On the contrary I want to befriend you more than ever. . . . Though our interests, as you have said, be apart, still we have the sentimental feeling of affinity which cannot be eradicated by time.'

Daisy could melt icebergs. If she now wished to return to court she would be received by Alexandra. Perhaps it was easier for the Prince to continue his affectionate surveillance because at this time Mrs. Keppel came into his own life—a lady so different from Lady Warwick, so discreet, so restful, so undemanding—the perfect mistress for an aging man.

In March 1898 Lady Warwick, who had not borne a child for thirteen years, gave birth to a son whom she named Maynard. His godfathers were Lord Rosebery and the great Cecil Rhodes, whom Lady Warwick deeply admired and who was able to inflame her mind with his ideas, particularly concerning Anglo-American friendship. By this time there seems hardly a continent or an aspect of social reform in which Daisy had not become interested.

But her heart—how was there time for her heart to be so grievously injured? Major Joseph Laycock, a cavalry officer, was among the richest men in England, owning huge estates in Durham and Nottinghamshire where he was as popular with the miners as he was with the soldiers he commanded. Perhaps I should start with the first description I ever heard of this magnetic gentleman: 'Well, he was the ugliest man I ever saw and the most attractive—ugly in that special way with eyes set very far apart, very lithe and yet very powerfully built and with such *vitality!* And he was such fun to talk to—up to the very end!'

Women who liked extremely masculine men could not resist him. After nine years of training the Prince to good works, Daisy was not looking for romance; it simply came her way and cruelly swept her off her feet.

Laycock—soldier, horseman, yachtsman, natural leader of men—had up to his thirty-fifth year managed to evade marriage, but he placed *a secret wedding ring on the finger of Daisy Warwick.*

After the Beresford experience she probably did not demand fidelity, but whatever she asked in return for her heart, Joe Laycock certainly gave her assurance. He contributed generously to her agricultural schemes and shared her feelings about the intolerable injustice of intense poverty. Lady Warwick's own finances had reached a perilous condition which she did not understand at all. As she had personally financed most of her good ideas her original annual income of £30,000 had in some puzzling way slid down to £6000. Trustees and lawyers got cross when she talked about it. They were so narrow-minded, such humbugs, they couldn't see what really mattered. While she raced from technical instruction committees to councils for workhouses, elementary schools, cripples' homes, financing all her own schemes, Joe Laycock's huge resources now proved a great relief. And how she enjoyed staying quietly at his large rambling house, Wiseton, near Doncaster, where he encouraged her to redesign the garden. Herbaceous borders and rose arbours spring up everywhere with terraces of sweet-smelling hedges—she had such taste!

Less peaceful was the fox-hunting season when Major Laycock was hotly pursued by other women. Among those who hunted with the same pack was intrepid Irish beauty, the Marchioness of Downshire: She had blue eyes like Daisy's and was twelve years younger. On one occasion when news came that Joe had suffered a bad fall and been carried to some house, Kitty D. rode straight cross-country to him, while Daisy, who had come out to watch in her pony trap, had to follow by road. When she reached the house where Major Laycock lay the maid informed her that Lady Downshire was already by his couch and had said that no one else was to be admitted. How angry Lady Warwick was, but she had to drive off.

During the difficult years of the Boer War Daisy worked away in a tangle of philanthropy and entertaining at Warwick Castle. Determined to unite England and America in good feeling, she took to flying the Stars and Stripes above Warwick Castle when American tourists arrived. But the Prince would not be involved, writing evasively: 'I heartily wish for an "Entente Cordiale" with America but during this unfortunate war we must not be drawn in.' So she goaded W. T. Stead: 'I would suggest your going to America to find a millionaire who simply wants a motive given him for spending his hordes . . . stir up a wild ambition in some man of millions to help to found an ideal union between the whole English-speaking race.' After Lord Warwick became Lord Lieutenant for Essex in 1901 Daisy caused consternation by publicly proclaiming her sympathy for the 'brave little Boers.' But she hid her private heartache from the world.

The several hundred letters which Lady Warwick wrote to Joe Laycock and which he left, some of them unopened, in a cupboard in his home, Wiseton, must be touched with reverence. The very dust on the old envelopes seems like tears crystallised. When one opens the little doors of a red velvet frame holding her photograph and notices its decoration, especially made in wrought metal and described in a letter to him—forget-me-nots, rosemary for remembrance and lover's knots—the sentiment does not make one smile. Daisy cares too deeply.

Most of the letters are sealed with red wax and stamped with her personal (not very discreet) signet *'Pensez à moi.'*

There is one early undated note in which her reference to August 12, the sacred date on which grouse shooting starts, amusingly depicts Englishmen. 'I send you this letter, my Joe, by messenger boy as I don't know how posts go about a camp. . . . If you are free from drills in the afternoon (as a Major I suppose you *are* fairly free?) perhaps an afternoon would be possible? I expect you have to be at "mess"—or I could give you a picnic dinner here? Brookie will be back August 6th and off shooting on 12th—but so will Joe— No women exist—wives or mistresses after August 12th.'

On Sunday, May 24, 1901, she writes from Warwick Castle: 'My dear one . . . I know you will forgive me when I tell you that the mere suspicion has clouded all these weeks in London and although I am always surrounded by a crowd I am living in an agony of suspense until I hear from you . . . for *your* sake. . . . Oh say it is not true and that I am a beast to have thought it. . . . I am sick with suspense about you know what . . . but which I won't believe possible till I hear it from *you.* . . . I want you so to see my Easton garden and you will forgive me for doing what we settled we would never do, believe stories we heard of each other. Tonight I've a huge dinner and enclose you a list and a dance after. . . .'

The dinner list for thirty-six included her son and daughter, the German Ambassador, Mrs. Willie James, George and Jennie Cornwallis-West and other well-known personalities.

It was very trying for a woman to have to entertain on this scale while seriously carrying on her work of reform, and at the same time knowing that Major Laycock was getting involved with Lady Downshire. In September that year she tried to reconcile her agitated feelings: 'I am your old love—but I don't think that is a reason to expect you to sacrifice your *own* feelings? If I am *very* pretty (I know you think so!) Lady Downshire is also, perhaps prettier—and we are both so different as women, that it is quite possible you could care for us *both*—only differently? Anyway darling I am not going to be unreasonable and selfish any more. I feel most dreadfully that I did not tell you all this instead of being tiresome and snappy. . . . I will be the truest friend to you that any man ever had.'

She really meant it. She was trying so hard to put the destructive torment of jealousy from her. But it was in a desperate state of mind that Daisy faced her fortieth birthday. Not only had Major Laycock wooed another woman, but he had allowed himself to be caught out by Lord Downshire's detectives—the evidence given by servants would reveal that with extraordinary carelessness he had stayed in Lady Downshire's hunting box and never even bothered to give the appearance of using his own bed. And the usual casket of indiscreet letters would be produced. The major was anything but pleased to be cited as co-respondent and as the Marchioness did not at all wish to be divorced Laycock was employing full-time detectives to watch Downshire in the hope that some dalliance might be observed which could stop the divorce. A long, detailed report written out in careful script by the detective survives among the Laycock papers. The poor man had found all vigils fruitless. Lord Downshire rose early, donned a butcher's cap and smock and then drove a cart around his estate selling mutton to his tenants: there was no sign of any female personage concealed in stables or elsewhere. In fact, as the detective dolefully concludes, his lordship does not seem to evince any interest whatever in the feminine sex.

Daisy was as anxious to stop the divorce as Joe Laycock and Kitty Downshire. She wrote unguardedly: 'Will you give me leave to say what I choose to Lady D? . . . She will refuse to marry you if she understands. . . . Meanwhile great pressure is being put on the D. family. I have every hope. But what is this statement made by them—(my information is through the King) that you have taken all her hunters to Wiseton. . . . Of course I have to deny your seeing her at present. . . . I have sworn that the only evidence Ld. D. has are a few silly letters of yours that can't really make a case if you choose to defend.' Although Lord Downshire's sister had knelt down in the road in front of her brother's pony trap imploring him to spare the family the disgrace of a divorce, his lordship now had that bee in his bonnet and he would not give it up.

Lady Warwick sensed she might lose her battle but she was determined to prevent Joe marrying Lady D. if the divorce went through. In one superb letter she told him that she knew perfectly well that a Mrs. C. had been absolutely furious when she found him in bed with some other lady. Only she, Daisy, could *understand* him and would always forgive.

From Warwick Castle, in the early spring of 1902, Daisy wrote one desperate letter after another. Some of them Joe Laycock did not even open, yet he kept them carefully. It was indeed a strange sensation to slit an envelope containing enclosures which Daisy asked to have returned—notes from King Edward and Charlie Beresford agreeing with her that it would be a pity if Major Laycock married Lady D.! Joe had never opened this letter. It was now seventy years too late to return the enclosures!

'My Joe . . . You know me too well not to realise that while a stone is to be lifted to stay your ill-fated *impossible* marriage, I am not the friend you know I am, if I didn't work for you. . . . It is no courage to sit down and let your lesser nature win; you may have a sensual, drifting, well-fed life with that woman—but "one needs must choose the highest where we see it" as Tennyson says. If our passion has been great so also has been our uplifting.'

No man relishes such effusions—especially not with references to sensuality and drifting. And yet he loved Daisy and admired her for all her works. Now, in the midst of this emotional pandemonium, on top of struggling to help hostels and cottage nursing, she set out to criticise Balfour's new Education Bill and naturally Joe received a draft of her attack—she was rather pleased with it.

'Again an acknowledged great defect in our educational system is that it does not provide means whereby children of the artisans and unskilled labourer class can stay at school over the ages of 13½ and 14. . . . It is disappointing to find that while dealing much with machinery, the Bill says very little about that for which the machinery is intended—Education.'

On reading this Major Laycock hurried to London to tell her how splendid she was—and once again Daisy felt the strength of those arms. The following week her letters expostulate—surely her charms are not purely physical? Is it possible that all these years it has been her mere body that men were after?

Well, of course, men are a rotten lot, and her sister Millie, Duchess of Sutherland, put it all too clearly in a letter (heavily embossed with her ducal coronet): 'Daisy darling, A little line to tell you how much I have been feeling for you these days. Please God the cup is not so bitter for you now but still you must be very low—and I *am* so sorry. Why does a woman lean to the worthless in man! It's an old question and will never be answered. Certain it is the good and worthy we cast away. . . .'

Unfortunately the worthy are not always very attractive. Even Lord Charles Beresford so lacked shame that he was now trying to get back into her favour—telling Lady Wilton that no woman existed for him but Daisy. But no man could exist for her after Joe. Yet she wondered if Charlie might not prove useful in the present battle.

Seeking maybe to arouse Laycock's jealousy, she sent him Charlie's notes. Here is one: 'I am so sorry to hear you are hurt—I meant all I said to Lady Wilton. There is so much wants explaining. I should love to meet you once again. Let me know when you come up to London. I shall be here a bit. Bless you—Charlie.'

But Joe Laycock's jealousy was non-existent. He cared only for sport and adventure. Daisy Warwick had been a great love, but his schooner, his hunting, his shooting and his soldiering meant more. Now she began scolding him for thinking of her lightly, and in her anxiety she grew very earnest: 'The King wrote me today, asking me to be one of his small committee for this ridiculous "Coronation Dinner" for the Poor!' (Edward spent £30,000 on jolly meals for the lower classes.)

On Whitsunday 1902 Daisy wrote from Warwick Castle: 'My dear one . . . I am so tired of the perpetual mischief and lies that you swallow as a lizard does flies—because if anything is said against me, you are glad to have *me* to bully and try to blame, so as to ease your conscience for the way you are treating me. . . . It's so lovely here, and the flowers and blossoms in masses and Tiny One never leaves me. . . . Wilkinson has bought me a lovely pony hack. It is too awful to feel what I have to go through. One pays for love, Joe! Your Daisy. P.S. I hear your sister is with you—you may show her any letters and tell her how I have loved you. D.'

This letter, which contained three stamped envelopes that Joe was to post on to friends if he approved of the contents, had never been opened; it probably felt so heavy and the major may have guessed it contained some scolding. The clean red halfpenny stamps bearing King Edward's head will never know a postmark.

So few of Joe Laycock's letters survive that it is difficult to make out exactly how he was handling the two women who had woven themselves into his life, but certainly he was seeing them both all through the dangerous spring of 1902.

In April the divorce case came up and was reported in detail in *The Times*. In the face of overwhelming evidence no defence had been thought possible, and the judge granted Lord Downshire a decree nisi. Kitty obtained custody of her daughter and the two sons went to that unusual Marquis. It was said in London, 'Greater love hath no woman than this, that she should lay down her coronet for her friend.'

Now Daisy's letters grew ever more incoherent, jumbling up her emotions, her welfare work and her enforced grand entertaining: 'Oh Joe, I wonder sometimes if you have any feeling or heart after *all* that lies between us two? . . . The King asked me to help entertain at Warwick some of the "distinguished foreigners" who come over for the Coronation. So I wrote to Mr. Joe Chamberlain (Colonies), Lord Lansdowne (Foreign Office) and Lord George Hamilton (India Office). I enclose their replies. Mr. Chamberlain's views about Rhodes are interesting.'

During the six months which had to elapse before the divorce became absolute Joe Laycock took to his yacht and his moors, while Lady Warwick, ill with worry, had to endure the London season for her daughter's sake. She attended the Coronation and Lord Rosebery wrote that 'for stately grace and absolute . . . beauty your entrance into the Abbey was next to that of Queen Alexandra.'

Joe's letters reached her by special messenger—often a tired boy whom she ordered to be 'put to bed.' It is hardly surprising that after travelling hundreds of miles to speak on old-age pensions for miners, meeting trade unionists and launching co-operatives, as well as taking her daughter to balls, Lady Warwick's health began to fail and when her doctor diagnosed nervous prostration, anaemia and exhausted brain power she departed for a much-needed cure.

Now an August 31 letter from Lady Downshire slips in. She is obviously far less demanding of Major Laycock: 'Dearest—What fun you seem to be having shooting—I am so glad—you do fly about don't you and it's lucky meeting so many friends.'

A week later, on September 6, Lady Warwick wrote sympathetically: 'My Joe—I love your letters. You are an angel about writing and it does help to make the time pass getting them . . . how I felt for you with that horrid nettlerash and keep on thinking of it and how fussed you must have been. . . . You will have to come "curing" with me another year—

'The post has just brought your letter. You say you will write every day—so you must realise what they mean to me.'

It is impossible to peruse her letters and not to feel for Lady Warwick. She is so genuinely swept away by her own emotions. When reading—'Joe. My Joe—if you could see how my hand shakes when I write your name'—how can one not shake a little in sympathy?

Right up to the end she was playing her cards frantically, and indeed all her friends, including King Edward, were distressed to see the torment Daisy endured. 'October 28 1902. My darling— I have such a rush to get home (to the Guild)—only just to say that the King more than nice to me—agrees about it all—only he says (as *we* do) you *must* go away a bit then "things will be alright" and "a pity a man's life should be ruined" etc. (He is very down on poor Lady D. but that I can *tell you*.) Anyway to my intense relief he accepts the fact that you and I are "friends" to an "unusual degree." I told him that love and all that was done with, that you were a man and a friend in ten thousand—that your advice and help and encouragement in all my work had helped me through these years . . . he will be our "friend" now I know.'

Actually, everyone was 'down on poor Lady D.' She had broken the unwritten law by getting found out. (Many said that this was due to Daisy bringing the Marquess' attention to notes Joe had written, in which case her deceitful act was rebounding on herself.) Whatever the case, the well-brought-up, sensitive Kitty Downshire suffered torments at being divorced and having all the details printed in *The Times*. Joe was far too much of a gentleman not to rue his own thoughtlessness and although he had not contemplated matrimony before, now he determined to re-instate the exquisite Kitty as well as he could. But how was he to break the news to Daisy? He continued delaying tactics even after she wrote: 'If your letter meant that you had chosen *her* and given me up, then leave Scotland, come and tell me so. . . . Your letters are always impossible to grasp.' Not until November 14 did he summon up the courage to spend an evening with Lady Warwick and inform her of his resolution. Despite her 'mad misery,' despite the ring he had placed on *her* finger, six days later he married the Marchioness of Downshire.

The honeymoon started at the Ritz in Paris. After three days a special messenger arrived to say that Lady Warwick had taken an overdose and only the sight of Major Laycock could save her life. Joe hastened back to London, where Daisy greeted him in great form, saying: 'I thought you'd had enough of that!'

Joe accepted recapture. But briefly. He returned to his wife and Daisy upbraided him angrily for forgetting her birthday on December 10—seventeen telegrams had arrived and a diamond and turquoise bracelet from the King, but nothing from the man who mattered.

Joe would go on seeing her, but the bitter fact had to be faced that Kitty was now chatelaine of Wiseton, had *her* hunters in Joe's stable and *her* choice of cretonnes draped the windows—and Daisy had designed rose pergolas for *her* benefit. As a divorced woman Kitty was out of London society, but nevertheless she had secured the most attractive and sought-after man as a husband and he also happened to be extremely rich.

A long letter from Warwick Castle is very Daisy-ish: '23 February 1903 . . . Yesterday in London Maynard said to the King "Mummy and I are going to Sicily to live close to a volcano but" he added "if you like to come with us we will take care the lava does not cover you." Then he sidled quietly to the door and I said,

"Where are you going?" He said: "To tell Nanny about the King."
Can you come to Palermo for a couple of days? Early in April I
join Brookie on the Riviera (where we are buying a villa) and then
to Paris for clothes—I have bought Studeley Castle, a beautiful old
place for my hostel.

'In London the last few days my visitors have been—Arthur Balfour (full of schemes), Lord Rowton (working men's homes), Sir
John Gorst (social work for children), Winston Churchill (to revise
and talk over every line of the speech against Broderick next week),
George Wyndham (full of Ireland—really Joe the settlement of
that question is nearer than ever).

'I have got a little house where my Labour friends and I can meet
and discuss problems under the shadow of Westminster! And a Labour sec: of my own!

'Sir John Gorst mentioned my name in the House of Commons
last Thursday—the *only* woman whose name has been mentioned
as to her work—in the House except Florence Nightingale! I am
also the *only woman* asked to speak at the Guildhall next Friday
when many of the cleverest men in England meet to discuss the
question of the Unemployed. The King comes to see me and writes
to me about innumerable state matters (never love and rot). You
see I need rest for a month before taking on London—Brook House
and a great Cosmopolitan "salon"—I have put all the "Past" away—
and all the "rotten" women and men out of my life for ever—the
scandal-loving cackling hunting lot are but mere acquaintances
(though I had some ripping gallops with the Pytchley this year and
enjoyed them). Queenie rides beautifully and looks so well on her
horse. . . . My last hunt tomorrow and Lord Ribblesdale, Lord
Lovat, Winston, Muriel Wilson are here tonight for it.'

There was no other woman like her—while entertaining the King,
Cecil Rhodes, Prime Minister Arthur Balfour and her Labour friends
she could still gallop across the country, redesign her own gardens
at Easton and (to the embarrassment of her husband, who was now
a popular Lord Lieutenant for Essex) publicly proclaim her sympathy for the Boers—bravest of underdogs.

Then she learned that Mrs. Laycock was expecting a November
baby. She wrote miserably: '. . . I can never describe to you the
strain . . . I have resolutely had to face my work, my life and to
keep all the threads in my hands. I have won—however I don't
choose to lose my health and my looks for any man! But eight
days of work in every week when one is physically weak from an
awful shock has made hunting almost impossible—and I am going
away for a month's cure to Sicily.'

To be too ill to go fox hunting was a tragedy that Joe might comprehend.

The emotional strain was telling and she could not find solace at sister Millie Sutherland's villa outside Palermo. Major Laycock, following her by yacht to the Mediterranean, received a wistful note in Malta: 'I have no one in the world but *you*—I mean in my life— God knows I have enough around and hanging on to me and belonging to me!! . . .'

For a serious social reformer to have to endure all this was intolerable. At the same time she was noting with disgust Sicilian conditions and writing to W. T. Stead: 'Bad government, bad art, bad ideals, an effete and miserable aristocracy, an ignorant, depraved, servile democracy living under conditions no better than animals. . . .' Returning slowly to England via the Riviera for the publication of her excellent book *Warwick Castle and Its Earls*,* she wrote to Joe: 'Cap Martin, 7 April, 1903. I never told you that I worked my best work during the nights at dear Wiseton when you were getting well from your accident. You used to be delivered up to your nurses early and I had that vague miserable instinct that something was between us—And I used to write and write until I was too sleepy to think, and tumble into bed and then in the morning come to you—quiet and cheerful . . . to see you better and to wheel you out in your chair and choose the cretonnes and patterns with you and bask in our garden . . . it was only in the nights that I got anxious and frightened again. . . . How I should love to see you on the Bridge in your oil skins and muddling over your charts and the wind blowing! I am always thinking of you my Joe—with the face I always love to see when you are serious and keen and *thinking. . . . I would sit* in a corner on a "camp stool" or on nothing—just be happy watching you.'

On Easter Monday she wrote ingenuously from the Ritz Hotel in Paris (the *only* place to stay, apparently!): 'I am so ashamed of the frivolous letter I sent you yesterday but I was in a bad "upset" mood and all these silly women, Gladys [de Grey] and Rachel and Georgie [Countess Howe] all thinking life is bounded on one side by Worth & Cartier and on the other by King Edward's court and bridge! . . . I've had letters this morning from my "workers" full of our Labour Education programme . . . John Burns asking me to supper in Battersea to discuss the new Bill for facilitating Land Transfer (awfully interesting) and I've been lazy so long I am going to get back to work, or at least as much as I can do with

* Reviewed by the *Athenaeum* as of 'absorbing interest and genuine value.'

that d—d London season to tackle as well!! My Joe—I can't flirt
and I can't love—and I'm cross with myself for drifting into this
stupid fashionable life here. *You* know I'm not writing this *"en
poseuse."* . . . It is a lovely day and if only you and I could drive
off to the Bois and lunch and talk and laugh again!'

In the following July this was exactly what they did do. Major
Laycock left his wife, who was five months' pregnant, for what he
no doubt regarded as a permissible excursion. A Rumanian valet
was hired for him by Daisy because 'he notices nothing but can
look after *les bagages.*' She envisaged 'mad happy hours in quiet
places' and Joe certainly enjoyed himself, because, unlike Daisy, he
did not dread the inevitable parting. Certainly it never entered his
head he might be behaving badly. Joe Laycock was a law unto himself, he swept magnificently through life, delighting his men friends
and letting the ladies fall for him if they wished, he went where he
pleased and courted as he pleased. Let us remember, however, that
the women he seduced were peeresses of the realm, rich in their
own right, and had already borne heirs for their husbands. He did
not demolish lives, merely hearts.

Soon after returning to England, Joe had another riding accident
at Wiseton which worried Daisy immensely. 'Dr. Fripp rushed in
here this morning when I was not up as he feared I should see the
papers. . . . What horse was it? . . . Oh if only you were not at
home but in London. To be far from you when you are ill is too awful.'

But Joe was tough, he had cracked bones before and he soon recovered. A far more serious happening had occurred. At the age of
forty-one Lady Warwick was expecting a baby. The pathos of her
letters increases. She keeps fainting on political platforms and is certain she is going to die at the birth. Then the Congress of Socialists
would have to get on without her, and those who had treated her
badly would regret it!

In January 1904 her daughter Marjorie (Queenie) married Viscount Helmsley† and she had to organise a big society wedding;
there were fourteen bridesmaids, one thousand guests and, among
the hundreds of presents to be acknowledged, a ruby brooch from
King Edward. Lady Warwick's doctor grew seriously worried as
she struggled with arrangements, and the fact that the bride's mother
was heavily pregnant did not fail to arouse malicious comment.

But she got through it, frailer and paler than anyone had ever
seen her, and it was not until late March that Mercy was born (so
named, Lady Warwick said, from her own exclamation on hearing

† Later 2nd Earl of Feversham. Killed in action 1916.

the news!). Just before the baby's arrival she wrote a letter to Major Laycock which she believed to be her last: '3 a.m. Monday 14th March. I send you a cheerful letter . . . but Joe, Joe, I'm not cheerful . . . I'm writing in night time—the nights are so awful and the time is coming so near and I'm quite alone, Joe. . . . The doctor thinks I will not have strength to keep going on much longer . . . do come and see me Joe. . . . Perhaps Thursday as there isn't much hunting that day?'

Is it possible that this man was *still* thinking of nothing but fox hunting? His own first child had been born five months before, so understandably the novelty of peering into a cradle could have waned, but he might have been a little less callous. A man of action, made to lead in battle, he was a rather young captain in the Boer War and a rather old general in 1914–18, but he would live to see his second son become one of England's greatest soldiers.‡

Now in 1904 he was tiring of romantic drama. Yet he could not quite tear himself away from Daisy until, through what he felt was his own fault, the exquisite Kitty was mutilated in a motor accident. Driving his De Dion-Bouton fast along a straight road near Paris, he overturned the machine and when he tried to lift his wife he saw that her leg had been almost severed. Wrapping her in a rug, he got her back to Paris, where during the operation a hot bottle was allowed to burn her arm badly. When she came to, in the double pain of amputation and burning, Joe Laycock looked down on the lovely woman who had suffered so much for his sake and knew that she was the supreme love of his life. He told her then he would finish with Lady Warwick.

So Daisy lost him. She never got over it. Now only her political activities remained. She worked with frenzy, joining the Social Democratic Federation headed by Hyndman, who preached total transformation of the social system. Not only did she practise what she preached, paying for cripples' schools, women's hostels (the first in history), agricultural training centres for those in misfortune, but

‡ Major General Sir Robert Laycock made his name as a daring leader in Middle East Commandos during World War II. In 1941 after a night raid on Rommel's headquarters in the Western Desert, Bob was missing for forty-one days. The news that he and his sergeant had made their way back on foot across the desert reached his wife Angela first. Overcome by emotion, she telephoned Bob's parents—the unbelievable had happened, he was alive! Joe, who answered the phone, said absolutely nothing, he just passed the receiver to his wife. Later, Kitty explained to her daughter-in-law that Joe had simply not been able to speak, tears were pouring down his cheeks. When Angela recounted this to Bob he said: 'How extraordinary! I never knew that Father cared for me particularly!' This very British story reveals something of the make-up of Daisy Warwick's adored Joe.

she toured the country making enthusiastic, if not always consistent, speeches. To the society she scorned, she was a traitor to her class, to the Miners' Union a heroine.

In early 1905 she visited Paris to meet the leading French Socialist, Jaurès, and that ardent Republican, Clemenceau. Hyndman recorded: 'They were both quite swept off their legs by her beauty (though forty-two, as she constantly tells people, she looks twenty-six).' Her frank *bonne camarade* ways were absolutely natural and the gorgeous clothes and furs she wore when addressing working-men's unions added to her popularity. It would never have entered Lady Warwick's head to 'dress down.' She was simply herself and the Miners' Union greeted her with brass bands and cheers. The workingman does not want dowdy do-gooders to represent him. 'We are having fine meetings with the Countess as a speaker or in the chair,' wrote Hyndman in March 1905. 'There is, of course, a lot of snobbery in this, but what matter? People come to see and hear her who would never come to see or hear you or me.'

The Countess of Warwick, wearing one of those enormous velvet hats, all flowers and ribbons, was an eyeful on any platform and they loved her for the show. Not so the Tory landowners. They thought that as the owner of several thousand acres and two splendid homes Lady Warwick ought to 'know her place.' Even Queen Alexandra, who had rather liked Daisy, wrote sarcastically after the 1906 election (which swept the Liberals into power): 'And what do you think of that charming Lady Warwick mounting a waggon at the corner of the street and addressing her "comrades," the scum of the labourers, and then taking off her glove to shake and feel their horny hands!'

What Daisy Warwick fought hardest for was the feeding of hungry children, and if in assessing her whole life one tries to pick out the time that really matters, the time in which she benefited humanity, then the years 1902 to 1906, years in which she herself was desperately unhappy, are those which win her a laurel crown. When she faced physical misery Lady Warwick became a practical humanitarian. Perhaps she herself did not realise how important and how successful her efforts were at this time. The physical deterioration of the English race had been noticed when recruits signed up during the Boer War and after a government committee estimated that in London alone 122,000 school children were underfed, Sir John Gorst led a campaign pressing for free school meals. Lady Warwick played a large part in the propaganda campaign and accompanied Gorst and a famous children's doctor on a surprise visit to a Lambeth council school where they discovered many boys had had no breakfast whatever, and others had been told not to go home for dinner as there was none. Marching straight to the Lambeth Board of Guardians, Gorst and Lady Warwick and the doctor persuaded them to pass a resolution *immediately* in favour of feeding these actually starving children.

In the *Fortnightly Review* Lady Warwick then wrote a résumé of the evidence assembled and claimed that 'no child should be allowed to fall beneath a certain standard of food and clothing' and that the school age should be raised to sixteen. She could put a case very clearly when she got down to it. 'One looks wistfully for a general recognition of the fact that it is exactly the poorly fed, ill clad, and therefore imperfectly educated children of today who become the ignorant, stupid, slovenly parents of tomorrow.' It was this tremendous two-year campaign which enabled the Liberals to initiate free meals and medical inspection of school children when the party came to power in 1906.

It was in the English middle class that her best-written articles aroused most jeers. In the *Church Socialist Quarterly* she appealed for unity in the struggle against poverty and wrote in the exalted strain so natural to her: 'Let us see that we have grasped the bigger truth that our political economy is only a concrete foundation for a superstructure of the life of the mind, which alone matters.'

Such idealistic statements were not considered suitable for a Countess famed for amorous conquests.

Among her lesser personal schemes was one which linked a desire to help inebriate dropouts with a vast redesigning of the garden at Easton Lodge. It was one of those glorious muddles which, to the amazement of critics, could prove enormously successful. Daisy was always very keen on the Salvation Army, who rescued human dregs from the slums and gutters of the great cities. She asked if she could employ men from their Inebriates' Home to work on the new garden. Wooden huts were built and sixty-seven ex-drunks, criminals and layabouts started to build walls and plant hedges. The men adored her, she had imagination, she wasn't condescending, she had that inbred gift of the natural leader of making them feel that they *mattered*. And when she gave them a Christmas party unhesitatingly Lady Warwick dressed up to the nines for their benefit.

Less successful were her attempts to mould and improve the Socialist Party. But Daisy Warwick in her fabulous gowns, trying so hard to make the world a happier place, will be remembered in human history when the names of her dour opponents are long forgotten.

In her forties, fifties and sixties she was a woman who cared about people being hungry and cold, a woman who loved animals and kept a sanctuary for wild ones as well as filling her house with dogs and birds, a woman who ignored the sneers of conventional society if she could help some unfortunate, a woman who became the toast of the miners and workingmen, a woman no lover could forget.

As eventually her huge fortune was dispersed in philanthropic schemes, she noticed with distress that beloved Easton could not be kept up. Old tenants and pensioners had always been looked after, rents forgotten during hard times. Her heart was easily touched, she never treated anyone coldly. Then Lady Warwick, looking vainly around for funds, considered the immense value of King Edward's love letters. King George V refused to buy them, regarding her offer as blackmail, but Arthur du Cros, an odd scamp with a lot of money, paid her debts and procured the letters, which were suddenly published a few years ago.

I knew her very slightly as a very old lady, but she still had the charm. My brother John Leslie often stayed at Easton Lodge when he was a Cambridge undergraduate and occasionally I went over with him. Lady Warwick still had a rose-petal complexion and wonderful eyes, but she was exceedingly plump. Her clothes were rather marvellous still, although she stoutly refused to wear trapped furs. The gardens were her joy and so were her animals. I remember a number of little circus ponies she kept on the lawns to give them a happy old age. It must have been in 1936 when my brother was twenty that one day at tea he scalded his hand moving the silver kettle. 'It doesn't matter,' he replied to her sympathetic exclamation. 'Oh, but it *does matter*,' she insisted in a voice so deep, so velvety, so full of concern, that to this day he remembers it and says: 'No other woman could have made one feel such a hero—so brave and splendid—for getting burnt at her tea table.'

As Elinor Glyn wrote, she possessed the indefinable quality of 'It.' Let her slip into history as she really was—may future writers try to imagine the guileless blue gaze, the velvety voice, the dignity, the quick compassion of Daisy, Countess of Warwick, who invented the welfare state—and tried to run it out of her own purse!

16

Jennie and the Prince

In writing of past love affairs only hard facts keep the pattern interesting. The fascination dies when invention creeps in. I do not believe that there is a person living who could swear to the physical relationship of Lady Randolph Churchill and the Prince of Wales. We have to guess. She must have told her sister Leonie, for they were as thick as thieves on such topics, but among all of my grandmother's whimsical and very basic revelations she dropped no hints on the ultimate note of this twenty-five-year friendship which began in 1885, when Jennie was thirty-one and the Prince forty-four, and lasted until Edward died in 1910. During all that time the Prince wrote many letters to Jennie, and I think she kept every one, but none begins as those to Lady Warwick do. '*Ma chère amie*' is H.R.H.'s usual form of address to Jennie and although this term can be deemed familiar, no 'darlings' creep in.

I wish I had asked my grandmother more outright questions. She told me so many funny stories without reticence. I can remember her shaking with laughter during one wet day in Ireland when my grandfather (aged over eighty) brought into her room the love letters written to him by certain ladies. He thought he ought to burn them, and he did so, but only after reading them aloud to his wife. This was some years after their golden wedding!

As my grandmother did not reveal more than the quality of Jennie's friendship with the Prince—she spoke of its warmth and how *clever* she was to hold his devotion while ignoring his advice—I honestly believe that one should not make the easy assumption that Jennie (in the term she would have used) ever surrendered herself.

No proof exists of a physical relationship. The likelihood exists that the passionate Jennie and amoral Prince kept their friendship on platonic lines. Of course, it was impossible for Jennie to talk to a man without flirting and using her eyes. Indeed, it was considered rude for a young woman not to affect an air of being a little carried away by the gentleman she conversed with, but it would have been so marvellous for the Prince to discover one immensely attractive human being who did not regard him as just a feather in her cap.

Before speculating further on this subject let us pass a microscope over their relationship from the very beginning, for each meeting is recorded in the Prince's engagement diary and hundreds of notes written by H.R.H. have been kept.

The Jerome sisters were first presented to the Prince and Princess of Wales in August 1873 during Cowes week. As Mrs. Jerome had spent several years at the court of the Emperor Louis Napoleon, it may well have been the Empress Eugénie who arranged for the American girls to make their curtseys. Having been officially presented, their names appeared automatically on a list for an official dance on the cruiser *Ariadne*, given in honour of the Tsarevitch and his Grand Duchess.

When the Misses Jerome were presented the Prince's quick eye must have registered two exceptionally lovely girls—one dark, one fair. If he spoke a word to them, the sisters did not record the fact —and they recorded a great deal.

Some months later, when the Duke and Duchess of Marlborough were trying to dissuade their younger son from making what they considered an unwise, precipitate marriage, the Prince spoke to them in favour of the nineteen-year-old Jennie. When in the following April Lord Randolph Churchill won his battle and went to Paris for his marriage the Prince and Princess of Wales, as was natural when the son of such old friends as the Marlboroughs chose a spouse, sent beautiful wedding presents—a gold Russian *coffre* and a locket of pearls and turquoises. The Prince's private secretary, Francis Knollys, who was a close friend of Randolph, acted as best man.

During the next months, when Lord and Lady Randolph were getting their first house ready in London or staying at Blenheim, the Prince saw little of them, for newlyweds were not expected to appear in public and Jennie was pregnant. She was presented to Queen Victoria at a drawing room, and indeed she did appear at Ascot wearing her lace wedding dress and a bonnet of pink roses, but the stern Tsar Alexander II of Russia snubbed her coldly at the ball given in his honour at Stafford House. '*Et ici déjà!*' exclaimed His Imperial Majesty.

As Jennie could not go out very much, her sister Clara's letters to Mama are chiefly about her own conquests and pretty dresses. On May 22 Randolph delivered his maiden speech in the House of Commons without in any way distinguishing himself, and most of Jennie's letters concern the embroidered baby clothes her mother was sending from Paris. Even Randolph seems obsessed by frilled pillows. Seven months after her wedding Jennie gave birth to a son at Blenheim on November 30—an event which she certainly did not expect so soon and which caused her to be seriously ill. She convalesced in the palace surrounded by the Churchill family until after Christmas.

If every letter and report is scrutinised, it does not seem likely that this baby could have been conceived before marriage. Mrs. Jerome never allowed her daughters to be alone with any man even in their own drawing room. Nor could they go for a walk unless accompanied by a maid. The Victorians were obsessed by sex. They took no chances.

The Duchess of Marlborough, and Randolph's aunt, Lady Camden, sat by Jennie during her accouchement, and the latter wrote a blow-by-blow account to her mother. An American author recently wrote: 'No one ever stated that the baby looked premature,' but a perusal of the letters of those present at the birth shows his to be untrue. The local doctor tried to stop the premature baby arriving, and both mother- and aunt-in-law, grim dragons as they were, obviously took it for granted that Winston was a seven-monther. The first letter to be written to Mrs. Jerome by the somewhat shaken father dotes: 'The boy is wonderfully pretty everybody says, dark eyes and hair and very healthy considering his prematureness.'

There is no way of proving any baby's conception moment unless it is artificially inseminated. Of course, it would be intriguing, in view of the trouble taken by mamas to prevent such occurrences, if one line in any letter intimated that Jennie had been so foolhardy as to slip the leash and ruin her reputation by disappearing with Randolph prior to marriage. But no such intimation exists. At that time it would have been such a *silly* thing to do. The Jerome girls told their descendants they all went to their marriage beds in the state men wished for their wives—ignorant not only of the facts of conception but of the more brutal facts of birth.

When Lady Randolph returned to her own little London house it was to practise the enjoyable role of a young hostess for a husband whose friends were the most amusing men in England. Although not yet wholly immersed in politics, Randolph was already a captivating conversationalist, and he liked to entertain. During Clara's long visits, paid over the next six months, her letters to Mrs. Jerome record: 'I don't know why but people always seem to ask us whenever H.R.H. goes to them. I suppose it is because Jennie is so pretty and you have no idea how charming Randolph can be when *il fait des frais!*' At the Duchess of Westminster's ball the Prince asked Clara for a dance and at Ascot Races the Prince gave his arm to Jennie in the royal enclosure. More flattering still, the Prince invited both sisters to a small 'Pack of Cards' fancy-dress dance to which he only commanded twenty-four ladies outside the royal family. Obviously H.R.H. liked the American sisters, but his engagement diary —written daily in his own hand since boyhood—reveals that he only met them on three occasions between January and October 1875, and there is no suggestion of any kind of an affair with Jennie—although, of course, he might have been toying with the idea in the back of his mind.

To appreciate Edwardian love affairs it is important to pick out the facts and get the perspective. The Prince never paid court to newly married women. It would have been considered bad taste and caused commotion. (His Royal Highness must have learnt *this* lesson in the Mordaunt and Aylesford cases when his innocent but complimentary letters caused so much trouble.) Young wives were expected to keep producing children for their husbands—for the first ten years, anyway.

Nor did H.R.H. lavish jewels on Jennie or anyone else! The Prince and Princess of Wales together sent expensive Christmas presents to their friends. The Prince's important lady friends wore their own family diamonds. On the one occasion that the Prince did see fit to help a lady in distress he merely lent financial backing to Mrs. Langtry's theatrical career. Her jewels were supplied later by American admirers!

Then in October 1875 the Prince left for India and when he returned in the following April the Aylesford scandal had blown up. After this he did not speak to Jennie or Randolph for eight years. So no 'early affair' could have occurred. Obviously the Prince liked the American sisters, but there were only three meetings. No comment was aroused and then came the boycott.

But eight years pass and we come to 1884—an important moment in Jennie's life. Queen Victoria and successive Prime Ministers had long wished to terminate the quarrel between the Prince and Lord Randolph, and on March 9 of this year the Prince finally agreed to meet him at a dinner party in the house of the Attorney General, Sir Henry James, when Mr. and Mrs. Gladstone would be present. All went well and on June 2 H.R.H. again agreed to dine with Sir Henry James. This dinner took place in Paris at the Café Anglais and both Randolph and Jennie were present, together with old Mr. Jerome's friend, the millionaire sportsman J. Gordon Bennett. Jennie was anxious to end the social ostracism which prevented her being invited to the best London parties and she played her cards perfectly. With naturalness and humour she set the company at ease. The Prince was charmed, and Randolph gave her full marks.

But not for another two years did the Prince condescend to enter the Churchills' home, thus making complete forgiveness clear, and when he accepted dinner with Randolph at 2 Connaught Place on May 16, 1886, he felt it incumbent to write to his son Prince George that after this quarrel of ten years' duration he had 'thought it best to be on speaking terms though we can never be the same friends again.'

The Prince was now forty-five years old—fat and short-winded, his health destroyed by gargantuan meals. Jennie was thirty-two and at the height of her beauty, mentally mature and alert. A great deal had happened to her in the last few years. After his spectacular rise to sudden fame, Randolph was now Secretary of State for India, and would soon be Chancellor of the Exchequer and Leader of the House of Commons. Europe expected to see him become the youngest and most exciting of Prime Ministers. At the same time as he soared to the top political flight he had deserted Jennie's bedroom and at this very time (May 1886) she did not yet know the reason. He had contracted syphilis.

Hurt and angry, she had herself fallen passionately in love with the delightful Austrian Count Charles Kinsky. Kinsky had met Jennie in 1883, just before he won the Grand National riding his own horse, Zoedone, and he must have been a real charmer. In photographs we see only a slight man with big eyes and a huge moustache, but we know he was irresistible from private letters and that he danced as well as he rode and that he was sensitive and musical. When Jennie introduced him to an unhappy, thwarted girl, Ethel Smyth, who was to become England's foremost woman composer, Kinsky arranged for her to study music in Vienna. Dame Ethel would write, years later, to my father that she had 'always wished Jennie had married Kinsky because he was so delightful.' In young men Kinsky evoked hero-worship. Jennie could not have found a more vitalising, virile lover to make up for Randolph's neglect. Exactly when they became lovers is not recorded. Jennie was still trying to regain her husband's affections at the time she gave this dinner of final reconciliation. But I suspect—or should I say I sincerely hope—that Kinsky had already become her lover in the full sense of the word and helped atone for her unhappinesses. It was a romance on the great scale and he admitted in old age that Jennie was the supreme love of his life.

So let us imagine Jennie's state of mind at this famous dinner—not only Randolph, but his brother, the outrageous Blandford, who had originally caused all the trouble, were present. She knew herself already on good terms with the Prince because when Winston had been in danger of death from pneumonia two months previously the Prince showed great solicitude, stopping the whole line of a levée to ask after the little boy, and Moreton Frewen had written her how 'glad H.R.H. had been to hear of improvement.' Indeed, the ordeal endured by Winston's anguished parents during the danger days had drawn them together. Randolph's daily letters to Jennie changed from 'My dearest' to 'My darling' during their twelve-year-old son's pulmonary crisis. In these circumstances it was easy for Jennie to show warmth to the Prince when he entered her house for the first time. She was in a truly grateful frame of mind—not just because Mrs. Jerome had written to her to thank God in prayer but because she so dearly loved her child. So all winds were set fair on that May evening in 1886. Blandford and Randolph excelled as raconteurs and the meal progressed successfully. When the electric light failed (worked from a dynamo installed by the scientifically-minded Blandford in the cellar), the hostess was able to make a joke of it. The evening party continued softly by candlelight and when the Prince left her doorstep Jennie knew that she had a genuine friend, although she could not know how soon she would need that friendship.

Now we come to the suspicious events. During the rest of that summer season Lady Randolph Churchill several times received the Prince for luncheon, and *alone*. Many people took it for granted that a physical affair had started. The Prince's daytime excursions were notorious. A woman who lunched alone with him must be ready to expect *anything*. Randolph, like most Tory politicians, lunched at the Carlton Club. At luncheon and at tea wives received whom they pleased—it was not husband-time.

Could an affair *not* have occurred at this juncture? We must remember that Jennie was both fretting over her husband and deeply in love with Kinsky. Did she add the Prince, who was not her type physically although as a man immensely interesting, to her distraught love life? It would have entailed going upstairs after lunch to the drawing room (not, in a private house, to the bedroom) and ordering the footman who had brought coffee to remove the cups and not reappear unless rung for. The feat *could* have taken place—chaises longues and sofas abounded—but oh, the complication of all those clothes! In that famous engagement diary Albert Edward always noted the name of the lady he lunched, dined or supped with, but nothing more.

I have tried in vain to discover the hour at which the Prince's brougham fetched him from Connaught Place. Lunch was at 1:15 P.M., so if H.R.H. did not emerge till 4 P.M. carnal suspicions might be justified. But if he left at 3 P.M.? Hardly time?

The Prince's letters are jolly but uncompromising. During this decade they change from 'My dear Lady Randolph' to '*Ma chère amie*,' but they remain charming, cheerful notes full of jokes we cannot comprehend. Obviously H.R.H. relished her company and they were particularly congenial, but would the undignified bother of a tumble—so simple in smocks in a haystack—have been what either wanted? Could a nervous lady turn the key in her drawing-room door when entertaining the Prince? Servants, chattering excitedly in the basement, would not have entered unless rung for, but the whole arrangement might have been displeasing to Jennie's clear-cut nature, and the Prince was surfeited with sex.

Soon after the reconciliation dinner came a General Election. Lord Salisbury succeeded Gladstone as Prime Minister and, by July, Randolph was Chancellor of the Exchequer and Leader of the House of Commons. Having campaigned for his seat, he had hurried off to Norway and he learnt of the Conservative victory while salmon fishing with his old friend Tom Trafford. Among the silliest legends recently broached concerning Lord Randolph Churchill is one suggesting he had homosexual tendencies and that Trafford was his partner. In fact Randolph and Trafford were both overenthusiastic about the ladies. Tom Trafford, as his family attest, was a gay rake busily dissipating his fortune on wine, women, song, private trains and expensive fishing—and both Churchills, being always short of money, were only too glad to share in the fun. Tom and Randolph kept their mistresses (who were friends, if not relations) in the same apartment in Paris (possibly considered an economy by the future Chancellor of the Exchequer). Trafford's lady presented him with two healthy bastards (a son and daughter whom his family eventually had to educate expensively and launch into the world —but that is another story). Randolph's mistress gave him syphilis.

I have asked a modern venereal disease specialist why Lord Randolph Churchill had to suffer such particularly terrible symptoms from a disease which must have smitten thousands. He said, 'We call syphilis the disease of exceptions. The woman may never have known she carried the germ. In some people it burnt itself out without treatment whereas others tried every available cure in vain.'

I have related the facts concerning Tom Trafford in order to illustrate the ease with which homosexual tendencies can be imagined. Does the keeping of mistresses in the same apartment really point to sexual inversion? Or, for that matter, does salmon fishing in Norway?

Two other fabrications might be dispersed at this point. One is that unattractive fantasy related by the notorious Frank Harris in his pornographic memoirs. This book is full of inventions concerning people who had ordered Harris out of their houses and amongst these is a story that Jennings—Randolph's past political friend—had revealed that Randolph caught syphilis as an undergraduate after being rendered *unconscious* by champagne, from an old hag with *one tooth that wobbled*. Even if the true story of Randolph's tragedy was not available I should have thought that one wobbling tooth proved the authenticity as well as the taste of the story to be doubtful.

The final nonsense concerning Jennie emanated from a recent paragraph about one John Strange Jocelyn, who in 1880 became 5th Earl of Roden. 'He was the kind of man who could climb up the drainpipe to a bedroom window, and did.' The innuendo was then made that Jennie's second son, named John Strange, must have been fathered by him. This revelation, gleefully taken up by the press, dazed both the Roden and Churchill families, who had never heard that their antecedents had been acquainted.

While in 1969 Jack Churchill's three children were woken up in the early hours by long-distance calls from gossip columnists asking what they thought of the idea of Lord Roden as a grandfather, the present Earl of Roden, who lives near us in Northern Ireland, a great-great-nephew of this hitherto unheard-of Don Juan, was interrupted in the midst of giving his views on Ulster's troubles by a journalist who queried: 'And what is your opinion of old Lord Roden shinning up a drainpipe into Lady Randolph Churchill's bedroom?'

Such questionings could not be ignored. Both families, dazed at first, decided to delve carefully and compare findings. The results were hilarious. John Strange Jocelyn, who it had been suggested must be the father of Jennie's second son, was indeed a friend of the Duke of Marlborough, and belonged to his generation and shared his views on the Deceased Sisters Marriage Act. He had been a noteworthy officer in the Crimean War and Lady Airlie's book* told an anecdote concerning John Strange when he was sixteen years old. He and his schoolboy brother had once shinned up a hotel drainpipe to avoid their angry parents. This episode had occurred some years before Jennie was born and no other climb had ever been recorded. Going through John Strange's letters to his father, it became apparent that he was of an unusually religious, even priggish, turn of mind, for when he visited Blenheim he criticised the atmosphere as 'worldly.'

This stolid old soldier was never a friend of Jennie's, nor was he a 'favourite riding partner during her three years in Ireland.' During those years the elderly Colonel John Strange Jocelyn (married to the daughter of Byron's friend Lord Hobhouse, and with a daughter of Jennie's age) was living happily, if dully, in England. The wickedest record about him reveals that he sometimes backed horses and lost.

When, within the month that Jennie bore her second son in Dublin, Colonel Jocelyn inherited the title of Roden and the Irish estate, he *then* came to Ireland and the new baby was named after him in order to please the old Marlboroughs. We all racked our brains to pick more out of these facts, but there really seemed no reason whatever to suppose that the beautiful Jennie should have preferred an old soldier of fifty-six to her lively twenty-eight-year-old husband—even if Roden *had* climbed a drainpipe some years before she was born!

However, as we had all got going on research in depth on this affair we did not drop it. Had the gossip columnists muddled up, perhaps, the worthy old Earl of Roden with the much younger 'Star' Boscowen, 7th Viscount Falmouth? Here, indeed, there might be something to rake over—for Jennie's letters were always full of Star. Had he not sworn when he first set eyes on her that he would never give up the chase, and did not Jennie herself write to Mama that he had 'the loveliest moustache'? One might be tempted to jump to conclusions on discovering that Star *had* indeed been in Ireland at the same time as Jennie, and certainly saw her often when employed as assistant military secretary to the Viceroy.

And then there was Randolph's friend Lord Powerscourt, who lived just outside Dublin and whose Christian name incriminatingly happened also to be John Strange. The biographers ready to

* Mabell, Countess of Airlie, *With the Guards We Shall Go.*

risk brain fever from surmises can have a field day, but the fact remains that, although Jennie was a tremendous flirt and always had admirers in tow, there is no shred of evidence to lead one to suppose that she preferred Star Falmouth or any other man to her attractive young husband during the years in Ireland.

Having dealt with these red herrings, we can return to Jennie at the point at which we left her, November/December 1886, with a frighteningly changed Randolph now Chancellor of the Exchequer, and her beloved Charles Kinsky flitting from one diplomatic post to another but always keeping his London flat, his string of hunters in Leicestershire and his heart for Jennie alone.

When Charles was away she suffered from what she called 'blues.' A letter from Leonie to her other sister, who knew of Jennie's difficulties with Randolph but not the reason for them, seeks to calm poor fussy Clara: 'Randolph is not the least devoted to Gladys de Grey . . . only as she has no flirtation on hand she suddenly notices his coldness. It has been like that for years . . . *Chacun à son goût.*'

Kinsky was out of England when, on December 22, Randolph's ill-timed, inexplicable resignation ended his career. From then on, during the bleak months in which the hope of a triumphant political return dwindled away, the Prince of Wales not only gave Jennie solace but dared to annoy his mother by trying to defend Lord Randolph's indefensible rudeness to the Queen.

During the next years Jennie needed friendship and support, and these the Prince gave her. Whether they were lovers or not, I think H.R.H. can be called her 'best friend.' Kinsky was the man of her heart, the man she burned for, the man who would hurt her.

But whatever actually happened during tête-à-tête lunches between 1886 and 1889, no amorous liaison could have continued after that date. For Daisy Warwick had captured the Prince, was entertaining him in her own citadels, and Jennie Churchill appears as a constant guest. Daisy adored her and wrote: 'One never thought of giving a party without her. She was as delightful to women as to men. . . . Lady Randolph was like a marvellous diamond—a host of facets seemed to sparkle at once.'† Would a woman of Lady Warwick's calibre incessantly invite a rival to her house parties?

When Lord Randolph died in heart-rending circumstances in 1895 the Prince's physician wrote privately to the Churchills' doctors asking for information and the Prince's note of condolence was the first to reach Jennie on that bitter February morning when the

† Countess of Warwick, *Afterthoughts.*

husband who had showed such promise breathed away his agonising life.

Jennie was now forty and free. Kinsky had, two months previously, married under his father's orders. She had lost him whom she 'craved as some people crave opium' and during her five years of widowhood, in which she conducted a series of tumultuous non-platonic affairs, the Prince continued to love, to compliment and to admonish. His letters to '*Ma chère amie*' after Randolph's death are very affectionate and full of jokes we can't quite see, and are signed 'Albert Edward' or 'A.E.,' not the more intimate 'Bertie.' The fact remains that, although Kinsky was now off Jennie's map, Daisy was definitely on the Prince's.

Albert Edward teased Jennie when she rushed away to Egypt to enjoy a serious romance with handsome Major Ramsden—and found him embracing the wife of the army commander. And how the Prince scolded her when she wanted to marry his godson, who was twenty years too young! He was determined to prevent her making a fool of herself, but when, against his advice, she finally had her wedding, King Edward invited her and her much too young husband to Sandringham house parties. Queen Alexandra loved Jennie. Mrs. Keppel, who replaced Lady Warwick, also loved Jennie. The twenty-four-year friendship with the King lasted until his death at nearly seventy. Jennie was then fifty-six. He had given her comfort in time of need and she had given him laughter and loyalty. It was Jennie who could lighten the King's sombre moods and raise a smile when depression hit him. Albert Edward's letters in that neat, exasperatingly difficult-to-read hand contain no indiscreet amorous references. The tone remains intimate and affectionate and amused, but the most eye-aching perusal must leave historians guessing as to what actually happened on the chaise longue.

17

*Arthur of Connaught and
'Beloved Leo'*

FROM JENNIE, we move to the romance of her sister, my grandmother Leonie, and Prince Arthur, Duke of Connaught, who was
Queen Victoria's third and favourite son. As their friendship lasted
over forty years, and the Duke wrote to her almost every day,
plenty of documentation exists, but I have not been granted permission to quote from any of these letters, which all begin 'Beloved
Leo' or 'Dearest One,' and are signed 'Arthur' or 'Pat.' Several hundred of the Duke's letters in boxes were handed by Leonie's son
Seymour to King George VI, who placed them under seal until
1993 in the Windsor archives. But a dozen or so of the intimate
postscripts were left by my grandmother in her desk, as were a few
particularly interesting letters, on heavy grey paper embossed with
crowns.

It is difficult to write without bias about a person one has loved,
and I have to *try* to visualise Leonie as she was before the searing
pain of World War I. When she entered London society as the chic,
graceful but not particularly pretty younger sister of a famous
beauty she had to overcome her own sensitivity to comparison. She
was far too intelligent not to register the flickers of fleeting surprise, sometimes of disappointment, that the gorgeous Jennie had
been followed by this elegant, lively but ordinary-looking chick.

Incapable of jealousy, Leonie determined to develop her own assets to perfection. She played the piano as well as her sister, excelling at Chopin, whereas Jennie liked to pound out more tempestuous feelings in Beethoven sonatas, and she had the quickest wit of her generation. But apart from her music and her *joie de vivre*, Leonie possessed an extraordinary talent for touching the emotional chords in human beings. She wanted people to like her—not an unusual trait —but she also understood the shy and the hopeful. She was genuinely interested in others, and as she grew older her sympathy and wisdom increased. Of course she was pleasure-loving—no one in that worldly throng enjoyed parties and dancing more—and she deliberately made herself the most desirable of guests, but intimates clung to her because of a unique charm which she dispensed in private and which held people of every kind in her thrall.

I have one letter written from Blenheim Palace in 1880 when she was an unmarried girl of twenty-one. She seems so callow and unsophisticated, describing with inordinate enthusiasm the telegram which arrived asking the Marlboroughs to send her to stay for a hunt ball. 'It was 12 o'clock. I packed and started by the 1 o'clock train—a long journey cross-country—having to change 5 times! I arrived safely at 7:30 at Melton Mowbray (Nothing but the name is fascinating!) Marie and I drove to Mrs. A's Wicklow Lodge and found her dressing for dinner.' Marie was, of course, the Jerome girls' French maid, without whom they would find it exceedingly difficult to prepare for a ball. In twelve closely written pages Leonie artlessly describes several of the personages of this book, but even then she finds the most charming companion is a certain Sir John: 'Besides being good-looking and agreeable he can talk on any subject—music etc.' I try to visualise my grandmother at this her first hunt ball—a starry-eyed mouse who had changed trains five times and was ready to dance till dawn: '. . . and it was broad daylight when we arrived home.' It is difficult to imagine that she was ever shy, but this evening seems to have given her self-confidence. She danced the cotillion with Bay Middleton, the famous horseman who led the Empress Elizabeth out hunting: 'It amuses me that they should consider me such a good dancer. I really think I must have improved. Bay said: "Well, it's not often one meets such a 'good mover' as you!"'

The statuesque Gladys de Grey she met as 'Lady Lonsdale—who is much handsomer than her photos, quite a queen! . . . her hair is brown and her eyes so soft—and her colouring so exquisite. Of course Lukie White was very devoted.' Leonie, agog, watched a young hoyden call Lady Florence Dixie: 'What a creature! As we came into the ballroom they were starting a quadrille—Lady Florence and Bay opposite to Lady Lonsdale and some man. . . . As she passed Lady Lonsdale she said, "Why can't I be as tall as you?" and gave a spring—jumping way up in the air and coming down with a bang—What a fright and such dressing—White tulle, black slippers—black gloves! Bay turned round and said to me—"Can't keep this little boy in order. Don't be shocked!"'

Mrs. Ronalds, formerly the flame of Leonie's father Mr. Jerome, now courted by the Duke of Edinburgh, was there: 'She nearly threw her arms around my neck and was very much astonished at "little Leonie" having grown up etc.' Then we have a brief vision of the plump debutante Miss Daisy Maynard, in charge of her mama Lady Rosslyn, who sat just in front of Charlie Fitzwilliam watching the cotillion: '. . . He saw his slippers were dusty, so putting his foot one side of the chair he caught hold of what he thought was the portiere and began wiping them. But the portiere turned out to be Lady Rosslyn's best frock! and she was furious. . . . It was such fun! I never enjoyed myself so much in my life! All those pink coats did look so jolly and everyone was so civil. I wore my white jet and looked my best, but for all that I can't account for my "success" as in New York I am so often a wallflower.'

During the next four years she would be wooed by the Hon. Charles Fitzwilliam, the unfortunate foot-wiper, in England, and rich Freddy Gebhard in America. Not until September 1884 did she marry her devoted young Grenadier officer John Leslie.

In that hard London amoral society into which she stepped as an American bride of twenty-five Leonie suffered a certain timidity due partly to the stern indoctrinations of a Puritan mama, but, of course, men did pay court to her. After three sons had been born within five years they probably thought it was time for the traditional fling, but whether she really lost her heart—she who had more heart than any woman I've ever known—I cannot be sure. I know only that there were hopeful marauders and that she was naturally attracted by the musical and poetical. Sometimes she would mention a gentleman's name and laughingly say to me: 'He used to make up to me, and he took it very badly when I said no.'

Mulling through the memoirs of the Italian Duchess of Sermoneta, I find Vittoria trying to record how much Leonie meant to her, and there comes a paragraph which must have hurt my grandmother had she come across it. Vittoria di Sermoneta was describing one of Gladys de Grey's famous musical evenings when Melba was to sing: 'I motored down to Combe with my dear Leonie Leslie. It was a delightful gathering, for Lady de Grey somehow managed to invite wives without their husbands and husbands without their wives, picking out the better of the two in each couple.'

Poor Leonie! She tried so hard to make her dear kind soldier husband feel that he was just as amusing as she was, that they were invited to the interesting house parties for his sake, not hers; the implication that Gladys de Grey (that scamp!) had chosen to leave him out would have hurt *her* feelings far more than his. To tell the truth, my grandfather could not bring himself to speak to the Letter Thief, but as Leonie took that affair more lightly and genuinely liked the musical Gladys, he would in his gentlemanly way assure her that he particularly wanted to dine at his club that evening and that she must feel free to go. That was how things were between Jack Leslie and his wife.

It was in the mid-nineties, when they had been married for about ten years, that my grandfather, who had served in the Guards Brigade under the Duke of Connaught, introduced the vivacious Leonie to his former commanding officer. H.R.H. immediately fell under her spell and remained so until 1942, when he died aged ninety-two. The Duke was a keen professional soldier, and the year 1895 contained a bitter disappointment, for he had hoped to succeed the old Duke of Cambridge as Commander in Chief. This depended on the possibility of Lord Wolseley preferring to go as Ambassador to Berlin. Unfortunately for Arthur of Connaught, Wolseley agreed to accept the army command.

So my grandmother entered the Duke's life at a moment when he felt the star of fortune turned harshly. Being a susceptible male, Arthur knew his heart shaken; and being a shy German princess, the Duchess reached out for the gaiety which the American radiated. As Princess Margaret Louise of Prussia, the daughter of estranged parents, the Duchess of Connaught had known a tormented childhood, hating and fearing her sadistic father, who punished his children by bending back their fingernails and digging his own into the quicks. When she arrived in England as a nervous prospective bride for Prince Arthur he had driven his fiancée down to Windsor *unchaperoned*, in an open carriage. This greatly shocked Queen Victoria, whose astringent pen later noted: '. . . young, shy, not a beauty.' The knowledge of her own failings froze the little Princess into a rigidity which in turn froze other people. With my grandmother this tenseness melted away. Leonie was the first warm, zestful human being who had ever approached the Connaughts. For decades she 'ruled the Duchess and ran the Duke.' It was a curious dependency, the happiest of triangles—or perhaps, thinking of Jack Leslie, of quadrangles. The key to this utopian emotional realm was my grandmother's gift for helping people to deal with themselves. The exact words of the Duchess of Connaught to a younger member of the royal family were: 'Arthur and I never had any *fun* until we met Leonie.'

How did such a situation come about? Lesser royalties, left out of the frolics of the self-admiring Marlborough House set, led a dull existence. The arrogant and amusing aristocrats did not trouble to build up house parties to entertain 'domesticated royals,' whose presence in a country house meant so much standing about, and that no one could slip out of the room if they had tummy-ache. It was exciting to have the Prince of Wales to stay. There would be goings-on. But minor royalties meant bother without glamour. Although tall, handsome Prince Arthur had what was called 'a perfect condescension,' he and his self-effacing, literary-minded spouse were outside the range of those great hostesses who were vying to receive the Prince and Princess of Wales.

It was quite a feat on the part of Leonie Leslie to open up an escape route into 'amusing society' from military duties and the opening of bazaars and asylums. Having no big house or large fortune, Leonie could not herself act as a great hostess; she belonged to the Prince's set only because of what she could contribute, she always made things go and in her company other human beings shone. She was thought the wittiest woman in London, yet her sayings go unrecorded. Her wit lay in the power of creating quick laughter. This kind of wit is as impossible to catch as the froth of champagne. Prince Arthur, the dedicated soldier, had been considered heavy, but now he began to show his natural polish, and eventually Lady Cynthia Asquith would assess him as 'the only gentleman royalty with manners and presence.' Leonie was a wonderful dancer, the best of the three Jerome sisters, who all waltzed like birds: the Duke said he never realised that he himself could dance well until he took the floor with her. Meanwhile Margaret Louise began to blossom in this warm atmosphere. Some poor, frightened princesses had to carry their inability to communicate into old age, but Leonie, said the Duchess, could hand you a key to unlock your own shell. It really was an extraordinary set-up, with the shy Duchess looking on, seeing it all, and only wanting to be cared for and understood.

Of course Prince Arthur was in love with Leonie—half London was. But would it have suited her clear-cut, analytical temperament to be the mistress of a man whose wife called her best friend? And would her magic touch have lasted for nearly fifty years if there had been in the relationship a strain which she or he considered wrong?

Many other Edwardian affairs, platonic and non-platonic, lasted through the years just because of this sense of balance. The surmise of columnists did not exist. Occasionally, resentful servants might write a little scandal for *Tit-bits*, but such publications were not taken seriously. The servants who really knew secrets enjoyed them in pleasurable silence. I think that my grandmother's bond with the Duke of Connaught is the most perfect demonstration of any Edwardian friendship—but maybe this is just because I know the details.

Leonie's albums, stuck away under sofas at Castle Leslie, contain photographs of her 1898 house parties—she and my grandfather and Harry Cust, and Violet, the artistic Duchess of Rutland whom he so admired, and the Duke and Duchess of Connaught and the sculptor John Tweed and Lord and Lady Antrim and a Baroness de Meyer (lightly pencilled under this name is 'daughter of Edward VII').* All are staying with the Ernest Becketts in hot June weather after Ascot. The gentlemen wear informal jackets and panama hats; the ladies, sitting around in wickerwork garden chairs under lovely old trees, wear light-coloured skirts, blouses with ballooning sleeves, and huge decorated hats. Further examination reveals thick-soled, laced walking shoes. This was correct country attire for a heat wave. Colossal frilled hats placed on high-piled hair showed you were a lady, stout shoes that you were a sport. No one ever ran barefooted or jumped into the lake for a swim.

Four years later we have a page of very clear indoor photographs taken in Dublin when the Duke was Commander in Chief. The Duchess reads in her chintz-covered sitting room, surrounded by bookcases, H.R.H. and Leonie sit on a settee in front of a mantelpiece that is draped in flounced material covered with knickknacks. They gaze at each other serenely. The backgrounds of these photographs are fascinating—for objects abound. Around 1899 Leonie started to take photographs with her own Kodak. She showed a quick eye for a situation but not much versatility with the lens. Her first photograph of nephew Jack Churchill boating is taken from an original angle.

In the discipline of their long correspondence the Duke and Leonie arranged that each ordinary letter should have inserted into it a *private* postscript to be removed if the main missive was to be

---

* She was Edward's goddaughter and sat in his private box at the Coronation. Her mother was the lovely Duchess di Caracciolo.

shown, or placed in the boxes deemed suitable for royal correspondence.

The Duke signed some of his letters 'Arthur' or 'A.,' but in most
he uses the nickname Pat, which seems to have been a joke between
them since Irish days. In them he expresses again and again his
loneliness and his longing for that 'beloved black head.' In the early
years the *amie adorée* is begged not to make him miserable by slipping away from London when he is there. Then later, when the
Duke becomes Commander in Chief in Ireland and it is easier for
him to see her often, the tone becomes calmer. The Leslies naturally paid frequent visits to the Connaughts' residence in Dublin,
and in summertime the Duke rented Castle Blaney, a large country
house seventeen miles from Castle Leslie, so the *va et vien* could be
continuous. Gazing at the photo albums, one wonders how Leonie
dealt with the emotional situation during these particular years
when H.R.H. was so eager to overstep the boundary of devoted
friendship. How did she manage to keep his adoration and the love
of the Duchess without hurting either? Was it because she was incapable of hypocrisy? How could a woman give so much to two
people in different ways and break nothing?

The eight or nine visits the Connaughts paid to Castle Leslie and
to our shooting box in County Donegal greatly diverted the ghillies
and gamekeepers, while the indoor staff took to hysterics or drink.
Occasionally Arthur came alone.

My father described the first royal visit when the Duke arrived
at Glaslough Station, delighted by porters who had insisted on
changing the foot warmers (large stone jars), although they had no
hot water. The warm ones were removed and new cold ones put in.
They felt it was not every day that the King's brother passed
through Clones Junction and when he did so orders *must* be
obeyed.

Poor old Sammy Adams, our butler, harassed by two large-
footed, country-bred footmen, demanded 'trained reinforcements,'
so a wire was sent to Belfast for the 'best waiter.' A hotel professional arrived in a state of alcoholic euphoria, and while serving at
lunch kept joining in the conversation, whispering to the Duke,
'Loyal Portadown is still keeping the blinds down for Your Royal
'Ighness' ma.' When the dessert arrived, a light soufflé, the pride of
the cook, he handed it to the Duchess with 'Your Royal 'Ighness—
will you try the puff?' Then he gave a terrific sneeze, blowing
away all remains from the dish.

Mr. Sammy Adams dolefully steered this aide from the dining
room. He was escorted zigzagging to the next train with a week's

salary in his pocket and happy if muzzy memories, material for many an anecdote concerning his services to royalty when back in 'auld Belfast.'

During the shooting season the Duke would be led out with his gun. When there was no shooting he entertained himself with a pot of white paint and a large brush marking trees he thought should be cut out to improve the view of the lake.

Indoors, strict discipline was enforced during royal visits, and this did not amuse Leonie's offspring whom she instructed sternly: 'Never sit down while *they* stand; never start the conversation; never change the subject; never ask a question—and don't touch the Bar-le-Duc jam!'

Seymour, when a teen-ager, was allowed to accompany the Duke on an inspection of the big military camp in Donegal. There was no need of security precautions in those days, and as the train passed each station it slowed down to walking pace to exchange the single-line iron 'staff' held out by a stationmaster standing rigidly to attention, chest inflated with his own importance. The next Liberal government was going to give them back the Dublin government which George III had taken away. Bitterness would soon fade away. So Irishmen believed in 1902.

What Leonie's sons did not suspect was the tension of the 'grownups' at this time. Only one letter of my grandmother's survives among the Duke's 'private postscripts' in her desk, either a draft or a note which she forgot to send. Undated, written on her embossed 10 Great Cumberland Place note paper, it explains their special method of communicating on intimate matters:

> I am so sorry *mon Bon Ami*, that there was no letter from me to welcome you back to Dublin Tuesday—but your Sunday letter did not reach me till a day late—and I did not like to write, not knowing for certain when you returned—I was glad to hear again from you yesterday—I like to know what you do each day and who you see—what you think—and who you like! Your letter is the event of the day, as I am very quiet here—just alone with the children and my thoughts—I think a great deal and shall never be able to tell you all I think. The Duchess has written me a most kind letter—and I hope I shall always be worthy of her friendship. I can't help writing postscripts. I like to feel I can speak *à cœur ouvert*—it is like shutting the door and having a quiet talk—instead of trying to make conversation before inquisitive onlookers! I found these lines which I think you will like—
>
> > *Le Bonheur—Etre seul avec toi porte chose,*
> > *Bien loin du bruit et des gens ennuyeux,*

Et rester là—tous deux ensembles, très joyeux,
Mais graves, dans un calme absolu, qui repose.
Nous écoutons en nous un rhythme qui ressemble
Au double battement d'aile d'un même oiseau—
Etre ensemble—oublier même qu'on est ensemble.

Will you write again *soon*—Best of friends,

Votre amie, L.

Out of the hundreds of letters she received and placed in tin boxes a dozen of the Duke's intimate postscripts survive in her desk. These give the 'feeling' of the relationship. The Duke misses her terribly. The joy of his life is gone when she is not there. She has taught him not to be cross and to try to make others happy even when he is sad himself. He cannot resist unburdening his heart to the beloved friend. He owes her so much.

Leonie was, in fact, always a peacemaker. The Duke did not get on with his elder brother and through Jennie she sought to improve the relationship. On February 4, 1902, Jennie wrote her from Invercauld: 'The King came over yesterday for a deer drive and got a stag. The day before I went to Balmoral and spent two hours with him, we walked all over the house and the place. He talked about you. Also of the Duke of Connaught but not very kindly—I suppose really that he and the Duke are not on the best of terms.'

The most unusual aspect of the friendship is revealed in letters from the Duchess of Connaught in the autumn of 1902 after a visit to Castle Leslie. The Duke had, during the last four years, been suffering from a great romantic passion which must have been a severe strain on a man with high ideals of honour and duty, but when Leonie had intimated that she believed she ought to fold up her tent Arab fashion and slip over the horizon he fell into despair. From the Curragh Camp on September 7 the Duchess wrote a letter that touches the heartstrings, saying that she had started and then torn up two letters in the desire to express herself clearly, that she was happy and grateful that Leonie cared for her, that she admired her power of self-denial, and missed her because she gave so much happiness. Then in a very long, very affectionate letter, Margaret Louise asked Leonie *not to fold up her tent*—the very idea had made the Duke miserable and although it sometimes seemed difficult to know how to *steer* for the right goal she had but to touch the chord of honour with the Duke and all was well. Margaret Louise (who signed her letters 'Your ever grateful and affec. L.') felt that it was perhaps easier to write than to speak; with a humble sweetness she said that she so understood dearest Leonie caring more for Arthur than herself, that she knew she still counted for something and was not put aside and that she would rather give up her life at once than lose him.

Then she went on to encourage Leonie in her piano concerts for charity (which always made her feel nervous), and sent her a little book, *The Roadmender*, 'specially bound with the Wagner motif† on its cover.' It was not only the Duke but the royal Duchess who rejoiced that they would shortly meet at Glenveagh Castle (in County Donegal where the American hostess Mrs. Adair had created a deer forest for snob stalking parties), at Blenheim and at Lord Desborough's Panshanger.

How beautifully these two women, the quiet German Princess and the sparkling American, steered their way around the perilous depths of love. Could any tribute from a wife be more striking than praise for self-control and high spirits, the wish that a third party could 'always be with us' and a sharing of the desire that 'the vulgar world' should not pry into a friendship it could not understand?

The Duchess chose the word 'steer' and it could hardly be bettered. The result of this delicate navigation was that Leonie and her husband accompanied the Connaughts to India when the Duke went to represent King Edward at the Durbar. On the journey out H.R.H. laid the last stone of the Aswan Dam, which entailed a week on the Nile where Leonie kept an eye on her nephew Winston, who, having been crossed in love over Pamela Plowden, was pouting on a donkey around the ruins of Luxor. A piano stood in the royal sitting room and Leonie could keep her fingers in trim with nocturnes when the moon silvered the great river. Incidentally, the Jerome sisters believed in reincarnation. Leonie wrote to Jennie: '. . . I thought of you when I saw the Sphynx—because you had been impressed by it—it *does* give one a strange, weird feeling.' Like so many other people, Leonie felt she had seen Egypt before—but unlike those who half remember themselves as pharaohs or priestesses, she felt that she had been a cruelly treated slave girl.

From H.M.S. *Renown* in the Red Sea she wrote her sister: 'The climate agrees with the Duke who looks ten years younger, is full of energy and too kind and amiable for words. The Duchess and I read a good deal together.' It was not only the climate that agreed with Prince Arthur—it was the presence of 'Beloved Leo.'

The Durbar of 1903 cost £5,000,000. From the Viceroy's Camp outside Delhi, Leonie posted Jennie detailed descriptions: 'The Curzons meeting trains at the station and all mounting their ele-

---

† Leonie took as her motif the 'Birdsong' from *Siegfried* and often signed her name in visitors' books over these few bars of music.

phants there and proceeding through the town. . . . There seems great enthusiasm whenever the "King Emperor's" name is mentioned. They make a kind of religion of their loyalty. We ride in the mornings and see the native camps—the mass of retinue is something marvellous—the lower classes are hardly human beings —they are so numerous—live on nothing—move about silently— and timidly. . . . The back view of the elephants at the processions reminded me of Madame Hirsch [wife of the King's financial adviser].'

All the princes of India were assembled in the great horseshoe-shaped arena, waiting for Curzon to open the proceedings of state, when a fox terrier belonging to a bandsman in a Highland regiment ran up the dais steps and jumped onto the Viceroy's throne where it sat barking. In England this incident would have aroused delighted applause, but Indians do not think dogs sweet. The native princes registered horror and feared a bad omen. (No Indian could have believed that little Queen Victoria's first act after her long exhausting Coronation had been to run upstairs to give her spaniel a bath, and that her last words in 1901 concerned the pet dog on her bed.)

An Indian wrote of this Durbar: 'The Duke of Connaught had good manners with the Indian princes; in this a great contrast with the others.' The same comment had arisen during the Prince of Wales's tour thirty years before. Princes have better manners than army officers—they are schooled that way.

The Durbar extended to the Western Frontier and on January 23, 1903, Leonie saw the Khyber Pass: 'Here we are in the heart of central India—miles away from any town—camp pitched in the middle of a jungle. . . . We each have a tent and then dine in the Duke's big tent—the luggage arrived by elephant five hours after us.'

There were still vast areas of jungle in India where tigers roamed, and to Edwardian minds wild animals were created to be shot. For ten days the men went out each morning to mount elephants which carried them to little stands built in trees. Leonie loved the jungle, 'beautiful in the evening light—weird trees and huge leaves and orchids hanging from the branches—no sound except elephants' heavy tread on cracking dead leaves.'

Today's tourists can pay to ride elephants through the cities of impecunious maharajas, but the jungle has receded to a few patches, so Leonie's description is of a vanished nature world, and I like her line on the magnificent dead tiger carried away on a litter of branches, 'like the swan in Parsifal.'

After the Durbar the Duke became Inspector General of the British Forces. In London he lived in Clarence House, St. James's, whence he wrote Leonie a daily note, as well as sending long meticulous letters when on his travels. It was the intimacy and the knowledge that she was absolutely trusted which my grandmother loved.

Despite the formality so necessary to the dignity of a long close friendship, the Duke was so dependent on her for advice that occasionally he dropped in to tea without warning. This was, however, a most unusual happening. She sometimes described one unfortunate occasion when tea had been cleared away and, settling down on her drawing-room sofa alone with a book, she unlaced the tight waist of her dress. The doorbell rang, steps sounded and the footman announced the unexpected royal caller, 'His Royal Highness. . . .' Granny was caught most embarrassingly. Not for worlds would she have dreamt of explaining her physical predicament—years of devotion did not alter the proprieties. Years later she would enact the way she half rose, half curtseyed, secretly trying to do up hooks with one hand while murmuring: 'How nice to see you, sir!'

Worse then followed. The five-year-old Lionel had slipped into the room with his new drum—it was Nurse's day off—and there he stood behind the Duke, beating a tattoo while Prince Arthur tried to confide the news which had caused him to call without warning. She could give a most comic rendering of her efforts to appear attentive while trying to lure her small son within range: 'Gracious, sir! How tiresome, sir! Now come to Mama and give her that lovely drum. . . . Do be a good boy. . . . Do you mind ringing the bell, sir . . . ?'

And then suddenly the lights went out. Her son Seymour, that delicate teen-ager, now intent on becoming an electrical engineer, had blown the house fuses. Taking advantage of the darkness, she slipped to the door, rang for candles and managed to retreat upstairs backwards while still assuring the Duke of her sympathy in the predicament of the day.

The 1904 letters from the Duchess of Connaught continue to tell Leonie how much good she does her, that to be with her is reposeful and a joy, and one letter thanks her for a 'golden hour spent with you this afternoon.'

Now, after all these years of what one might call deep bondage, the royal wife ends: 'Bless you dearest for all you are to me. Your devoted L.'

Since I started this book several people have said to me: 'Your grandmother was the greatest of the Edwardians,' and I think this may be true, for, although I myself regard Lady Warwick as the most complete Edwardian, she did not maintain the tradition of discretion, she danced outside the pale, whereas my grandmother remained within it. The several hundred letters which Leonie's son returned to George VI give a detailed picture of ordinary royal life —from them the future historian may learn of the parades, receptions, coughs, colds, sneezes, sorrows and jokes of forty years. Many of them bear no stamp, for during the London season a liveried footman rang the doorbell and presented a note by hand every day. This attention my grandmother greatly appreciated. It made her feel so important, so trusted, so near to the wheels which ran the Empire. She once said to me: 'If ever you care for someone write them a note every day—even if it is just one line.'

Another instruction handed out when we entered society was: 'Never mention illness, money, children or servants—subjects which kill conversation.' Leonie's contemporaries called her worldly, but I think she knew about more worlds than one. Certainly she managed to touch the Connaughts' lives with magic. Ten years passed, twenty years, thirty, forty—and it was never necessary to fold up her tent.

In one letter of April 1906 sent to 'Darling Leo' at Glaslough the Duke describes his report on the South African War which he has just sent to the War Office and fulminates as soldiers do about the depletion of artillery and cavalry in Egypt; then he relates a comic story about Leonie's mother-in-law (Lady Constance Leslie) who, on seeing a man fall into the pond in the park, jumped out of her Bath chair and called others to the rescue. Great was her disappointment on discovering the man was a confirmed drunkard. The local clergyman asked her to visit him and this Lady Constance did, reading the Scriptures aloud and imploring him to mend his ways. The Duke thought it exceedingly funny and wondered if the man was really glad at being saved.

The postscript to this long newsy letter is very tender. Leonie is his own sweet love, and many are the prayers he offers for her health and happiness for he finds life 'intolerable' without her. When in 1909 the Duke assumed command of the Mediterranean area it meant that the Jack Leslies went out to enjoy Malta, and scrapbooks grew heavy with photographs of polo ponies and parasols. It was, in fact, around this time that the Duke, who had many disagreements with King Edward over military matters, blundered into an unfortunate, much-talked-of incident during a big shoot at Windsor Castle. Some fourteen years previously Prince Arthur had inadvertently shot his brother-in-law Prince Christian of Schleswig-

Holstein in the eye. On this occasion, when he fired at a rather low pheasant, feathers waved in the Queen of Italy's huge hat! Edward swore furiously at his brother, accusing him of having fired dangerously low, until some bright courtier cracked a joke about the bird on the Queen's hat being out of season. It seems unbelievable that the soldier who had commanded the Guards Brigade at the Battle of Tel-el-Kebir could have disregarded elementary safety rules, but several versions of this story were current. The Connaughtites swore that the Duke had fired high and it was a breeze that ruffled the Queen's feathers.

The drama had blown over by November 16, 1909, when the Duke wrote a long letter from Windsor Castle thanking his 'Dearest One' for her pencilled note delivered after dinner. Now, he said, he must *pamper* her with *two* letters each day, for she was ill —they had been out shooting 559 birds, most of them brought down by his brother and nephew Georgy (shortly to become George V). At the investiture of Knights of the Garter, Georgy and he had brought in King Emmanuel looking nice in his white breeches and silk stockings so as to enable the Garter to be buckled under his knee. Queen Alexandra wore her robes and all but four Knights of the Garter were present and he, Arthur, was the oldest royal Knight after His Majesty. The banquet for a hundred and fifty presented a fine sight. Queen Ina, sitting next to Leonie's nephew Winston, was charmed by him, and he himself had made the acquaintance of 'very pretty Mrs. Winston.' The Duke of Marlborough (who had married Consuelo Vanderbilt) was present at the investiture but not asked to dinner, 'being in great disfavour.' Mrs. Lloyd George dined, but not her husband. Arthur supposed there were 'too many Dukes for him.' How sad it was to think that he would be passing within one hundred yards of Leonie's house at ten o'clock on the morrow, in his own carriage on his way to the Guildhall, and would not see her; he would send this letter off by hand of his valet who was fetching clothes from London: she must keep six o'clock free for him on Saturday (and, of course, the policeman standing outside her front door would deter other callers!). There were blessings for the beloved one from her own obedient Pat. And so it went on, year after year, the sharing of joys and annoyances, the little detailed stories which only interest those who really care.

When Queen Victoria died in 1901 the Duke had told Leonie how light his mother's body felt as he lifted her into the coffin— the weight of a little child. And when King Edward died in 1910 he wrote of the pain (made more poignant, no doubt, by the memory of quarrels) when Queen Alexandra took him to gaze on his brother's face for the last time—so calm and beautiful and natural. 'One line beloved friend to thank you for all your sympathy'—he was longing to see her (this was the Saturday after King Edward's death) and, knowing this, the ever thoughtful Margaret Louise had unknown to him telephoned her to come to Clarence House.

When Leonie's son Norman, a captain in the Rifle Brigade, was challenged to a duel by an Egyptian Pasha (he had been caught making assignations with the Pasha's wife) it was the Duke who held secret conferences at Great Cumberland Place with Lord Cromer concerning the dilemma—duelling was forbidden in the British Army, but Norman would lose the respect of the Egyptians if he did not fight. Granted long leave, Norman practised with an expert sabre master for weeks and the duel took place in Paris—in sufficient secrecy to avoid court-martial while satisfying Eastern custom. A slight wound inflicted by the brilliant swordsman Youssery Pasha ended it.

In 1913 the Duke became Governor-General of Canada and within hours of sailing he was scribbling letters with private postscripts which called down blessings on the 'precious black head' of that 'dearest of friends.'

Soon after this, war broke out and Leonie's son Norman was killed, as were the sons of almost all her friends. As Norman charged up a railway bank, he was shot dead by a German sniper, and his sword, a gift from the Duke, fell and lay in the Flanders mud for nearly twenty years. Then a farmer's wife found it and, deciphering the engraving, she had it returned to the Duke of Connaught. It was a strange touching moment when he could hand back to my grandmother the sword he had once handed her son.

In 1915, to help assuage their grief, Jack and Leonie paid a visit to Ottawa. After their departure the Duke wrote a long letter, which reached Leonie on board ship, stressing what her company had meant to him, speaking of the calm and encouragement she had brought to him despite her own grief, and telling her of the flowers he had had sent on board for her birthday (her fifty-sixth—she wore the years with grace).

In 1917 when the Connaughts had returned to England and the Duchess grew seriously ill Leonie called daily at Clarence House and was asked to break the final news. Her diary for March 12 reads: 'The Duchess is much worse—only a miracle can save her. I try to comfort the Duke by telephone—I go to Clarence House at 2 and sit with him till Princess Louise and Queen Alexandra come— then he walks up here—is told. He seems stunned. I tell him there is no hope—he is so silent and patient in his grief—does not want anyone with him. He has the sympathy and love of all Canada—and of every soldier in the Army—and still he is the loneliest man I have ever seen—God knows what he will do without her. I think of her lovely hands—I trust they won't let her suffer—"

The Duke allowed Leonie to take violets to his dead wife. On March 16 her diary briefly records: 'Revolution in Russia, I go to Clarence House at 5, he clings to what remains. Pcss. Louise came to see him and we both tell him how near she is.'

Throughout the next twenty-five years Leonie would continue to cheer and amuse her Prince. On one or two occasions a slight fear arose that certain ambitious ladies had designs on the handsome old widower. My grandmother would then be asked if she could not hurry off for a 'little rest' in his villa in the South of France. 'We send you out like the Fire Brigade.'

In one torn letter written by my grandmother—maybe to the Duke or maybe to one of her sons—she disapproves of a certain influence and wisely analyses the reasons. 'If you fear to speak your mind freely to a person you see often, that person's mind dominates and rules *you*, though such a person may be greatly your inferior— if you are much with that person, you will absorb and partake to an extent of that person's passions, prejudices and even ailments—besides being ruled by them and thwarted in your aims—True such persons may seem your friends—but there are in the world thousands of unconscious tyrants and tyrannies in the name of friendship. People who call and believe themselves friends *only* as long as you do what they wish, and as long as you give them your society so you allow them to drag you in their direction—who are sore if you do not call on them as often as they desire, or if you seek other associations—If you tolerate and endure this tyranny—if they enjoy their way—and you only endure their way, then you are not only their slave, but you are being injured in body, mind and fortune through the absorption of the inferior thought element you are continually receiving as you think of them.'

Right up into the 1930s the Duke drove around in a sedate electric brougham. As my grandmother had no car of her own in London, this silent vehicle would draw up at 46 Great Cumberland Place, once or twice a week, to collect her for a small dinner party at Clarence House. Sometimes she would murmur next day: 'Rather hard work—such silence—all Royals except me—I had to *faire les frais* for the Duke.' She had moved to 46 Great Cumberland Place when number 10 was pulled down. 'Poor house—it looked so desolate being demolished. I threw a rose into its ruins as I walked by for memory's sake. . . .'‡

And so the years rolled by. From 1898 to 1936 she nearly always spent Whitsun at the Duke's house at Bagshot. In the abdication crisis she wrote to Seymour: 'Today Queen Mary lunched. I never saw her more cheerful, we walked in the garden and returned to tea. I cut a huge slice of chocolate cake for her and the Duke reproved me ("Cut it in half!"). And she ate every scrap and a lot more, what a digestion! And what strong nerves. The King has a party nearby, the usual guests! . . .'

We know the rest of the story. Edward VIII was about to desert his throne and Queen Mary was suffering intensely.

One of the sweetest notes the Duke wrote was almost the last—a firmly penned hope to 'Beloved Leo' that they will meet often in the coming year to enjoy the long friendship which they *both can look back to with so much gratitude*. It is signed 'With Warmest love, ever your own devoted Pat.'

The relationship became quite comic in the end, for although the Duke was only ten years older than my grandmother, he got very slow and deaf, while she carried her years lightly. By the time she was seventy and he eighty, they were no longer of the same generation, and although the loving correspondence continued, she regarded her weekly visits to Bagshot as rather a chore.

Occasionally she took me or my brother to give variety to the conversation, which by now had to be conducted through an ear trumpet. He was a perfect pet, and said nice things which put us at our ease in front of other grownups. We adored him in fact—but by now Leonie enjoyed the company of 'young men' such as Somerset Maugham and Noël Coward, and sometimes she got rather cross at the long drive down to Bagshot—yet it was a duty from which she would not seek to disentangle herself. The Duke wanted her, and to the Duke she would go. According to her code, you didn't let people down who expected you—had indeed been expecting you for nearly fifty years! But I remember she could show ill humour. We were driving home after a slightly soporific visit, and I remarked innocently that I had liked the Duke's tartan dressing gown and might get one myself. 'You'll do no such thing,' snapped my grandmother, 'nothing looks shabbier than tartan. We're all sick of that old dressing gown. He is so obstinate about it.' I saw she was shaking with annoyance. For once her advice had not been taken.

When war broke out in 1939 the old Field Marshal proudly re-

‡ She told this to André Maurois, who based a story on a like incident.

sumed uniform. Now he felt of use once more, for he could inspect troops and hearten dazed recruits stamping on the parade grounds of Aldershot.

My brother Jack, an officer in the Irish Guards, felt greatly honoured when asked to lunch alone with the Duke. They sat in his dining room at Bagshot—the Field Marshal of nearly ninety and the lieutenant of twenty-two—talking of the grim shadow of Hitler which was darkening Europe. When my brother returned to barracks he was asked what he'd had to eat. 'Sausages and mash,' he answered, 'but quite *different*, delicious!'

I'll leave the story there. Maybe some future historian will be allowed to delve through those hundreds of letters which H.R.H. wrote to 'Beloved Leo'! I like to think of the little flutter they always caused her, and of the happiness she was able to give in return. All the usual rumours were afoot, of course, but of what interest is rumour when a shy Prussian Princess attests: 'We never had any fun until we met her'? To be fun for fifty years, to be the inspiration of a man throttled by sense of duty, to be the friend his wife thanks for a 'golden hour,' to give and give and never wonder what the return may be—it really was an art. Such civilised living is not all that easy. My grandmother had a favourite motto which she caused to be painted on ashtrays: '*La fumée s'envole. L'amitié reste.*' But in the end, of course, '*L'amitié s'envole. Les lettres restent.*'

18

King at Last

ON JANUARY 22, 1901, eleven months before his sixtieth birthday, Albert Edward became King. It was very late in the day. Had Queen Victoria died ten years earlier he could have taken a place which he well understood, and served his empire with sagacity.

The footling disruptions of Tranby Croft would surely have been avoided. A King constantly in consultation with his ministers could not have been thoughtlessly involved in a debate concerning a cheating offence. The repercussions of Tranby Croft swelled out of all proportion, and it was ungracious of *The Times* to remind readers, on the day after Queen Victoria's death, that like many former Princes of Wales this one had been 'importuned by temptation in its most seductive forms' and 'must often have prayed not to be led into temptation with a feeling akin to hopelessness.' Yet after this moralising even *The Times* admitted that 'he had never failed in his duty to the throne and the nation.'

George Wyndham described the first proclamation: 'A mediaeval ceremony of a most impressive kind and quite apart from the vulgarities of modern life, there being no reporters or outsiders of any sort, a return to the reality of ancient days when the King and his Council were the sole legal Government of England.'

At the traditional Accession Council at St. James's Palace, where the oath was administered by the Archbishop of Canterbury, the new King, in a spontaneous address, announced that he would drop his father's name—for there could be only one Albert—and

be known as Edward VII. So by that very simple, very English
name he shall be called henceforth, but in the family and among
intimates he remained, of course, Bertie, and his letters to lady
loves continued to be signed A.E., not Edward R. When in June
1902 the Coronation had to be postponed, Wilfrid Scawen Blunt
drove through the city all decked with red cloth and wrote in his
diary: 'A bolt has fallen from the blue. . . . The King is ill, to
undergo an operation—. Passing through the park I found Rotten
Row crowded, not a trace of trouble on any face, though the newspapers talk of general gloom. On the contrary, streets are full of
gay sightseers, satisfied to look at the decorations since there will
be nothing more. Returning after dark I found the park still
crowded but almost exclusively by lovers who occupied each
bench in pairs, reposing according to the native London custom,
in each others' arms.'

Appendicitis and death level all men into equality. Ordinary
people enjoy seeing their monarch in a situation where they *have*
to be sorry for him. Two months later in the heat of August, when
all the important foreigners had gone away, came the ceremony
and again the King's subjects thronged the streets and took advantage of those kindly park benches. Even Blunt, who was prone to
criticise the 'vulgarity' of admiring Edward, let his pen rip: 'At last
came the famous eight cream-coloured horses, drawing the antique golden coach, through the crystal panels of which could be
seen the King and Queen. . . . Popular enthusiasm knew no bounds,
and a mighty roar of continuous cheering echoed from the Palace
to Westminster.'

Inside the Abbey certain conveniences were inadequate and the
Duchess of Devonshire caused consternation by taking a mighty
tumble in her anxiety to reach the Ladies' before anyone else. After
the long ceremony she tried to hurry out in the wake of the royal
procession, but found herself stopped by a line of Grenadier
Guards. Leonie and Jennie, who were descending from the King's
special box, heard her upbraiding the officers in front of all the
other peeresses, many of whom were themselves most uncomfortable. Then, trying to push her way past them, she missed her
footing and fell headlong down a flight of steps to roll over on
her back at the feet of the Chancellor of the Exchequer, who
stared paralysed at this heap of velvet and ermine. The Marquis
de Soveral swiftly took charge of the situation and had her lifted
to her feet while Margot Asquith nimbly retrieved the coronet,
which was bouncing along the stalls, and placed it back on her
head. It was a moment in which younger women naturally had to

give precedence to an angry Duchess. The organisers of sanitary arrangements received good scoldings later—but the cheering street crowds never knew what the ladies in the Abbey had to endure.

Now that His Royal Highness had become His Majesty, we can glance at the great ladies of that famous Marlborough House set and find that all of them were now over forty, most over fifty, and a few like Louisa Devonshire had passed seventy. They had lived their lives strenuously and splendidly, in the wake of this warm-hearted, restless, lovable (or at least impossible to dislike) royal profligate. They had felt the pulse of the world's most powerful empire as they lay beside—though never for gymnastic reasons in the arms of—the heir to the throne. And now they were middle-aged friends—devoted friends—able to call on the King when in trouble, for loyalty lay deep in his nature, his memory was good and his impulses remained generous. Instinctively he tried to help —but physical romping had become rather an effort. Despite the laborious work put in by Sophie Hall-Walker during spa time and various titillating accounts of afternoons out of view in Marienbad forest and visits to Parisian houses of ill fame; despite the determi-nation of that wicked old Leopold II of Belgium to introduce his stylish mistress Emilienne d'Alençon—'*Je vais en Ecosse chasser le grouse. Viens avec nous. Tu t'appelleras la Comtesse de Songeon et je te ferai connaître mon cousin Edouard*'—the King had ad-justed his senses to a more sober rhythm. I think the reminiscences of Mistinguett and the maître d'hôtel of Maxim's must be taken with a grain of salt.

Cocottes and madames of gay establishments would naturally fall on their knees to obtain a glance from Edward and talk about it for ever more, but according to Elsie Gill's eyewitness account of nap time in Marienbad, seduction could be hard work, and many props were needed. Before taking for granted that King Edward's visits to Paris always included fornication let us ponder Jean Coc-teau's description of famous cocottes he watched dining:

'It was no small affair: full armour, shield, yoke, sheath, whale-bone, shoulder pieces, thigh pieces—gauntlets, corselet, halters of pearls, shields of feathers, baldricks of satin, velvet and jewels, coats of mail—these knights bristling with tulle, and eyelashes, these sacred scarabs armed with asparagus tongs, these samurais of sable and ermine, these dreadnaughts of pleasure from dawn to dusk harnessed and caparisoned by sturdy wenches—seemed strangely stiff in front of their host as if unable to extract from an oyster any-thing except its pearl. . . . The idea of undressing one of these

ladies seemed an expensive enterprise which would have to be organised like a household furniture removal.'

Think of the bother of bedding such a bird—a glance and a
laugh, yes—but the King was busy and he had acquired the habit
of sleeping with well-bred ladies.

Robert Hichens described him in *Yesterday:* 'Night after night
as I sat in my stall at the opera and saw him coming into the
omnibus box and taking up his opera glasses to survey the glittering
women in the first and ground tier boxes, I saw a man who looked
I thought, extremely genial and satisfied with his position in the
scheme of the world.'

Most of the ladies of the Prince's set now had grown-up children,
and during his ten years' reign they would be busily engaged in
arranging important marriages for their daughters. Lady Warwick's
eldest daughter would, as already recounted, become Countess of
Feversham, Lillie Langtry's daughter would become Lady Malcolm,
Mrs. William Cornwallis-West (Patsy), the beautiful heartless
Irish tigress who had enjoyed the Prince's favour in the eighties,
would deliberately enlist Edward's aid in marrying her youngest
daughter—His Majesty's favourite 'little girl'—to England's richest
man, the Duke of Westminster. As the gentleman proved slow in
proposing, Patsy Cornwallis-West arranged a house party for the
King where her daughter and the twenty-two-year-old Duke, who
had known each other since childhood, were left alone together on
several occasions. Nothing happened. So Mrs. Cornwallis-West
teased His Majesty into taking Bendor Westminster aside to urge
him into action. The King spoke in plain but kindly fashion: 'My
boy—you can't keep looking at a girl like this and you compromised her last night—her mother tells me she found you both
alone together in the garden . . . ! If you're a gentleman you will
ask her to marry you. . . .'

The young man acquiesced. Bendor related this to my father
many years later, and said how angry he had been when he learned
that Patsy Cornwallis-West had boasted of her cunning in stalking
the unsuspecting pair and then pouncing from behind the bushes in
simulated horror. Jennie Churchill was also at this house party and
told my grandmother the details. I fear she found them amusing.

Louisa Manchester's daughters had married, as she dictated, three
elder sons—the Duke of Hamilton, the Earl of Derby and the Earl
of Gosford. Gosford Castle, a colossal rambling Victorian edifice,
lay in Northern Ireland, some twenty miles from Castle Leslie, and
my uncle Seymour, who as a boy was sometimes driven over in a
'sociable,' found Louisa Gosford most intimidating and wondered

how she could have emerged from that glamorous Manchester House. Later on he learnt that the famous Duchess of Manchester had been a hard mother; her daughters became emotionally frozen while she pursued her worldly successes. The surpassing beauty of country homes is not always sufficient aid to a girl's development.

Lady de Grey's only child, the Lady Juliet Lowther, was tall like her mother, but less beautiful, painfully shy and cruelly neglected. She married a Baronet and bore two children to whom she was in turn exceedingly unkind, often mocking them in front of her luncheon guests till they felt they could die from shame.

As for my grandmother, she had no daughters, only four sons—the last being born in 1900. Because she proved an asset to any party, this slim, dark, musical American had become the most sought-after woman in English society (even more so than sister Jennie, who, as she grew older, was inclined to think of *herself*, and did not always pull her weight when parties grew sticky).

Jennie Churchill had no daughter. She would have been wonderfully understanding with a temperamental girl. As it was, she dearly loved her only niece, Clare Frewen, who was to be the first rebel against the conventions of that era, the first society woman to break away, becoming a journalist and then a sculptress, the friend of kings and, finally, of dictators.

Throughout Edward's reign, Jennie—now happily married to George Cornwallis-West—would be slaving to help her two sons, Winston and Jack, and pouring out her affection and energies to them equally, for a true mother's heart does not alter when one of her offspring gains fame. In my biography of Lady Randolph I did not sufficiently stress the deep bond that lay between Winston and his brother Jack, or the fact that Jennie had no favourite son—she cared for them equally.

Having done all in his power to induce Jennie not to marry a man twenty years younger than herself, and taken George, his godson, aside to explain what an utterly ridiculous match this was, King Edward forgave them after the *fait accompli*. He often invited the curious couple to stay at Sandringham. Thus it was that Patsy Cornwallis-West's son (to whom she had always been horrid) became, in his twenties, a figure in Edwardian society amidst important personages twice his age. Jennie, of course, was just Jennie—ageless, stimulating to the young, amazing to the mature, and a source of disapproval to the old.

She and George never had a penny—or not what counted as a penny in English society—but they did not let this matter. Jennie's sisters-in-law had made the richest of marriages, and she thought that ought to suffice for one family. Jennie and George tried to *make* money in a number of ways, and although they groaned a lot about finance, they had the tremendous asset of *themselves* to fall back on.

How did they ever meet? The story is typical of what can occur at a great Edwardian house party. Towards the end of her liaison with the Prince, Daisy entertained him at Warwick Castle rather more than at Easton Lodge. Jennie would always be invited because she kept the Prince laughing, and as he grew older Edward's liverish depressions made the task of amusing him ever more onerous. On this particular occasion Lady Warwick had also summoned a Guards officer who would not in the ordinary course of events have been asked—he was far too young—but the Prince expressed a desire to see his twenty-two-year-old godson and so Lieutenant George Cornwallis-West was released from regimental duties. Knowing Daisy Warwick, I have a notion that she probably intended George to meet and marry Miss Muriel Wilson, a suitable heiress who was also in the house party. (Incidentally, Jennie entertained hopes that Miss Wilson might marry Winston!) All these plans came to nought. The unexpected happened. George Cornwallis-West took Lady Randolph boating and fell violently in love. Three years later, against a crescendo of advice, he married her. It says a great deal for Jennie's capacity to hang on to friends that Queen Alexandra and King Edward continued to invite her to Sandringham where they only suffered people who were personally congenial. After the marriage George had to come along also. He was a first-rate shot, but as he admits in his own memoirs, *Edwardian Heyday*, no one else of his age group entered the sacred portals.

Only personal friends were invited to Sandringham. There were many important people longing to go there rather than to Windsor for a ball or official function, because it would show they were *intimate* with the King, but in their own home it was clearly understood that only people who were congenial to Alexandra as well as Edward should come to stay.

Occasionally the King would pay a visit to some country house for the first time, and on these occasions the host and hostess sometimes lost their heads in snobbish excitement and spent much more than they could afford on unnecessary redecorations, painting and plastering whole wings and hanging new curtains in every room. My grandmother was present at one of these weekends where very intensive preparations had taken place. On the first morning the hostess anxiously enquired if His Majesty had been quite comfortable. Never having seen the house before, Edward had not no-

ticed the new brocades and cretonnes. He thought for a moment
before answering: 'You might put a hook for a dressing gown on
the bathroom door!' Of course, he had not *meant* to deflate her,
he was merely trying to be helpful: it *is* very aggravating to be
unable to hang up a dressing gown! The ambitious hostess retired
shattered. It was the *first* royal visit; she had taken such pains,
spent so much money! My grandmother tried to comfort her, saying the King would be *so* delighted to find a hook next day. But the
lady, whose feelings he would not have dreamt of hurting, never
quite recovered from the blow.

Lord Knutsford has published the letters he wrote from Sandringham six months before Queen Victoria's death. The Whitsun party
that year included Lord and Lady de Grey, De Soveral, whose
caustic wit always lightened Edward's humour, Tosti, the famous
baritone-songwriter (Alexandra and her daughters were so musical—
strumming away *à quatre mains* while Tosti's voice made chandeliers
vibrate in after-dinner songs), the Hon. George Lambton (racing
trainer), and Lady Randolph Churchill, 'just back from her hospital
ship which had been a boon in South Africa, but fractiously insisting
she is going to marry George Cornwallis-West.'

Lord Knutsford describes the chattering guests travelling in that
special train coach from St. Pancras to Wolverton Station where the
house party was met by royal carriages with officious flunkeys in
red livery who dealt with the luggage—and *such* luggage! Big trunks
had to be brought for a few days' stay so that the correct attire
could be produced for every meal and outing.

How exciting to drive through a forest of rhododendrons and to
disembark in front of Sandringham House. The royal host and
hostess stood in the hall to welcome their guests. After handshakes
Queen Alexandra sat down to pour tea. Dinner was at 9 P.M. (at
Sandringham all clocks were kept half an hour ahead of time).
Footmen informed the gentlemen what waistcoats were to be worn.
Ladies' maids scurried to the ironing rooms. At nine, having assembled in the drawing room, each man was told whom he must
escort into dinner and where to sit. This saved hesitation and embarrassment. On this occasion Knutsford describes the Prince giving
his arm to Lady de Grey, while Alexandra walked beside De Soveral
and Lord de Grey escorted the unmarried Princess Victoria. There
were, of course, no cocktails, but exquisite wines accompanied
each course. The Prince never drank more than a glass or so of
claret at dinner and a brandy after the last course.

When the ladies left the dining room cigarettes and cigars were
brought by footmen. Heavy drinking was never encouraged, and

after half an hour the gentlemen moved to the drawing room to chat with the ladies, until Alexandra rose and they retired to their bedrooms where the ladies' maids would be waiting to unlace them from their gorgeous satin and velvet gowns. Hard as the existence of a servant might be, they were perhaps consoled by the colossal meals offered in recompense for late hours. A five-course breakfast could be consumed by every scullery maid if she so desired, and many a working-class mother strove to 'get her daughter's knees under a good table.'

When the ladies had disappeared upstairs the men went to the billiards room, where the Prince, who idolised his dogs, would roar with laughter when his black bulldog nipped the legs of players. No one could go to bed before Edward, but at twelve-thirty he would certainly retire. There was no thought of any hanky-panky after hours at Sandringham. That would have been considered bad taste and an insult to the royal hostess.

On Sunday morning the breakfast gong sounded at 10 A.M. Then came church and a stroll in the garden until lunch at one-thirty. After a fairly heavy meal the ladies went upstairs to change into walking skirts and strong boots. The whole party then underwent a slow three-hour walk to the kennels and stables and farm. Talk was almost entirely about animals—dogs, pedigree cattle and, of course, race horses. Knutsford noticed Alexandra's 'touching girl-like love' for every stone and corner of Sandringham. She reminded him of 'a bird escaped from a cage.'

Certainly the royal pair were never so happy as in this big Norfolk house, which they regarded as home, but guests grew weary of trying to do the right thing. Knutsford found dinner very wearing, with the conversation in mingled English and French: 'they drop from one to another in the same sentence.'

Then came the local Whitmonday sports. Off drove the house party—Lady de Grey and Holford in the first carriage with Edward. Knutsford found himself in the second carriage with Princess Victoria and Lady Randolph Churchill and Lady Musgrave. The ladies wore coloured blouses and contrasting skirts and jackets over their blouses, white gloves and feather boas. A brisk wind nearly blew off their huge hats. Lady Musgrave in particular had difficulty with her concoction. 'Send it to the bazaar!' cried Alexandra, and everyone roared with laughter.

Sandringham parties were called 'informal,' but what a relief, nevertheless, when they all got back to the station in those regal carriages followed by the four horse-drawn vans of luggage.

In this spring of 1900 the visitors departed to their homes full to the brim of food and anecdote. Jennie, who had been argumentative all weekend, would almost immediately marry her young George. Gladys de Grey would get on her newly installed phone to admirer number one, the Hon. Reginald Lister, or if he was not available to admirer number two, Sir John Lister-Kaye. Ladies were now able to ring the men up and guardedly converse instead of sending dangerous notes. Servants might overhear but there would be nothing *on paper.*

My uncle Seymour describes his mother Leonie and his aunt Jennie as among the first to instal the expensive novelty of a telephone, and being excitable Americans, they even indulged in the rare extravagance of extensions to their bedrooms. As a boy he watched them sitting rapt during long confidences, the receiver (into which they also spoke) clamped to an ear while a maid would stand by with hot tongs attempting to curl their hair.

And, apart from telephones, cars were creeping in. Two years after the house party just described the Sandringham luggage wagons were replaced by motors and the King owned a Daimler and a Mercedes. Queen Victoria would not have been impressed. To the Duke of Portland, Master of the Horse, she had spoken frankly: 'I hope you will never allow any of these horrible machines to be used in my stables. I am told that they smell exceedingly nasty, and are very shaky and disagreeable conveyances altogether.'

How right she was!

19

Mrs. Keppel
and Miss Keyser

Two REMARKABLE WOMEN would remain as dominant companions of the King throughout his reign. One of these, Miss Agnes Keyser, was a wellborn girl who devoted her life and her personal fortune to nursing, and then during middle age gave her affections to the aging monarch, without anyone knowing except his family and closest friends. But the famous personage of Edward's reign, and the most perfect mistress in history, was, of course, Mrs. Keppel. The fame of this liaison resounded throughout Europe and gave her terrific *réclame* in France, where the power of a wise mistress has always been regarded with respect.*

Curiously enough, Edward met both Agnes and Alice in 1898, and they each established an immediate though exceedingly different hold over his affections. He was fifty-eight at the time, little Miss Keyser was forty-six and the voluptuous Mrs. Keppel was twenty-nine.

The daughter of Admiral Sir William Edmonstone and the wife of the Hon. George Keppel, younger brother of the Earl of Albemarle, Alice Keppel was a close friend of my grandfather until the

* In this book I use the term 'mistress' in the European rather than the American sense—*une maîtresse* is the one who rules and gives favours, not merely a woman who sleeps with a man out of wedlock.

Prince of Wales whisked her away into more important realms. H.R.H. first set eyes on the delectable Alice when he was inspecting the Royal Norfolk Artillery in which her husband was an officer. He asked the Colonel Lord Leicester who she was and requested she be presented to him. A few days later, at Sandown Races, the Prince noticed my grandfather strolling happily along with lovely Mrs. Keppel on his arm. Waving his stick in salutation, the Prince summoned him for a chat, but his eye continued to rest on the lady at his side.

'May I introduce Mrs. Keppel, sir?' asked my grandfather.

'I am Colonel-in-Chief of her husband's regiment and we have met,' answered the Prince, never withdrawing his gaze. Then, in the most gracious way possible, H.R.H. gave Leslie to understand that his presence was no longer required. Whimsically, my grandfather used to describe that certain look—blending shrewd appraisement and admiration—that crossed the Prince's face as his eyes travelled over Mrs. George Keppel's lovely face and fashionably curved figure. Aware that he had been dismissed for the afternoon, John Leslie strolled meekly off to watch the horses in the saddling enclosure. In fact, he saw little of Alice Keppel henceforth, for she responded to the Prince's overtures and remained his constant and extremely busy companion for the next twelve years.

Only mature women could now interest the King, and although nearly thirty years younger than her royal lover, Mrs. Keppel proved the ideal mistress for such a monarch. She took her post seriously and her well-bred, handsome husband raised no objections. Alice Keppel was liberal in outlook, quiet, affectionate, and absolutely discreet. Always intelligent and well informed, she became even more so as King Edward's intimate companion. Queen Alexandra accepted her as a friend, and she and her husband were often invited to stay at Sandringham—an occurrence which would have been out of the question with Lady Warwick.

It is difficult to discover a sour word concerning Mrs. Keppel in contemporary letters. True, in 1902 Lord Carrington, the Prince's intimate, comments with coolness, 'A good many Mrs. George dinners lately,' and the new Prince of Wales sounds unenthusiastic in letters to his wife from the royal yacht *Britannia* during Cowes Regatta. 'Alas, Mrs. K. arrives tomorrow and stops here on a yacht, I'm afraid peace will not remain'; and the future Queen Mary writes back, 'What a pity Mrs. G.K. is again to the fore. How annoyed Mama will be!' But these slighting references fade into insignificance when one reads the assessment made by Lord Harding of Penshurst, head of the Foreign Office, in his private file: 'I used to see a great deal of Mrs. Keppel at that time, and I was aware that she had knowledge of what was going on in the political world.

'I would like here to pay a tribute to her wonderful discretion and to the excellent influence which she always exercised upon the king. She never utilised her knowledge to her own advantage, or to that of her friends; and I never heard her repeat an unkind word of anybody. There were one or two occasions when the king was in disagreement with the Foreign Office, and I was able, through her, to advise the king with a view to the policy of the government being accepted. She was very loyal to the king, and patriotic at the same time.

'It would have been difficult to find any other lady who would have filled the part of friend to King Edward with the same loyalty and discretion.'†

After this, it is hard to add to the legend of Alice Keppel, but sidelights reveal a pleasing warmth about this relationship—for although she was obviously enthralled by the great power she wielded, at the same time she genuinely cared for the King. He was gross, he was still sensual, he was indeed still unfaithful all round, but he remained extraordinarily endearing—a man of sensitivity, a man who could laugh at small joys and weep at his friends' sorrows, a man whom it was hard to know and not love. When Edward's niece, Princess Alice of Albany, came to stay at Sandringham, she found Mrs. Keppel delightful. 'She never flaunted herself or took advantage of her position as the king's favourite. Queen Alexandra was very fond of her and encouraged the liaison. There was a lot of gossip and public disapproval of their relationship and unnecessary sympathy for Aunt Alix, who did not need it as she welcomed the arrangement.'

When Princess Alice confessed that she found it difficult to keep up a consecutive conversation with the King owing to his habit of fiddling with the cutlery, Mrs. Keppel advised, 'Don't worry about that. We all experience that trouble. He likes to join in a general conversation interjecting remarks at intervals but he prefers to listen rather than to talk himself. Often he starts a discussion but he prefers to listen to others rather than continue talking; as soon as he can get others involved in it he is content to listen and to make occasional comments.'

This reluctance to make small talk was quite natural. Edward had an immense amount on his mind. Wishing to conserve energy, he disliked having to chat, but he was interested in other people's opin-

† Published in Sir Philip Magnus' *Life of Edward VII.*

ions and reactions. He preferred to gain information through people
rather than through reading reports. Mrs. Keppel understood this.
She spared him the effort of keeping conversation going by instruct-
ing everyone, including his shy young niece, to keep talking. The
King would take in what they said and the cutlery would lie undis-
turbed. Mrs. Keppel noticed what tired His Majesty and told people
how to entertain him. Everything seemed easier when she was present, therefore he wanted her constantly to hand, at every house
party and every dinner, and to be alone with at the end of a tiring
evening.

The working classes appreciated Mrs. Keppel. There is the famous story of an occasion when, urgently summoned to the country, she sent for a hansom cab. Stepping in with her luggage, she
gave the directive to the station: 'King's Cross.' 'Is he—oh dear,'
said the cabby, whipping up his horse.

Mrs. Keppel had one little girl, Violet, who was four years old
at the time she met Edward. The other daughter, Sonia, was born
in 1900, so her earliest memories are of being dressed up and given
firm injunctions by Nanny before going down to the drawing room
of 30 Portman Square. 'Be sure to curtsey to the King,' Nanny
would say, but the child dared not raise her eyes above the gentlemen's midriffs, and she sometimes curtseyed to the protuberance of
Sir Ernest Cassel by mistake. 'Kingy,' as she was taught to call His
Majesty, enjoyed children. He allowed Sonia to horse-race pieces
of bread and butter down his trouser leg (possibly to the displeasure
of valets?). Meanwhile Mrs. Keppel would look on, her turquoise-
coloured eyes alight with maternal pride. Sonia can remember her
mother pouring tea in attire proper to the occasion—a black velvet
dress with a huge black-feathered hat. As jewelry she wore a high
pearl dog collar, pearl earrings and drop-brooch.

The Keppels were particularly good parents, mounting to the
nursery floor each evening in full evening dress to kiss their daughters good night. And in the morning little Sonia would be allowed
to breakfast with them, to watch Papa curl his moustache, and
Mama in frilly petticoat and lace bed jacket having her glorious
hair brushed. The impressions of a child brought up close to Alice
Keppel have been lightly strewn through Sonia's book *Edwardian
Daughter*. She was well aware of having a most extraordinary
mother—one whom important gentlemen like Lord Alington were
proud to take out in a carriage. Mrs. Keppel would deliberately
insist on Lord A. driving her to the East End of London to view
the slums he owned: 'Next year there will be such a difference,

19. Zena Dare

20. Daisy, Countess of Warwick, with Maynard (Sir Joseph Laycock's favourite photo, which he kept with her letters)

21. Joe Laycock

22. Daisy, Princess of Pless

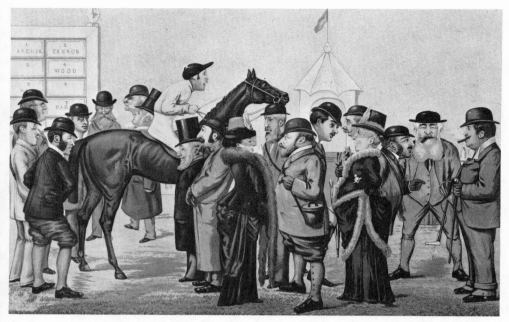

23. Newmarket, 1885. Cartoon by Spy from *Vanity Fair*. The centre group consists of the Duchess of Manchester, the Marquess of Hartington and the Prince of Wales. To the right, partly hidden by the Duchess of Montrose, is the Marquess of Londonderry. The jockey is Fred Archer.

24. Count Kinsky on Zoedene, Grand National winner. Autographed for Jennie Churchill

25. Arthur James Balfour when Prime Minister

26. Lady Elcho

27. Lady Warwick's home, Easton Lodge

28. Rotten Row, Hyde Park

29. 1902. Mrs. Adair's stalking party at Glenveagh Castle, County Donegal. Back row, left to right: John Leslie, the Duke of Connaught, Mrs. Adair (sitting), Leonie Leslie, the Duchess of Connaught, Princess Margaret of Connaught, the Duchess of Abercorn, her daughter. Front row, left to right: three unidentified men and the Duke of Abercorn

30. The Earl and Countess of Fingall with family

31. Alice Keppel, from a drawing by Ellis Roberts

32. Margot Asquith in 1911

33. Leonie Leslie

34. The Duke of Connaught with daughters and Lionel Leslie at Bagshot

35. A gathering at Ascot, 1898

36. Mr. Balfour getting into carriage. Left to right: Harry Graham,
Hugo Baring, Katie Cowper, Lord Cowper

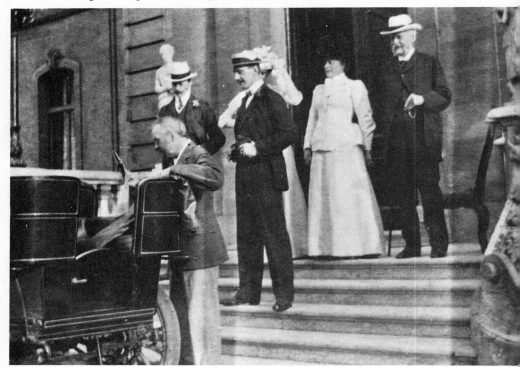

37. An Edwardian scene

38. Leonie Leslie, Nancy Astor, Anne Islington, Princess of Pless and Evie Pelly

39. Balcony of boathouse at Blenheim

40. Leonie's first photographic attempt. The rear view is of Jack Churchill

I'm sure . . .' and the fearless blue eyes would gaze straight into his, as the horses clopped back to Portman Square.

To keep going in King Edward's set necessitated enormous outlay, and George Keppel was often heard to mutter about financial crises. 'But,' writes Sonia, 'throughout her life, Mamma was irresistibly attractive to bank managers.' There was one in particular, a most useful Mr. Montagu of the Westminster Bank at Victoria Gate. Mrs. Keppel always took her little daughter with her on banking occasions. She would walk across the park 'with the tirelessness of a Scots gillie' to visit Mr. Montagu in his private office. 'Once inside it, he would place Mamma opposite him, with myself between them, and make his opening remarks in a reverently low tone as though he was praying in church. Usually whatever the season, Mamma was veiled. Placing her umbrella or parasol on the table, then she would lift her veil, and Mr. Montagu seemed to catch his breath a little as he beheld her beautiful face.'

Mr. Montagu knew, of course. All England knew. Lucky was the bank manager whose prosaic day could be enhanced by the presence of such a lady. How utterly delicious became the usually sombre discussion of overdrafts. Her requests would be granted, of course, and then she would graciously sweep out with the little girl at her side, leaving the manager pensive at his desk, unwilling, or maybe unable, to return to accounting while the faint smell of spring blossom, the smell of 'fresh green sap' which was Alice Keppel's personal odour, lingered on in the dark office.

Then, each Easter, there would be a three-week holiday at Biarritz in that Atlantic air so beneficial to cigar-choked lungs. Violet and Sonia had to be specially outfitted for this—light dresses and straw hats—black stockings for the older girl, white socks for the smaller one. Such excitement. Mama's luggage filled the hall: 'studded wardrobe-trunks standing up on end, and high enough to stand in; hat boxes; shoe boxes; rugs; travelling cushions, her travelling jewel-case . . .' And the journey would never resemble the journeys made by other little girls off to the seaside with their mothers; an indefinable something filled the air—a sense of drama, of importance, of mystery. 'At Victoria a special carriage was reserved for us; and a special cabin on the boat. And at Calais Mama was treated like royalty. The Chef-de-Gard met her and escorted us all through the Customs, and the car-attendant on the train hovered over her like a love-sick troubadour.'

This was no ordinary passenger—this was a lady whose smile could keep the railway officials jaunty for weeks, vicariously sharing royal pleasures, as they counted the sheets and wrote out their passenger lists. France uses the historic title proudly—*la maîtresse du roi* was travelling, and obeisance must be made to that which makes life more charming. There would be two double sleepers, Nanny and Violet in one, Sonia and Mrs. Keppel in the other. From her upper berth the child would watch her mother climb into a voluminous nightgown, push her chestnut hair into a mobcap, grease her face, swallow a sleeping pill and then with a black stocking tied around her eyes fall into oblivion. Sonia was too frightened of the dark roaring train even to creep down the ladder to the lavatory, and the blue light made her mother's face so strange—would dawn never come? Meanwhile the sleeping-car attendant offered yet more *couvertures,* and whispered to other passengers: '*Mais oui —bien sûr—c'est Madame Keppel dans le seize.*' And the whole train chuffed and puffed and whistled and rocked itself into a state of euphoria.

Soon after daylight, cups of steaming hot coffee would be brought in by an elated breakfast-car man, so busy, so helpful, while trying to repress the inevitable gasp as the black stocking was removed and he looked at close range into those sleepy turquoise eyes beneath the mobcap.

At Biarritz Mrs. Keppel would stay with Sir Ernest Cassel, who always rented the Villa Eugénie, which had once belonged to the French Empress. It was like a large conservatory, with carpetless floors and glass doors. Nanny did not care for Biarritz: 'Our clothes were hard put to it to compete with those of Sir Ernest's grandchildren, Edwina and Mary. And I suspect that Nanny put in several clandestine hours overtime washing and ironing, sensitively conscious of the inferior quality of the lace on our knickers.'

'Kingy' would be in particularly good form at Biarritz, however, and enter into nursery games with an enthusiasm of which Sir Ernest was incapable. 'Always he was accompanied by his dog Caesar, who had a fine disregard for the villa's curtains and chair-legs, but a close regard for me.'

On Easter Sunday, after presents of lovely little Fabergé jewelled eggs had been distributed to the children, as well as to the grownups, 'Kingy,' with a host of courtiers, would set forth for a mammoth picnic.

'Kingy' liked to think of these as impromptu parties, and little did he realise the hours of preliminary hard work they had entailed.

'First, his car led the way, followed by others containing the rest of the party. Then the food, guarded by at least two footmen, brought up the rear.

'"Kingy" spied out the land for a suitable site and, at his given word, we all stopped and the footmen set out the lunch. Chairs and a table appeared, linen tablecloths, plates, glasses, silver. Every variety of cold food was produced, spiced by iced-cup in silver-plated containers. . . .

'For some unfathomed reason, "Kingy" had a preference for picnicking by the side of the road. On Easter Day inevitably, this was packed with carriages and the first motor-cars, all covered with dust, and when we parked by the roadside, most of the traffic parked with us.

'Much of "Kingy's" enjoyment of these picnics was based on his supposed anonymity and, delightedly, he would respond to an assumed name in his deep, unmistakable voice, unaware that most of the crowd was playing up to him.'

On the way back to England a few days would be spent in Paris. Again Mrs. Keppel and her daughter would be the guests of Sir Ernest Cassel. Diplomatic circles as well as the nobility accorded her the utmost respect. While His Majesty visited old acquaintances and received semiformal visits from ministers, Mrs. Keppel ordered new gowns at Worth. The sewing women peeped through curtains to watch fittings and admire her curves, while a buzz of excitement ran through the whole establishment. Just as Lord Alington felt proud to be seen driving 'Alice K.,' so Monsieur Worth could not restrain his pleasure in dressing her. And every year Sonia would be presented with a little satin dress for her doll. The Keppel girls, who would have to grow up into the desolation of the Kaiser's war, would look back on this early dream world with nostalgia. King Edward would probably have exerted pressure, had he lived, to marry them grandly; as it was, the debris of the old aristocracy lay at their feet. Sonia's choice would be typical for her shattered generation—she married a youthful officer whose three elder brothers had been killed.

I was fourteen when I met Mrs. Keppel in 1928. My parents drove me up to Ombrellino, her ancient richly adorned villa on a hill above Florence. It was springtime and she wore a huge white cartwheel hat and a romantic white muslin dress. Although approaching sixty, she looked wonderful even to my unappreciative eyes, and as the hired fiacre slowly descended the hillside, with the driver shouting imprecations to his slipping horse, I listened puzzled and uncomprehending to my parents discussing her past.

My uncle Seymour (who is eighty-two as I write) remembers Mrs. Keppel's extraordinary attraction of *manner* and her 'deep throaty voice like Garbo.' He last talked with her in the Ritz air raid shelter during the blitz of Hitler's war. An old lady, white-haired and soignée, she sat bolt upright, her back straight as when she poured tea for King Edward, and, as the Nazi bombs smashed London, over the face of Alice Keppel, that face which had never shown scorn to any human creature, there crept an expression of utter contempt.

Had Edward lived longer, he might have merited his name of 'Peacemaker'—for he perceived the terrifying determination of German military minds, and he feared his nephew's ambition. At least he might have reiterated warnings to those politicians who appeared so *surprised* in 1914. My father has written of him: 'From the wisdom of businessmen and the wit of beautiful women he learned how to deal with men.'

Certainly he cared for wit and wisdom, but another craving lurked deep in his make-up. The most restless and tireless of men, he yet longed for quiet.

Miss Agnes Keyser gave him this, and held a unique position in the King's life. The daughter of a prominent member of the Stock Exchange, she had, to the bewilderment of her rich respectable family, insisted on taking up nursing as a career.

To understand Agnes Keyser's character it is necessary to reflect on the tremendous pressure put on girls of her class to marry and keep within the conventional rails. Any form of 'career' was discouraged and because so few possible jobs existed, young women were caught in the net of their family's will. Miss Keyser, being financially independent, could break away from the usual pattern and follow her own bent for nursing, but it was not easy. She had been a pretty young girl and for a time she was made to follow the conventional social round, but she would not marry and she put up a firm fight for independence in her twenties. And it would hardly have been possible for the King to conduct an affair with an unmarried woman had she not been literally matron-in-chief of her own establishment! The set-up is unique. Miss Keyser was the only 'bachelor girl' in the King's life and she really loved him.

Agnes Keyser had no time for women. She liked men, sick men, wounded men, impecunious men, men she could dominate and scold and pamper. She liked men stretched out in bed or in wheelchairs; best of all she liked to hold their hands as they went under the anaesthetic. The nursing staff feared her, and so did ladies who visited her patients. There were a few extraordinary exceptions, all characters in their own right. The wealthy Miss Grace Maple, heiress of Maples Furnishing Company, and the famous Rosa Lewis were women she tolerated, and so, strangely enough, was my grandmother.

When the Boer War broke out, Miss Keyser and her sister had tried to establish a nursing home for officers at their own expense in their large private house, 17 Grosvenor Crescent. This proved beyond their means, so the King set up a trust and asked his rich friends to send donations. Sir Ernest Cassel, Arthur Sassoon, Nathaniel Rothschild, Lord Burnham, Lord Sandwich, Lord Iveagh and the banker Hambro subscribed handsomely, and in time Miss Keyser's house proudly bore the name of King Edward's Hospital for Officers. Gentlemen from the Household Cavalry and the Guards Brigade were especially welcome and if they were short of funds they could in a way sing for their supper by recounting regimental gossip which Agnes Keyser knew would amuse the King.

Grosvenor Crescent lay beside Buckingham Palace (*so* convenient) and there the King visited Miss Keyser regularly for twelve years. He seems to have found absolute contentment with this handsome, formidable, middle-aged woman, especially in moments of stress when he could dine alone with her without arousing gossip or envy. Agnes Keyser cared nothing for society; the furious pace of ambitious hostesses vying to entertain the King bored her. Unknown to the public, except as a sort of minor Florence Nightingale, Agnes Keyser made Edward feel that he was welcome to drop in at any time. She would always be at his disposition, ready to listen to his worries, ready *and able* to take his pulse! She was calm and sympathetic; there was no nonsense about this lady, and she gave Edward a sense of security he could find nowhere else. Certainly she was uncoquettish, she simply loved the King and he was the only man in her life. Edward had never known the cosy comfort of an English nanny—Agnes Keyser was able to give him that fireside glow which most of his subjects had enjoyed in childhood. The fact that she offered complete devotion, avoided all publicity and exacted nothing except help for her 'home' earned her the respect of the royal family. What Mrs. Keppel thought of her I do not know, but Rosa Lewis gave her much praise for making the King 'induce his snob friends to dole out.'

Throughout all these years, during which she ran 17 Grosvenor Crescent and saw King Edward almost every day when he was in London, Miss Keyser managed to keep the press at bay. The staff, and indeed the military inmates of her home, must have had some knowledge of the King's regular visitations, but wisely, or out of loyalty, they kept their mouths shut. And a very efficient establishment the house became.

The tender depth of this extraordinary relationship is demonstrated by the fact that when in January 1901 the doctors stated that Queen Victoria was failing and the Prince of Wales had to hang around London awaiting news, the only person he could bear to visit was Agnes Keyser.

The political position of the heir to the throne was at this moment unbelievable. Even now, when he was a grandfather of nearly sixty years, the Queen had not confided in him. Indeed, he had just been staying at Chatsworth with the Duke of Devonshire (now nine years married to Louisa Manchester), and it was Harty-tarty, a member of the Cabinet, who casually informed the man about to become England's King that urgent discussions concerning an Anglo-German alliance were afoot. Knowing that great responsibilities were to be his at last, the Prince left Chatsworth (where the Keppels were in the house party) to fidget around Buckingham Palace, until on the evening of January 18 he was advised to travel to Osborne to be with the dying Queen. On this dramatic and moving night Edward wished to see no one except Agnes Keyser. He dined alone with her at Grosvenor Crescent and left at dawn by special train for the Isle of Wight. Two days later he was King.

Not only did Miss Keyser fulfil an emotional need, but she tried to discipline Edward's appalling eating habits. Instead of stuffing him with rich food as eager hostesses did, she struggled to reduce his diet to what in those days was considered healthy nursery fare. Miss Keyser told my grandmother that her usual choice for his dinner was Irish stew and rice pudding, heavy enough to our way of thinking, but at least plain and wholesome. Edward obeyed her orders like a small boy. If Sister Agnes had obtained complete control of the King's fare he might have lived longer.

Indeed, Edward was seriously interested in medical discoveries. He had deeply resented the agonies undergone by his sister Vicky and her husband the Emperor Frederick, both of whom died of cancer under the callous gaze of German doctors who did not approve of pain-killing drugs. In 1908 Edward wrote to a friend: 'My greatest ambition is not to quit this world till a real cure for cancer has been found.' His own wheezy chest kept him in constant discomfort and Agnes Keyser's ministrations eased this strain.

A wonderful picture emerges—there sits the greatest libertine of that amoral age in the large, respectable mansion, spooning up his milk pudding and being scolded if he asks for second helpings. Starched nurses scurry on the upper floors, starched maids carry in and out the dishes. Miss Keyser, also starched, gently imposes her will of iron. The King is at home. The King can relax. And if the worthy matron of this charitable establishment occasionally thinks it is time for a lie-down—well, *honi soit qui mal y pense.*

20

The Tennant Sisters

IN VICTORIAN and Edwardian peerages birth dates of the feminine sex are not recorded. It was considered bad manners *ever* to refer to a lady's age, and the years in which such characters as the Lady Gladys Herbert and the Lady Theresa Chetwynd-Talbot entered this world have to be guessed at by their brothers' recorded births, and the dates on which they married such illustrious persons as the Earl de Grey and the Marquis of Londonderry. But turning over the pages of *Burke's Peerage* or *Burke's Landed Gentry* for the seventies, eighties and nineties gives many intriguing pictures of the history of England since the Conquest. Perfectly written summaries depict the background of these aristocratic English ladies who carried on so naughtily under Edward's indulgent gaze. These short family histories reveal that nearly every big family had obtained their lands through the Norman Conquest, but occasionally we read of a squire whose name 'argues him to have been of the old English stock,' and there is terrific assurance in such statements as 'eighteenth in descent from this Saxon Thane is Mr. Shirley of Ettington.' The Norman conquerors are then put in their place, and reminded that Shirleys were lording it in Ettington when Duke William's forebears were just river pirates.

The Williamses who produced Hwfa and Edith Aylesford and her five sisters, who all married titles, are an ancient Welsh family descended from unpronounceable fifteen-syllable chieftains and culminating in that Colonel Owen Williams, the Prince's friend, who vainly tried to tame his infatuated sister. Not in the *Burke's Landed Gentry*, but in my tailor's scrapbook, I read with delight: '1866, Captain Owen Williams of the Blues introduced into modern use the red swallow-tail coat for hunting—(similar in shape to the orthodox coat for evening wear, but buttoned in front). Smart but offers no protection to the legs in case of rain.' But what gentleman cares about rain when he can jump the hedges with long red coattails flying?

Out of the green fields and woods of England had emerged this pastoral aristocracy which surrounded Edward, but he was by nature a liberal man and he kept his personal world open to newcomers of every type, even to what the landed gentry considered foreign financial adventurers. A Scottish laird whose ancestors had been slaying neighbouring clans since long before the Conquest wrote out a motto for outsiders who aspired to enter Edward's set. 'Get on. Get honour. Get honest.' Edward thought this funny. Maybe Baron Hirsch and Sir Ernest Cassel did not.

But although intelligence and financial success counted with the King, people in England were still judged mainly by the standards of country gentlemen who had inherited land from generations of ancestors. Rich industrialists strove to copy them. Everyone wanted roots. Those who had none bought acres on which to grow them. Because of this earthiness, this bond to the soil, the English aristocracy remained entirely different from continental brands. While retaining a taste for the oddities of antiquity, it was not as woodenly snobbish.

Yet a certain harshness concerning class distinction had crept in with the German kings. The scorn of the English country gentleman for 'Hanoverian-made lords' is vividly expressed in *Tom Jones* and the career of the old Duke of Cambridge, who was Commander in Chief for over thirty years, gives an astonishing idea of what snobbish un-English ideas could be imposed. Having bravely commanded the First Division in the Crimean War, this royal Duke spent the next three decades defending obsolete systems and fulminating against the growing tendency to promote *for merit alone*. In his view highly trained Staff College men were 'a nasty lot of "fellas" and many of them dirty.'

Under his command the British Army remained mentally static up to the Boer War. Among regiments, the Horse and Foot Guards and Rifle Brigade each considered themselves a cut above one another and really produced a show of intolerable vanity. When an effort was made to break this conceit by interchanging officers these gentlemen suffered mental trauma. The battle to alter the military machinery so that the ablest commanders could lead England in war was a long and hard one. Queen Victoria finally demanded the old Duke of Cambridge's resignation. She liked him personally while disapproving of his private life. He had always been handsome and a true lady's man, fulminating that he would never marry one of those ugly German princesses considered suitable for such as he. He carried on many love affairs in and out of society, and eventually married an actress, Louisa Fairbrother, without the royal consent required by English law. Queen Victoria pretended the marriage did not exist, and never received his three sons who carried the usual bastard surname of Fitz-George and could not succeed to the title. King Edward, distressed by such needless embarrassment, employed one boy as his A.D.C., but not until 1959 did *Burke's Peerage* even mention the wedding—although it was a religious one legally valid in every country except England.

Queen Victoria may seem sticky on this point but, according to Princess Alice, the protocol of the Prussian court made her drawing rooms seem like an informal garden party. In Berlin all had to make their bow in strict precedence: the Prince of Weid, being only a *Serene* Highness, would be separated from his wife because she was a *Royal*. After a faultless minuet performed by nervous courtiers there would be waltzes for the young, with no sitting out allowed. Married people were not expected to dance, and one couple who did so because they so enjoyed it were severely criticised. This was the German scene at the time that England was veering towards a great series of liberal reforms which would culminate under Prime Minister Asquith.

In her extraordinary memoirs—much of which are fussily contradicted in the margins in my grandmother's handwriting: 'This conversation imaginary'—Margot Asquith gives a vivid description of her early days as the daughter of a Scottish laird before she became the talkative, megalomaniac wife of the great Asquith, 'a town-bred man of working class origin.'

Margot's father, Sir Charles Tennant, was, however, not the usual 'bonnet laird.' Having doubled his own inherited fortune, he came rather suddenly to the ownership of wide acres where his wife, a pioneer of feminine liberty, allowed her daughters a most unusual amount of freedom. In London it was still considered saucy to walk out shopping with 'only a brother of nine and a footman as chaperones,' but at Glen, their Highland home, the Miss Tennants were permitted tête-à-tête conversations and lonely walks over the hills with gentlemen who aspired to marriage. 'Old fogies' like Sir Charles Dilke, however, received short shrift. When, during a visit to Glen, Dilke met the eighteen-year-old Laura Tennant in a passage on her way to bed he said (it being the male custom never to miss an opportunity): 'If you will kiss me, I will give you a signed photograph,' to which she answered: 'How good of you, Sir Charles, but I would rather not, for what would I do with a photograph?' At least this is the story which Margot repeated.

The 'unrestrained manners and freedom from conventions' of the Tennant girls attracted many suitors and one of these, a certain erudite Mr. A. G. Liddell, known as 'Doll,' recorded his wooing of Miss Laura Tennant in a diary—the amorous passages written in transparent cipher in Greek have been translated by Oliver Lyttelton (Lord Chandos).* No wonder girls were not usually allowed to be alone with members of the opposite sex. The moment they were unwatched such a lot happened and Mr. Liddell was out of his mind about Laura and when staying at Glen he wrote incessantly of '. . . a long talk with occasional fondling—an attractive time.'

She played him up heartlessly, while letting herself fall deeply in love with Alfred Lyttelton, the nephew of Mrs. Gladstone. During a visit to Stanway, the home of Lord and Lady Elcho, she wrote: 'Of our conversation Alfred is the salt, Arthur Balfour the pepper, St. John Brodrick the bread and Hilda Brodrick the dessert. I feel rather like the milk.'

In January 1885 Mr. Liddell, whose diary is full of poetical as well as amorous description, tried all out to force an assent from his young lady while he was on a visit to Glen. He walked with Laura in the woods: 'I took her in my arms: a quaint time and place, the grey night falling in and the snow dripping on us through the trees. Going back she said she kissed Alfred Lyttelton. I was torn with jealousy and folly, we both made ourselves very wretched and kissed and almost cried.' On the following day he departed: "One long last kiss. For five minutes I sobbed, very nearly missed the train.' That night Laura accepted Alfred Lyttelton. Eleven months later she died in childbirth.

Now came a most extraordinary repetition of this romantic pattern. For several years the bereaved Lyttelton suffered acute loneliness while Liddell endured we know not what despair. Then Liddell (who had great physical attraction) began to flirt with Edith Balfour, a friend of the dead Laura. His diary records every sensation. On a walk she put her handkerchief in his pocket. 'Query: is this devised or a common dodge? It gave me such a start when I

* Lord Chandos, *From Peace to War.*

felt a hand putting a handkerchief in my pocket.' Falling violently
in love once again, he proposed and was refused. 'Although she
kissed me on the lips deliciously, her eyes were hard as flints.' Edith
was twenty-three and years later she explained that this was the first
time she had been kissed—'it was a shattering experience, I mean to
my self-control, and I longed to see him again.' But she sensed she
ought not to marry Liddell: 'Something tougher and stronger than
my passion held me back.'

She was thinking of Alfred Lyttelton. In the following year
Liddell, who seemed to specialise in Highland settings for romance,
took her walking in the hills where she drank from a burn: 'She
took up the bright water in her hand and I kissed her pretty lips.'
A few months later Edith, or D.D., as she was called by her friends,
was staying along with Arthur Balfour at Stanway where the
Pembrokes and De Greys were among the guests—also George
Curzon, who caught her and kissed her as she hurried from one
room to another. Her letters were calculated to make Liddell jealous.
Then in 1890 he joined a large Balfour family party in the Tyrol
—Edith's mother regarded him as an accepted suitor and was indignant with her daughter when she learnt there was no proper
engagement. Liddell was sent away. More kisses, moonlight and
tears. And in the following year Miss Balfour married Alfred
Lyttelton! For the second time poor Liddell had his sweetheart
captured before his eyes and in the diary he wrote: 'I should have
hated Alfred Lyttelton but I could not.'

Margot Asquith, the most famous of the Tennant sisters, is such
a personality, riding roughshod over the prejudices of her time,
that we see the merging of the classes, the rocking of the old
structures, parliamentary and social, and feel the passions of liberal
thought which, despite his outward grandeur, King Edward deeply
cherished. As King, he could not side with any political party,
but, as far as he was able, Edward backed the new reforms. Sir
Charles Tennant was a rich, partially self-made baronet, not old
aristocratic stock, and Lady Tennant did not belong to society at
all, but Margot describes the usual rich girl's education: 'I received
the scrappy, superficial upbringing that was given to the well-
to-do in the 'eighties. Pianos with magenta pleating behind maple-
wood fretwork were thumped; hard paints out of wooden boxes
were used to copy flowers and fairies on weekdays and illuminate
texts for school children on Sundays. English history was taught
and retaught from Alfred the Great to Queen Elizabeth and we
recited French fables in the presence of Swiss governesses to pained
but interested parents after tea in the evening. The mildest ques-

tions put to any of our teachers were called "impertinent"; and it was only because my father had a fine library, and we were fond of reading, that I learnt anything at all before I was sixteen. . . .

'There was not a stone dyke, peat bog, or patch of burnt or flowering heather with which I was not familiar, and I made friends with wandering tramps and every shepherd, farmer, fisherman on the Border. . . .

Nature has a life of her own which she cannot share with town-bred people. . . . The Asquith family were of necessity town-birds. They never had the fortune, leisure or circumstances to live in the country. Until I was seventeen, we knew few people in high society, and had never lived in a town. Apart from this, two more different natures and temperaments than Asquith and Tennant could not have been found. We were born adventurous, familiar, gay and unselfconscious. . . . The Asquiths were cool, intellectual and shy. . . . They were not at ease with simple country folk and I never saw one of them go inside a cottage, or talk to a villager on any of the estates which we rented for the summer holidays. If you are not bred in the country, you may admire the views, enjoy the walks and love the holidays; but you are not in touch with the lives of the men who are part of the soil, and I have watched with pity the unemotional scrutiny that betrays those who only know the country from outside. Early contact with people of one's own class in life sharpens the intellect but does not develop the emotions in the same way as the daily contact with poor cottage people.

'Though the library at Glen was full of priceless first editions of unread books, there were many strange volumes that my sister and I dipped into—chronicles of crime and witchcraft, obscure Memoirs. . . . No one at Glen took much interest in what we *knew* or what we *wanted* to know, much less interest in what we read, and it was only after Lord Napier of Ettrick drove over the Border to visit Glen that my reading received a check.

'Observing me tucked up on a sofa reading *Tristram Shandy*, he warned my mother that it was imprudent of her not to supervise my reading. I was outraged by his interference, and when my mother—who only cared for chronicles upon gardening—remonstrated with me, I hid the works of Sterne and Ouida under the pillow of my bed. . . .

'My father knew nothing of our intellectual struggles. Though a man of many tastes, his ear for music was impartial, and his knowledge of literature limited. He denounced all the modern books with which he was unfamiliar; praised "the classics"—whatever this may mean—and read in a quivering voice long passages from

Grattan's speeches, Pitt and Burke. . . . After observing the impassive expression on our mother's quiet countenance, it was not surprising that we fidgeted about upon our chairs and watched our brothers sorting their salmon flies.'

When Margot and her sisters left the Highlands to 'come out' in London, her mother offered a few maxims: 'Men hate to be run after.' Margot queried this, but not the useful admonition: 'You can do what you like in life if you hold your tongue but the world is relentless to people who are found out.' She repeated this years later to my grandmother, who looked at her quizzically. 'But, Margot, you can't hold your tongue!'

'I know, my dear,' sighed Lady Oxford and Asquith, her long leprechaun face wrinkling up, 'that is why I have had to be more virtuous than I intended.'

What Margot called her 'earliest lover'—meaning suitor—'was a man of no occupation except buying horses, boxing, gambling and keeping himself physically fit. But, like most idle people, he was always engaged and hated to be kept waiting, and upon a rare occasion when I was unpunctual I watched him smash a Chippendale mirror, an antique chest, and a valuable chair in my London boudoir.'

A more understandable burst of temper is that she witnessed in Sir William Eden, the father of Anthony Eden, who as a Master of Foxhounds understood the importance of retaining popularity with the farmers of his county. 'I saw him fling himself upon the floor when he was told that strangers had been seen riding across the newly-sown seeds of his favourite farmer.'

As a very young woman Margot encountered Lord Randolph Churchill and his friend Lord Rosebery. She comments freshly: 'No one was better company than Lord Randolph Churchill. He was like a prima donna who expected bouquets to be thrown at him from every part of the theatre.' The friends would throw shafts at each other: 'Don't look at me with your poached-egg eye, my dear Rosebery,' said Lord Randolph. At which Lord Rosebery gave 'one of his rare and lovely smiles.'

In old Lord Salisbury, three times Prime Minister, Margot found 'the most fastidious, least prepared sense of humour of any orator that I ever listened to.' But Lord Salisbury remained what the Edwardians called 'stuffy.' His home, Hatfield (which had been Queen Elizabeth's), was, except for Arundel Castle, the only country house to which Mrs. Keppel was never asked to accompany the King.

Of Winston, Margot wrote before his days of fame: 'There are some people whom you cannot change; you must either swallow them whole or leave them alone. You can do something with talent but nothing with genius and Mr. Winston Churchill has a touch of—what we all recognise but can never define—genius. . . .'

Margot knew all the famous older ladies, of course. She liked Gladys Ripon and could not bear Lady Londonderry (partly because of the Londonderrys' abhorrence of home rule for Ireland which Asquith strove to enforce).†

Although Margot's memoirs were considered indiscreet when they appeared, no one could guess from reading them of the intensity of drama behind the scenes. Margot makes occasional pertinent remarks: 'It is surprising since the question of sex dominates the destinies of half mankind how wearisome too much dilatation upon it can become. . . . All sense of fatigue disappears when Jane Austen takes us into her elegant and forgotten world of comedy without foot lights, conduct without crime and love without sex.'

When she was over thirty—after a very horsy, uninhibited girlhood—Margot became engaged to the recently widowed Liberal politician Asquith, and her mother took her to Monsieur Worth to buy smart gowns for her trousseau. The funny little English dressmaker, who designed for all the rich beauties, strutted about in a flowered waistcoat and purple velvet jacket, 'scolding, smiling, draping chairs with material.' He gave Margot a rainbow-coloured gauze gown as a wedding present, and Margot, being an unselfconscious Scot, asked that all the women who had worked on it might come down so that she could dance for them. Then she married the great Liberal leader and became what was called in those days 'a political animal.'

Days of political battle were indeed looming—the issues of Irish home rule, tariff reform and the smashing of the remaining powers of the House of Lords lay ahead. They were days of tremendous interest and opportunity—as young Mr. Winston Churchill when he joined Asquith's Liberal Party stringently observed. He was, in stern Tory strongholds, called an 'insupportable pup' and 'a traitor to his class,' and the Duke of Beaufort wished he could see him torn to pieces by his pack of dog hounds. But then Winston had likened the noble Dukes to goldfish peering

† In 1913 my mother was enjoying a magnificent political reception at Londonderry House when Lady Londonderry swept up and dazed her with the following greeting: 'I should like to see your husband [Shane Leslie, who had stood as Nationalist candidate for Londonderry in 1910] cut into small pieces or slowly burned in oil.' As a newcomer to London society the American bride felt bewildered.

through a glass bowl—able to see dimly but unfit for the fray without. Hardly polite words for a young politician, himself the grandson of a Duke.

Margot Asquith must have been the most unpopular Prime Minister's wife in history, pert, original, overtalkative and oblivious to the effect she created on the stodgy middle class whom she offended by smoking in public, saying whatever entered her head and inviting Maud Allan to dance at 10 Downing Street *in bare feet.* This was some time after the Duchess of Sermoneta had received a scandalised letter concerning Maud Allan's Rome debut: 'I examined her most carefully through my opera glasses and—*she does not wear tights!*' Bare legs were in those days considered overexciting, or at least they evoked a sensation of surprise, just as *we* feel surprise when people wander on the stage naked. We aren't accustomed to it. *We notice.* It is perhaps difficult to envisage the consternation caused by Maud Allan's performance in the sanctuary of England's Prime Minister. She danced as a nymph to Mendelssohn's 'Spring Song,' and in grey draperies to Chopin's 'Funeral March'—in which my grandmother said her toes were wonderfully able to express sorrow. But long faces were pulled in government quarters—*bare feet at 10 Downing Street!* And worse was to come. In the following year Maud Allan danced with a jewel in her navel (glued in, I suppose, and visible through the transparencies). Even I can remember the 'shock' caused by Margot Asquith's memoirs in the late twenties. She mentioned things which were considered too intimate for print—the physical and mental anguish of losing a stillborn baby, for instance. I can recall my grandmother's comment: 'I wish Margot did not feel she must even publish her birth pangs,' and Great-Aunt Mary Crawshay's immediate rejoinder: 'My dear, Margot would publish her hiccoughs.'

21

Majestic Middle Age

'I CAN STILL SEE King Edward at the State balls at Buckingham Palace, leading out his partner in the opening *quadrille d'honneur*. I do not think any other man could walk through a quadrille with so much courtly grace as he did. Sometimes he wore gorgeous uniforms, sometimes a kilt, sometimes court dress with breeches and the diamond Order of the Garter sparkling on his shapely leg. . . .' Thus he appeared to the eyes of the young Italian Duchess of Sermoneta. He was increasingly popular with the people and he could still enjoy balls—but the kind of entertainment which the King would attend must not be confused with the dances of today. A ball was a splendid and formal affair. People did not give a 'coming-out party' for a daughter, they merely allowed her to accompany them to a grown-up ball and stand beside them in her white gown with her dance programme to be filled in by the approved young men. There were certain annual customs. On Derby Day the King gave a large dinner at Buckingham Palace for members of the Jockey Club. The Duke of Devonshire, as a Steward, would always attend this dinner, while Louisa gave a dinner for Queen Alexandra at Devonshire House prior to her annual ball, to which the King and his guests would come on from the palace later.

Lists for these mighty goings-on were carefully kept and although many longed for invitations no one would have dreamt of going unless bidden. The idea of gate crashing did not exist. As everyone wanted to attend Louisa's splendid parties she held great power still, and her zest for political intrigue never diminished. In 1901, when Joseph Chamberlain was striving to negotiate an Anglo-German alliance, she summoned Baron von Eckardstein to Chatsworth: 'As we shall have a house party of fifty or sixty or so for the theatricals you will easily get an opportunity of a quiet talk with the Duke and Joe. It is true Asquith and some other leading members of the Opposition will be with us too, but that will not matter, for there are in the "Schloss" plenty of rooms where you will be able to talk without anyone noticing it.'

The attempt to reconcile German and British aims failed, and in 1903 King Edward paid his first state visit to Paris. Because of the ill feeling aroused by the Boer War he had not been there for four years. England and France had not been on friendly terms for a decade, but King Edward was determined to solidify friendship with France. He had long ago invented the term 'entente cordiale,' now he was going to put the idea across in person. He succeeded magnificently. The sour cries of *'Vivent les Boers'* which greeted him on the first day turned to *'Vive Edouard!'* on the second, and finally to that cry so inappropriate in republican France of *'Vive le roi.'* It was a personal triumph for Edward. His graciousness, his dignity, his brilliant admiral's uniform, appealed to the royalty-starved French nation. Here was a King who played his part to perfection. With that ease of manner born in him, King Edward asked President Loubet to take him to see a new play rather than Molière at the Comédie Française—'I have seen *Le Misanthrope* a dozen times; they really must not treat me like the Shah of Persia.' There were a few hisses from the audience when the King arrived, but he ignored these and during the entr'acte he strolled through the foyer on his own. It was here that he so charmingly complimented actress Jeanne Granier, who blushed with pleasure, and by dawn all Paris knew of that spontaneous remark.

Two months later President Loubet came to London—the first time a French President had crossed the Channel. Owing to his absolute refusal to wear court breeches instead of trousers, Monsieur Loubet could not receive the Order of the Garter (impossible to tie a garter around a trouser leg!), but henceforth England and France were committed: if war came, if the unbelievable happened and Germany forced the issue, they would fight together. How jolly! What a lark! sighed the sons of the great Edwardian ladies —those boys who were growing into eager, excitement-craving young men.

King Edward had five grandchildren by now, and practically

every lady whose name had been associated with him would during his ten-year reign become a grandmother. As they grew older, plumper, more interested in the beautiful gardens of their country homes, many of them were content to sit back benignly watching the intrigues and amorous dalliance of their safely married daughters. But not so Daisy Warwick, who was never to escape from the throes of her own passionate nature, and not so Gladys de Grey, who could not live without a love affair. She was, however, prone to that complaint so common among the middle-aged of expressing horror at the moral laxness of younger people. 'In my day we used to hide the pictures of our lovers, and put our husbands' on the mantelpiece. Now it is the other way around.' A mantelpiece laden with photographs of the lovers of the Countess de Grey might perhaps have appeared overdecorated. However that might be, she was now shocked. Most of the glimpses we get of Gladys in her fifties are chiefly in her box at Covent Garden Opera, or giving musical parties at her house at Kingston, or at the grandest house parties where her husband—the best shot in England—can bang off all day with his gun. Mrs. Hwfa Williams describes ecstatically the gala nights at the opera organised by Lady de Grey, the men in uniform or court dress if a foreign royalty or president attended, the women in tiaras. Lady Londonderry would receive her friends in one box, Lady Charles Beresford owned another, 'always filled with people but among them all she could be distinguished with her various pieces of coloured chiffon and beads around her neck.' The Painted Lady had successfully hung on to her Red Admiral. After a special opera Lady de Grey might invite the performers down to her house, Combe Court, and Melba and Caruso would sing there till dawn.

Once a year she invited all the stars of Covent Garden Opera to a dinner party 'as her personal friends, and it was considered a great privilege to be included in her list of guests. She used to plan it all very carefully and ask people two months ahead, so as to be sure of getting exactly who she wanted, and the evenings always ended with delightful music as all the singers relaxed in her tactful presence.' The Duchess of Sermoneta was exceedingly impressed, and my grandmother, who was so musical and loved these parties, was far too discreet to tell her the reason that my grandfather (who luckily for him was not musical or he would have missed a lot) took himself off to the Guards Club, shaking his head disapprovingly, when an invitation arrived to Combe Court.

As the first aristocrat to become a serious patron of music and ballet, Gladys de Grey should not be passed over lightly. Her efforts to aid the Covent Garden Opera will not be forgotten.

The late love of Lady de Grey's life was, according to a reliable French authority, the Hon. Reginald Lister (a younger brother of Lord Ribblesdale) who became British Minister in Tangiers. My informant visited him there in 1910 and describes him as handsome in a melancholy way, adding: '. . . As for Lord de Grey, I always heard he had no sense of smell, but in exchange his sight was so piercing he could catch the eye of a thrush nesting.' This phenomenal eye enabled him to bring down many thousands of high-flying pheasants while his wife's sharp eye followed a different kind of game.

Miss Edith Balfour describes the boredom women suffered during Monday-to-Saturday shooting parties. One morning at Panshanger, where Lord Desborough had a famous shoot, she woke at seven and, having finished her book the night before, she put on her dressing gown and descended to the library to seek another. There she found Lord de Grey drilling his two loaders and practising changing over his three guns. 'He was not pleased at being discovered, for in those days it was considered more praiseworthy to excell by unforced aptitude.' Trying too hard was not the thing.

In 1909 the De Greys became the Ripons (he succeeded his Viceroy father as 2nd Marquess). A letter of Lord Knutsford's, written after a 1909 Sandringham shooting party during which Queen Alexandra celebrated her birthday, gives a fair idea of the greatest shoot in England. The Sandringham larders had been built to hold seven thousand head of game. On the first day over two thousand pheasants were shot, 'as usual,' and five hundred rabbits. 'Tea over, I come to my bedroom to write this. A hairdresser arrives tonight to dress all the ladies' heads as they have to wear tiaras. . . . Thirty to dinner . . . Lady Ripon in salmon pink with a sort of shawl. . . . They all had tiaras and every jewel they possessed . . . Dighton Probyn got up and said, "I give you the Queen's health" and "May God bless her" (very earnestly, he is so devoted to her) and drank her health. We all stood up and did so too. She seemed touched.' Then the Russian Balalaika Court Orchestra played 'like the wind whistling through violin strings, very lovely and very exciting!' Knutsford was intrigued by a picture in his bedroom. It showed an angel warning all nations of the Yellow Peril and was signed, 'To my dear Uncle Bertie from Wilhelm.' In 1909 the Kaiser's Chinese phobia was considered comic.

Next morning at ten-thirty the shooters went out. Knutsford, a fairly good shot, felt nonplussed at being placed between Prince

George and Ripon, the 'star turns.' The men returned to a terrific tea at five. The King, who did not greatly care for shooting, came in very sorry for himself and complaining he had had to sit through a council with his ministers (Salisbury, Derby, etc.) with toothache, and a dentist had arrived to pull the tooth out. 'Just cocaine,' said the King. 'I can bear pain.'

Queen Alexandra came down to tea in 'a white teagown covered with lace and splendid jewels.' At dinner she wore black velvet with diamond spangles and a high collar of diamonds.

Every person who visited Sandringham wrote of the manner in which Edward spoiled his dogs, and of Alexandra's gracious attention to her guests. She was still the most frivolous and unpunctual Queen, but in her own home no woman could be more delightful. Lord Knutsford, like all around her, felt captivated by her irresistible girlish charm. It is interesting to note that King Edward never allowed her to see the official boxes, a privilege he granted his daughter-in-law who was to become Queen Mary. May of Teck and Mrs. Keppel were the women he considered trustworthy, and whose judgment he took seriously.

The signature of Gladys de Grey or Ripon in old country house visitors' books gives one an idea of her continuous social life. But what more can one learn? Her early photographs look ludicrously coy and stories of her practical jokes on her husband do not seem as funny now as then. She once bought a huge tea service and had the footman drop it behind Lord de Grey so that he thought his priceless china collection had been smashed. Lady Desborough, in a little privately printed book, writes of Gladys' good looks which 'had a trick of making other people look insignificant, and, in a sense, it was the same with her personality. . . . Life was an endless adventure, and the freshness of her curiosity never abated. . . . She grasped whatever she took up with passionate interest.' Ettie Desborough's praise is never mean. She saw Gladys at her best, working for the revival of opera at Covent Garden where she 'performed the double function of being the most practical and discriminating patroness and also the most beautiful object in the house.' When Diaghileff brought his Russian Ballet to London, Lady Ripon was the first to wax enthusiastic and to help it become a success. Sargent drew Nijinsky's head and gave it to her as a tribute and Sir Osbert Sitwell describes Gladys Ripon in what one would hesitate to call her old age: 'Alas, I never knew her well, but I met her sufficiently often to be able to admire her unusual beauty, personal dignity and intelligence. She carried herself with the supreme grace of her generation, and with her grey hair and distinguished features of so pure a cut, she remained, though no longer a young woman, the most striking individual to look at in any room she entered.'* One might imagine that this elegant aristocrat had mellowed with the years, but she was unkind to her only child, the shy, tall Lady Juliet Lowther, who had made the unpardonable mistake of being born a girl instead of Earl of Lonsdale; and, according to a great-nephew of her admirer Sir John Lister-Kaye (described by his own family as 'that rascally bounder'), the Marchioness of Ripon's relationship with Nijinsky was extremely curious. Sir John (a tall thin man who proved irresistible to several gracious ladies) took a poor view of Nijinsky and grumbled: 'She says she is good for his dancing—utter rot.' Her love letters to Lister-Kaye lie in a remote Irish castle.

Lady Ripon made herself the ballet's 'social manager' and instructed Diaghileff which invitations to accept or refuse. 'I must have Vaslav for the weekend,' she would say when commandering Nijinsky, and off she would drive him to lovely places where he could wander the gardens alone. As Vaslav Nijinsky could not speak a word of English he probably enjoyed being organised and the jealous Johnnie Lister-Kaye was just being waspish. As she grew older many people admired Gladys Ripon, but she would never win forgiveness from Lady Londonderry, and in the end— and this reveals a human streak in her nature—forgiveness was what she desired.

* Sir Osbert Sitwell, *Great Morning*.

22

Arthur Balfour
and Lady Elcho

As THE YEARS CAST a silvery mist over Edwardian heads we cannot continue to unravel romances concerning splendid fifty-year-olds. It is time to glance back through the file and pick out the one love affair which can be described from start to finish—from 1883 up to 1918. Dozens of liaisons must have existed, but there were two men who caused devastations in the dovecots whom I feel I know personally—Arthur Balfour, who was Prime Minister when Edward became King, and his younger friend Harry Cust. They were both acquaintances of my grandmother and the lovers of her closest friends. So she heard everything. I myself never saw Lady Elcho, but I met Lady Desborough, her rival, and her daughter-in-law, who was born Lady Violet Manners.*

The affair between Lady Elcho and Arthur Balfour was one of those which continued in the grand Edwardian tradition for many, many years—from the year of her marriage, 1883, until he died in 1922. She was the sister of George Wyndham (another charmer well known in Ireland where as Chief Secretary he launched the famous Wyndham Land Act). When Arthur Balfour, nephew of that great old Tory Prime Minister Lord Salisbury, went to Ire-

* She was the daughter of the 'Soul' Violet, Duchess of Rutland, loved by Harry Cust, and the sister of Lady Diana Cooper.

land, George Wyndham was his private secretary, so it was natural that Balfour should stay at Stanway, the Elchos' home in Gloucestershire, whenever he returned to England. In addition to this, Arthur Balfour had been made a trustee for Lord Elcho after he got into financial difficulty during a rather wild youth. Mary had met Balfour before her marriage to Hugo Elcho, but he did not propose. He was a curious, erudite, musical personality, able to sparkle and to philosophise, but not to lead or consolidate in politics. Many women loved him, and two he loved back with sufficient ardour to make him flee the suitable young girls paraded for him—for the nephew of the great Salisbury was for many years considered a very eligible gentleman; but he would die, as Earl Balfour, unmarried.

Margot Asquith recounts that the press erroneously announced her engagement to Lord Rosebery, who greeted her with 'frigid self-suppression,' and later the press repeated this annoyance, naming Arthur Balfour, who treated the rumour with his usual 'insolent indifference' and replied airily to a questioner: 'No, that is not so. I rather think of having a career of my own.' Margot's scatterbrained relationships with men are difficult to assess from her memoirs, but she liked Balfour's reaction to the press rumour: 'Seeing me come into Lady Rothschild's ball-room one night, he left the side of the man he was conversing with and in an elastic step stalked down the empty parquet floor to greet me. He asked me to sit down next to him in a conspicuous place; and we talked through two dances.'

Of course, Lord Rosebery was being bombarded by women who wanted to marry him (their love letters have been kept, but not published, so his embarrassment when meeting the talkative parakeet Margot is understandable), but Balfour retained his 'elastic step, and deliberately sat in public with her. Margot goes on to say that A.J.B. was 'difficult to know intimately, because of his formidable detachment. The most that many of us could hope for was that he had a taste in us. . . . He was blessed or cursed at his birth, according to individual opinion, by two assets—charm and wits. . . . His social distinction, exquisite attention, intellectual tact, cool grace and lovely bend of his head made him not only a flattering listener but an irresistible companion.'

My grandmother and my great-aunt Jennie, who were both musical like A.J.B. and had therefore a natural link which did not necessarily entail coquetting, said he liked to stir up emotional warmth, to love and be loved, but that he was unmasculine—not homosexual, just a man who liked a lot of smoke and rather little fire. 'Too many white corpuscles in his blood!' commented my grandmother, who used medical terms metaphorically.

Whatever the virility of A.J.B., he could charm the birds off the trees, and the ladies into and out of their boudoirs—whichever seemed convenient. They fell in love with him and they could not seem to fall out. A line penned by Dilke in 1878 simply states: 'Arthur Balfour is present, I am the greatest of admirers of his "charm." It was much spoken of in his youth.' Much later on, Lloyd George, when asked what place Balfour would take in history, answered: 'He will be like the scent on a pocket handkerchief.'

Although Mary Wyndham's feelings for Balfour were aroused before her marriage at nineteen to Lord Elcho, and made themselves manifest during the earliest years of her married life, the story had better begin in 1888 by sketching that group known for many years as 'the Souls,' which consisted of a group of people who revelled in each other's company and considered themselves an intellectual elite, immune to worldly pretensions and interested in discussing only 'the worthwhile.' Their name was bestowed on them by Charles Beresford during a dinner. Turning to Arthur Balfour, Harry Cust, Mary Elcho, Margot Asquith and Violet, Duchess of Rutland, he said, 'You all sit talking about each other's souls, I shall call you "the Souls."'

The name stuck, and other congenial aesthetic types, such as Lord Curzon and Wilfrid Scawen Blunt, drifted into the group. The trouble was that during the next ten years 'the Souls' so often discovered they had bodies too.

Letters written by Laura Tennant, just after she had married Lyttelton, describe the atmosphere when she visited Stanway: 'We found Hugo and Mary in good form. He is very amusing and completely unscrupulous. Arthur is the most interesting of them all . . . because he lives with his windows shut and has a few false windows.' When writing to her sisters she sums up Mary Elcho precisely:

'I am sure Mary is good and I know her very well, but I am sure she deceives herself; the truth is not in her about her own affections. I don't think M. is subtle enough to think out for herself what you say about the desire everyone has to get at Arthur *per se*. She likes him—he fascinates her—her attitude is that of looking up in wonder—not of standing on the same ground with him and piercing him with her understanding. Her weapons are weaponless worship. . . . Then she feels she *must* not disappoint him—she is at the top of her bent with him. She listens to him and he is not strong enough to withstand the easy delights of constantly pleasing and never annoying, jarring or disappointing her. If he did what I should say was unArthurian, she would say since *he* did it that it *was* Arthurian and her affection for Hugo is strangely mixed up with her affection for the man she knows can, will and does help Hugo more than anyone else does. Were I or you in her position we would cancel our engrossment. As it is she is not able to do so and is the most "*à jour*" woman I ever met. What Arthur should do is very easy to see. He should deny himself the gratification of the luxury—but few men make extra commandments for themselves, feeling I presume that their duty is done if they obey the Decalogue.' A nice assessment of many a love affair.

During the years 1887 to 1891, while Balfour was Chief Secretary for Ireland, he could conduct his liaison with Mary Elcho ardently but delicately. He was a man, I think, who preferred distance. When Balfour visited the Elchos' home, Stanway, a rambling sixteenth-century house of golden Cotswold stone in Gloucestershire, he invariably found a superb juxtaposition of ill-assorted guests, for Lord and Lady Elcho liked entirely different types of people. Thirteen years after her marriage Mary wrote to Balfour: 'If only you had married me in 1881!' This aroused no vehement protestation; instead Balfour sent flattering remarks concerning her husband: 'Hugo has just made one of the most amusing speeches I have ever heard in the House.'†

While Mary Elcho's brother acted as private secretary to Balfour it was so easy—indeed natural—for A.J.B. to visit Stanway. Amidst the surprising Elcho house parties his presence must have added calm and lustre. Indeed, there was not a house in England which did not covet Mr. Balfour for his conversation; he was an important man with a first-class brain. From 1891 he led the Tory Party in the House of Commons and from 1902 to 1905 he was Prime Minister in continuously rough political weather.

Sir Harold Nicolson describes him at this time: 'His patrician temperament rendered him unsympathetic to the cruder men who were by then ousting the old territorial aristocracy from the control of the Conservative Party. His philosophic aloofness had induced in him the habit of mind, so dangerous in any politician, of being interested in both sides of a case. It was not that he lacked the courage of his convictions: few statesmen have manifested such physical and moral audacity: it was rather that he classed convic-

† Viscount Elcho sat in the House of Commons, being the son of the 10th Earl of Wemyss, who lived till 1914.

tions with deliberate forms of belief and much disliked all deliberate forms of belief.'

The sixteenth-century gables and mullioned windows of Stanway, its 'restful shabbiness and gentle dilapidations,' must have meant a romantic refuge to Arthur Balfour for nearly forty years. In winter it was icy, but that did not prevent the family loving the old place, even if the log fires did scorch one half of the human body while leaving the other side blue with cold. Wind whistled through the big rooms with their endless intercommunicating doors —one bedroom had five doors—maybe useful at times but always draughty. Stanway had beauty and atmosphere; it was a happy home.

Mary Elcho wrote to Arthur Balfour describing her own sitting room, the East Room, as 'the right paradise for both of us,' while his letters remained more abstract. As the years slipped by, it became obvious that *he* was the pursued, and yet he continued to visit Stanway, to be chased and cajoled and entreated by this lovely woman—when he was not slipping off to visit Lady Desborough at Panshanger, where the utterly delightful Lord Desborough, scholar and athlete, welcomed his conversation and ignored the overtures —much spoken of—made to his enchanting wife.

Sometimes Mary Elcho wrote petulantly to A.J.B.: 'You love me as much as a man can love a woman he has loved for ten years.' This is an ignoble wail for either wife or mistress. It ill behoved Lady Elcho to be sorry for herself at this stage. She was surrounded by adoring friends, her husband was gentlemanly and grateful for the children she bore him, her coachman insisted on the feudal call, 'Make way for her ladyship,' in the local inn yard, and she was admired by her father-in-law, old Lord Wemyss (of whom Matthew Arnold said, 'to my mind, indeed, the mere cock of his lordship's hat is one of the finest and most aristocratic things we have').

In addition to these pleasant things, for many years she kept a firm hold on Arthur Balfour, whose attentions so many other women hankered after. When Lady Elcho complained, maybe it was because she became run down—she had to run Stanway and a five-story brick mansion in London (only open for three months a year) on rather little money, she bore six children between 1884 and 1896, and she was not very strong.

When I read in Mr. Kenneth Young's *James Arthur Balfour* that she had in 1898 written to Arthur Balfour concerning a self-induced abortion I took the trouble to check up on this occurrence which I had never heard of in Edwardian circles. I think the choice of words gives an erroneous impression. What Lady Elcho actually

did was to bicycle like mad uphill and down dale hoping to dis-
courage yet another baby. Fair enough. Bicycling is not abortion
and should not be called so. I am not seeking an argument with the
medical profession, merely clarifying the phrase. Mary's seventh
and last child, Irene, arrived four years later. No suggestion was
ever made that any of her children were not Lord Elcho's. The
love affairs of the Edwardians were certainly not platonic, but they
usually started on poetic levels and intensified physically as the ladies grew older and less likely to produce difficult-to-account-for
children.

Through the long years Lady Elcho and Mr. Balfour enjoyed
strolling, bicycling and playing tennis together. Balzac has said:
'Great love affairs start with champagne and end with *tisane*'—but
in England they end with croquet and tennis.

When a high-strung, brilliant, rather delicate man is the focal
point for many women's affection it is intriguing to analyse the
spell he casts. Certainly in the House of Commons A.J.B. proved
an alert and dexterous dialectician, his ordinary conversation was
always stimulating, and Oliver Lyttelton (Lord Chandos) wrote:
'Part of the charm of Arthur Balfour seemed to arise from his
presumption that what you were saying was at least on the level of
his own thought.' But why were so many women mad about him?
And why could he never bring himself to marry? Was it entirely
owing to his devotion to Mary Elcho and Ettie Desborough? Or had
he a basic disinclination for the final feminine domination? He
showed an irritating propensity to jeer at women who tried to
educate themselves. When a group of Lady Elcho's friends attended
a class of ethics he teased them unmercifully.

'But, Mr. Balfour, nobody could be more humble than we are
about it.'

'Humility is good but it is not sufficient for the study of ethics.'

An annoying man, although light in hand. He did not, however,
belong to the practical-joke brigade and for King Edward and
Queen Alexandra he was far too serious and highbrow. When Balfour attended the last Chatsworth house party, given for Their
Majesties in 1907, the Duke of Devonshire and Louisa celebrated
Twelfth Night with crackers and old-time festivity. Mr. Balfour
sedately put a paper cap on his head, but such nonsense was plainly
anathema for him. Not so Queen Alexandra: 'She was wonderful
at this sort of thing and made everybody play up so that the fun
became fast and furious.'

A.J.B. liked fun, but not this kind. The boisterous romping in
which Alexandra could partake so gracefully left him cold. He

once said: 'An omnivorous, universal and insatiable curiosity to know everything that can be known is a pleasure that lasts longer than any other.' Maybe these words reveal him. Being sensitively adjusted, he may have realised that omnivorous, universal and insatiable curiosity is not likely to be the perfect cement in matrimony.

While Mary Elcho discovers 'paradise' in the East Room with A.J.B. one might wonder if his lordship does not deserve some commiseration. But not at all. Hugo loved his vague dreamy wife who bore him all those children, and if she blossomed when the soulful Balfour was around—well, he could himself see the fellow's charm. The beautiful tubercular Hermione, Duchess of Leinster, had been in love with Hugo before she died and as time went on he found a suitable soul mate for himself in a married woman fourteen years his junior. Lady Angela, youngest daughter of the Earl of Rosslyn and half sister of Daisy Warwick, had been a keen hunting girl, brought up traditionally in the stableyard. When James, the son of Sir Charles Forbes of Aberdeenshire, who also rode like smoke, asked her to become his wife, she had immediately answered: 'Yes, if I may have your chestnut horse.'

The marriage was successful for seven years and two daughters were born. Then in 1904, on the most amicable terms, the Forbeses separated. Lady Angela went off with an allowance, the family emeralds (and presumably that chestnut horse—getting rather long in the tooth).

She was a tough, vibrant personality, 'whose language could make a trooper blush,' and while Mary Elcho read poetry with Mr. Balfour, the more down-to-earth Hugo relaxed with horsy Angela. These two liaisons, which did not upset each other, lasted 'till death us do part.' There were ups and downs, of course; ups in the mellow years when A.J.B. was Prime Minister (although Mary always had to share him with Ettie Desborough, who was 'all electricity no man could switch on or off'), and down when Lady Angela (whom Elcho sometimes had to share with Lord Ribblesdale) brought a case against her husband's trustees. When she overspent her allowance these tiresome lawyers asked her to return the family emeralds as 'surety.' This she refused to do 'except for the little ones I do not care for'—so very understandable! Eventually she brought a court case in which both her lovers, Hugo and Ribblesdale, gave evidence on her behalf and were ticked off by the judge for encouraging 'a very ill-advised action.'

But to get the real flavour of this kind of love affair—one in which for twenty or thirty years the parties involved steadily visited the same country houses, wrote each other letters and shared pains and joys—one must slide forward into the terrible summer of 1915. For over thirty years Arthur Balfour had courted Mary Elcho, stayed at Stanway and dined during the summer months at her large, 'so difficult to run' red brick house in Cadogan Square. At sixty-six he was, with some distress, about to take over the Admiralty from a miserable Winston Churchill after the Dardanelles debacle. Mary was herself in her fifties, with three married children and several grandchildren. Passion had turned to simmering devotion. Arthur Balfour still attended Lady Elcho and Lady Desborough, but now it was with bowed head, striving to find some word of comfort for them.

Within the first six months of war Ettie Desborough's two sons had been killed—the poet Julian Grenfell and the athlete Billy—and so had Mary Elcho's nineteen-year-old son, the 'joy giver,' his father's favourite, his sisters' favourite, just out of school. Soon the eldest would be killed as well. Elcho's daughter Cynthia (married to Prime Minister Asquith's second son) wrote in her diary: 'Oh why was I born for this time? Before one is thirty to have known more dead than living people.' And, when Lady Desborough came to stay at Stanway, trying to help others with her own philosophy: 'The same old extraordinary zest still unimpaired, and the exaggerated interest in everyone and everything. One almost begins to wonder and think it inhuman, but directly she is alone with one she is just a simple, effortless woman with a bleeding heart. Tears pour down her cheeks, and she talks on and on about the boys, yet preserving such wonderful sympathy for others. . . .

'She says she thinks it illogical to be so unhappy with her conviction that they would not mind and are happy. She seems to have no qualms about immortality, and cannot account for the fearful pain of their loss.'

What did Arthur Balfour say to these two bereft women? He was always about, in and out of their houses, inviting them to dinner, distracting them with interesting war news, but what, in the end, could he drag from his heart? What could he say? He was not a father, like Hugo Elcho, sitting in Cadogan Square 'heartbroken and just like a child . . . tears streaming down his cheeks and so naively *astonished*.'

Lady Angela was the right medicine. Having no worries over her own teen-age daughters, she had plunged into war work of the most boisterous kind. No jobs had been organised for women except bandage-rolling and acting in matinees, but Lady Angela went off to a Paris hospital which dealt with the worst cases from the Battle of Mons. She calmly set to, working in the operating theatre. Then, appalled by the unattended wounded she saw lying on the quay at Boulogne, she impetuously opened two British soldiers' canteens, starting with a personal £8 order from Fortnum and Mason, and kept going by newspaper appeals.

These canteens, called *Angelinas,* were most popular with the troops, but Lady Angela's habit of dispensing with red tape maddened officialdom. On one occasion she was reported to the Adjutant General for saying 'damn' at 5 A.M. while trying to serve several thousand men with hot tea. During all her skirmishes with officials Arthur Balfour backed her to the hilt. When the War Office finally decided she must not be allowed to return to France because of her immoral habit of washing her hair in the canteen ('only hot water available—so insanitary not to!'), Mr. Balfour, as First Lord of the Admiralty, arranged for her to travel secretly to Boulogne. Through the anguish they stuck together—Hugo and his Angela, Mary and A.J.B.

The picture of this curious, deeply loyal foursome, who had lived so hotly in early years, is typical of the end of many Edwardian love affairs. It reveals the quality of their relationship, the depth of their caring.

In Mary Elcho's house there had always been happiness and security for the children. To break up a home was the price *never* to be paid for romance. After the nineteen-year-old son was killed his elder brother wrote to his mother: 'The only sound thing is to hope the best thing for one's country and to expect absolutely nothing for oneself in the future. . . . We were a damned good family. . . . I couldn't have had more joy out of anything than I have from my family. . . . I am awfully sorry for Papa who loved him. He must write his sons off and concentrate upon his grandchildren, who, thank God, exist. . . .'

But Hugo Elcho could never recover from the loss of that gay youngest son—his own and everybody's favourite—the boy who had revelled in his few weeks of military training and written elated letters of the men marching with 'a thousand singing legs.' The Germans were employing a tough professional army, men bred as serious warriors whose families were adjusted to the cold honour of death. Germany did not fight her way with Rupert Brookes and Wilfred Owens and Julian Grenfells—the golden boys, the poets of the race.

Within a year the Elchos' eldest son was reported wounded in Mesopotamia; there followed two anguished months of fleeting hopes, contradictions and finally the news that he had been seen to disappear in a shellburst. His body was never found, which allowed

Violet, his wife, half demented with grief, to indulge in wild impossible hope that he might have 'crawled off wounded.' It was one of those particularly cruel cases offering long-drawn-out faint gleams of hope. In a way it seemed less terrible to lose a son who was over thirty, who had achieved something in his life and who left two little boys—but Mary Elcho had to face a new torture, for her daughter-in-law could not bring herself to accept her husband's death. After two months on the alert, after being lifted 'from Hell to Heaven' on a false report and flung down again, Lady Violet could not bear the final 'bad news.' If she could not see him 'just once again' she wished to die. A strange final misery hit her when, sending for her small boys, she explained, 'Daddy is never coming back—you do remember him, don't you?' and it became obvious they didn't—they were too little.

Mary Elcho drove her daughter-in-law down to Stanway—that should have soon been her happy home—and in the lovely old house, which now seemed *aching*, Mary knew the desolation of having to bear a mother's grief while trying to lessen a wife's. Through all this Mary and her husband wrote each other sustaining letters and Arthur Balfour was always there, while Angela, back from a new skirmish with the War Office, gave all her animal strength to Hugo.

After a final 'cruellest moment,' when Lady Elcho received back from the Red Crescent her own last letter to her son and for one moment the Turkish writing looked as if it might be his 'if weak and sick,' Cynthia, inwardly blaming herself for allowing her own heart to leap, accompanied her mother to Brighton where Mr. Balfour and Lady Desborough were staying, 'in order to give Mr. B. a healthy holiday—the first time he has left London since he went to the Admiralty.' Cynthia had a long discussion about her mother with A.J.B.: '. . . We agreed that she didn't like completely passive submission, but, as Mr. B. said, successions of gentle rearguard actions.'

In London, Cynthia at dinner sat next to Winston, who was fuming at having to impotently watch the mismanagement of the Dardanelles. He said it was 'like being bound hand and foot, and watching one's best girl being—well, I won't say what.'

From 1916 on it seemed all the more terrible to belong to a large, closely knit family, for the pain of having to break the news to so many and to watch them suffer. Cynthia describes the stricken face of her thirteen-year-old sister Irene when handed £93—her share of the tiny fortune left by the adored young brother, who had been in such a hurry to leave Eton and who had lasted three weeks in France. An occasional 'sleeping draught' was administered by the family doctor, but real sedation was unthought of.

Lady Elcho's fortitude almost frightened her daughter, while Violet kept saying, 'I know I am going to die, but I just want to be finished off like a shot animal. I must know exactly what happened, so that I can feel it with my senses.' But no one would ever know. The younger boy was killed by six bullets, if that was consolation, but the elder had simply vanished in a shellburst.

Cynthia's diary makes painful reading; one sighs with relief when she notes: 'Mamma went off to Brighton with A.J.B.' November came and Cynthia took the train back to Stanway for a weekend: 'I am in Mr. Balfour's room, which I hate—very uncomfortable bed.' Mary Elcho was vague, but this *is* a curious sidelight, she did not even bother over A.J.B.'s mattress! Later came a weekend at Stanway when Ettie Desborough travelled down with Mary Elcho and Hugo with Angela. After dinner they played a game, inventing the most surprising titles of books certain people might have written. This suddenly reveals what they thought about each other. For Lord Elcho—*Tina's Bible Stories for Tiny Tots;* for Mr. Balfour—*Three Girls and a Horse;* for Mary Elcho—*Talks About Chaps* (she was slightly piqued); and for Lady Angela—*Ragged Homes and How to Mend Them.* Cynthia wrote: 'Angela's face quite withered and Papa said they couldn't see the point; it was terribly double-edged, the house-breaking inference, which I don't suppose she would mind much—and the raggedness of her own home.'

Lady Desborough was still what they called a 'tuning fork' at a party. She set the note for conversation. Cynthia went 'a delicious walk' with her. 'We discussed "lovers" and their compatibility with happy marriages. She said she was not monogamous in the strict sense of the word, and had never been in love in the way which *excluded* other personal relations. To be at her best with one man she must see a great many others.'

It is interesting to note how astringent a lady of the old school could remain after terrible sorrow. Ettie Desborough's courage and compassion for others were a legend with which I grew up.

Throughout the war Cynthia dined at 62 Cadogan Square with her mother and Arthur Balfour, or with her father and Angela. Occasionally they were all playing tennis together at Stanway. On one evening in London A.J.B. came to dinner with Mary and tactless Hugo did not go out. Then Lady Angela came in to make four—she was 'thirsting for help' in her various troubles, and Mr. Balfour, who wanted rest from Admiralty worries, did not have the evening he expected.

Cynthia's diaries (published in 1968) present a unique period piece. She had much of her mother's appeal and frankly describes her dependency on masculine admiration, although she remained devoted to her husband Herbert Asquith. She kept her spirit alive with two lovers to whom she wrote daily when they were in the trenches, and who when on leave were permitted to stay 'late at night' in her flat—Lord Basil Blackwood and Lord Alex Thynne. Both were killed before the war ended, and so was Asquith's elder son Raymond, but Cynthia's husband, Herbert Asquith, often ill but always struggling back to the front, coughing and writing poems, survived.

After Basil Blackwood's death Cynthia records: 'Some sort of very vague but serious religion—quite unformulated—makes it all bearable for me. Would it be easier if one hated the Germans? I feel them—poor devils—to be our wretched allies fighting against some third thing. The whole thing *must* be the means to some end, and that no political one.'

Then: 'The post has become a bitter pang. I cannot believe that I shall never have another of Basil's letters. He has been a very great deal of the wind in my sails for the last five years. . . . Everything makes me realise how I miss him. . . . Nothing is without an association with him. . . . A whole language gone.'

She was at a nursery tea in the house of Raymond Asquith's widow Katherine (daughter of Lady Horner, whose memories dot some of these pages) when the nanny handed her a note to say that the only surviving Horner boy had been killed. Cynthia, not quite thirty, writes: 'Soon there will be nobody left with whom one can even talk of the beloved figures of one's youth.'

The country houses of England, always cold, were almost fireless now. Asquith's third son Arthur, having had his foot blown off, got engaged to the daughter of Lord Manners. Her father, inspecting her trousseau, was shocked to see *transparent* lawn nightdresses, but the bride-to-be replied firmly: 'It doesn't matter. I shall wear my combinations under them.'

The pacifist-minded D. H. Lawrence saw Cynthia constantly and wrote to her outraged: 'I feel as if the young grass growing would upset all the cannon on the face of the earth, and that man with his evil stupidity is often all nothing—the leaves just brush him under. The principle of life is, often, stronger than the principle of death, and I spit on your London and your government and your armies. Pah! What are they? Lloyd George and Haig and such-like *canaille? Canaille, canaille,* the lot of them—also Balfour, old poodle that he is.'

Cynthia could not help laughing when Lady Angela held forth on the immorality of young women of today, and we see exactly what war work was turning her into. 'Dined in with Papa, Angela and Flavia [Lady Angela's provocative-looking, badly behaved flapper daughter]. Poor Angela, quite in her worst form. She is again in deep trouble with the authorities—her Ambulance Convoy being held up—and she was very hoarse and indignant.'

The humorous side was also evoked whenever Grandpapa, as Hugo had become, arrived home and a five-year-old grandson, eager to be helpful, rushed out with the news a child guessed would most interest him, 'Lady Angela isn't here!'

Despite her genius for organisation, Angela did not treat women workers with tact. One of them, sacked for drunkenness, sent a round-robin complaint about Lady Angela's morals. This somehow reached the Foreign Office just after the ghastly Battle of Cambrai and, with the rumour of forty German divisions being moved to the Western Front, Angela had insisted on the subject of herself, her ambulance and her work canteens being brought up in the House of Lords! Her former lovers, Hugo (now Earl of Wemyss) and Lord Ribblesdale, were to speak in her favour and Lord Derby, Secretary of War, solemnly prepared drafts of the debate for them to study in advance. Lord Ribblesdale will ask the questions and will be followed by Lord Wemyss. In their speeches they will *not* attack the War Office, but they will be at liberty to eulogise the work of Lady Angela and to make reference to the necessity, in the interest of military discipline, of the centralisation of the control of huts.

Lord Derby will reply in the following terms: 'The noble Lord is quite right, etc. etc. I quite recognise the valuable and difficult work done by Lady Angela and the closing of her canteens was not intended in any way to reflect on her management of the huts, or upon the zeal and ability she had shown in discharging her onerous tasks. . . . I hear of many wild rumours in regard to this case—and for these I beg to assure the noble Lord the War Office is not responsible. I hope the incident may now be considered closed, and these much-to-be-deprecated rumours should cease.'

Cynthia sat with Angela in the gallery during the debate. 'Atmosphere strangely sleepy after the House of Commons. The peers are a scratch-looking lot. . . . Papa spoke with great eloquence in his best sanctimonious cathedral voice. The Lords either had great control or else they didn't see the absurdity of the situation.'

It seems unbelievable that, a month before the Battle of the Somme, the Secretary of War should be rectifying rumours about this brave but obviously maddening woman, when the whole House of Lords knew that Ribblesdale and Hugo Wemyss had been her lovers! Three days later Cynthia recorded: 'Angela sobbing down the telephone to Papa—quite distraught, poor girl. . . .'

Lord Derby, who had been put out by all this rumpus, had not renewed her working permit! How glad she was when he lost office shortly after. Years later Edith Sitwell would describe Lady Angela Forbes as 'an elderly gorilla affected with sex-appeal.' But sometimes that is just what gentlemen like.

The year 1914 broke up the Edwardian world, but in the agony of losing husbands and sons, no one realised that it had gone forever. In 1918 Cynthia ended her diary with the words: 'I am beginning to rub my eyes at the prospect of peace. I think it will require more courage than anything that has gone before. . . . One will have to look at long vistas again, instead of short ones, and one will at last fully recognise that the dead are not only dead for the duration of the war.'

23

Harry Cust

AFTER THIS HARROWING excursion into the next reign let us return to Edwardian heydays. The holocaust of sons occurred in the first two years of the war. After 1915, except for newly fledged schoolboys, the aristocracy of England had no young men left to send to the trenches.

Going back to the decades before the deluge, we find the sentimental dalliances of Mr. Arthur Balfour were nothing compared to the havoc created by his much younger friend, Mr. Harry Cust, heir of Lord Brownlow. Here the charm was less elusive—Harry's sex appeal was the kind which words *can* describe: clever, amusingly amorous and with a face which in ancient Greece would have been called beautiful; he was both poetic and essentially male—an enticing combination which women fall for in every age.

I have been somewhat shocked at that eminent historian Sir Charles Petrie referring to this delightful philogenist as 'the most notorious lecher of the day.' Harry Cust was no more lecherous than ninety per cent of the men around him. He merely happened to possess—quite unfairly, of course—an enormous attraction for women. Conquest came too easily and he could not steel himself to the strong-minded 'No.'

Considering the disaster that his thoughtlessness had caused when, as a very young man, he allowed Lady Londonderry's letters to fall into the hands of Gladys de Grey, one might hope that he would have grown more careful in the future. But the Bad Fairy had attended Harry's christening, and when all the other assets were doled out she handed her cruel gift: Harry Cust would be a man who disappointed himself.

When still a schoolboy he had written charming verse:

> Grey grows the glimmer on an April even
> And, as the sunset glory fades away,
> There comes to float upon the clouds to Heaven
> The burden of the day.

His tutors delighted in his erudition and his contemporaries found elation in Harry's company. But these talents, added to shining good looks, resulted in his eventual downfall—or rather to a drift into fading sunset glory where the burden of the day weighed heavily on a might-have-been.

No sooner did he emerge into the London social scene than he became a most sought-after spare man for country house parties, where he could both quote the classics and get a difficult horse across the country.

Lady Augusta Fane in her hunting reminiscences describes young Harry finishing off a day's sport by kissing a lady on top of the Devil's Punch Bowl silhouetted against the evening sky. That famous Master, Mr. Beaumont Lubbock, whose eye missed nothing, expressed the wish to meet this fellow: 'Such a sportsman!' Lady Augusta decided to set this right. Having described Cust as 'a very clever rising politician, the hope and admiration of a certain very high-brow set,' she related Harry's reactions to her announcement that Mr. Lubbock was requesting an introduction: 'With juvenile pride Harry said, "Of course I shall be delighted. No doubt he has heard of my writings and speeches."

' "No, he wants to know you because you are the only man he has seen kissing a lady not once but twenty times on top of the Punch Bowl." ' Harry looked so deflated!

Then students of Arthur Balfour's life will find that eminent statesman seeking legal advice on how to extricate the overgallant Cust from a serious entanglement with a lady-soul whose husband was sore displeased, on returning from a long trip abroad, to find a new baby which he could not possibly have sired. This kind of predicament created an impression of irresponsibility most undesirable in a Member of Parliament. A friend of Harry's would write: 'He tossed off the cup of life without fear of it containing any poison'—but poison lay in the dregs and would in the end taste bitter.

With that curious masculine vanity inherent in men of the time,

Arthur Balfour kept the love letters which Mary Elcho wrote to himself, but, after dealing with Harry's troubles, he burnt all the Cust papers 'to spare the butler's feelings.'

The dispersal of the Souls as a literary coterie did little to cool Harry. Ladies of poetic persuasion continued to meet him by moonlight and starlight and sunset, and those wonderful blue eyes kept on appearing in nurseries where they did not rightly belong. This was what his men friends called being 'deficient in will power.'

Cust's nephew, the Orientalist Sir Ronald Storrs, has written that he himself 'passed under his spell' and, with an intensity of feeling unusual even when recalling a dearly loved relation, Storrs has tried to pass on the magic of that 'golden emergent individuality.' An Eton master who had taught in succession Rosebery, Curzon and Cust told a colleague that of the three he had chosen Cust as the most likely future Prime Minister.

Despite the recurrent danger of scandal, Cust remained for several years a Tory Member of Parliament. When women raged, men closed their ranks to defend Harry, who lent so much grace to life. With Curzon, George Wyndham, Lord Crewe and others of intellectual bent, he stayed for a week each summer with Wilfrid Scawen Blunt at Crabbet, to contend in verse and talk and games. Blunt defined the Crabbet Club to my father as a meeting 'to play lawn tennis, the piano, the fool, and other instruments of gaiety.' There were no ladies in this joyous band, so that on the evening when Harry was awarded the silver goblet for his Aristophanic poem the members could talk through the night, swim at dawn and then play tennis stark naked till breakfast—Harry and Curzon, the future Viceroy of India, defeating George Wyndham, future Secretary for Ireland, and their poet-host Blunt.

In 1892 William Waldorf Astor, after listening to Harry Cust through a dinner, rose and offered him the editorship of the *Pall Mall Gazette*. Without any former experience, Cust plunged enthusiastically into this endeavour. He gathered around him such contributors as Rudyard Kipling, H. G. Wells and the poetess Alice Meynell. No other evening paper has attained such literary renown. Harry's own leading articles may have been composed while he dressed for dinner, but they set the highest of standards and, what with Alice Meynell's elegantly composed essays, and competitions for new poetry, and Arthur Balfour's reflective political notes, this journal soon aroused amazement in Fleet Street. The inscription which the freethinking H. G. Wells wrote on the flyleaf of *The World Set Free* is revealing:

To the Honourable
H. C. Cust,
Noblest and Best of
Editors,
Inventor of Authors,
Friend of Letters
from his affectionate contributor
H. G. Wells

Harry Cust's humour was quick. Cornered in a protectionist controversy, he stated that he had 'nailed his colours to the fence.' Winston in *Thoughts and Adventures* tells of an unnerving moment during a rowdy political meeting when an enormous man suddenly started to advance on Harry Cust in a threatening pugilistic attitude. Cust took off his coat and squared up to the enemy with clenched fists, while at the same time imploring his companions: 'Hold me back! Hold me back!'

He could choke friends and foes alike with laughter.

There is another story of Cust's insouciance when he came to the rescue of Prime Minister Asquith, who was being physically attacked by suffragettes on a golf course. Harry stepped forward, calmly announcing that, whatever dispute the ladies had with the Prime Minister, he as secretary of the golf club (to which he did not actually belong) must ask them not to walk *on the grass*. So impressive was the request, or so attractively was it delivered, that they all glanced down at the turf and stopped battering poor Mr. Asquith.

'To be with him was delight—the hint, the flash of shining treasure unrevealed. . . . Never could he be at less than concert pitch. . . . Harry read the *Georgics* driving in his dog-cart to the Meet. Like Charles James Fox he would cap quotations from Horace while walking down St. James' Street after a dance at three in the morning.'

Is this the man to be dubbed merely 'the most notorious lecher of the age'?

His nephew Ronald Storrs, who used to stay with us in Ireland during the thirties, was himself the most stimulating talker, as well as being a gifted if excitable writer—I remember my grandmother remonstrating with him for splattering ink on the mauve curtains of the best guest room. I only half listened when he was comparing the men who had enthralled him most in life, but he often talked of T. E. Lawrence, whom he had known so well, and 'that fount of joy—Harry Cust.' Years later I found his written reference to these

two: 'Twice only have I felt myself close to the springs of life'—
these moments were during long talks with Lawrence and Cust.

Harry's mind was too sharp not to be pricked by sadness. With
such gifts he must have known that he should have attained far more.
His nephew found pencilled in one of Harry's many copies of
Goethe: 'Crooked eclipses against his glory fight.' Harry knew all
right—he was not to make the grade that all who loved him expected, the grade he must have expected of himself.

And women could give him pain. Here is some unpublished verse:

> O Little face of heaven,
> O little heart of hell,
> If all love's sins were seven,
> You've made me sin them well.
>
> Sin well and suffer greatly,
> And still to grace my state,
> You've scored your eighth point lately,
> And taught me how to hate.

Those unmoved by the romantic impulse may perhaps find
Harry endearing because of his poems to dogs. Here is one written
to his bulldog Lo-Bengula, who had been stolen and recovered from
Bethnal Green Dogs Home.

To Lo-Bengula: On His Redemption from Slavery, and on the
Occasion of His Approaching His Third Birthday

> Burst from the bondage of a brigand tomb,
> Thou comest—Alcestis-wise—from Bethnal Green,
> O rare Lo-Ben!—what day yon sun has seen
> Two cycles since thy summons from the womb.
> Our mined hearts are full: yet there is room
> Even so, to meditate thy marriage-queen,
> And—like the Thane of Cawdor's—cross the scene,
> Horrid, thy awful generations loom.
>
> Thou heritor of hideousness divine,
> Now thro' thy pulses peals the passionate pain
> Which Shakespeare knew, and Goethe; there shall be
> Wonderful things made new, a lordly line,
> Waking eternal ugliness again,
> Of little loathsome lovèd Lo-bengulae.

Eventually, slightly against his will, it seems, Cust married. It is
a curious story as recounted by Lady Horner—most highbrow of

Edwardian hostesses. In 1893, when Harry was thirty-two and, according to Lady Horner, 'on the verge of a dazzling engagement' to some girl with a huge fortune (name not recorded), he went to stay with Lady Horner and met the twenty-six-year-old daughter of Sir William Welby-Gregory, 4th Baronet. According to Lady Horner, she was 'not his type, plain, highbrow, awkward,' but my grandmother described her as a beautiful bluestocking. Whatever transpired at the house party, this determined young lady made up her mind to force Mr. Cust to relinquish other thoughts and marry *her*. She set about this endeavour by writing to Arthur Balfour and Lord Haldane, both high in the government, saying that as *she* was with child by Mr. Cust the other marriage must be stopped. Balfour, who had guided him out of hot water before, now prevailed on Cust to capitulate and marry Miss Nina Welby-Gregory.

But the fear of pregnancy proved unfounded. By strange and bitter chance his wife would be one of the few women who came under Harry's spell and did *not* bear him a child. He deserted Nina frequently for other women, but she remained wildly, almost crazily in love. Artistic by inclination, she studied sculpting, and carved immense equestrian statues of Harry for her bedroom. He gave her a large house in Hyde Park Gate, where they entertained a group of intellectual friends. Harry travelled a great deal and on occasions they went to country house parties together.

Lady Horner described Harry as 'golden-haired, well-born, irresistible—not to me—but to most women.' Countess Benckendorff, the Russian Ambassadress, noted: 'I find his hair vulgar but his face seduces me.' And Margot Asquith compared him to the Prime Minister's eldest son (younger than Cust and to be killed in battle): 'With the exception of my stepson Raymond Asquith, Harry Cust was the most brilliant young man that I have ever known. He had a more unusual mind than George Curzon, and a finer sense of humour than George Wyndham, and if he had not had a fatal fascination for every woman that he met, might have gone far in life. But he was self-indulgent, and in spite of a charming nature and perfect temper, he had not got a strong character. . . .'

Charm is an asset to women; I think it usually saps a man's ambition. It is the sting of not succeeding easily with the feminine sex which has driven many on to fame.

Margot Asquith could see Cust's blind spots. 'I sometimes think if he had been a Liberal and my husband had been his Chief, he would have done more to stand by Cust when his self-indulgence got him into the trouble that ended his political career. . . . He was a brilliant suggestive talker, more faithful in friendship than in love and by his intellect a stimulant to the circle called the "Souls." '

Here, of course, Margot is beating about the bush—he may have been a stimulant to the male Souls but he was positive dynamite to the women.

Lord Curzon, himself the most erudite and pleasing of talkers, regarded Cust as a serious friend, and he was the only journalist invited to Curzon's farewell dinner before he departed as Viceroy of India. Some of Harry Cust's verse was published in anthologies and one lament reached the *Oxford Book of English Verse*. It is a love poem ending:

> Not unto us, O Lord:
> Nay, Lord, but unto her be all things given—
> My light and life and earth and sky be blasted—
> But let not all that wealth of loss be wasted:
> Let Hell afford
> The pavement of her Heaven!

Another poem he wrote was to Pamela Plowden, the early love of Winston Churchill, and perhaps the lines refer to her own wistfulness when she decided to marry Lord Lytton instead of Winston. However that may be, the verses show the quality of Harry Cust himself.

> Beautiful face!
> Is your heart broken that you look so sad?
> Is there no heart on earth that once made glad
> Your heart, to hearten yet your flower of grace?
> Is God untender towards you? Or can Man,
> Loving such dear eyes,
> Or, save despairing,
> Far too much caring,
> Grudge his uncrownedness in the race he ran,
> And squandered life and lived and lost the prize?
> They pay the worthiest cost
> Whose lives for you were lost.

A woman's man entirely, one would say, but skipping forward to 1909, we find a cool masculine assessment of Harry Cust in the diaries of Wilfrid Scawen Blunt, who had also been a member of the Souls and held many of their gatherings at his Sussex home.

In October of this year Mr. Blunt and his wife, the Lady Anne, held a house party and among the guests were the Harry Custs and the Winston Churchills. Winston was twelve years younger than

Harry. Blunt's diary records: 'In the evening we had another great discussion of the fundamental of politics, each of us holding our ground. . . . Harry Cust with all his cleverness was quite outclassed by Winston in the discussions, who has studied all these problems thoroughly, and is wonderfully quick in defending his position. He has just his father's talent of seizing the points of a situation and driving them home in his replies.

'Cust, though less attractively brilliant than Churchill, is wonderfully well equipped for talk, having a far greater knowledge of history and literature and a real poetic side, which in Churchill is wanting. His knowledge of poetry is wide, and he has himself written quite excellent verse. Both have wit and quickness of repartee and the power of epigram. It is first-class sword-play between them.'

Here the man is clearly depicted and one cannot be so brutal as to smile at the epitaph his wife eventually caused to be engraved above his marble effigy. 'Of all sorts enchantingly beloved.' Nina had returned to Harry when he lay dying in 1917 and she wrote to my grandmother in her grief: '. . . I have still to learn to live without him. I try to go on with his work. It is the only morphia. And I try to remember that as I have been the happiest conceivable woman on earth, so now I am the richest in beautiful memories. He was so fond of you dear Leonie. You were such a good friend always. . . .' Nor can one be sorry, now that the fury and the spark have subsided, that so much of the Cust strain entered England's peerage and that from such a number of cradles there gazed babies with eyes like large sapphires instead of the black boot buttons of their legal fathers.

24

An Injured Wife

BEAUTIFUL, VIRTUOUS, feather-brained, unpunctual, adored by the equerries, feared by her ladies-in-waiting—such was Alexandra, the most publicly cheated wife in Europe.

'But I was the one he loved best,' she is reported to have said to a member of the Seymour family. And this may indeed have been true. Albert Edward had fallen in love with that seventeen-year-old girl at first sight, and he remained an affectionate, admiring husband throughout his long years of infidelity.

The little Danish Princess had been selected by Queen Victoria entirely on account of her looks. From the political point of view no more embarrassing marriage could have been made, but after Albert Edward's adventure on the Curragh his mother conducted her search among European princesses as if holding an audition for a beauty queen. Every reason existed to avoid a link with Denmark, a small country bitterly disliking Prussia, but as Sir Charles Phipps, Keeper of the Privy Purse, wrote: '. . . It is of the *first importance* that the Princess of Wales should have beauty, agreeable manners and the power of attracting people to her and these the Princess Alexandra seems to possess in a remarkable degree.'

Queen Victoria's eldest daughter Vicky, the Crown Princess of Prussia, admitted herself to be very impressed by this girl and although the Crown Prince spoke of such a marriage as 'the very worst that could happen to us,' yet even he softened when he met Alexandra, and grudgingly he admitted that her education 'seems to have been a good one, i.e. a natural one—one of the heart.' But it was the reports of her great loveliness which caused Queen Victoria to decide that here lay 'a pearl not to be lost.'

The news that the most beautiful of princesses had been selected for his appraisement could not have been disagreeable to a somewhat overvigorous young man of twenty. When Albert Edward first saw Alexandra at Lachen he did not have to try to fall in love.

The wedding, in March 1863, three months after Alexandra's eighteenth birthday, has already been described. England went out of its mind about the royal family's new acquisition and although Queen Victoria was soon to note 'very clever I don't think she is,' yet Her Majesty must have felt that she had done the right thing in risking an unfortunate political connection. When the most beautiful of princesses married the lustiest of princes, trouble ought to be forestalled. And for a time it was. But exquisite wives have never prevented men looking around. *L'appetit vient en mangeant!*

The Prince's younger brother, Alfred, also fell in love with Alexandra. Indeed, he had hoped that if the marriage did not materialise he might get her for himself, and Queen Victoria's eagle eye did not miss the dangers inherent in this situation. When Alfred began to hang around Marlborough House she wrote: 'He is far too *épris* of Alix to be allowed there much without possibly ruining the happiness of all three.'

Of course, the gusto with which the young couple plunged into frivolous enjoyments worried the Queen, and so did their health. Alexandra's first baby was born prematurely after she had been rushed home in a sledge. *Punch* published a comic lullaby beginning:

Oh hush thee my darling, thy Sire is a Prince
Whom Mama beheld skating not quite five hours since. . . .

The second son also arrived prematurely, so this tendency may have been inherent in Alexandra's constitution, but Queen Victoria never ceased to remonstrate with Bertie over his carelessness in allowing dearest Alix to get fatigued. The Prince and Princess of Wales lived with the gay abandon of two children suddenly set free on a floodlit stage, with all the scenery and gorgeous costumes to play with. They went to balls every night of the season, they dined in the houses where Queen Victoria advised them not to go, they attended the opera and theatre dressed in glittering outfits, and gave the crowds their money's worth.

All went smoothly with the Prince and Princess until November 1867. Then Alexandra, being again pregnant, could not accompany Bertie to St. Petersburg for the wedding of her sister to the Tsarevitch Alexander (they were making big marriages, these penniless little Danish princesses). It was during this six-week absence at the Russian court that Albert Edward first aroused comment by paying inordinate attention to the sirens of St. Petersburg. He had been married for four years, and his rather delicate wife was producing a third child. It may not have been nice but it was natural that a robust young man, chased and flattered by passionate Russian women, should succumb to temptation.

When he returned to England it was to find Alexandra exceedingly unwell. Within three days she developed rheumatic fever and she suffered agonies from leg and hip during a confinement which had to take place without chloroform. After the baby daughter, Louise, had been born on February 20, 1867, she continued to be seriously ill for months.

A wife's sickroom is, alas, not the most advantageous spot in which to nurture fidelity. Albert Edward was twenty-five years old, and the exotic treatment meted out in Russia had filled his head with notions as conducive to pious sympathy as tzigane music is to religious meditation. Of course, he was terribly sorry for poor Alix, but young men of randy disposition fly from sickroom whispers and reproachful glances. Lady Macclesfield, Alexandra's mother's lady in waiting, recorded: 'The Princess had another bad night *chiefly* owing to the Prince promising to come in at 1 A.M. and keeping her in a perpetual fret, refusing to take her opiate for fear she should be asleep when he came. And he never came till 3 A.M.!' This situation would repeat itself.

In May, three months after the baby's birth, while his wife was still an invalid, the Prince had to officially open the International Exhibition in Paris. Sir William Knollys recorded gloomily: '. . . The accounts I subsequently heard of this visit were very unsatisfactory; suppers after the opera with some of the female Paris notorieties, etc. etc.'

By August the Princess felt well enough to travel with her husband for a cure at Wiesbaden. The three tiny children went with them accompanied by twenty-five servants and the usual suite. Queen Victoria had counselled ominously against this trip and indeed, from her point of view, it proved a disaster. Albert Edward grew restless. From his younger sister, the Princess of Hesse, he received a lecture which she admitted he accepted 'most good-humouredly,' but two months' rest in a spa by the side of an invalid wife was enough to irritate the most docile young man. Queen Victoria had agreed with the Queen of Prussia that Baden society was such that 'no one can mix in it without loss of character,' but, just as his mother had predicted, the Prince of Wales found his way to the racecourse of Baden to bet on horses and indulge in even less seemly activities. When his elder sister the Crown Princess also remonstrated Bertie wrote his mother quite crossly: 'I know that Vicky has written to you on the subject, but one would imagine that she thought me ten or twelve years old and not nearly twenty-six.'

Yet more serious, from Queen Victoria's point of view, was Alexandra's unwise refusal to receive the King of Prussia. As a Dane, she hated Germany for annexing Schleswig-Holstein, but the insult came from a future Queen of England. Queen Victoria wrote to her Prime Minister: 'The Queen trusts that Lord Derby will take an opportunity of expressing *both* to the Prince and the Princess of Wales the *importance* of *not* letting any private feelings interfere with what are their public duties. Unfortunately the Princess of Wales has *never* understood her *duties* of this nature.'

Although the Wiesbaden cure helped Alexandra's knee, she suffered from a joint stiffening for the rest of her life, and a far worse affliction had been triggered off by the rheumatic fever—a form of hereditary deafness which was to spoil her middle age. She produced two more daughters and a sixth baby, a son, who lived only twenty-four hours. After the age of twenty-six Alexandra never bore another child.

Apart from a steadfast refusal to curb his sexual appetites, Albert Edward treated his wife with affection and consideration. As the Prince's infidelities became increasingly well known, Alexandra gained a popularity never previously accorded a royal consort. The country idolised her—so beautiful, so pure, so badly treated. In the public imagination she combined the appeal of Cinderella and Andromeda. Marvellously dressed, radiant, gracious, pouring forth smiles—who could fault this paragon? Yet the hardheaded old Queen wrote, when Alexandra continued to be rude to Prussian royalty: '. . . Good as she is—she is not worth the price we paid in having such a family connection.'

Had the Prince of Wales been faithful, Alexandra would not have obtained so much popularity. Had he insisted, as many Victorian husbands did, on forcing her to continue bearing children, while appearing to remain within the pale himself, she would not have received the thunderous ovations accorded by the mob to a 'wronged wife.' No one pitied the Duchess of Abercorn, who gave her stern, bearded husband fourteen children!

It would be impertinent to surmise on the Princess of Wales's private inclinations, but for a woman who so obviously thrived on admiration there must have been compensations when Albert Edward went on the tiles. Although there could never be any question of a Princess of Wales retaliating by a move from the straight and narrow path, she was always surrounded by men who were head over heels in love and this must have been a poultice to hurt feelings. To a certain extent the whole nation was in love with her, and she enjoyed the situation. And when with great propriety she conducted a long, exalted love affair with a man she adored, the Prince understood and respected both her feelings and the wholehearted devotion shown by his equerry, Oliver Montagu.* Curiously enough, this attractive, rather wild young officer who, according to his own brother, led a rollicking life in the company of 'a noisy, sporting lot of people,' had originally been criticised by Queen Victoria as an unsuitable companion for the Prince—but she never raised any objection to Montagu's 'pure and noble love' for Alexandra.

Oliver Montagu was the Princess of Wales's constant companion and gallant cavalier for twenty-five years. His unhidden feelings never wavered, nor did they evoke criticism. There was a place in the Victorian world for romance without pawing. Montagu would have served his lady ill had he allowed a breath of scandal to arise.

Louisa, Lady Antrim, describing her own debut into society, gives us the picture: 'The Princess of Wales floated through the ballroom like a vision from fairyland. She went out a great deal, and chief among her cavaliers was Oliver Montagu. Her husband by this time was living in a very fast set, indulging in many flirtations. It is surprising that, young and lovely as she was, the Princess never gave any real occasion for scandal. I think it must have been due to Oliver Montagu's care for her. He shielded her in every way, not least from his own great love, and managed to defeat gossip. Oliver Montagu was looked upon with awe by the young as he sauntered into a ballroom, regardless of anything but his beautiful Princess, who as a matter of course always danced the first after-supper waltz with him. But she remained marvellously circumspect.'

Although he was quite a rip when away from royal circles, Captain Montagu had breeding and he knew the art of conducting a platonic love affair on this high level. From 1868, when he became an equerry to the Prince, until he died in 1893, his devotion never flagged and although he may have set the fashion for falling in love with Alexandra (a proceeding which made young men feel interesting without entailing responsibility), Montagu's intense passion was very real. All other women were set aside (from the point of view of courtship) by this chivalrous knight. He had chosen a fair prin-

* The Hon. Oliver Montagu, a captain in the Blues, younger son of Lord Sandwich.

cess, placed her on a pedestal, knew her untouchable and was content to worship at a distance—a very short distance, let us admit, but although he saw her all the time, although he could waltz with her, teach her to fish for salmon and let his shining eyes tell what he felt—that was all.

The knowledge of her own breath-taking beauty and her power to arouse enthusiasm in the English people must have eased the Princess over jolts—over the Mordaunt case when she was clapped while the Prince got hissed; and during the humiliating tangle of Tranby Croft, and the open scandal of Lady Warwick's reign.

Frivolous, merry, childishly obstinate, often beguiling, always dignified and unaffected—such was the lady who stood gallantly by her husband's side during his many peccadilloes, and he paid her generous tribute.

When, in 1898, Lady Warwick, wishing to return to court, asked the Prince if he could induce Alexandra to receive her now that their affair had become platonic, he ingenuously asked his wife if she would care to associate herself with one of Daisy's philanthropic schemes. Alexandra smiled sweetly (perhaps she felt a little deafer than usual that day) and expressed sympathy. Albert Edward immediately wrote to his former mistress: 'Certainly the Princess has been an angel of goodness through all this but then she is a Lady and never could do anything that was mean or small.' But at this very moment Prince George was writing to his wife: 'In case you should hear from Lady Warwick asking you to become President of a Charity of hers, refuse it, Mother dear has done so and wishes you to do the same.'

'Mother dear,' as all the family called Alexandra, knew how to play her cards. If it ever entered her head to punish Albert Edward, she never showed it. With grace she went her own way, doing just exactly what she wished, keeping the Prince waiting for important functions, snubbing the German royalties she did not like, and not quite hearing if the old Queen sent some complaint. She was the fairy doll on the top of England's Christmas tree—glittering with diamonds, blue-eyed, golden-haired—she appeared to be overflowing with kindness, sometimes in fact she overdid it and embarrassed people, but her acts always seemed to be spontaneous. She was as she was—making no attempt to alter herself in any way.

The Prince deserved to be rather frightened of her. He treated her with deference, and however angry her unpunctuality made him he could never bring himself to speak really sternly to her. She henpecked—not viciously but peremptorily. And what else?

At what point does the Fairy Queen transform into a heartless tyrant?

From the beginning Alexandra frightened her maids of honour. She liked to be attended at public functions, such as Ascot, by the taller ones, perhaps to emphasise her own fragility, so the short girls saw only dull events such as gloomy private services at Frogmore Mausoleum. No one dared to suggest this rota was not quite fair. And I have heard of several surprising instances when the Princess of Wales berated her ladies unmercifully on returning from some function at which she had just been radiating charm and gracious smiles. More extraordinary still, my grandmother was told by an eyewitness of how, after one of those glamorous drives around London on Alexandra Rose Day when the populace lined the streets to cheer her open carriage, the Queen actually beat her lady in waiting with the long steel umbrella which she used in lieu of a walking stick.

But members of the royal staff *can* resign if they wish (though not perhaps the ugly Miss Knollys, lady of the bedchamber, who had a fixation on her gorgeous mistress). The human beings who were totally, inescapably, in Alexandra's power were her three daughters. From the start her love for her children appeared to be unhealthily possessive. For although she took clothes seriously, and had the luck to be extremely musical, it was to the nursery that she turned for pleasure. Extraordinarily unintellectual compared to the Prince's sisters, she never read a book and regarded education as rather a bore. The letters she wrote to her son George after he went into the Navy contained baby talk even after he became a commanding officer. Fortunately for the boys, they were at thirteen removed from her clutches, but the three girls remained imprisoned in their mother's boudoir. They delighted her as toys delight a child —but children are not always kind to their toys, and even her favourite son Georgie would write to his wife, 'Mama, as I have always said, is one of the most selfish people I know.'

All the memoirs of that epoch stress the extraordinary *girlishness* of Alexandra—she thrilled guests and courtiers by her ability to frolic without losing dignity. Right up to her sixties she could charm with this unaffected *girlishness*. All visitors to Sandringham, in their reticent, decorous memoirs, used this same word.

Her unself-consciousness amazed those who suffered from this complaint. But did she never notice the effect she had on her daughters? Once they ceased to be tiny girls the scamperings of a mama they could not emulate petrified them. While Alexandra, accustomed

to being the centre of attention, could enchant her public by lark-
ing, her serious-minded girls felt themselves turning into ugly duck-
lings. Although they had good features, none of them possessed their
mother's deep-set violet-blue eyes, and no one ever told them they
were pretty. In agonies of embarrassment they watched that glorious, lighthearted 'Mother dear' romp through after-dinner games
while their own limbs grew wooden. They just could not copy her
—and did Alexandra really want them to? Was not the limelight *her*
place?

As Louise, Victoria and Maud grew from shy teen-agers into
stiff, obedient little Princesses, their grandmother and their father
discussed possible husbands. Queen Victoria remained a romantic;
she made no bones about the importance of sexual fulfilment in a
girl's life. When a tentative marriage for her own plainest daughter,
Helena, had fallen through, she wrote frankly that either Helena
must remain 'in single blessedness which would be *most unfortunate*
or we must find someone else.'

Alexandra, however, refused to see anything 'unfortunate' in the
single state. True, *she* had been a much-admired, extremely independent, married woman since the age of eighteen, but why should
her daughters expect similar roles? In 1886 Princess May wrote
that her brother Alge would 'come here on Saty 20th to go up with
us to Marlborough House to a *children's party* for Louise's *19th*
birthday! Does that not seem too ridiculous?' Is it possible she never
noticed the girls were not quite as good at playing high jinks as herself—that Louise was agonisingly self-conscious and Victoria of
intellectual bent?

All well-bred girls were trained to speak softly but these isolated Princesses reduced their personal comments to whispers and
constantly used the adjective 'poor' when discussing even the jolliest
relations. As a result their conversation concerning human beings
became so muted, so full of meaningless concern, that it had an
idiotic quality.

As they entered their twenties Alexandra announced point-blank
that Princes from German courts (the usual source of supply for
English Princesses) were not to be considered. Why indeed should
her girls marry at all? They were perfectly happy at Sandringham;
did they not ride nice horses and walk into dinner with eminent
statesmen and watch the world's prettiest mama being dressed, and
play duets on the piano with her? What more should they want?

The old Queen grew increasingly distressed at the prolongation
of this macabre innocent fun, while the Prince of Wales remonstrated with his wife in vain. She knew what *she* wanted and that

was that. After an altercation concerning his daughters Albert Edward had to report Alexandra's argument to Queen Victoria: 'Alix found them such good companions that she would not encourage them marrying, and that they themselves had no inclination for it.' Queen Victoria did not believe this.

After much procrastination, Louise, shyest of the lot, married a Scotsman and became the recluse Duchess of Fife. Maud, the youngest, fell in love with Prince Frank of Teck, an attractive rotter who remained infatuated with an older woman, and it looked as if she would never find a husband but eventually King Edward insisted that she should be allowed to marry an athletic Viking Prince. In 1903 Maud became Queen of Norway—rather unhappily so, because she had not been brought up to realise that a Princess who marries a foreign King *has* to live out of England.

The one who never escaped from the horrific gilded cage of Sandringham was the most intelligent of Alexandra's children, the Princess Victoria. With the hot blood of the Hanoverians in her veins, she must have suffered intensely during the long years of her hidden, blighted life.

All human beings must be judged by the way they treat those who are in their power, not by casual or dramatic acts of kindness to those who lie outside their orbit. The Princess of Wales was genuinely appalled by the bad conditions she found in hospitals when making unexpected visits and she rightly determined to improve conditions for nursing sisters, but such action, laudable as it may be, cannot excuse her cruelty to the eager girl whose fate lay irrevocably in her mother's hands. There were several members of the royal family who summoned up courage and tried to tell Alexandra what harm this infantile domestic imprisonment must do to any normal creature, but an entrancing smile and her deafest ear would be the reward.

Lady Geraldine Somerset had once called little Victoria '*very* sharp, quick, merry and amusing,' while Queen Victoria's verdict was 'exceedingly naughty.' The brief descriptions make it all the more poignant to read of this Princess turning into the embittered hypochondriac of later years.

As the pool of German princes (where all shapes and sizes of husbands could be found) was out of bounds, the Princess Victoria, who remained lively even under the domination of her mother, took to falling in love with commoners. Here was a girl who craved romance, needed a husband and ought to have been a wife and mother.

After being forbidden to think of Lord Revelstoke's son John

Baring, who first captured her young heart, Victoria fell lightly for an equerry, but that was also stamped on. Alexandra, herself the cynosure of a million admiring eyes, had no wish to lose her playthings, and certainly not to *non-royals*. The idea that her daughters had any right to lives of their own, to become 'Mother dears' in their turn, she brushed aside.

By 1894, when Victoria and Maud were twenty-six and twenty-five, the Crown Princess of Prussia wrote to the Queen: 'With regard to darling Bertie's sweet girls . . . Of course I would write to Bertie with pleasure—I am only so afraid of displeasing dearest Alix —or of appearing to meddle in her family affairs—but it really is *not* wise to leave the fate of these dear girls *dans la vague* for years longer.' But this was exactly what their egocentric mother intended.

When the unexpected occurred and a fascinating older man tentatively pressed his suit to Princess Victoria, her mother expressed horror. The Esher papers reveal that, around the time he became Prime Minister in 1895, Lord Rosebery, who had become a widower several years previously, aspired to marry Princess Victoria. A succession of important ladies had tried to tempt him into matrimony. Many of their letters—written without false modesty—lie in the archives at Dalmeny, but although he must have enjoyed these proposals (or why should he have kept them?) Rosebery evaded all traps. His friend Lord Esher, when staying with him in March 1895, describes his terrible insomnia in a letter: 'He complains of loneliness. Marriage frightening him. He cannot believe in a fresh, disinterested affection. As if that mattered to anyone who understands love! I tell him that he dried up at the fount by becoming a man too soon. Pascal said that the happiest life—the life he would choose—begins with love and ends with ambition. R. has reversed the order. He has—while in the prime of life—everything that men toil for, wealth, power, position, everything. Yet he is a lonely sleepless man!'

In his journal Reginald Esher wrote: 'He has been satiated with the sweets of life, and the long process has left him longing for affection, universal approval, omnipotent authority. He denies that he was always "grown up" and reserved from early youth. But it is true nevertheless. He ought to marry again. He requires companionship.'

Esher is so human. He can see that Rosebery needs a relationship in which he can *give*, not take. Obviously a stupid wife would never have suited him—but a young shy sensitive wife such as the Princess Victoria could have given him the chance of moulding her life. She needed affection and understanding and freedom. Might not the joy of giving have broken down the tensions which kept him sleepless through whole nights? We shall never know, for Alexandra 'would not hear of it.' No thought was given to her daughter's feelings.

It is easy to imagine what the poor Princess had to suffer when she was in her late twenties and this attractive older man tentatively made his offer. The Prince of Wales and Queen Victoria could have dealt with the difficulties inherent in the situation when a statesman marries into the royal house. Alexandra must have made Lord Rosebery feel embarrassed at pursuing what on the surface might have appeared an ambitious marriage.

In his youth Rosebery had given Sir Charles Dilke the impression of being 'the most ambitious man I have ever met,' but it could not have been ambition that motivated him at the time, for the hand of a royal Princess could only have been a handicap in the political form. No, he must have desired her companionship. It would have been a surprising match but sensitive and intelligent. The Princess had to forswear not only a delightful husband but the interesting life at his side. Rosebery owned four beautiful country homes, where a contemporary describes him as '. . . at Mentmore, the English squire, at Dalmeny the literary man annotating his books, at Durdans breeding and training his race-horses in the grand manner of the eighteenth century, at Rosebery the sportsman enjoying his moors, and at his house in Berkeley Square the Liberal statesman entertaining and feeling the political pulse of the Empire.'

Rosebery never remarried. Both he and Princess Victoria remained lonely individuals.

By curious chance, I know the end of this story, which has not previously been published. In the early thirties the two husbandless Princesses, Victoria and her cousin Marie Louise,† often went to tea with my great-aunt, Mrs. Crawshay (Mary Leslie). One evening I went to her house, 75 Upper Berkeley Street, just after the elderly royal ladies had departed. They had been reminiscing about the past and my aunt Mary (who was an astringent old lady; she always said that self-pity was 'like sitting in wet shoes') sat bolt upright presiding over her silver teakettle with the saddest expression. 'If you knew what royalties have to endure and never show it,' she said. 'The poor dears were talking about their past, and Princess Victoria told me there had been someone perfect for her, but they

† Princess Marie Louise has in her memoirs explained how her own early marriage to Prince Aribet of Anhalt was arbitrarily declared null and void by her German father-in-law, leaving her unable to remarry because of her Church of England vows.

wouldn't let her marry him, and if you could have heard her voice break when she said, "And we *could* have been so happy." '

I always remembered the words and my aunt's tone of voice as she repeated the phrase. But thirty years passed before I learned the names of the men who could have given her life—John Revelstoke and Lord Rosebery.

The Grand Duchess Olga, who came on visits to Sandringham, describes the life which Princess Victoria led henceforth.

'Mother dear' had now metamorphosed into a tyrant who kept a bell at her side to ring whenever she wanted her daughter: 'Poor Toria was just a glorified maid to her mother. Many is the time a talk or game would be broken off by a message from my Aunt Alix, and Toria would run like lightning, often to discover that her mother could not remember why she had sent for her and it puzzled me because Aunt Alix is so good.'

Particularly deadening were the family visits to the dull little court of Darmstadt which Alexandra so enjoyed. May of Teck, although a most dutiful Princess, noted: 'the 6:30 dinner is our despair and the endless evening afterwards with *cercle* is a bore.' Certainly the future King George V understood what his unmarried sister had to endure. He wrote of 'the dawdle and waste of time' and a letter to his young wife commiserates: 'Yes alas, poor Toria has of course to go to D. with Mama, it will certainly do her no good I fear and she hates it so.'

As the long frustrating years passed and Princess Victoria grew plainer, more bitter and waspish, her mother remained undeservedly lovely. Victoria had an expressive, delicately boned face, but it never had the chance to light up with the knowledge she was loved. The adjective 'selfish,' used by 'Darling Georgie-boy' in a calm assessment of his 'Darling Mother,' too lightly censures the treatment of that chained creature 'Toria.' What anguish she must have endured at Sandringham during the endless childish excursions and vapid endearments which her mother so enjoyed. The place for this young woman was at the head of her own dinner table, in the company of intelligent men. Rosebery, with his splendid homes and the most interesting friends in Europe, would have been surely the perfect husband for a clever Princess. He was no ordinary Prime Minister. Daisy of Pless assessed him thus: 'It always seemed to me that his detachment from the more trivial side of Party politics, his independence, great wealth of intellect and his silver tongue and magic pen gave him a unique position in European affairs.' Married to this erudite, witty older man, Victoria could have struggled out of the constraint of her early upbringing. Amidst Rosebery's friends she would have developed into a mature woman, known joy, accomplished something. But no life of her own was ever permitted.

Lord Esher once wrote to Rosebery: 'He ought to marry because I suppose in these days a Prime Minister cannot have a mistress.' But the idea that a Prime Minister should woo a Princess of England, merely because it would not look well to take a mistress, is comic. No, it would have been a strange match but an interesting one. He might suffer ill health, but with such a mind *any* woman who married him must have been called lucky. During the following decades many great ladies desired to marry him and wrote without modesty proposing to him. Georgiana, Countess of Dudley, led this band and the love letters—which he kept—might be compared to battering rams. But he remained a widower.

Boredom can in the end become physical pain. The congealed mind turns to psychosomatic illness, and amidst the nagging and the silliness of 'Mother dear's' entourage, the Princess Victoria, perplexed maybe at her own malaise, slowly stifled until physical ills became her only solace.

Maudlin courtiers describe the jollities of Sandringham; the way in which Alexandra can squirt her son Georgie with soda water without ever losing her dignity is a marvel—but such feats hardly compensate for deliberately destroying her daughter's whole life.

Wading through anecdotes, one is occasionally touched perhaps by Alexandra bursting into tears when she meets a blinded Highlander returned from the Boer War, or by her sudden compulsive kindness to servants, but she is for ever giving her nieces 'inappropriate presents,' and does anything show up more clearly the selfishness of the donor? One begins to wonder when Alexandra will become *real*. Can this royal lady, 'dazzlingly beautiful whether in gold or silver by night, or in violet velvet by day,' think at all? Does she care to attempt thought? Or is a glance in the mirror preferable?

In 1902 Alexandra, aged nearly sixty, was still able to bring tears to the eyes with her beauty when, dressed in black with a small diamond crown on her high-piled fair hair, she attended the first state opening of Parliament. But the Grand Duchess Augusta wrote in a letter: 'I had a talk with Victoria, so sensible, glad to have a rest by herself alone, how odd that her mother doesn't feel that at thirty-three one requires a little freedom.'

When an elderly relation died, leaving vacant a suitable small house at Kew, her mother would not hear of the unfortunate Princess moving there. Victoria became a sick old lady before she was allowed her own apartments in Kensington Palace.

Georgina Battiscombe in her *Life of Queen Alexandra* attributes this hard attitude toward the daughters, who were so completely within her power, to lack of imagination rather than selfishness. But the simplest peasant woman realises that daughters must be allowed to leave the nest. No excuse can be found for a Queen.

I will not go on about the secret tears of a thwarted Princess, but because of her daughters it is impossible to *like* the Alexandra whom the nation idolised, and it is equally hard not to like the much-caricatured Edward. After all, he merely wanted to go to bed with a lot of women and took advantage of unparalleled opportunities. Would many men act differently if put in his place?

Mabell, Countess of Airlie, when lady in waiting to the future Queen Mary, saw King Edward and his wife at very close range, and her observations, though discreet, give a clear picture of the wilful Alexandra and her unpardonable unpunctuality on important occasions: 'Keep him waiting. It will do him good,' the Queen once told an equerry sent to implore her to be on time for an official function. Yet Lord Esher, often maddened by her waywardness had to admit that Alexandra's 'mixture of ragging and real feeling' was attractive, and she was at her very best when the King got ill or had trouble with one of his mistresses. Early on she must have realised Edward could not be faithful and she decided to let him rip, while keeping the whip hand at home.

Alexandra's purity could never be suspect, but as the years rolled by and her skin remained delicately rosy, a rumour arose that she *enamelled* her face. On this score Daisy of Pless testifies as an eye-witness: '. . . A lovely figure and a straight back, and fresh red lips that are *not* painted, as one sees they are always moist. And I have seen her at Cowes in the pouring rain, and she certainly is not enamelled—and all that nonsense as the people say.' But seasick attendants knew irritation when after a rough voyage the Queen, untouched by this affliction, stepped forth looking as if 'out of a bandbox.' And how she would laugh if a big wave knocked the ship and plates fell onto the floor. She didn't have to clear the mess.

After the death of Oliver Montagu, Alexandra chose as her favourite cavalier the Marquis de Soveral, Portuguese Minister in London (and reputedly the illegitimate son of Edward's friend, King Carlos of Portugal). Now it became her habit to dance the first waltz at every ball with him, and he took the trouble to speak in a carefully pitched tone she could understand. Known as the 'Blue Monkey,' Luis Soveral was considered one of the wits of London society. When asked if he had seen *The Importance of Being Earnest*, Soveral, who had remarked Cassel's rise in favour, quickly answered: 'No, but I have seen the importance of being Sir Ernest Cassel!' Certainly the Prince enjoyed his sparkle and treated him as an intimate. He had a dreadful reputation as a Don Juan, but Alexandra was Caesar's wife, beyond reproach. Her preference for Soveral's lively company was considered perfectly natural. No breath of gossip arose—King Edward held the monopoly for that.

Let this chapter end with a picture of Alexandra, the injured wife, at her best. Never would the brave side of her nature show up more admirably than during the crisis of June 1902 when Edward was stricken with appendicitis on the very eve of his Coronation. The city was decked with flags, thousands of visitors had arrived, preparations were finalised. The day before a state drive back to London he had enthusiastically but unwisely spent several hours showing a large party, which included Mrs. Keppel, around Windsor Castle (if only Agnes Keyser had been present, she would have put a firm stop to *that*). On the following afternoon the King drove to Buckingham Palace in an open carriage, concealing his agonising pain while Queen Alexandra forced herself to smile to the cheering crowds.

That night she had to attend a dinner for two hundred guests without him, and then face a palace reception at which Princess Victoria crept around whispering: 'Dear Papa is very ill.' But nothing was said officially and eyes kept turning expectantly towards the King's entrance. Meanwhile three doctors had decided they must operate in the morning, and the King, still pathetically insisting he must go to his Coronation if it killed him, had been given an opiate.

Early next morning the Queen walked calmly to the operating room and it is typical of her royal courage, as well as of her medical innocence, that she thought the doctors expected her to remain beside her husband while he was cut open. Indeed, she helped to hold him struggling during the administration of chloroform. Then, as Treves the surgeon wrote later, 'I was anxious to prepare for the operation but did not like to take off my coat, tuck up my sleeves, and put on an apron whilst the Queen was present.' When requested to leave, Her Majesty released her hold on the unconscious figure and walked quietly out to wait with her son and two daughters until it was over.

Alexandra never allowed herself to show the strain she had been forced to undergo. For this performance she must be given full marks, and it is pleasant to read of her two months later, when the Coronation did take place, wearing a dress of golden Indian gauze, glittering in state jewels, with a sceptre in either hand, walking slowly up Westminster Abbey, her fantastically long violet velvet train behind her, a canopy held over her head by four tall Duchesses.

The peeresses in robes and coronets had thronged to their appointed places; and for those dear ladies, whose rank did not automatically entitle them to a place in the Abbey, King Edward had provided a special box. Jennie and Leonie were there and Mrs. Keppel and Daisy of Pless (whose mother Patsy had been a *chère amie* in the long ago), but this was Alexandra's hour.

The most beautiful Queen England has ever known was deeply religious; she accepted the Coronation ceremonies reverently and she prayed devoutly as the oil was placed on her brow. She must have known that she had won all round.

25

Marienbad

As THE FRENCH SAY, *Vieux le diable se fait hermite!* Naturally, the fires were burning less hotly after 1900 and the very number of women who wished to be able to *say* they had kidnapped the royal affections for an hour may well have helped to cool the blaze still further. To be the 'smart thing' in this sense for year after year must be wearing to the most manly ardour. But the King remained a kind gentleman, loth to withhold favours from those who genuinely desired them.

Sir Frederick Ponsonby in *Recollections of Three Reigns* has described the torture he personally underwent when having to inform Germans that the numerous decorations they expected during Edward's state visit to Kiel in 1904 would not be forthcoming: 'Orders and decorations played a great part in German life and the Germans were unable to understand British customs . . . on state visits foreign Sovereigns scattered three to five hundred decorations, whereas the King only gave about thirty.'

It seems a pity really that, as Edward was so softhearted towards feminine aspirations, no one advised him to pander to this quite natural masculine longing for medals which, as the Germans were seldom out of uniform, could impart so much pleasure at little cost. If anything might have lessened the tensions of those last years of peace, surely it would have been worth dressing the Kaiser in a kilt as colonel-in-chief of a Highland regiment, and loading the breasts of his cohorts with stars which they might have been loth to fling away in the advent of war. As it was, many powerful Germans were enraged by what seemed to them to represent deliberate slights.

On the state visit to Berlin in 1909 Ponsonby held a very embarrassing session with a Prussian general who showed lists of what had recently been bestowed by the Kings of Sweden and Spain, and suggested that there should be an English repetition. When Ponsonby explained that King Edward would only be giving thirty decorations, according to English custom, the General gasped and said there must be some mistake. He then enquired if the Garter was to go to General von Plessen as Lord Roberts had received the Black Eagle. Ponsonby had to explain that the Garter was only given to foreign crowned heads, and the English possessed no equivalent to the Black Eagle: 'We had, on the whole, an unpleasant interview.'

Obviously, these state visits which were intended to augment good feeling had the reverse effect. As Ponsonby noted: 'There was always a feeling of thunder in the air whenever the King and the Kaiser were together.'

King Edward did, in fact, distribute more medals of the Victorian Order than the English press considered expedient. A strong feeling existed in England that British medals should not be made cheap. But the *reason* for a state visit is to improve relations with foreigners, not to please the press at home. If King Edward could not give the same number of decorations as other monarchs he ought to have stuck to the non-official ritual of the August cure at Marienbad, where he would join four thousand other stout people to sip the waters and diet. The royal suite at the Hotel Weimar— bedroom, sitting room and dining room—was specially furnished each year, and when the King departed the hotel sold off pictures and furnishings for high prices, so eager were people to own something King Edward had sat on!

The equerries found it a relief to reach this spa each year and find 'the same rooms, the same servants and practically the same people. It was always an advantage to have people to walk with the King as he really had quite enough of us at other times.'

Ponsonby says that Sir Charles Gill (the eminent lawyer who was counsel to the Jockey Club) and Mrs. Hall-Walker (later Lady Wavertree) 'were particularly useful in this way.'

Before writing the eyewitness account given me by Sir Charles Gill's daughter of *how* useful Sophie Hall-Walker could be, I will draw a few more incidents out of Ponsonby's book.

Considering the general magnificence of the Prince's life, it seems unfortunate that the equerries should have thought it important or even advisable to query bills in a foreign country. Everyone likes to make a bit of money and when the Prince of Wales travelled it was rather natural that he should have been charged heavily for every item. After a legal battle with the local chemist, a town councillor, who had hired him a car which broke and then asked for a 'warrant of appointment' or a decoration in lieu of payment, Ponsonby related the whole story to the King 'and His Majesty was very much amused.' But the embittered feelings of the little man who so desperately wanted to make himself important can be imagined.

Later on, Ponsonby decided to break down the expenses of a Marienbad visit, and asked a chartered accountant 'to dig out what the food at the King's table had cost per day, what the servants' food had cost, what the hotel charged for the rooms, and what was the cost of the hired chauffeur and his keep. He spent some days extracting this and then came to me with startling information. Although the food had necessarily to be quite plain on account of the cure, and although only a little light hock was drunk, the cost of the food was enormous. The charge for the rooms was not excessive, but the hire of the motor for three weeks came to more than a new motor. In addition to the chauffeur's keep (and he appeared to have lived like a prince, drinking the most expensive wines at each meal), the bill for renewing worn-out parts came to over £1,500.'

What *did* they expect?

'Life at Marienbad was very hard work, as I spent so much time seeing people who were difficult to get rid of. For instance, one day I saw an Austrian Countess who wanted to take her dogs to England and thought I could give them a pass to prevent them going into quarantine. She was followed by an American who had some place in Austria; while the Abbot of Tepl, who was a great talker, wanted my advice on how to attract English people to Marienbad; other visitors were an officer who had invented a scabbard which telescoped up when the sword was drawn, a sculptor who wanted to do a bust of the King, and last, but not least, a beautiful lady from the half-world in Vienna who wanted to have the honour of sleeping with the King. On being told that this was out of the question, she said if it came to the worst she would sleep with me, so that she should not waste the money spent on her ticket; but I told her to look elsewhere for a bed.'

If this was the true ending, I consider it most ungracious. The Prince of Wales had a reputation. It was too late in the day to grow stingy about any kind of favours. The tiresome councillor ought to have been given some kind of warrant of appointment he could proudly hang over his door, and some gallant should have obliged this generous-hearted courtesan so that she did not return to Vienna feeling rebuffed. However there may well be more to this story than Ponsonby relates. The King was amused by adventuresses.

Now let us return to Edward's friends who accompanied him during exercise and dined at his table—or sometimes gave him a private dinner in the hotel. Ponsonby describes Sophie Hall-Walker's various efforts to 'amuse' the King. Sophie (a Sheridan of Frampton in Dorset and a direct descendant of Richard Brinsley Sheridan) had married a very rich man much older than herself who was to become the 1st Lord Wavertree. He bred race horses by astrological calculations—in fact he bred Minoru, who won the Derby for King Edward. Sophie Hall-Walker had no children and suffered from boredom and bad temper. I knew her years later when, as Lady Wavertree, she had become an enthusiastic tennis player, handsome still and surprisingly agile for her weight and age, leaping about the court and perpetually trained by a tough young professional. At the turn of the century she was a lovely young woman, with much wealth and rather little to do. Serious tennis had not yet entered her life, so she took cures and entertained the King.

One night she told the equerries that she had asked the new dancer, enchanting Maud Allan, to dance before His Majesty as Salome. Ponsonby fussed, he had heard that Miss Allan danced 'more or less naked' and was afraid the press might get hold of the story and use it to the King's detriment. However, Mrs. Hall-Walker insisted, and after dinner two pianists were concealed in her sitting room (one of them the correspondent of the *Daily Mail* sworn to secrecy) and out tripped Maud Allan to shed diaphanous veils. Ponsonby had to admit she was wonderful, '. . . and, although I cannot say she wore many clothes there was nothing the least indecent about her performance.'

There was only poetry and music about Maud Allan. His Majesty graciously watched, graciously praised, and indeed graciously allowed the fact he had viewed and approved to be used to secure the Lord Chamberlain's licence for a London performance.

That was how on one occasion Mrs. Hall-Walker entertained the King after dinner. But what had gone on *before* dinner? Did they have naps? Yes, they did. In the afternoon a stroll was compulsory, then full of fresh air and righteousness everyone returned to their hotels for tea and a 'quiet time.' Recently I had the whole routine explained to me by the daughter of that Sir Charles Gill who, to the relief of the equerries, was 'always able to interest the King.' Elsie Gill when in her late teens used to accompany her father to Marienbad, not to do the cure but as company for him and to learn

German. In 1970 Elsie Gill, transformed into a splendid old lady, Mrs. Denton Carlisle, lunched with us on her eighty-fifth birthday and told me to write down everything she said. She had a great sense of history and was able to impart a marvellous description of Marienbad at the turn of the century. The King always invited Elsie to accompany her father to dinner where she used to be the only young girl sitting at the royal table. She rather enjoyed this and knew how to take her cue. When the King's Messenger arrived with despatches she would hastily finish her dessert, rise to make her curtsey, and slip away to bed.

One year Lady Cunard, the birdlike American hostess who was the inamorata of George Moore, was also staying in Marienbad and the King invited her to dine. Among properly brought-up people a tremendous difference in conversational tone took place when *une jeune fille*—forgotten phrase!—was present. Lady Cunard did not notice Elsie's presence or else she did not trouble to trim her talk. Chirping as was her wont, Emerald Cunard (whose party manners have been likened to those of an 'inebriated canary') sought to amuse the King by discussing Elinor Glyn's novel *The Visits of Elizabeth*, which depicted the bewilderment of a young girl on hearing the corridors creak at night in a country house, and the yet more risqué *Three Weeks*. The Prince looked thunder, turned his shoulder on Lady Cunard and changed the topic with determination. Elsie pretended to notice nothing, but she heard later that an equerry had been sent to Lady Cunard with a reprimand which kept her banished to her own hotel for several days.

Innocent, but observant, Elsie Gill found much of the time spent with older people at Marienbad extremely tedious. In the afternoon, when the cure-takers were having the 'obligatory stroll' and Elsie was supposed to be studying, she would close her grammar and tiptoe from her room to accompany the housemaids who were preparing the larger suites for informal visiting at the tea hour. Listening to their gossip was a much more entertaining way of learning German than running over the allotted phrase books. And astonishing indeed were the preparations made in the suite of Mrs. Hall-Walker.

Elsie would watch mystified as the excitedly gabbling hotel maids prepared these rooms for the tea visit of King Edward. Sweet-smelling flowers in huge vases were not enough—the rooms had to be *sprayed* with perfume, and then the curtains were pulled. Mrs. Hall-Walker received Edward, who must have been thirty years older than she, in a setting suitable for the Arabian Nights. It was many years before Elsie realised what the preparations were *for—*

she had, as a schoolgirl, simply thought that was how you received princes at teatime: in almost total darkness with lilies and scent sprays. What makes this revelation so interesting is the fact that Sophie was rich, young, attractive and keen on sport. How curious that the attentions of the elderly monarch could have added prestige to her life. It meant only that no *other women* had him—on that particular afternoon!

26

Daisy, Princess of Pless

THERE WERE THREE well-known Daisys in Edwardian society—the famous Countess of Warwick, the Irish Countess of Fingall and the Princess of Pless.

The last-named was a tall blonde whose Irish mother, Mrs. William Cornwallis-West, had been among the Prince's flirts in the eighties. This Daisy had the rather doubtful luck of finding herself married off, aged eighteen, to the richest young Prince in Europe. Her ingenuous diaries, revealing the differences of aristocratic life in Germany and England, are all the more interesting because they were never intended for publication. She writes frankly that 'Dear Diary' is to receive her outpourings as if she addressed 'a rather dotty friend.' The writer reveals more than is consciously intended.

I never met the Princess of Pless, but I knew her sister Shelagh, Duchess of Westminster, and her brother the handsome George Cornwallis-West who married Jennie Churchill. Finally her son 'Hansel,' who grew up in the vast castles where the Kaiser was an annual visitor, has corrected this chapter. It is so easy to flounder into inaccuracies concerning the atmosphere of the Prussian and Austrian courts.

Patsy Cornwallis-West, the mother of Daisy, Shelagh and George, had been a beauty who bore all her children before the age of twenty-one. Thereafter she devoted herself to pleasure, living chiefly in Ruthin Castle in Wales and Newlands Manor in Hampshire, and spending the summer season in London where she continued a liaison with the Prince of Wales for several years. She was in fact the exception to his rule of avoiding very young married women.

While George was sent to the usual horrific boarding school, her two daughters were brought up like other girls of their class, running wild in the country, with a smattering of history and a lick of French and German, administered by a poor old governess in the schoolroom.

As the Prince of Wales, as well as Lord Charles Beresford (so prone to poach on each other's preserves), frequently came to stay, Daisy met both these gallants as a little girl. At the age of seventeen, knowing little except how to jump a horse and climb trees, she was brought to London, put into a long dress with a train and taken to curtsey to Queen Victoria. Then she was 'out' and at the end of the three-month season of 1891 she found herself engaged to be married to Prince Hans of Pless: 'Prince Henry proposed to me at a masked ball at Holland House. I did not know what on earth to say or do. I realised that my mother was ambitious and desired the match. In those absurd days it was a big feather in a mother's cap if she could marry a daughter off during her first season.' And the lovely Mrs. Cornwallis-West 'was much too much accustomed to homage and admiration' to want daughters clinging to her skirts. They had no dowries, but the Prince of Wales kept an eye on both girls and his opinion carried weight. Advised by His Royal Highness, the heir of Pless would marry pretty Daisy and the richest Duke in England her sister Shelagh. Only George rebelled against the Prince's wishes when he insisted on the impecunious, much older Jennie as his bride. Daisy was easily dazzled. 'I was to have hunters, jewels, castles, two ladies-in-waiting, visit England every year . . . it all sounded splendid and romantic. . . .'

As the blue-eyed tomboy, now a Countess of the Holy Roman Empire, wearing a diamond coronet, walked out of St. Margaret's, Westminster, for the huge wedding reception arranged by her triumphant mother, she saw the Prince of Wales's kindly, almost proprietory eyes, light up. His farewell words were, 'Learn to speak German and be a good subject.'

'I began my married life totally unprepared for any of its experiences, duties or responsibilities. Literally, I knew nothing.'

So without any knowledge of the facts of life the eighteen-year-old drove off with the handsome but rather frightening stranger who had suddenly become a husband, and found herself mistress of a palace in Silesia containing over six hundred rooms, and estates larger than most English counties. Powdered footmen stood outside her bedroom door, *Jägers* followed when she galloped through the forest, the famous seven-yard-long rope of Pless pearls was wound around her throat and historic tiaras and necklaces were laid out for her, but she found the rigid etiquette of Berlin a dismal contrast to England.

Decorous manners prevailed in French and English society, but here she had to be taught that no man must be allowed to sit on a sofa beside a lady—that would be too intimate, insufficiently respectful—he must bring up a separate chair for himself. Only a very elderly relation might share the sofa for a talk. It was impossible to go out driving in a carriage unless accompanied by some older lady, and only inconspicuous dark dresses could be worn when walking in Berlin. What could be more unlike Hyde Park?

In each capital city the upper classes lived by rule, but London could be termed free and easy compared with Berlin and Vienna. And how did these two differ? The Prussians were hard and efficient and tough and—according to Daisy's son 'Hansel,' who certainly ought to know, for his father's principality was governed from Berlin—lacking in charm, whereas the Austrians were artistic, gay, cultured and attractively flirtatious. The Emperor Franz Joseph and the Kaiser had mistresses who were well known and could, in our jargon, be called 'steadies.' But how, in either capital, might a love affair blossom between a wellborn married woman and a man who was not her husband? Divorce did not exist. To meet alone was extremely difficult. So what happened?

'Hansel,' who was a boy of fourteen when the First World War broke out, helps clarify amours in these old empires. He says that when a man fell in love with a woman of the upper class his first thought had to be protection of her reputation. He would not automatically try to seduce her, for that was a grave matter, and a gentleman did not necessarily feel he was a failure because he never reached his lady's bed. Yet romance floated in the air. Because a man may not show his feelings by touch or word or glance, because lovers never let their eyes meet in the ballroom, does not mean passion is lessened—on the contrary Great Love keeps well on a pedestal, and affairs of the heart which broke no outward rule were respected in Berlin and Vienna rather more than in the looser social structure of England.

For historical and temperamental reasons the moralities of German and Austrian women differed. The morality of Protestant Berlin was based on strict discipline; that of Catholic Vienna on the rules of the Roman Church. The fact that English upper-class women now regarded discreet husband-swapping as a sport slightly shocked Germans and Austrians.

Despite, or perhaps because of, the apparent impossibility of illicit love affairs developing, the Kaiser's sons, the Crown Prince and the younger Prince Joachim Albrecht, made passes at Daisy whenever they got the chance. 'Dear Diary' learns when a hand is slipped into hers under the carriage rug, and when her elbow is taken rather closely to guide her to examine a picture. In the palace Prince Joachim in fact behaves quite idiotically, stealing her handkerchiefs, which he carries away in sentimental ecstasy, and so on. Hans, her husband, never seems jealous. He is busy being unfaithful in Vienna. 'Dear Diary' learns this when Daisy makes herself miserable by opening a letter by mistake. But then Hans is a man, one could not expect *men* to be faithful, they are different, they don't represent the *home*.

Whatever frowns Hans causes his wife, she herself remains firm with the Crown Prince, reprimanding him for little indiscretions and insisting that some at least of her stolen handkerchiefs are retrieved from the doting Prince Joachim. Amidst all the grandeur it is interesting to note that the daughter of an English country gentleman was considered a fit mate for any prince in Europe. From rambling entries we get sidelights concerning the England for which Daisy is homesick. That ambitious mama works hard to marry her second daughter. In 1896 Daisy makes this entry: 'Gerry Cadogan has proposed to Shelagh but of course it wouldn't do; he has only a thousand a year.' (The 6th Earl Cadogan owned a slice of fashionable London, but rents were small in those days.) Later on: 'The Ilchesters are quite anxious for her to marry their son, he is too shy to propose, and Shelagh says he is too young and will not encourage him one bit; he is only twenty-two but I think she is throwing away a good chance, as a woman is almost bound to fall in love with the man who gives her everything—houses, jewels, horses, every penny she has, and later on her children; in fact the one to whom she owes everything—just as Hans gives me everything, and is so good and dear. . . .'

Eventually, England's richest duke would swim into sight, and the story of how he got hooked has been related.

This marriage took place in February 1901, but in spite of the fact that 'Bend Or' Westminster (named after his grandfather's Derby winner of 1879) gave his bride 'presents not unworthy of an Empress' the end of the story was not as Daisy predicted must be the case when a man gives a woman 'every penny she has.' After the birth of three children and the sad loss of an only son, the Duchess divorced her 'great catch.'

Effortlessly, the Princess of Pless describes the disappointment that most wives know at some time, when they have been romanticising over an absent husband and the wretch returns home exhausted and bilious. 'I was asleep when Hans arrived—very tired and rather liverish. . . . I wanted him to take me in his arms and be very dear to me, but—he was just as usual; he might never have been away at all.'

Daisy had been married eleven years before 'Dear Diary' learns of a persistent lover. But she destroyed his letters over five years, although they were 'perfect examples of devotion,' and finally he moved on to Vienna: 'At last he has made up his mind he cannot live like this and he will take his pleasure in Vienna. He will probably live with some woman—possibly even a lady I may know. But this has nothing to do with me . . . nor do I care more for him because I know he has been living almost a saintly life all these years; sometimes I have let him kiss me on the forehead.' Later she writes: 'How I wish I had kept or could keep all the love letters I receive,' but virtuously she adds: 'I have always refused to accept even playful admiration from a married man.'

Despite unshakable rules of behaviour in both capitals, Vienna presented the climate for romance whereas Berlin tended to spread a frost. The Crown Prince naturally considered England the gayest place. He told Daisy: 'My mother is always in a fever if I or my father go to England,' and she laughed thinking of the prudish Empress in a black frock with a large, untightened waist; '. . . she must have an extra supply of breath to enable her to gasp at her fantastic notions of all the horrible temptations that her husband and son have to resist in the dangerous little isle.'

There were very real dangers for silly princes, however. During a ball given by Shelagh Westminster in old Grosvenor House the Crown Prince disappeared. Embarrassed equerries and detectives eventually tracked him to a bedroom where he was taking a rest from official duties with a certain notorious peeress. Next day His Imperial Highness sent a magnificent jewel to this lady without realising it was one of the German Crown Jewels and not therefore at his disposal. The Kaiser furiously demanded the jewel back through the German Ambassador. The lady said 'No.' Ambassadors grew red-faced during this 'scandal of the season,' but it was finally settled without the press finding out. The Kaiser won.

Living in Germany, Daisy of Pless saw her own country with a fresh eye. She praised the English habit of separating husbands' and wives' bedrooms. When Hans came to her room 'he was quite pleased with himself, and then we laughed and talked together, and he said, "I shall see you tomorrow—Oh, I forgot you were my wife." The sentence explains what I mean; there was something unusual in his having to come right along a passage past other doors and then leave quietly on tiptoe as if he (and I too) had been doing something wrong; and there is a little air of mystery about it which is amusing and therefore more tempting.'

This is a truly Edwardian point of view. Throughout the whole epoch no sound is more exciting than the creak of a board in a corridor late at night.

On January 6, 1903, comes a long entry written at Chatsworth where the Plesses joined a large house party and we see the famous Louisa in the pomp of her old age. 'Arrived here late last night, dressed in a great hurry but got downstairs in good time. The Duchess of Devonshire is marvellous and *looks* marvellous for her seventy-four years. Always very décolletée in the evening with dresses that only a woman of thirty should wear, and yet she really does not seem dressed too young; she generally has a wreath of green leaves in her hair (or rather wig!). The evening being Twelfth Night we all danced around the Christmas Tree, Soveral leading the Duchess, then the girls and I ducked for an apple.'

The 'girls' consisted of the Duke of Connaught's two daughters Margaret and Patricia; other guests included the Tecks (Queen Mary's parents), Lord and Lady de Grey and the Desboroughs, along with 'Mr. Balfour, bland, smiling, and with a rare, rather old-fashioned courtesy towards women which is sweet.' They cut a cake containing charms and 'the Prime Minister, Mr. Balfour, got a little golden heart—perhaps to make up for the real one that he missed years ago!' She must mean Mary Elcho.

The Italian Violetta di Sermoneta, who came to England every year and also stayed at Chatsworth, gives us a last picture of the great Louisa: 'Talking of racing makes me think of the old Duchess of Devonshire, who was a great personage in King Edward's set, and attended every race meeting. She was very old when I knew her and always stiffly corseted, whilst her face wore the fixed expression of a monk. I was very frightened of her, but fascinated at the same time, as I had heard so much of her wonderful beauty and charm, so I used to study her from as near as I could to see if I could discover any traces of this.

'At the races she always sat on a bench like a stone image, quite immovable and stupendously dignified. One day I was rewarded by seeing her pull up her skirts and produce a purse from a bag secreted among her petticoats. "Put two pounds on *Cream Tart*," she said to one of her satellites. It sounded like the voice of an oracle. . . .'

In these days after the turn of the century the Duke, who had always been somnolent, dropped off to sleep rather too easily on public occasions. He once recounted a splendid story about having had a terrible nightmare that he was making a dull speech in the House of Lords, and waking up to find it was true!

During her week in London Daisy dined with the young Duchess of Manchester (Louisa's American daughter-in-law) to meet King Edward. 'He told me I was *très en beauté*, I always feel rather shy when he talks like that.'

Except for Mrs. Keppel, the other women at the dinner were also Americans—Lady Lister-Kaye and Lady Essex. The King let himself go, speaking 'very freely (too freely) about Germany. . . . On several occasions the other women turned apologetically to me, but the King said, "Oh Daisy doesn't mind; being married to a German does not make her change her national feelings." I thought neither does it make one insensible, so I let them go on arguing and talking about everything, and when they had finished I *had* my say *at* them, and then dropped my fan and, someone coming to pick it up, caused a change in the conversation.'

The fact that Daisy scribbled nightly in a diary not intended for publication makes her feelings about King Edward, whom she had known so long, and the Kaiser, who visited her every year, very interesting. After all, these two men were the only human beings capable of influencing the forces which were leading to that war of 1914.

Daisy of Pless once witnessed the Kaiser's chagrin at the discord between England and Germany. 'He said, "Oh, I am always misunderstood, there is no one living to tell the truth to me," and a tear fell on his cigar. I was at once touched and antagonised. The act of weeping into his cigar, so typically German, somehow put me off.'

And yet she liked him, and he could be very funny about the discomforts of staying in her castle in the past. Of his icy, carpetless bedroom he exclaimed, 'Did they think I wanted to skate!' Daisy comically described his moustache waxed up until it nearly went into his eyes, and his dozens of uniforms. She thought she must find out if he had one for 'the private occasion' when alone in his wife's bedroom.

'The mornings were spent stalking or shooting. Luncheon began at three-thirty and went on for an hour and a half or even two hours. . . . Dinner began at ten o'clock. . . . The men wore uniform, the women wore their smart clothes, the contents more or less of the family jewel chest and tiaras and both men and women Orders and Decorations. I loathed these meals. I do not for a moment wish to insinuate that the Kaiser was a tedious guest. Far from it, he was always delightful. It was the proceedings during his stay which were such a bore. King Edward, naturally genial, human and unassuming hated the Kaiser's pose and swagger, which, by the way, was largely assumed. When the Kaiser unbent he could be most human and interesting and it was well known that with his own particular male cronies he could be very unbent indeed.'

In June 1903 she wrote: 'I lunched with Alice Keppel before leaving for Berlin; three or four of the women present had had several lovers, and did not mind saying so, but I can generally *placer* myself in any *milieu*. Alice is fascinating.'

On the day after her twenty-ninth birthday, which she spent at Kiel, Daisy lunched on the *Hohenzollern* with the Kaiser and his Empress, who 'all paid me extravagant compliments over my toilette. I would not wear a feathered hat on the sea, so wore a lace and embroidered frock with pink around my waist and a pink bebe washing hat with pink ribbon. My dear diary, I am really not vain, for honestly I cannot see where my beauty lies. This is what I am really like: I would look much plumper if I did not wear long and well-made French corsets; blue eyes with fair eye-lashes which I make black; pretty coloured fair hair; good eyebrows; straight yet somehow turned-up nose; short upper lip with the two front teeth rather longer than the others (like a rabbit or a mouse I think), thick bottom-lip and a very slight double chin—which I keep in hand by dint of frequent massage. There is nothing to boast about in that, is there?'

As she matured, Daisy tried to encourage a happier relationship between the German royal family and the German-hating Queen Alexandra. When the Kaiser's stodgy wife, who looked so much older than her spouse, would gather the ladies around her, it resembled a Quaker meeting. Daisy wrote: 'They were all so shy with her, but I never am; I saw she liked it if one kept the conversation going quietly, for nothing is so awful as a dead silence in such gatherings; until someone coughs or giggles, and then a brave one mumbles faintly something which no one hears, and everyone says, Hem! What! and it turns out that whatever she had said was not worth repeating; then everyone looks at everyone else to see who is going to speak next.'

There is an amusing description of the first rich Americans to bring their yachts to Kiel. The Cornelius Vanderbilts arrived on their *North Star,* and the Plesses dined aboard. Later the men left for beer drinking ashore, 'but in about an hour, to my astonishment, the launch reappeared with several men *and* Prince Henry [the Kaiser's brother] who disappeared below with Mrs. Cornelius Vanderbilt, our hostess, a fascinating (though snobbish) little American, but with much charm; I always imagined the Prince stiff and shy, certainly without a *soupçon* of flirtation but—still waters run deep: I think, too, he saw a good deal of her during his visit to the United States.'

Vivacious American women with their huge fortunes and elegant clothes could lead most European noblemen by the ear, but no American heiress wanted to marry a German—the great prize was an Englishman. Daisy remarked about young Miss Goelet who was to marry the Duke of Roxburghe later that year. 'How I should hate to be May Goelet, all those odious little Frenchmen, and dozens of others crowding round her millions.' An English duke did not *crowd around*—he merely *accepted* a millionairess.

At Fürstennstein there were large shoots on the English model—eight hundred pheasants shot in a morning—and in the evenings music and dancing. Daisy not only sang in public but did Spanish dances for the astounded German nobility. Anxiously her mother-in-law told her to be careful to catch only the top skirt, 'for once or twice you caught the underskirt too, and one could see up to your knee.' How lucky were men in those days when the mere sight of an ankle could heighten their blood pressure. Daisy's diary record of the Chatsworth house party of January 1904 stresses how the people of Edward's set, the people of this book, kept meeting over and over again in the same great houses.

On this occasion the Duke and Duchess of Devonshire gave their Twelfth Night party for Edward and Alexandra: 'The Queen is as charming and beautiful as always, and the King very well and in good spirits. . . . The King has his Bridge with Mrs. Keppel who is here—with lovely clothes and diamonds—in a separate room, and in the other rooms people are massed together, also of course playing Bridge. Generally, to amuse the Queen I am made to go and sing and dance in the corridor where the band is. . . .' The Elchos and Desboroughs were present among the twenty or so house guests, with two of Louisa's own granddaughters and Princess Victoria—now thirty-five.

'The last evening was very cheerful: the Queen danced a waltz with Soveral, and then we each took off our shoes to see what difference it made in our height. The Queen took, or rather kicked hers off, and then got into everyone else's—even Willie Desborough's old pumps. I never saw her so free and cheerful—but always graceful in everything she does.'

But there was nothing graceful about the sharpening Princess Victoria, as she watched this asinine gambol. She belonged nowhere, not with the Duchess's granddaughters—simpering virgins awaiting proposals from well-propertied eldest sons—nor with the young marrieds whose conversation had to be adjusted slightly when a spinster was present. Perhaps she found contact with Lady Maud Warrender and Lord Howe, who were both musical; or with the King's intelligent Parsee friends, the Sassoons—but she could never be relaxed, nor was she ever out of her mother's sight.

Daisy of Pless has been married twelve years by the time 'Dear Diary' gets on its pages a certain old friend. 'When I shut my eyes and think of Cairo, I walk in that desert sand with him; or I lean from the window of my room to look at the purple sky in bright moon, the shadows of the palm trees, I see him waving us goodnight, and I hear his steps and the clink of his spurs down the silent path. Then he was a soldier; now he drudges in the City to make gold. . . . On arriving here [Grosvenor House, London] I found another letter asking if he might come and see me. I shall let him come to tea. . . . I cannot think what is the matter with me lately. . . . I feel something in me that aches to emerge and meet something deeply responsive. . . .'

She was too naïve to analyse her discontent.

The personages of this book are always staying at Chatsworth. By 1907 Queen Alexandra looks 'just as she has for the last sixteen years. . . . Princess Victoria has never become much known to the general public. In spite of her reserve, fastidiousness and natural shyness she is full of fun and cheeriness and can be a great asset at a house party. . . .' This poor little Princess carried her pathetic remnant of gaiety on to the end. Again we hear that Lady de Grey is expressing disapproval at the new habit of placing lovers' photographs on the mantelpiece while relegating husbands' photos to drawers.

'Mr. Balfour was urbane, smiling, amused, and took a surprisingly intense interest in everything that went on. Somehow one does not expect a great philosopher statesman and writer to be human! As for dear Alice Keppel, she was inimitable. What spirit, wit and resilience that woman has! . . . The Queen was as charming and sweet as ever and gave me a dear little fire-opal and diamond brooch for Christmas. She is a darling. It was the same huge party as usual, only Soveral was furious; he was rather the man out, which as a rule he never is. . . . Soveral generally went down and smoked a cigar alone in the smoking-room. . . . Lord Elcho, Lord Desborough and Muriel Wilson played dominoes with Lady de Grey.'

As was usual at all big house parties, when royalty was present the women wore tiaras at dinner and the men wore their orders and decorations. Sir Frederick Ponsonby, attending his royal master at this Chatsworth winter party, recorded: 'I sat next the Duchess a very clever shrewd woman who pretended to be the reverse. She was in a delightful mood, most witty and amusing, and she told me many stories of the old days.'

Ponsonby describes the amateur theatricals: 'Lady Maud Warrender sang, but she seemed too big for the tiny stage and certainly her voice was too powerful for the room. But Daisy of Pless looked lovely—singing dressed as a geisha, and then in white fur and short skirts while snow fell on her.'

Ponsonby gives us one final view of the Duke of Devonshire, who was now seventy-one and had quitted politics after much bother over tariff reform. He was, according to all who worked for him, the most courteous and thoughtful gentleman with a great feeling for people and a desire to let others enjoy the treasures he had inherited, but social activity bored him. 'While everything was beautifully managed anything left to the Duke to decide was invariably forgotten. . . . With so large a party it was impossible for all the men to shoot, and yet the Duke never selected the guns till very late at night and so the list was only made known the next morning. No one could discover the principle on which the guns were chosen, but of course there *was* no principle. If the Duke happened to be sleepy he simply said "The same guns as before." '

Lord Rosebery once left Chatsworth in a fury because he came down to breakfast in shooting clothes only to be informed by his valet that he had better change as he was not on the shooting list. Of course the Duke proffered apologies when he learnt of the incident but it shows how casual he could be. Maybe it might have been possible for 'Skittles' to catch him in a sleepy mood and get herself married to him in the long ago. It would indeed have been extraordinary if the Liberal statesman had been lassoed by that equestrian cocotte. He did not like to be bothered and let Louisa boss him right up into old age. He had never read Milton, and when he found *Paradise Lost* in the library one day, he began to read it to the librarian, exclaiming at intervals at his discovery: 'How fine it is —how very fine.' But Louisa entered and poked him with her parasol. 'If he starts reading poetry he will never get out for his walk.'

No one realised that this party at Chatsworth was the last of its kind, for in the spring the Duke would die at Cannes, and his property would be inherited by a nephew. As he lay dying he seemed to be reminiscing to himself. His last words were: 'Well, the game is over and I'm not sorry.'

Daisy of Pless had acquired a critical foreigner's eye: 'It always interested and astonished me to note how much more truly King Edward was appreciated abroad than at home. . . . The King's great flair for foreign affairs arose from the fact that for thirty years he had watched the eddies of international politics from a position of great eminence divorced from direct responsibility. . . . The European press saw in his Continental visits nothing but social jaunts whereas they were, behind the façade of amusement, serious missions.'

During the summer of 1909 (the last of the King's reign), Daisy of Pless made her most perceptive entries. On July 24, while staying at Cliveden with the American Mr. and Mrs. Astor (who were both to enter the British House of Commons—Nancy as the first woman Member), she wrote: 'The house is full of people, among them being Sophie Torby and the Grand Duke Michael (morganatically married), and Winston Churchill, who sat next to me at dinner. I am awfully sorry for him, he is like a race-horse wanting to start at once—even on the wrong race-track; he has so much impetuousness that he cannot hold himself back, and he is too clever and has too much personal magnetism. . . . At present his politics are all personal, the politics of an American advertiser. He is not happy if he is not always before the public, and he may some day be Prime Minister—and why not, he has energy and brains.'

Later on that summer Daisy went to Cowes and sailed in the *Britannia* with Mrs. Keppel. King Edward had casual good manners. When he asked Daisy to stay on a day she hesitated because all her clothes were packed, and he did not insist . . . 'he is so nice always —and said, "Think it over and do what you like." '

In December 1909 Daisy visited her sister Shelagh Westminster during the King's last visit to Eaton Hall. She mentioned the Kaiser's eagerness for a treaty between England and Germany. ' "Yes," said the King with a laugh, "and what would France and Russia say?" ' Being a mere woman, Daisy thought France ought to be delighted as, if war did break out, the Kaiser's forces would have to march through French fields and French towns.

One afternoon, when Mrs. Keppel had wished to accompany Daisy on a drive to visit the latter's grandmother—Lady Olivia Fitzpatrick, the mother of Patsy Cornwallis-West—King Edward insisted on accompanying them and they arrived unannounced; 'he made outrageous love to the old lady and in a few minutes they

were both flirting desperately. Granny never could resist flirting
and neither could the King. He asked, "Is it true that my Mother
sent you away from Court for trying to flirt with my father?" "I
can't quite remember, Sir; most likely I wanted to—he was a very
good-looking man—besides all the Coburgs inherit a roving eye."
This shaft the King did not try to parry.'

When six months later news of Edward's death reached Germany, Daisy would write: 'As well as a great King he was the kindest gentleman and truest friend . . . the face of England has
changed overnight.'

The Prince of Pless corroborated this, in a solemn statement:
'You will go there to see your parents and I to get my breeches,
and that is all.'

27

Rosa Lewis

THE YEARS ROLL BY and new heroines creep into the Edwardian scene, but they continue the processional of London balls and country house parties in much the same way. As they depart from London for the long weekend, boarding the train which has been selected by their hostesses (no casual choice of arrival time permitted), each lady clasps the large green leather, lockable 'travelling bag' from Vickery's in Bond Street, which contains precious love letters, while her maid nervously clutches a smaller matching leather jewel case.

The way of life continues in a pattern set nearly fifty years before, but these new beauties are too young to amuse the King; his fingers drum with boredom when he sits next to them at dinner; small talk is not in his line, the bilious grey eye rolls past the fresh pretty faces to some mature woman with whom he can converse.

Some of the older houris have become eccentric in old age. My father had already seen the formidable Louisa through the unadmiring eyes of a small boy. 'Of Devonshire House, I recall the Duke [Harty-tarty] standing like a somnambulist at the top of the stairs while my mother called on the famous wicked Duchess, who played the new game of Bridge in a yellow-red wig, and was named "Grand Slam."' Daisy of Pless's diary records: 'The Duchess of Devonshire was at Monte Carlo, and they say that in the gambling rooms she was always followed by detectives and carefully watched by croupiers in case she tried to snatch any money.' The snatching habit apparently remained from the days when important gentlemen were her meat.

For young girls the drill remained unchanged. They were 'flappers' with flapping hair until the day it was put up, they were then 'out,' and could at the opera be permitted to sit in the lower open boxes, with grown-up ladies in evening dress carrying lorgnettes and fans. Up until 1914 if a girl of seventeen, with her hair down, went to the opera in Paris or London she had to be sent up to one of the high balconies and her chaperones would have to wear dark day dresses. The rules were exasperating, but people must have liked this rigidity, or they would have changed it.

A few rebellious expressions could be perceived. Lady Randolph Churchill's niece, Clare Frewen, who would become a sculptress and journalist, caused consternation by walking across Hyde Park wearing a bright-coloured chiffon scarf around her neck accompanied by a Borzoi instead of a maid. After this 'exhibition' she was told that no *nice* man would want to marry her, and indeed even the nice man who did so requested Clare to 'refrain from drawing attention to herself.' And the quiet, sensitive Miss Sackville-West of Knole was gathering the material which would one day emerge in that classic *The Edwardians*.

The great old ladies, the real Edwardians, all in their fifties and sixties, continued to hold power. In October 1903, when the question of army reform was being debated, King Edward held a Council at Wynyard while staying with Lord and Lady Londonderry and he delighted the august Nellie by insisting that all official documents should be headed in medieval fashion 'at our Court at Wynyard.' The Duchess of Devonshire and Mrs. Keppel were present at this party. The raddled old Duchess and fresh young mistress played bridge every night with the King and his equerry while the other guests preferred poker.

Sir Almeric Fitzroy was sitting in his temporary Privy Council office when Lady Londonderry crept stealthily in. 'She had apparently left her room on a voyage of discovery, and having found somebody to talk to, ensconced herself in my arm chair, and was eloquent on fifty subjects in half the number of minutes. The zest with which she throws herself into the political interests and movements of the hour will help her to keep the position won by her beauty.'

What energy, determination and nerve she must have had.

To slip down from these scenes of grandeur, one might now outline the career of one who, although no lady, must certainly be called a great Edwardian, for she lent much to the scene and indeed helped to hold the social edifice together. Mrs. Rosa Lewis of the Cavendish Hotel was aiding aristocratic love affairs right into World War II, and she began this splendid service in 1901—no mean record.

Born in 1867 to respectable working-class parents, Rosa was a skivvy at twelve, a little maid of all work with her hair hanging down her back. She rose at six in the morning to light fires with old newspapers in which she avidly read the Court Circulars concerning court balls, royal race meetings, etc. And she worked until bedtime.

At sixteen, with good references, she changed to a new employer —a real nob—the Comte de Paris, pretender to the French throne, who was living in exile at Sheen House near London. From scrubbing floors, Rosa rose to the status of washer-up of the precious Sèvres dinner service and sewer-up of stuffed poultry—tasks for dexterous fingers.

The Comtesse de Paris, a disciplinarian, keen on deportment, took to inspecting the kitchen on her way to the morning ride, and she would tap with her riding whip any kitchenmaid who slouched, just as she did her own daughters. *'Tiens-toi droit, mon enfant.'*

By the age of twenty Rosa was head kitchenmaid and had learnt to speak French, to cook exceptionally well, and to carry herself like a swan. There are varying descriptions of how the Prince of Wales first set eyes on the blue-eyed, pink-skinned girl whose Cockney backchat was to become so famous. One story tells of her being sent up from the kitchen to sing in her lusty natural voice after dinner, but the version that she herself used to recount (during her jolly, long-drawn-out dotage) described the morning of a shooting party some time after she had left Sheen House. A cold collation had been laid out on the sideboard and Rosa was standing in the dining room surveying her handiwork when the Prince slipped in for a snack, saw a handsome young woman alone and, after a few amiable words, gave her a kiss. When luncheon was served he asked his hostess where a certain lovely guest had vanished to—a tall woman in a white dress with a wonderful complexion. 'Sir, you mean Rosa the cook?' 'And after that,' she'd say when an old woman, 'I was the Queen of Cooks, I was.'

By this time Rosa had embarked on a new career—that of temporary cook to be hired out for an evening or a country weekend. It was Mrs. Murray Guthrie (my great-aunt Olive Leslie of earlier chapters) who first employed her for those huge dinners in Stratford House (which still stands off Oxford Street). Olive knew nothing about food, and her own cook wilted when asked to produce ten-course dinners for twenty or more people. From Mrs. Guthrie, Rosa got an introduction to Lady Randolph Churchill who throughout the nineties was frequently entertaining the Prince of Wales, and the latter let it be known that Rosa's delicious, complicated, but never sickly dishes were his favourite fare. Naturally Rosa became much in demand. Hostesses vied to obtain her services for country house parties, and so she travelled throughout England, staying at those 'stately homes' which are now open, with tea and buns, to paying visitors. She could ask big fees, for it soon became *essential* to get her when entertaining the Prince. Only she understood his predilections (from his valet she learned how much he disliked gravies that spilt on his shirt!), only she could create the subtle surprise, and it was Rosa who insisted, against Victorian prejudice, that a dash of sherry should be put in the consommé as what she called *un amuse gueule* (can I vulgarly translate this as tummy-tickler?).

At the age of twenty-five Rosa married, rather snobbishly, Mr. Excelsior Lewis, the illegitimate son of a gentlewoman, and he had become butler to Sir Andrew Clarke, Bt. Her personal description of her spouse was: 'He was a bit of a dud, but other people loved him.' They had no children and the marriage failed for alcoholic reasons. It is worthy to note, however, that Rosa, like the grand ladies who employed her, kept whatever lovers she may have had a dead secret. Cook or countess—they did not wish such arrangements to be scrutinised or discussed by the 'mob.'

As she grew more important Mrs. Lewis employed a chorus of handsome girls to travel with her—they were dressed exactly as she was, in spotless white with tall chefs' hats and high laced 'cooking boots' of soft black kid, to support the ankles during the long hours spent preparing dishes. 'Can't concentrate if yer feet aches.'

With the zeal which differentiates a good cook from a superb artist, Rosa always rose at five in the morning to choose her own fresh vegetables at Covent Garden Market and, on the afternoon of a London dinner party, she and her girls would move into the kitchen of the house where they were to work, bringing many partly prepared delicacies with them. The regular servants were banished—genius does not like to be interrupted or watched!

During the Coronation years of 1902 Rosa produced twenty-nine suppers for big balls, often only getting home for a couple of hours' sleep before it was time to be up for the marketing. With the money saved during this year she bought the Cavendish Hotel in Jermyn Street, an establishment which became different to any other in the world. Having got rid of Mr. Lewis, whose inebriated muddles made accountancy impossible, Rosa proceeded to organise most splendid catering arrangements. With perspicacity and definite courage, she divided her hotel into suites, each with its own bathroom (the tubs were encased in mahogany like those she had seen in grand country houses) and its own dining room. This made possible an extremely attractive form of private entertaining; but of course the Cavendish was not open to the public, only to the gentlemen Rosa selected, and she had strong views. The Prince of Wales kept his own permanent suite where he could dine peacefully with whomever he wished, and when Rosa acquired the houses and gardens at the back, these formed a private courtyard with four doors through which hasty exits could be made in emergency.

Rosa Lewis deserved the fortune she earned by catering to the vital needs of the aristocracy—she produced delicious food and complete privacy. In time a public dining room was added—a long, quiet, panelled room to which the swells could bring their lady friends at a time when there was no such thing as a good London restaurant.

Secrecy, unique cooking and Rosa's Cockney wit kept the Cavendish Hotel famous for forty years. She had an inbred aversion to scandal and gave caustic advice about burning love letters: 'No letters, no lawyers, and kiss my baby's bottom' was her adage.

The two sporting gentlemen who moved into permanent suites—Sir William Eden, the father of Anthony Eden, and Lord Ribblesdale, lord in waiting to Queen Victoria in 1880 and Master of the Buck Hounds 1892—caused much comment but there was never proof that Rosa had taken a lover. Certainly she followed her own proverb and left no indiscreet letters—her famous corsets signed by King Edward and other gentlemen of note were not proof of *anything*, and I fear they disintegrated before a museum could acquire them.

The sporting Sir William Eden was indeed a great original, a skilled water colourist and most erudite. He and Lord Ribblesdale simple settled down in the place they liked best. Ribblesdale, growing melancholy after the death of his wife (the gay, hard-riding sister of Margot Asquith), and losing his eldest son in action in Somaliland, lived in the Cavendish for years.

Incidentally, Lady Ribblesdale, being one of the Tennant sisters and brought up in that unconventional way, had had a brief affair with Lord Curzon which her husband forgave and referred to merely as a 'clumsy indiscretion.' When Curzon first met Charlotte Ribblesdale and made strong advances, as was his way with all pretty women, she kept him in his place, writing him: '. . . I have not changed my views on the subject of Christian name. . . . I don't wish you to call me by mine and I would sooner not call you by yours.'

A year later this entirely changed and she was writing: 'My very beloved George . . . I do not regret it now, for how should I ever have got to know you as I do now? I look upon them as three precious hours well spent . . . in which I have gained blessing, for what greater blessing can there be on this weary earth than a friend who loves one? Mind—I recarnalise this word as much as you do a kiss.'

All the Tennant girls knew how to express themselves on paper and in a later letter Lady Ribblesdale attempted to philosophise: '. . . I always feel friendship is so one-sided, one gives and the other receives. I don't mean the time-honoured adage of "*un qui baise et l'autre qui tend la joue,*" I am afraid I have committed both these hideous enormities but what I mean is . . .' etc.

'Clumsy' is hardly the suitable adjective for this particular indiscretion, but it ended with no bones broken, and then death took the gay naughty Charty.

After losing both son and wife Lord Ribblesdale found the outspoken humorous Rosa Lewis to be exactly the companion he craved—a down-to-earth human being who could make him laugh. There was no nonsense in Rosa. Once when Ribblesdale brought her home from the theatre, friends called out to ask what the play had been like. Quickly she turned and answered: 'The sort of play you'd take your cook to.'

She could throw a good mood over a man like a garment, and she agreed with Ribblesdale's statement: 'To be a lord is still a popular thing . . . to be pleased with yourself may be selfish, or it may be stupid, but it is seldom actively disagreeable. . . .'

During the 1914 war Rosa would arrange girls and champagne for penniless young men on leave, and if comfort was possible she gave it to Lord Ribblesdale when his second son was killed in 1916. Sir William Eden died in the Cavendish Hotel during that war in which three of his sons were killed. To him it was 'home.'

For nearly thirty years after the King's death Rosa remained an extraordinary 'Edwardian' personality. My father used to take us to visit her as children—to munch strawberries out of the grownups' champagne glasses in that sitting room whose walls were lined solidly with photographs of her friends and the friends' offspring. We were quick to notice that *our* parents were never allowed to pay for champagne—corks would pop and then some bewildered millionaire would be led into her parlour for the *honour* of signing the bill.

And what a snob she was! In the fashion of the day, she did not regard artists or writers fit for high society. Lord Ribblesdale and my father had to be forgiven literary output because of their breeding, but she firmly shared the views of Lady Falmouth who, when my grandmother announced with pride that her son had published a book of poems, exclaimed coldly: 'What odd things people do nowadays!'

When the Kaiser, with a retinue of ninety, rented Highcliffe Castle near Bournemouth for a month in November 1907, King Edward suggested he ask Rosa Lewis to accept the post of head cook, and the idea appealed to her.

The Kaiser, who had just made his 'blood is thicker than water' speech at the Guildhall in London, enjoyed a good reception and word went about that he was studying the English people in order to work out methods of remaining amicable. Rosa gave him French dishes although he insisted on German wines—at that time she considered His Imperial Majesty as 'a bit of all right.' Her views would change in the future, when her favourite gentlemens' sons were wiped out in the trenches. Lord Ribblesdale's splendid portrait by Sargent hung for many years on the stairway, and we have all seen her raise her champagne glass to toast him: 'To Lordy —the greatest gentleman of them all!'

To appreciate the atmosphere of the Cavendish Hotel prior to the 1914 war, it is necessary to read the novels of Elinor Glyn and to realise that *Three Weeks*, which sold five million copies, did not merely appeal to the romantic aspirations of kitchenmaids but to the kitchenmaid in the heart of every great lady in Europe. The story of a Balkan queen who clad in diaphanous garments receives her lover while lying on a tiger-skin is extremely well written and contains a plot which today must rouse the mirth of twelve-year-olds, but women were unsophisticated in 1908—the success of this book proves it. Mrs. Glyn received immense acclaim and was invited to stay in the Court of St. Petersburg so that she could do a story about imperial Russia. Princes and princesses felt it intriguing to meet her, and the great Lord Curzon, Viceroy, Foreign Secretary, and so nearly Prime Minister, became her enamoured escort. I myself will never forget reading the forbidden *Three Weeks* which I found in a guest room when I was about fourteen years old—I thought it was true! And although we did not actually understand what went on in the Cavendish, my young brother and I appreciated the atmosphere of mystery and intrigue as we explored the long creaky corridors and peered into the dusty bedrooms with their chintz curtains and sporting prints and huge gold mirrors. We considered it a strange tantalising old house, a unique house. And this childish assessment was perfectly accurate.

28

∽

Lord Esher and His
Daughter-in-law

In the summer of 1971, while walking down the King's Road in London, I was ruminating on whom I personally would pick as the most fascinating man of Edwardian times—despite the alluring Harry Cust and the impact of Joe Laycock and the erudite charm of Rosebery, I came to the conclusion that the febrile, mysterious Esher, with his razor-sharp perspicacity, would make the most entertaining companion of the century. He was never sad like Rosebery and his sense of humour packed harder punch. They said he had a gift for friendship when he was young, yet you would have to seek him out, for Reginald Esher was an elusive character, loving power but loving it secretly, refusing all high office, refusing to be Minister of War while he was in fact reorganising the armed forces, and finally even refusing the honour of being Viceroy of India.

The official posts he did hold were accepted merely for convenience' sake; they were posts which enabled him to organise efficiently from behind a smoke screen, and kept him near to the throne. No wonder he aroused the envy and dislike of politicians, generals and courtiers who could not fathom his intentions or understand why he held the ear of the Prince.

He had been born the eldest son of Viscount Esher, a Master of the Rolls, and he caught Queen Victoria's eye as a very young man. She was fond of Reginald's French mother, and she soon found the youth could write neat reports. A very astute old lady, she had learnt to assess potentiality quickly. Those who could be useful must be used. And Reginald Esher's genius lay in writing confidential memoranda for sovereigns. His lucid, humorous mind seized the bone of the matter and his clear, concise pen could sketch out the alternatives, the pitfalls, the remedies, as a great draughtsman can outline any subject with a few bold strokes. He would place on paper all that was needed—and no more. Uncluttered by detail, the reader could grasp the immediate issue and the alternatives, but if detail could be helpful it would be there, accurate, precise.

He was good-looking. Even the curling moustache of the period could not hide that mobile mouth—the quick half-smile. And who had loved him? Most especially Millie, Duchess of Sutherland, I believe. She who is described in every memoir, standing in her diamond tiara at the top of the staircase in Stafford House, St. James's, receiving her lines of mounting guests while the strains of waltz music floated from the ballroom. Millie Sutherland, always listed among 'the beauties,' made more impression than any other hostess in the reception of her guests; they never seemed able to dissociate her from that staircase! But apart from the knowledge that there was caring, and that Lord Esher could not have been the only gentleman whose heart missed a beat when he saw the tall figure shimmering with diamonds, I know nothing more. Although the Duchess of Sutherland was Daisy Warwick's half sister, she did not resemble Daisy in untamable passions. She kept to the true Edwardian tradition—she was discreet.

And Lady Esher, who lived in her husband's shadow, was, to those who managed to know her, a delightful woman who used to say, when on the topic of husband-keeping, 'You must make the tea-kettle exciting.' She meant that a wife must make ordinary life so alluring that a man *wanted* to come home.

I thought of this, and of the clarity of Esher's writings in the six volumes of his *Journals and Letters* which I had recently been reading, volumes which I had picked up with a sigh, and then found myself riveted by the perfection of his comment—how fair he was, how just! An early letter to Lord Cowper, Lord Lieutenant of Ireland, applies so perfectly to freedom of speech as Englishmen view it! 'I hope you will have nothing to do with suppressing agitations in Ireland by force or by law, call it which you will. I do not maintain that the principle of absolute freedom of speech is a good thing everywhere, but I am convinced that wherever you have to do with

Englishmen, either as a dominant class or not, you cannot afford to ignore it. Observe how in India the experience of the last few years has taught us that it does not do to yield to the very natural desire to prevent people saying what is disagreeable and what may be dangerous.'

He was a very young man when he wrote this—*ordering* the Lord Lieutenant to observe what he had observed! For a time he worked as private secretary to Lord Hartington, and for five years he remained a Liberal M.P. Then for ten years he appeared to be idling contentedly, but his mind worked hard and his prescience increased. In beautiful handwriting he sent out directives to those in high places telling them in the most delightful casual letters, interspersed with witticisms, how to run the Empire! He lived as an English gentleman of moderate means, uninterested in society, untouched by court intrigues, doing apparently just exactly what he wanted. While others strove to build up pheasant shoots and to give big house parties, Reginald Esher preferred to retire to his Scottish estate and go out with a gun accompanied by two dogs. The 'smart thing' had no appeal. He was independent of what people thought, and yet he did not stagnate. He was not indifferent to life, but to triviality.

In 1895 Lord Rosebery persuaded Esher, who had reached the age of forty-three, to accept a post which placed him in charge of much royal property and made him responsible for the organisation of Queen Victoria's Diamond Jubilee celebration. One would think this a headache. But Esher could organise without ruffling a feather, as if he was playing patience with himself—a card here, a card there, a reshuffle. To use his talents amused him.

In 1902, pressed by the King, Esher accepted membership of the Royal Commission ordered to analyse the disasters of the South African War. Two years later he became the chairman of the War Office Reconstruction Committee, which, in fact, enabled him to fulfil his own ruling passion—the reorganising of Britain's defence forces. From behind the scenes he zealously supported naval revolution and army reforms, and naturally he encouraged the King to support them too.

In 1905, after he had refused the War Office but accepted permanent membership of the Committee of Imperial Defence, King Edward exclaimed: 'Although you are not exactly a public servant, yet I always think you are the most valuable public servant I have.' Esher enjoyed this compliment, for he wrote to his younger son Maurice, '. . . and then I kissed his hand as I sometimes do.' This

was a curious, spontaneous, un-English but to him absolutely natural
reflex.

Now he was indeed the King's 'best friend,' the power behind
the throne, and many important people did not like it. Jealousy
sprang up. Lord Carrington, who had been Edward's companion for
years, noted grumpily in his 1905 diary how he was awaiting a summons to the King's private room when 'the door opened and in came
Esher. He certainly is an extraordinary man, and has a wonderful
footing in Buckingham Palace. He seems able to run about it as he
likes and must be a considerable nuisance in the household. He is a
clever unscrupulous man, who might be dangerous; and he is not
trusted by the general public, who look on him as an intriguer.'

In fact, the general public could neither trust nor distrust a man
they knew nothing about; it was the ministers of the Crown who
grew incensed and called him an intriguer. As they knew him to be
capable of prejudicing the monarch prior to cabinet decisions, their
rage was understandable. And Esher would not become one of
them. It was exceedingly irritating to ambitious generals to see him
dining at Brooks's Club with the King's other favourites, Admiral
Sir John Fisher, Private Secretary Francis Knollys and the anti-
German Soveral. Esher would hearten the occasionally downcast
Admiral Fisher by assuring him that His Majesty had 'two receiving
plates in his mind,' one retaining lasting impressions of people and
their relative value, and one merely recording '*things*.'

As the King sometimes had to listen to Fisher's fulminations
about naval inadequacies for five hours at a stretch, it is perhaps
natural that he switched off one receiving plate. However eager the
King might be to give full attention to his cabinet ministers, it was
inevitable that Esher's witty comments and succinct memoranda
should make concentration easier to sustain.

Esher was a truly extraordinary man—completely self-sufficient
in that he wished to use his first-class brain to run England without
the tedium of accepting ministerial office. He did not want to do
nothing, he wanted to do a great deal—but without being noticed.
His ambition was the reverse of ordinary ambition. He wished
to attain power without recognition, without applause—his enemies
said without responsibility.

Ponsonby, the private secretary, who must often have been put
out by Esher's talent for domination, has written what he intends
as a compliment: 'I always think that Esher's strong point was that
he never minded who got credit for any measure he devised so
long as it was adopted by the authorities.'

Esher's very subtlety helped to make him unpopular. He was so different from the rest who, nice chaps as they make themselves out to be and probably were, hankered for recognition of loyal service, and longed for well-deserved honours to flow in their direction. It must have been so teasing to realise that the most beguiling man in England, the one who could have had *anything,* preferred tramping his Scottish moors alone.

Such were my reflections while walking down the King's Road with a sheaf of copied Esher letters in my pocket. And then I noticed a tall, graceful figure moving lightly over the pavement—scarves flowing, head held high—and I caught up with my father's friend Zena Dare, the most magnetic of eighty-five-year-olds, a lady who carried herself more gracefully than anyone else in the street. It was a chance to learn something more, for sixty years ago Miss Dare, star of London's musical comedy, had married a Guards officer who was the younger son of this extraordinary Lord Esher. What could it have been like for her?

We lunched together and I plied questions. Having soared to fame in 1905, she could give a lively account of theatrical life during Edwardian times, and her own upbringing in sedate middle-class circumstances vividly revealed the prejudices of various layers of society. Her musical mother had longed to be an actress; this was never permitted, so she married a lawyer who was Clerk of the Court, an interesting if unremunerative employment. There was never quite enough money, a fact which would make it easier in time for the daughters to attempt careers. Zena's mother insisted that her two girls should be well educated—far better than if they had been stuck with one old governess in an aristocratic country house—and they were taught to dance and sing.

At eleven, Phyllis, the younger girl, went into pantomime and her treble voice aroused comment. Zena had to continue schooling until Seymour Hicks, the famous actor-director, noticed her waiting for her sister. He spotted her quality immediately and taught her to act—'No tiresome dramatic diplomas needed then—one just *went* on the stage!' Within a year Seymour Hicks had her playing opposite him in a musical, and in one night Zena's name reached the headlines—'Success is such fun at seventeen. My school friends came around with clippings and we sat on my bed reading them. I realised I had suddenly become famous, and then it was that I knew nerves for the first time.'

The Catch of the Season, in which she won acclaim, had a Cinderella plot. Zena Dare played the part of a girl whose family will not allow her to go to a ball, so disguised as an entertainer she gets in to play her banjo and sing and dance. . . . 'Keep your legs down,' said Mr. Hicks when she tried to show off her high kicks. 'Girls get paid a lot for charm, very little for tricks, *so keep your legs down!*' 'I've always remembered those words,' said Miss Dare.

It was in her dressing room that Zena first met Lord Esher and his son Maurice Brett. 'All the Bretts loved music and the theatre —there was something bohemian in them.' Lord Esher, like King Edward, had many friends in the theatrical profession. When Esher took his son behind the scenes to congratulate Seymour Hicks, they were naturally introduced to the new leading lady.

So there they stood, father and son, two gentlemen in top hats and opera cloaks with their gold-knobbed canes, looking at the young star. She had no idea what they were thinking, but years later they each told her. Maurice was thinking: 'I'm determined to marry her.' And Lord Esher was thinking: 'What a fool the boy is. That's the girl I'd marry if I were him.'

Six years passed. During this period Zena Dare went from one success to another and received the extraordinary adulation of the time—hundreds of postcards of her in different costumes were sold and sent by her fans for signature; every Sunday would be spent posting them back.

'You can't imagine the glamour of being an actress in those days —the stage door was romantic, exciting. No one had publicity agents. One's contact with the public was natural, so warm and close. Every night there would be a long line of hansom cabs with gentlemen waiting to take us out to supper—no night clubs existed, of course, just a meal at the Savoy or Carlton Grill and then by 1 A.M. I had to get back to our house in St. John's Wood where my mother would be waiting with a candle ready to say, "The play ended at eleven-thirty and the restaurants close at one and it's fifteen minutes past. What *have* you been doing?" Oh, it was all very respectable—but the young men who took us out felt such dogs— to be *seen* giving supper to an *actress!* And the flowers we would get! And not only flowers, for often a present would be hung in the bouquet—one had to look carefully in case a trinket got lost. Sometimes these were valuable diamond brooches and brace- lets which had to be returned to the sender—if you were a *nice* girl, that is. I was allowed to keep a pekinese puppy that jumped out of a huge bunch. The Gaiety girls were rather different, they *kept* jewels! Perhaps that is where the line of respectability could be drawn—between those who kept and those who sent back dia- monds!'

And so the years passed and the Hon. Maurice Brett was just a Guards officer among many others who courted Zena Dare.

It is an interesting fact (not given me by Miss Dare but by another member of the family) that Lord Esher continually encouraged his son not to lose heart. At a glance he had recognised that show-stopping quality which he himself possessed. People who saw him tell of Lord Esher's extraordinary *presence*—when he entered a room there would be a moment's hush and heads would turn his way. Some indefinable quality aroused interest and he in turn responded to this trait in a girl.

If a Guards officer married an 'actress,' he had to resign, however respectable she might be. The Prince of Wales thought this perfectly ridiculous where Zena was concerned, but even he could not sway the Guards Brigade. Captain Brett, most promising of soldiers, had to resign. 'So lucky as it happened—his regiment was wiped out at the beginning of the war and Maurice then joined the Black Watch!'

Zena Dare talked on about the strata of society which in those days never met. 'Had I not gone on the stage, had I remained an ordinary solicitor's daughter, I could never possibly have met Lord Esher's son. Our paths would never have crossed. We lived in completely different worlds.' And yet when they married and the newsboys were shouting, 'Secret marriage of Zena Dare,' there was no mention of the groom!

Rather naturally, we got on to the many-faceted topic of love. 'I have loved deeply in my life,' Miss Dare said, 'but I know that I have never actually *fallen* in love—not, that is, into the state in which I have seen other women—hysterical, reckless, weeping all night. I may have missed something. I don't think so. I have known great love, but not that other thing—I stepped into love, I did not fall.

'Maybe it was the discipline of the theatre which prevented it—maybe the atmosphere in which I lived after my marriage. I saw a great deal of my father-in-law, and I suppose I learned to love with the mind—to care for the person and not just for the mood. Isn't that sort of wildly giving way to being in love rather like indulging in a tantrum? But I have known real love all right.'

We seemed to have drifted away from Lord Esher.

But had we?

29

The End

No one dreamt that the end was approaching. Despite fits of depression and a chronic cough, and the fact that he was short-tempered at bridge when his cards went wrong, Edward showed no serious symptoms. Perhaps his bulk and heavy breathing should have been recognised as mortal afflictions, but the King seemed so alive and energetic, and he was standing up well to the tense political struggle concerning the House of Lords. Although Asquith had written: 'The Cabinet were all of opinion that, as far as possible, the name of the Crown should be kept out of the arena of Party politics,' Edward knew the Prime Minister might demand the creation of several hundred Liberal peers in order to get the Home Rule for Ireland Bill passed.

Edward, the most popular monarch in Europe, continued to find personal happiness in giving presents and doing kindnesses. He found that he could shoulder great responsibility without flinching. 'He was one to come to decisions by instinct not by logic, and rarely made a mistake in his judgement of men. On the whole, he preferred the society of the female sex, and was never happier than in the company of pretty women. He always thought a men's dinner party was tiresome and dull,' wrote Ponsonby. He ruled over a swiftly changing scene and the contrasts excited him. During the years since Queen Victoria had died, cars had replaced horse-drawn vehicles, telephones the hand-delivered note and electric light the paraffin lamps. But the adage stood: 'You should not choose women or linen by candlelight.'

Osbert Sitwell has in *Great Morning* evoked the atmosphere of England in these exuberant years. 'In London, in the streets, you still saw a few carriages, but they diminished day by day, and seemed to be part of life's decoration . . . mine was the first generation in which the young men were allowed to take their sweethearts for drives—only the fastest of actresses had ridden in tandems. . . . All classes still believed in absolute progress—and the loss of this certainty has whittled down more than anything else, the feeling of life's joy. . . . Young men from the prosperous classes, such as my brother officers and myself, would find themselves invited to as many as five or six entertainments in a night. An air of gaiety, unusual in northern climates, prevailed. Music flowed with the lightness and flash of water under the striped awnings and from the balconies; while beyond the open illuminated windows, in the rooms, the young men about to be slaughtered, still feasted, unconscious of all but the moment.'

A few of the great Edwardian characters had fallen by the wayside, but aristocrats of individuality still abounded. Houses grew slightly more comfortable, the drains of Londesborough, where long ago the Prince of Wales had caught typhoid, now conformed to the rules of hygienic plumbing, but the Earl of Londesborough remained an eighteenth-century personality, and the 'gloss, speed and style' of Londesborough's carriage horses had been transferred to an electric brougham. Londesborough's relationship with the Deity was intensely familiar. During shooting parties he would sometimes address the sky, as prophets did in biblical times, with, 'Oh, God, you know how much I like shooting. Why won't you allow me to hit these partridges?' And one wet summer evening when a ball was to be held at his London residence, Hanover Lodge, in Regent's Park, and the garden had been decked with Japanese lanterns, Lord Londesborough looked up at the rain, angrily exclaiming, 'Oh, God, how like you!'

In January 1910 King Edward attended a shooting party at Elvedon, the Suffolk home of the Earl of Iveagh, who owned seventeen thousand acres. Daisy Fingall said the great hall must have been the coldest room in England. Everyone assembled in it for tea after a shoot, and sat there in the evening. There was only one large fireplace, and this had to be allotted to His Majesty. Yet the grandeur was tremendous and even belowstairs the ladies' maids were waited on by footmen. The King liked Lady Fingall. 'Jolly little lady,' he would say when he found her name submitted to him for a party, and he never scratched it out.

She found, in fact, that she nearly always had a bedroom allotted to her on the same floor, and it was somewhat embarrassing to pass the men in red livery standing outside the royal door, in order to reach the large icy bathroom. When Queen Alexandra visited Elvedon she brought a maid, a dresser and a sergeant footman. The magnificence was only equalled by the discomfort, and in Daisy Fingall's case by nausea at the slaughter of so many birds.

On the last of King Edward's visits to Elvedon the guests included the King's intimates, Marquis de Soveral, Mrs. Willie James and, of course, Mrs. Keppel. Through her maid, Lady Fingall heard that the King was not well and had to be given oxygen in his room. Yet he went out with the guns for a short time and appeared to be himself at mealtime. On the last night Daisy Fingall sat next to him at dinner and he teased her about being a suffragette. 'You can get all you want without the vote,' he said. Edward thought the suffragette movement unbecoming to the fair sex and enjoyed repeating the story of an M.P. who, when the ladies chained themselves to the railings of Westminster and said they would stay there till they got the vote, expostulated: 'I might as well chain myself to St. Thomas's Hospital and say I would not move till I had a baby.' Daisy backed her sex bravely until, at the end of this particular meal, the King said on a more serious note, 'I want to speak to you after dinner.'

Later, when the men joined the ladies, the King walked up and led her to a corner of the drawing room. She wondered what was coming. 'I want to tell you,' said King Edward, 'that one of your friends has hurt me deeply.' He mentioned a sister of Douglas Haig who believed that she could communicate with the dead through automatic writing. Daisy felt stunned. 'Oh, sir, she would never think of hurting you willingly. What has she done?' Edward continued: 'She knows how much I loved my sister Alice, and she has written to me giving a message which she says was sent through her brother George.'

Lady Fingall quickly recollected the tiresome admonitions which usually came through George Haig on the planchette board—in fact a friend had been driven to remark: 'Well, George was a bore when he was alive. But he's a much worse bore now he is dead.'

Then Daisy saw His Majesty was not smiling. 'What was this message, sir?'

'It was, "The time is short. You must prepare." '

Daisy recoiled; she felt, however, that her friend would only have transmitted such a message to the King if she had believed it to be her duty.

'But did she give you any proof that this message came from Princess Alice?'

'Yes,' he said huskily, 'she said that I was to remember a day when we were on Ben Nevis together, and found white heather and divided it.'

The King requested Lady Fingall once again to inform her friend how deeply *hurt* he had been by her wish to transfer this confidence from the other world.

'Sir, I could not do that.' Daisy was Irish and fey; warnings from another world seemed natural to her. In a daze, she returned to the other guests, who chaffed her. 'You were catching it hot about the suffragettes.' She found it hard to laugh as she replied: 'Yes, the King hates suffragettes.'

The party broke up next day, and Daisy Fingall never saw King Edward again. Within four months he was dead.

In the elections of January 1910 the Liberal Party suffered a reduced majority. This setback determined them even more bitterly to reduce the powers of the Tory House of Lords. When King Edward, with the Queen at his side, opened the new Parliament on February 21, he knew that Prime Minister Asquith was likely to advise him to use the royal prerogative to ensure the passing of an act to restrict the veto of the Upper House. The Liberal Government was absolutely set on Home Rule for Ireland. The Lords could prevent it.

While his doctors kept urging King Edward to go to Biarritz, he insisted on remaining in London, attending to his numerous duties, until the Prime Minister assured him that no immediate crisis was imminent. Crossing to Paris on March 6, this sick, overworked King, instead of resting for a few days, went to the theatre and caught a chill. He travelled to Biarritz by special train two days later and on arrival at the Hotel du Palais collapsed and had to remain in his room with bronchitis. For two weeks he received hardly any visitors except Mrs. Keppel, and Soveral, who never fatigued him. From the Mediterranean, Queen Alexandra, who was about to embark for a cruise on the new royal yacht, wrote him to leave 'that horrid Biarritz' and join her, but King Edward felt that he must remain within easy call in case the Government should resign. If this happened, Arthur Balfour, Leader of the Opposition, said that he would ask for an immediate dissolution and again appeal to the country in a General Election. As the atmosphere at Westminster grew tenser the young Home Secretary, Winston Churchill, enjoyed his task of writing daily reports of the debates in the House of Commons in his own special style for the sovereign's perusal. 'Very interesting and instructive reports,' Edward called them.

When, at the end of April, the King travelled back to face the political blow-up, he stayed as usual for a few days in Paris. He asked his old friend the Comtesse de Pourtalés to walk with him once again in the Jardin des Plantes, and he called on the Comtesse Greffuhle. It was on this occasion that he said to her: 'I have not long to live. And then my nephew will make war.'

After reaching London on April 29, the wheezy but dauntless monarch attended *Siegfried* at Covent Garden Opera, and next day he travelled to Sandringham for the weekend. It is typical of King Edward that he should struggle not to disappoint his steward and employees by cancelling his usual Sunday inspection of the farm. An icy east wind caught his lungs, only half cleared after bronchitis, and it was a very sick man who returned to London next day. He dined quietly with Agnes Keyser in Grosvenor Crescent. Distressed at his appearance, Agnes begged him to take a day's rest in Buckingham Palace, and this he did. On May 4 he wrote in that engagement diary he had kept since boyhood, 'The King dines alone.'

On the following day he attempted to give audiences, and defiantly insisted on donning his formal frock coat. He would *not* give in. Although breathing with difficulty, he managed to partake of a light lunch and a large cigar. Then, while standing by an open window playing with his pet canaries, King Edward suddenly collapsed. Queen Alexandra, who had just returned from the Mediterranean, was summoned by Princess Victoria. After five doctors had examined the King they stated that hope must be abandoned. He had tried to ignore the discomfort of his swollen abdomen and choked lungs, but no heart could stand the strain of all that eating and smoking. The King was going to die. The news leaked out from the palace to the nation. His subjects were unable to believe that good old Teddy was leaving them.

My grandmother, who had spent the afternoon of May 2 playing bridge with Mrs. Keppel, knew, of course, that His Majesty looked badly, and Agnes Keyser had been exceedingly reticent on the telephone. Obviously she feared for the King, but there was nothing she could do. With these two sources of information, and guarded telephone calls from the Duke of Connaught, my grandmother knew as much as anyone in England. With her sister Jennie and her son Seymour she waited in Great Cumberland Place. There was much whispering for, as when scandal hovered, the servants were not supposed to be alerted. All that evening they waited, and at intervals the phone rang. Seymour remembers his mother coming back to the drawing room with tears in her eyes, saying, 'They can't get him out of his armchair. Alice has been sent for.' By this time her eavesdropping lady's maid, also in tears but intent on the 'proper thing to do,' had rushed to the attic and was sorting out the heavy mourning which everyone kept for bereavements.

Late that night the Connaughts telephoned to say that during a lucid moment the Prince of Wales had told his father that his two-year-old horse Witch of the Air had won a race at Kempton Park, and the King had murmured, 'I am very glad.' These were his last words. Slipping into a coma, he died just before midnight.

Next morning the country knew. Blinds remained down and the entire nation went into black, while every social event of the London season had to be cancelled. Town houses were closed and families returned to the country.

With that graceful generosity which came to her naturally where the King's ladies were concerned, Alexandra had led Alice Keppel into the King's room to say goodbye. Later the Queen laid a sheaf of red roses on his coffin for Agnes Keyser.*

Meanwhile, the country waited stunned, and impending political battles were laid aside.

While King Edward's body lay in state in Westminster Hall with his people filing past paying their last respects, Wilfrid Scawen Blunt, who had been the first Englishman to go to prison for Ireland's sake, asked a few people to stay at his Sussex home; among them was my father, a twenty-five-year-old poet intent on seeing the Irish Home Rule Bill forced through. He proved the star-turn guest during this long Whitsun weekend, being able to recount the intimate details which everyone wanted to hear, because, as Blunt wrote in his diaries, he 'has heard the story of the King's last days both from his mother and from Winston.'

Then Blunt went on to quaintly describe my father, who was about to stand as Nationalist candidate for Londonderry. 'May 15: I have had a long talk with Leslie about Irish affairs and think he may eventually take a lead in them as he has the wit to join the Nationalist party. Young and being of the landlord class, a tall, good-looking fellow with much intelligence and heir to a baronetcy, and, Meynell tells me, an excellent speaker, he may even

---

* On the anniversary of Colonel Oliver Montagu's death, Queen Alexandra always visited his grave and laid down flowers as a tribute to her own chivalrous cavalier.

have Redmond's succession some day. It has always astonished me that no great landlord of them all should have come forward long ago in this way, even out of ambition. Leslie has been at Eton and Oxford, but is nevertheless, as far as I can judge, a quite sound Nationalist. . . .' Then, Blunt added: 'They tell me the new Court is going to be a very moral one, but they hope it will be saved from dullness by becoming intellectual.' This hope did not materialise.

The story of the Edwardian romantics might well be rounded off with the long entry in Blunt's diary for May 20, 1910. 'Today the King was buried, and I hope the country will now return to comparative sanity, for at present it is in delirium. The absurdities written in every newspaper about him pass belief. He might have been a Solon and a Francis of Assisi combined if the characters drawn of him were true. In no print has there been the smallest allusion to any of the pleasant little wickednesses, though his was not even in make-believe the life of a saint or in any strict sense a theologically virtuous man. Yet all the bishops and priests, Catholic, Protestant and Non-conformist, join in giving him a glorious place in heaven, and there were eight miles of his loyal and adoring sub-jects marching on foot to see him lying in state in Westminster Hall. For myself, I think he performed his public duties well. He had a passion for pageantry and ceremonial and dressing-up, and he was never tired of putting on uniforms and taking them off, and receiving princes and ambassadors and opening museums and hospi-tals, and attending cattle shows and military shows and shows of every kind, while every night of his life he was to be seen at thea-tres and operas and music-halls. Thus he was always before the public, and had come to have the popularity of an actor who plays his part in a variety of costumes, and always well. Abroad too, there is no doubt he had a very great reputation. His little Bohemian tastes made him beloved at Paris, and he had enough of the *grand seigneur* to carry it off. He did not affect to be virtuous, and all sorts of publicans and sinners found their places at his table. The journalists loved him; he did not mind being snap-shotted, and was stand-off to nobody. If not witty, he could understand a joke, and if not wise he was sensible. He quarrelled with nobody, and always forgave. He disliked family scandals, and spent much of his time patching up those of the Court and whitening its sepulchres. In this respect he had every right to the title of "Peacemaker."'

While Jennie Churchill and Leonie Leslie paid their visits of con-dolence to Queen Alexandra and quietly held the hand of Mrs. Keppel, who to escape condolences had immediately moved from Portman Square to the house of Mrs. Arthur James in Grafton

Street, my father sat down and penned a 'Ballad to Mrs. Keppel,' of which the refrain was: 'Send for Alice.'

In Paris His Majesty's old friend the Comtesse Edmond de Pourtalés wrote in her diary after attending the memorial service in the English Church: 'So ridiculous to think that everyone considered I had an affair with him—*on ne prete qu' aux riches!*'

Over five decades many women had sought to link their names with this King. Now they were sighing over their memories, wishing they had given a little more or a little less. Some would be surprised at their own warm tears. As the bells of London tolled they knew an age was ending. There could be no more Edwardian romantics.

Bibliographical Note

A DETAILED BIBLIOGRAPHY concerning Edwardian society is difficult to compile because the memoirs of those who belonged to the Prince's set are so stiff and discreet, and most of the books written by outsiders are studded with errors. Apart from those books from which I have quoted, the volumes which have given me personally most pleasure are:

King Edward the Seventh by Sir Philip Magnus; *Victoria R.I.* by Elizabeth Longford: *Life of Queen Alexandra* by Georgina Battiscombe; *Queen Mary* by James Pope-Hennessy; *My Dear Duchess: Letters from Lord Clarendon*, edited by A. L. Kennedy; *Life of the Duke of Devonshire* (two volumes) by Bernard Holland; *Four Studies in Loyalty* by Christopher Sykes; *Edward VII and His Circle* by Virginia Cowles; *Letters and Journals* (6 vols.) by Lord Esher; *Disraeli* by Robert Blake; *Asquith by* Roy Jenkins; *Gladstone* by Sir Philip Magnus.

Several of the personages of this book have been depicted under other names in V. Sackville-West's novel *The Edwardians*, a volume which caused some consternation among living Edwardians when it was first published in 1930.

A.L.

Index